Approved by OCR for CLAIT Plus

CLAIT PLUS
LEVEL TWO
IT User Qualification
Student Workbook

ALAN CLARKE

Orders: please contact Bookpoint Ltd, 130 Milton Park, Abingdon, Oxon OX14 4SB. Telephone: (44) 01235 827720, Fax: (44) 01235 400454. Lines are open from 9.00 - 6.00, Monday to Saturday, with a 24 hour message answering service. You can also order through our website at www.hodderheadline.co.uk

British Library Cataloguing in Publication Data
A catalogue record for this title is available from The British Library

ISBN 0 340 849096

First published 2003
Impression number   10 9 8 7 6 5 4 3 2 1
Year   2007 2006 2005 2004 2003
Copyright © 2003 Alan Clarke

Printed in Italy for Hodder & Stoughton Educational, a division of Hodder Headline Plc, 338 Euston Road, London NW1 3BH.

Contents

Acknowledgements

To my wife and sons for their help and support and particularly to Peter for his practical assistance and suggestions.

The author and publisher wish to acknowledge CorelDraw and the Microsoft Corporation for the use of screen captured images.

OCR does not endorse the use of one software package over another, and all CLAIT qualifications are written in generic form. This book is written using the Microsoft Office suite as examples, simply to provide clear support to the majority of candidates who will be using that package. The use of any other form of software is equally appropriate and acceptable to OCR.

Introduction

In a modern society it is essential to have Information and Communication Technology (ICT) skills and knowledge. OCR have developed a suite of ICT user qualifications at levels 1, 2 and 3. This book covers the content required for the CLAIT Plus qualification.

CLAIT Plus is a level 2 qualification for Information and Communication Technology (ICT) users. It forms part of the suite of ICT qualifications with New CLAIT (level 1) and CLAIT Advanced (level 3). To achieve the full CLAIT Plus qualification you must achieve four units comprising of the mandatory unit and three optional units. You have a choice of twenty optional units covering areas such as spreadsheets, electronic communication and computer art.

There are no formal entry requirements for CLAIT Plus. However, the course assumes that you have the skills and knowledge of ICT provided by New CLAIT. This book is based on Microsoft Office 2000. However, a large part of the material should be suitable for Office 97. Only the Computer Art chapter employs another application. CorelDRAW 10 is the basis of this chapter. The mandatory unit and twelve optional units are covered within the book.

Please Note: Figures do not necessarily appear on the same page as their first mention in the text, but all figures are easily referred to as they are marked out in grey.

Create, Manage and Integrate Files

This chapter will help you to:

- Use a computer's system safely and securely to create and manage files and directories/folders

- Use an input device to enter data accurately from a variety of sources

- Work with datafiles using database and/or spreadsheet facilities to select and export data

- Create and print an integrated document, combining text, numeric tabular data and an image or a chart

- Format page layout and manipulate text according to a house style

This chapter covers the content of Unit 1 of the CLAIT Plus course which is mandatory. There are no pre-conditions for studying this unit. However, its content does assume that you have the skills and understanding which are provided by the OCR Level 1 ICT course New CLAIT (e.g. Unit 1 - Using a Computer).

Assessment

After studying Unit 1 your skills and understanding are assessed during a 3 hour practical assignment. This is set and externally assessed by OCR. If you are unsuccessful then you can be re-assessed using a different assignment.

Files and Folders

All information stored on a computer is held in a file. Each file has an individual name and they are often stored within folders. Folders are also sometimes called directories. Both folders and directories serve essentially the same function as paper folders do in filing cabinets, that is, they allow records to be stored in an organised and systematic way. Computer files need to be organised for similar reasons that paper files and records do. You need to be able to locate them so you can read, update (change), copy, remove or move a file.

Microsoft Windows operating system provides a range of functions that allow you to:

• Create and name folders (directories)

• Open, close and save files

• Delete files and folders

• Move files and folders

• Copy files and folders

• Rename files and folders

• Print the file structure

The file management application provided within Microsoft Windows is called Windows Explorer, shown in Figure 1. The Explorer's application window is divided into a number of areas. These are:

• Title bar (e.g. Exploring - C:\My Documents\Alan\CLAIT Plus)

• Menu bar

• Toolbar

• Address (i.e. shows the location or path of the highlighted folder)

Example

C:\My Documents\Alan\CLAIT Plus

This shows that on the hard disk (shown by letter C:) is a folder called My Documents within which is another folder entitled Alan. There is then a further folder called CLAIT Plus within Alan.

• Folders (left hand side of the display) - showing the structure of folders stored on the hard disk, floppy disks, CD-ROMs or other storage media. The plus sign indicates that the folder has more folders stored within them. If you click on the plus sign, the structure will be opened up to show these folders. The

FIGURE 1
Windows Explorer

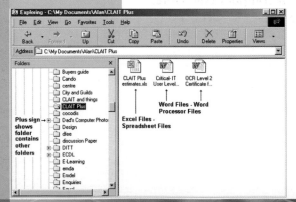

revealed folders can also be shown with a plus sign, indicating further folders stored within the revealed ones.

• Contents of the folder (right hand side of the display). This shows the files and folders stored within the highlighted folder.

FIGURE 2
**Structure
of Folders**

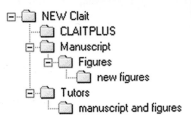

In order to locate files using Windows Explorer you need to understand the structure of the folders. Figure 2 shows the structure of some folders. It is displayed in the way that Windows Explorer shows them in its left hand window.

Files are stored in folders. However, folders can also be stored in other folders. Figure 2 shows that within the folder NEW Clait there are three folders CLAITPLUS, Manuscript and Tutors. Within the folder Manuscript is the folder Figures which in turn has new figures folder stored within it. The Tutors folder has the folder manuscript and figures stored in it. This structure is shown by what is called the path and the examples below are based on the folders in Figure 2.

Example:

C:\NEW Clait

C:\NEW Clait\CLAITPLUS

C:\NEW Clait\Manuscript

C:\NEW Clait\Manuscript\Figures

C:\NEW Clait\Manuscript\Figures\new figures

C:\ NEW Clait\Tutors

C:\ NEW Clait\Tutors\manuscript and figures

FIGURE 3
**Within
Folders**

Folders and files are stored on a variety of media which is indicated by the letter at the beginning of the path. On new computers a compact disc writer (CD-RW) is often provided on drive E: while a DVD (i.e. Digital Video Disc) is installed on drive D.

Example:

A: Floppy Disk
C: Hard Disk
D: or E:CD-ROM, DVD or CD-RW

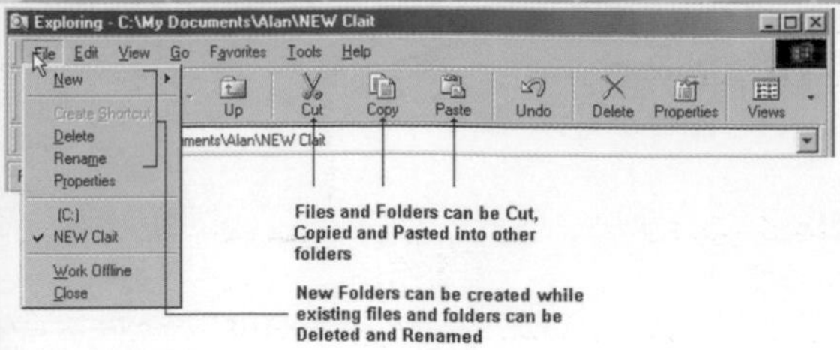

FIGURE 4
**Manipulating
Files and
Folders**

Figure 3 shows Windows Explorer's view of the NEW Clait folder. In the right hand side of the Explorer window you can see the three folders and a range of files stored within NEW Clait folder. The folders are shown as yellow index card icons while files vary in appearance to show they are different types. The folders and files can be opened by double clicking on them with the mouse pointer. The files will only open if an application which is able to read the file is present on the computer system. If no suitable application is identified by the system then a message will appear asking you to identify the correct application.

In order for a file to be opened requires the presence of the application which created it. Microsoft Excel needs to be available to open spreadsheet files created with it and in a similar way text files need a word processor application, database files an application such as Access and image files an application such as CorelDraw.

When windows is unable to locate a suitable application, it offers you the opportunity to select one in which to open the file. If you consider the file extension (discussed later) you can frequently identify the correct application.

When a new folder opens within Windows Explorer the display changes to show the contents of the new folder. To return to the original folder click on it in the folder structure shown on the left hand side of the display.

Exercise 1

Windows Explorer

1. Open Windows Explorer by clicking on the Start button, highlight Programs and select Windows Explorer. The application will appear (Figure 1) either in a window or filling the whole screen.

2. Explore the folders display by scrolling the display up and down to browse the whole range of folders stored on the hard disk.

3. Click on a plus sign to see the folder open up to reveal what other folders it contains. Explore the different folders and watch how the right hand side of the display changes. What files and folders appear in the display?

4. Double click on a file and see if it will open. It will only open if a compatible application is present on the computer system. To return to Windows Explorer simply close the application which has been loaded to open the file (e.g. close using the windows buttons in the right hand corner of the window).

5. Continue to explore until you are confident that you can move around the folders and open files.

6. Close Windows Explorer by clicking on File Menu and Close option.

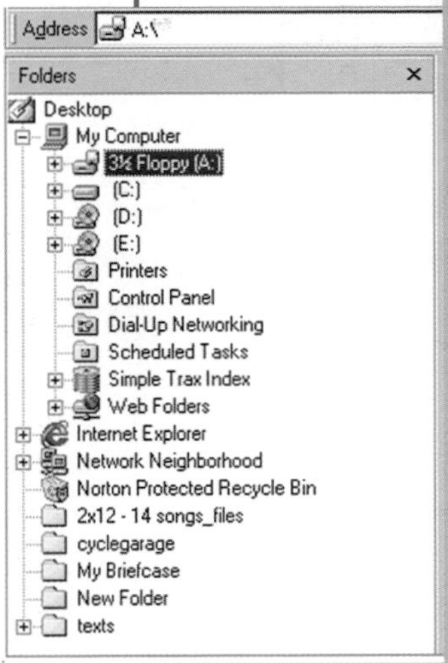

Windows Explorer Functions

Windows Explorer provides the tools to create new folders and delete, rename, move, copy and save files and folders. These functions are available on the File menu and toolbar, shown in Figure 4. The toolbar options of Cut, Copy and Paste are also available on the Edit menu:

New - create a new folder in the folder currently being viewed in Windows Explorer

Delete - deletes the file or folder highlighted

Rename - allows you to change the name of the file or folder highlighted

Cut - allows you to cut out a file or folder with the intention of moving it to a new location using the Paste option

Copy - allows you to copy a file or folder to a new location using the Paste option but leaving the original file or folder unaffected.

Paste - allows you to place a copied or cut file or folder in a new location

These functions allow you to control your files and folders. They allow you to administer your files and folders in a similar way that you could move paper files and folders in a conventional filing cabinet. When you have hundreds of folders and thousands of files it is essential that you are able to control them. When you initially start a task it is natural to create an individual folder to store the files you create. Later it will often be found that the folders relates to other folders. You may need to move the folders so that the relationship is reflected in the structure.

You could create a master folder and then move all the related folders so that they are stored within the master. Windows Explorer allows you to restructure the folders in anyway that is appropriate. Moving or copying folders and files is a frequent task that you will need to undertake to ensure that the structure meets your needs. The alternative is that you may find it difficult to locate files or folders and thus work less efficiently.

Address A:\

Folders ×

Desktop
My Computer
  3½ Floppy (A:)
  (C:)
  (D:)
  (E:)
  Printers
  Control Panel
  Dial-Up Networking
  Scheduled Tasks
  Simple Trax Index
  Web Folders
  Internet Explorer
  Network Neighborhood
  Norton Protected Recycle Bin
  2x12 - 14 songs_files
  cyclegarage
  My Briefcase
  New Folder
  texts

FIGURE 5
Drives

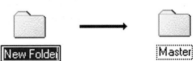

New Folder → Master

FIGURE 6
New Folder

FIGURE 7
Master Folder Open

Desktop
  My Computer
    3½ Floppy (A:)
      Master

FIGURE 8
Structure

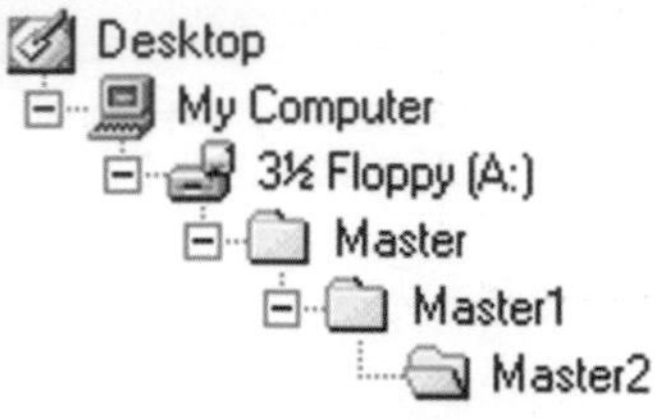

Desktop
└ My Computer
  └ 3½ Floppy (A:)
    └ Master
      └ Master1
        └ Master2

Exercise 2

Manipulating Folders

1. Insert a floppy disk into the drive.

2. Open Windows Explorer by clicking on the Start button, highlight Programs and select Windows Explorer. The application will appear (Figure 1) either in a window or filling the whole screen.

3. Click on the Floppy option (Figure 5) and if the floppy is empty then no files or folders will be shown on the right hand side of the display. If you cannot see the Floppy option then scroll up the window. Floppy is at the top of the list.

4. You are going to create a new folder so select the File menu, highlight New and click on the Folder option. A new folder will appear on the right hand side of the display with the name New Folder. The cursor will be flashing in the name box and you should enter a name for the folder from the keyboard. In this case call it Master. Figure 6 shows New and Named Folder.

5. The Master Folder is stored on the floppy disk because this was the drive selected when the folder was created.

6. Double click on Master and you will see the right hand side is clear because this folder is empty. However, on the left hand side the Master Folder will appear (Figure 7) and because it has been selected, the folder icon is shown open.

7. Create a new folder and name it Master1. Open Master1 and create another new folder called Master2. You now have three folders stored one within another. Figure 8 shows the structure.

8. Highlight Master1 folder by clicking on it, then select File menu and Rename option and you can change the name to New Master. Repeat the process for Master2 and rename it Modern Master.

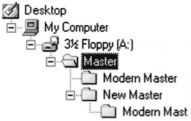

Desktop
└ My Computer
  └ 3½ Floppy (A:)
    └ Master
      └ Modern Master
      └ New Master
        └ Modern Mast

9. Highlight Modern Master (single click) and then select the Copy tool. Highlight Master folder and select the Paste tool. You will see the Modern Master folder copied into the Master Folder. The original Modern Master folder is still in place. Figure 9 shows the new structure.

10. The process of using the function has now been illustrated. You must highlight the folder you wish to operate on and then select the function. Now practise using the other functions:

FIGURE 9
New Structure

a) Delete a folder

b) b) Cut and paste a folder in order to move it to a new location (e.g. move original Modern Folder to place it in the new Modern Folder using cut and paste).

11. Continue trying the different functions until you are confident.

12. Close Windows Explorer by clicking on <u>F</u>ile Menu and <u>C</u>lose option.

Types of Files

Different types of files are shown as different sizes of icons or described in text. Figure 10 compares the appearance of different types of files. File names normally end with a full stop and three letters. This indicates the type of file and helps you to distinguish between them.

Example:

.doc	-	Word document
.bmp	-	bitmap image file
.jpg/.jpeg	-	image files
.txt	-	text document
.htm	-	hypertext markup document (i.e. web page)
.exe	-	application file (i.e. an executable file)
.ppt	-	PowerPoint presentation (i.e. Presentation Graphics)
.mdb	-	Access Database
.xls	-	Excel Spreadsheet

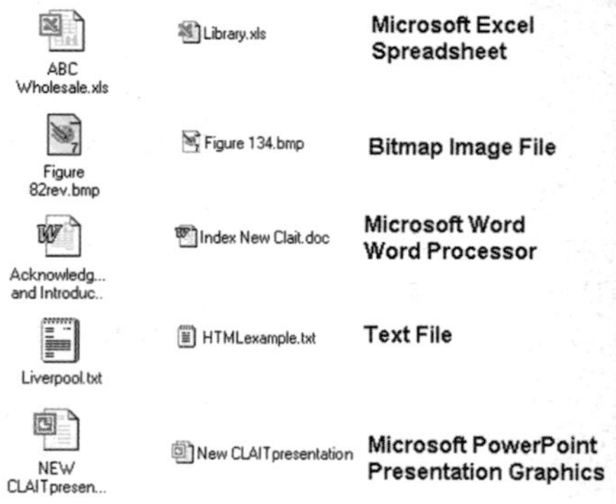

Most files can be opened by double clicking on them if a compatible application is available on the computer. An executable file is one which launches an application and does not rely on the presence of a compatible application.

FIGURE 10
Types of Files

Library.xls	Microsoft Excel Spreadsheet
Figure 134.bmp	Bitmap Image File
Index New Clait.doc	Microsoft Word Word Processor
HTMLexample.txt	Text File
New CLAIT presentation	Microsoft PowerPoint Presentation Graphics

ABC Wholesale.xls
Figure 82rev.bmp
Acknowledg... and Introduc...
Liverpool.txt
NEW CLAIT presen...

Printing Windows

If you wish to obtain a permanent record of a file structure or the contents of a window then Windows provides a standard function to allow you to produce a printout of the contents. If you hold down the ALT key and then press the Print Screen (sometimes Print Scrn) key then a copy of the window contents are held in the Clipboard. This is a special area in the computer's memory used to store information. You can then paste the image into a document (e.g. in Word) and print it using the normal functions of the application. If you want to capture the contents of the whole display then you only need to press the

Tools

✓ Spelling and Grammar...	F7
Language	▶
Word Count...	
📄 AutoSummarize...	
AutoCorrect...	
Look Up Reference...	
Track Changes	▶
Merge Documents...	
Protect Document...	
Online Collaboration	▶
Mail Merge...	
📧 Envelopes and Labels...	
Letter Wizard...	
Macro	▶
Templates and Add-Ins...	
Customize...	
Options...	

FIGURE 11
Word Tools Menu

Print Screen key and then paste the image into a document.

Entering Data

You will probably have applied for a bank account, credit card or simply changed insurance company. The forms you complete are often used to enter your information into the company's computer systems. Almost every organisation keeps records on their customers, clients, staff and suppliers. These all require people to enter data into the computer and many forms are now designed to assist the process.

Computer data can be used for a variety of purposes once it is entered into a system. It forms the basis for managers to make decisions which affect both the organisation and the individual or company the records refer to. If incorrect, a great deal of harm can potentially result. Many organisations check that both the input documents and the data entered are correct. Proofreading documents and screen displays are important skills to master.

If you are entering thousands of documents then even a small reduction in the quantity of data to be entered will make a substantial improvement to productivity. This is often achieved by encoding the data so that a single letter or code represents a chunk of information.

Example:

A overdraft limit up to £250
B overdraft limit up to £500
C overdraft limit up to £1000

Spell and Grammar Checkers

Applications can often assist you with checking the accuracy of your documents. Most modern wordprocessors, spreadsheets and databases provide spell and grammar checkers.

Microsoft Word provides both. These are available in the Tools menu as the Spelling and Grammar option (Figure 11). This will check the document starting from the position of the cursor and work towards the end of the document before going back to the start. When the option is clicked then a dialogue window (Figure 12) appears and works through the document stopping each time it locates what it considers an error. This can take several forms such as:

• Punctuation

Spelling and Grammar: English (U.K.)   ? ✕

"That" or "Which":

Finally select Column Chart type and the default sub-type which is in the top left hand corner.	Ignore
	Ignore Rule
	Next Sentence

Suggestions:

type, which	Change
———OR———	
type that	

☑ Check grammar

?	Options...	Undo	Close

FIGURE 12
Spelling and Grammar Checking

- Capital letter
- Grammatical error
- Spelling mistake

You need to decide if you want to take the advice the checker is offering (i.e. Change button) or if you are going to ignore it (Ignore button). In some cases the checker will offer more than one answer and you need to choose which is correct or whether they are all wrong. When you make your decision the checker acts then moves on to stop when it finds another item that it considers to be incorrect. This process continues until it has considered the whole document. It will tell you when it has completed the whole document.

Spell and grammar checkers only suggest changes to you. You need to decide if you want to act on them. They may be wrong so that simply agreeing with the advice will nevertheless add errors to the document. You must be sure that the change is correct. However, checkers are very good at locating typographical (data entry) errors.

English Date Formats

The way dates are presented in different countries varies.

For example

In Britain dates are shown as: day, month and year while in the USA they are presented as month, day and year. Obviously there is room for confusion if they are mixed or used in an inappropriate way. In addition there are several different ways/formats of presenting English dates such as:

13 February 1952
13/02/1952
13-02-52
13 Feb 52

FIGURE 13
Save As

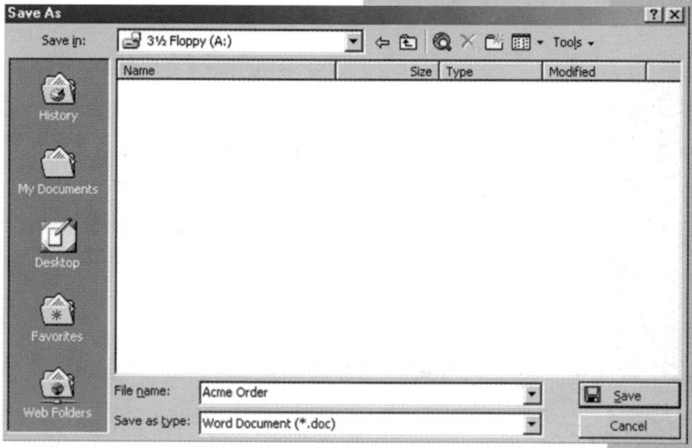

Often when you are entering dates the format is specified and it is critical that you follow the specification. If you do not then it is likely that the application (e.g. database) will not recognise the date format and thus be unable to locate it. This will produce errors.

Font Families

CLAIT Plus uses the term font families. There are two types called Sans Serif and Serif. A serif type font has small projections on the ends of the characters while a sans serif type font does not. You might say that serif fonts have more fancy characters or that sans serif fonts have plain characters.

The exercises sometimes use font names rather than families so below are shown some examples of sans serif and serif:

Examples

Serif

E Courier New

E Times New Roman

Sans Serif

E Arial

Exercise 3

Data Entry

1. Open Microsoft Word by clicking on the Start button, highlight Programs and select Microsoft Word option or double click on the Word icon on the Windows desktop.

2. Enter the data input sheet below:

Name: Janet Jenkins   Date: 12/01/02

Area: South-East

Visit - Order

Order taken during visit to Acme Engineering for period 1/04/02 to 30/06/02. Stock to be called off with delivery within 72 hours of request for stock.

Order

Part No. 123	64
Part No. 789	23
Part No. 901	74
Part No. 314	17

Discount 5% for volume purchase

Standards terms - payment of order within 30 days of delivery

3. Note that the layout of the information, the standard format of the dates and the use of codes rather than describing the stock ordered (e.g. Part No. 123). There are several different ways of formatting dates and some applications will only accept particular ways so it is important to get it right.

4. Systematically check your document against the input sheet to ensure that it is correct. If you find an error then move the cursor to the error by clicking once at the desired location. You can delete the mistake using either the backspace (deletes to the left) or delete keys (deletes to the right) and enter the correction.

5. Check the spelling and grammar of the entry (select the Tools menu and Spelling and Grammar option).

6. Insert a floppy disk into the drive and save your document by selecting the File menu and the Save option. This will reveal the Save As dialogue window (Figure 13). Change the Save in: box to Floppy (A) by using the down arrow at end of box to show a list of options. Save the document as File name: Acme Order. When you are ready click the Save button. You have now saved your document as a file called Acme Order.

7. Close Word by selecting the File menu and the Exit option or continue with Exercise 4.

Amend Documents

A key advantage of a computer application is that it allows you amend your documents. Microsoft Office applications allow you to delete, insert, copy and move information within a document. These functions operate in a similar way in all Microsoft Office applications. They are available in the File and Edit menus. The functions operate in the following ways:

FIGURE 14
Open Window

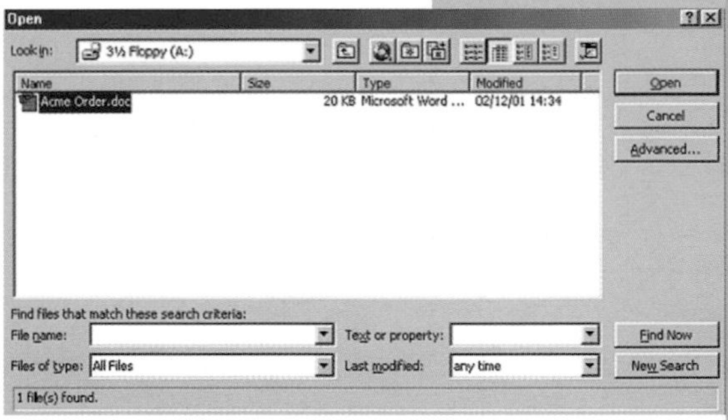

Delete – insert the cursor before or after the word or phrase you need to remove and then use the delete or backspace key on the keyboard. The backspace deletes to the left while the delete key works to the right. Alternatively highlight the word or phrase and press the delete key to remove the selected items.

Insert – insert the cursor in the desired location and then enter the new information. This requires that you position the pointer at the new location and click the mouse button. However, on the keyboard is an Insert key (i.e. Ins). When this is pressed any data entered from the keyboard will overwrite existing information. This occasionally happens by accident and can be confusing until you realise the key has been pressed. To cancel the key press it again.

Copy – highlight the word or phrase you want to copy and then select the Edit menu and click on the Copy option. Move the cursor to the location where you want to copy the information to and then select the Edit menu and the Paste option. The copied items will now appear at the new location and will remain at their original place.

Move - highlight the word or phrase you want to move and then select the Edit menu and click on the Cut option. The word or phrase will disappear. Move the cursor to the location where you want to move the information to and then select the Edit menu and the Paste option. The cut (moved) items will now appear at the new location.

Exercise 4

Amend Document

1. Insert your floppy disk into the drive

2. Open Microsoft Word by clicking on the Start button, highlight Programs and select Microsoft Word option or double click on the Word icon on the Windows desktop.

3. Open the file Acme Order by selecting the File menu and the Open option to reveal the Open dialogue window. Change Look in: box to Floppy (A:) using the arrow button at the end of the box. This will reveal the files stored on the floppy in the central area of the window (Figure 14). Double click on the file Acme Order or single click to highlight it and then click on the Open button.

4. The document Acme Order will appear in the Word work area.

5. Figure 15 shows the input sheet after it has been proofread.

6. Make the changes indicated by the proofreading:

a) Insert a new paragraph between the sentence ending "to 30/06/02" and sentence beginning "Stock to be".
b) Insert 24/ so that it reads 24/72 hours of request for stock
c) Insert letters (2 tabs from numbers e.g. 64), as below:

Order		
Part No. 123	64	A
Part No. 789	23	B
Part No. 901	74	C
Part No. 314	17	C

d) Indent the line starting with Order one tab

e) Indent the line starting with Discount one tab

f) Delete the letters so that Standards now reads Standard

7. Revised document should now look like:

Name: Janet Jenkins   Date: 12/01/02

Area: South-East

Visit - Order

Order taken during visit to Acme Engineering for period 1/04/02 to 30/06/02.

Stock to be called off with delivery within 24/72 hours of request for stock.

Order

Part No. 123	64	A
Part No. 789	23	B
Part No. 901	74	C
Part No. 314	17	C

Discount 5% for volume purchase

Standard terms - payment of order within 30 days of delivery

8. Save your revised document as file Acme Order Amended by selecting the File menu and the Save option.

9. You have now amended the document in relation to the proofreading corrections. This has allowed you to practice deleting and inserting information. You now have the opportunity to practice copying and moving text around the document. Try:

a) Reordering the list of parts so that they are presented in numerical order

e.g.	Part No. 123	64	A
	Part No. 314	17	C
	Part No. 789	23	B
	Part No. 901	74	C

Use the Copy, Cut and Paste functions to achieve this result.

b) Using these functions to move and copy text until you are confident that you understand their use.

10. Close Word by selecting the File menu and the Exit option.

FIGURE 15
Proofread Document

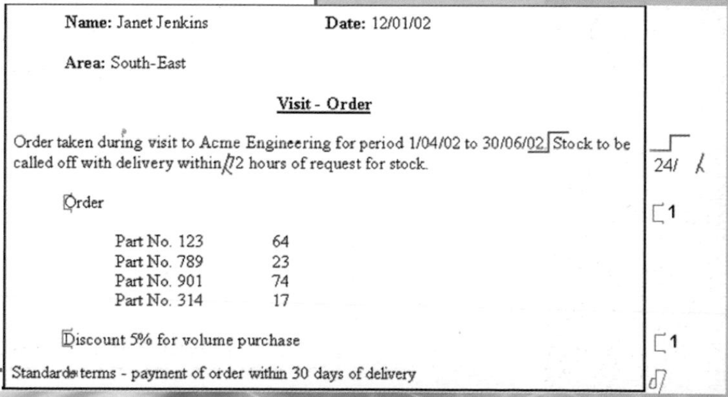

Name: Janet Jenkins   Date: 12/01/02

Area: South-East

Visit - Order

Order taken during visit to Acme Engineering for period 1/04/02 to 30/06/02 Stock to be called off with delivery within 72 hours of request for stock.   24/

Order   1

Part No. 123	64
Part No. 789	23
Part No. 901	74
Part No. 314	17

Discount 5% for volume purchase   1

Standards terms - payment of order within 30 days of delivery

Proofreading Symbols

Proof readers employ a number of symbols to identify changes they are recommending. The symbols are written on the document and then other symbols are placed in the margin to explain the nature of the amendment. Figure 16 gives some examples of the main common symbols.

Creating a New Document

One of the most useful computer applications is word processing. Modern word processors such as Microsoft Word provide users with functions to precisely layout documents including:

• Margins, line spacing, page and paragraph breaks
• Headers and footers
• Bullet point lists

Many organisations want to present a standard appearance to their clients and therefore adopt a defined house style for all their documents. This normally includes:

• Font (e.g. Times New Roman)
• Character Size (e.g. 12)
• Different fonts and character sizes for headings and the main body of the text
• Leaving a blank line between each paragraph
• Line spacing (e.g. 1.5)
• Size of margins
• Use of Headers and Footers (e.g. page numbers and date inserted)

If you are working within an organisation you need to understand what the house style is and how to apply it.

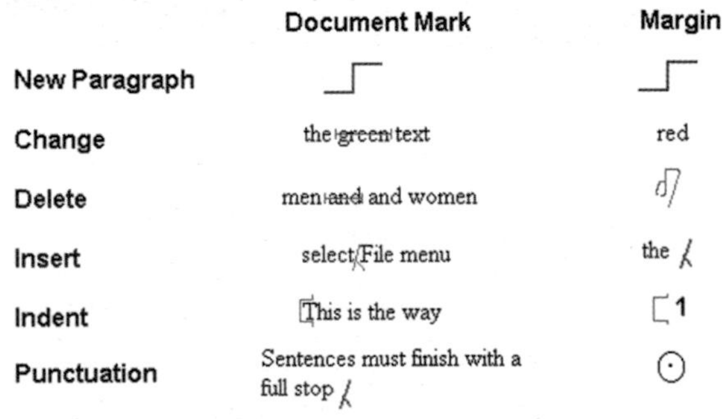

Layout and Formatting Functions

Microsoft Word and many other word processors offer you many functions to control the layout of your documents. These include:

• Page Breaks
• Paragraph breaks
• Line spacing
• Margins

A page break is the means of starting a new page. Word will automatically start a new page

FIGURE 16
Proof reading Symbols

	Document Mark	Margin
New Paragraph	⌐	⌐
Change	the green text	red
Delete	men and and women	∂⁊
Insert	select File menu	the ⋏
Indent	This is the way	⸢1
Punctuation	Sentences must finish with a full stop ⋏	⊙

when the old one is full. Page break is the means of starting a new page when the last one is not full. That is, you are controlling the layout of the document. Page Break is available in the Insert menu as the Break option.

FIGURE 17
Page Setup

There are several ways of indicating a new paragraph and Word allows you select them using the Format menu and the Paragraph option. Within this option you can also change the line spacing of the text. That is, the space you want to leave between the lines of text. If you are creating a document which will be proof read then often you will double space the text so that the proof reader has space to write notes on the document.

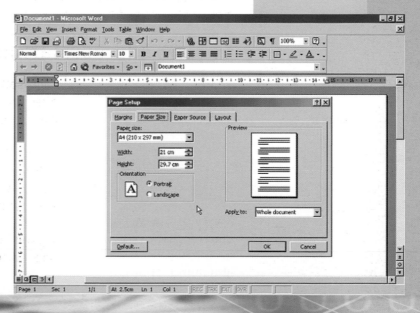

Margins are the spaces at the left, right, top and bottom of the document in which you are entering information. Word allows you to change all four margins in any way that you want. Margins are changed using the File menu and the Page Setup option.

Page Setup

When creating a document it is often useful to start by setting up the layout of the pages. You are free to alter this later if you change your mind. Once you have opened a new document the layout can be established using the File menu and the Page Setup option. This opens the Page Setup dialogue window (Figure 17).

FIGURE 18
**Portrait
and
Landscape**

The Page Setup window allows you to change the right, left, top and bottom margins of your documents and to preview how the changes affect the appearance of the document. You can also change the size of the Header and Footer. These are special areas at the top (header) and bottom (footer) of the document in which you can place information which will be repeated on all pages of the publication. Headers are often the place to put the title of the document so that it appears on all the

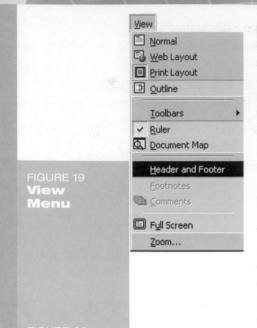

pages. Footers often contain details of the author. In both locations you can insert automatic fields which change, such as page numbers.

Page Setup has several tabs on the top of the window which, if clicked, reveal windows providing more options. By clicking on the Paper Size tab, the options shown in Figure 18 are shown. You can select the orientation of the page, either portrait or landscape.

Headers and Footers

You can insert either or both a header and a footer depending on the type of document you are designing. The function is available on the View menu (Figure 19). Select the Header and Footer option which opens a header area on your document and a toolbar providing extra options for the header. If you scroll down the page you will find the footer area at the bottom of the page.

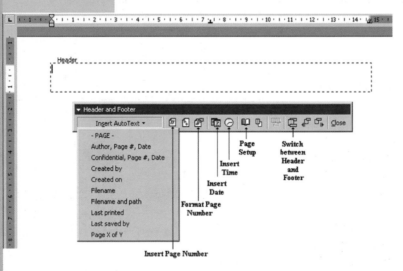

Once the Header or Footer area is visible (i.e. the area enclosed by a dotted line) you can enter text. This will appear at the cursor which you will see flashing in the top left hand corner of the area. To insert a field within the area you need to click on the menu options of your choice (e.g. Insert Page Number). The menu has wider functionality including providing access to the Page Setup dialogue window. At the start of the menu is a button, Insert Autotext that allows you to insert a range of information including the author's name, the last date the publication was printed etc. Figure 20 shows many of the options to add extra information and fields to either the Header or Footer area.

Bullets and Numbering

A very useful way of presenting information is a list, which is easy to read and understand. Word provides you with the means of producing bullet point lists which start with a symbol, letter or number so that the information is structured. They are accessed by selecting the Format menu (Figure 21) and clicking on the Bullets and <u>N</u>umbering options. This opens the Bullets and Numbering Window (Figure 22).

Figure 22 shows some of the different bullet point options available. The window is divided by tabs. If you click on a tab (e.g. <u>N</u>umbered) you can see a range of other options including numbered, aphabetical and indented lists. To select a bullet you single click to highlight it and then click on the OK button, or you double click the selection.

Special Symbols

Word provides a wide range of special symbols which you can insert in your text.

Example: ♪ ☺ ϕδ®©✍Ü

These are accessed by selecting the Insert menu (Figure 23) and clicking on the <u>S</u>ymbol option. This will open the Symbol window (Figure 24). The window provides access to a large number of symbols which are selected by highlighting the symbol by clicking on it and then on the <u>I</u>nsert button. The symbol is then inserted into the text at the cursor.

Search and Replace

It is important in any word processed document to be able to locate words or phrases in a document and to replace them with an alternative. You could simply read through the passage and find each word or phrase and then replace them by deleting the original words and entering the new ones from the keyboard. The problem with this type of approach is that it is easy to make errors (e.g. incorrectly spell the new word) or miss one of the words you are seeking to change. Word provides you with a means to automate the process.

If you select the <u>E</u>dit menu (Figure 25) and click on the <u>R</u>eplace option, the Find and Replace window (Figure 26) will appear. Enter the word or phrase you are seeking in the Fi<u>n</u>d what: box and then enter the words you are replacing them with in the Replace with box. Start the process by clicking on the Find Next button. The function will search through the document until it locates a match. You then have the choice of replacing the words with your new selection. Clicking on the Find Next button will move the search through the document. This systematic approach will ensure no errors are made.

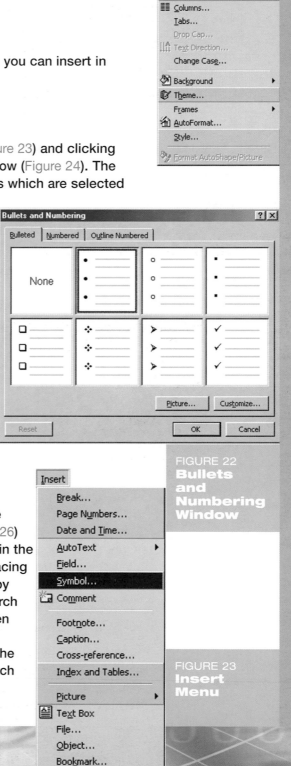

FIGURE 21
**Format
Menu**

FIGURE 22
**Bullets
and
Numbering
Window**

FIGURE 23
**Insert
Menu**

Widows and Orphans

FIGURE 24
Special Symbols

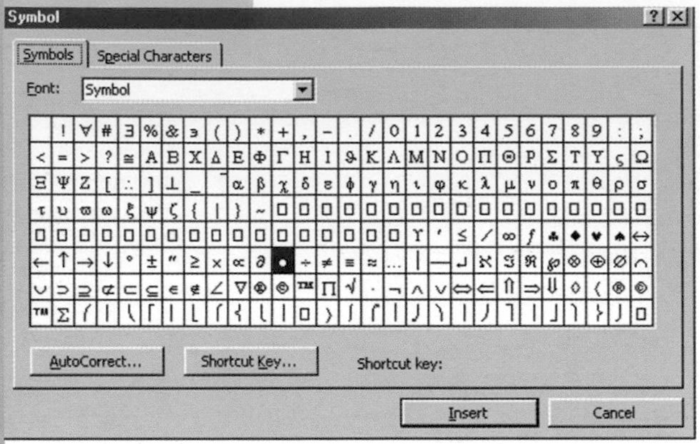

When creating a document there is always the risk that you will produce widows and orphans. These are isolated words or sentences on pages. The page break may leave an isolated word or phrase on one page while the text it relates to is on another page. This is poor presentation and Word provides you with a variety of ways of avoiding. Some ways of avoiding or removing them are:

• Page breaks to avoid leaving text behind which relates to the new page
• Change the font or the character size so that the amount of text which can fit on a page is altered and may avoid widows and orphans
• Change the line spacing so again the volume of text which fits on a page changes

House Style

Word processing allows almost everyone to write letters and other documents. This provides considerable flexibility to organisations but it does make it difficult to ensure the quality of documents. Organisations have addressed the problem of quality by setting standards which are often called house styles. This normally sets a standard for:

• The layout for letters (e.g. position of address, date and size of margins)
• Fonts
• Character Size

FIGURE 25
Edit Menu

This provides a standard look and feel to documents so that a minimum quality standard is established.
Organisations often spend considerable effort to develop a house style to ensure a common standard for all documents. They insist that all employees follow the standard.

FIGURE 26
Search and Replace

Exercise 5 below is intended to help you practise laying out a document in accordance with a defined house style.

The house style is:

Margins (Left, right, top and bottom)   3 cm
Portrait Orientation
Header   Text Centred
Footer   Automatic Date Field And Automatic Page Number - one
line below date, both centred

Single line spacing

Body Text   Times New Roman and size 12, left justified
Bullet Text   Times New Roman and size 12, left justified
Tables   Times New Roman, size 12, left justified
Column Headings, Times New Roman, size 12, Bold and
Centred
With Gridlines

This house style should also be applied to exercises 6, 7 and 8.

Exercise 5

Layout

1. Open Microsoft Word by clicking on the Start button, highlight Programs and select Microsoft Word option or double click on the Word icon on the Windows desktop.

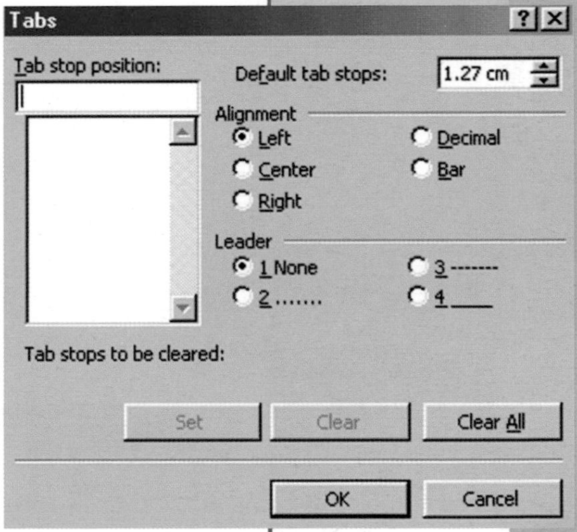

2. Using the File menu and the Page Setup, set the four margins to 3 cm and both header and footer to 2 cm.

3. Enter the passage below which includes using a bullet list in accordance with the house style:

The Solar System consists of the Sun and nine planets which are in orbit around it. The Solar System began life 4,500 million years ago when the planets condensed out of an immense cloud of gas. The nine planets are:

- Mercury
- Venus
- Earth
- Mars
- Jupiter
- Saturn
- Uranus
- Neptune
- Pluto

FIGURE 27
**Tabs
Window**

FIGURE 28
Paragraph Window

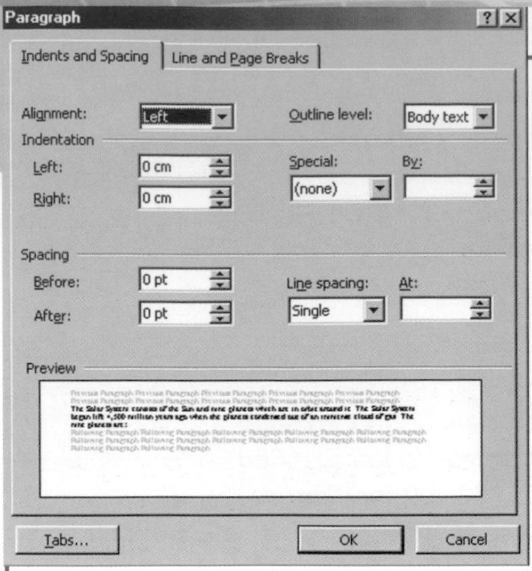

FIGURE 29
Table Menu

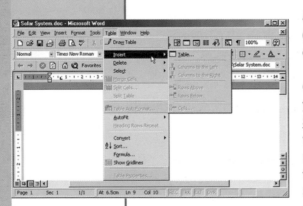

FIGURE 30
Insert Table Window

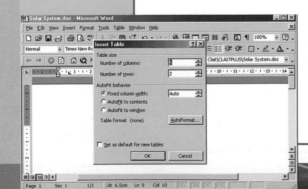

In addition to the planets there are approximately 63 moons and many thousands of asteroids. Moons orbit the planets while the asteroids orbit the Sun. Asteroids vary in size from several miles across to simple lumps of rock. They are often irregular in shape and have strange orbits.

The planets are divided into two groups. Those planets which orbit close to the Sun (e.g. Mercury, Venus, Earth and Mars) are called the inner planets. Planets that are further away from the Sun such as Jupiter, Saturn, Uranus, Neptune and Pluto are called the outer planets.

4. Systematically check your document to ensure that it is correct. If you find a mistake then move the cursor to the error by clicking once at the desired location. You can delete the mistake using either the backspace (deletes to the left) or delete keys (deletes to the right) and enter the correction.

5. Check the spelling and grammar of the entry (select the Tools menu and Spelling and Grammar option).

6. Enter your floppy disk into the drive and save your document by selecting the File menu and the Save option. This will reveal the Save As dialogue window. Change the Save in: box to Floppy (A) by using the down arrow at the end of the box to show the list of options. Save the document as File name: Solar System. Click the Save button. You have now saved your document as a file called Solar System.

7. Now add a header and footer to the document. The header should read Solar System, in Arial font with a character size of 16. The title should be centred. The footer should show the page number centred on the page and one line below the date.

8. Save your document again by selecting the File menu and the Save option.

9. Close Word by selecting the File menu and the Exit option.

Indenting Text

In any document you may wish to indent your text. There are several ways of doing this. The most straightforward is to use the tab key on the keyboard which will indent the text. You can set the size of the tab by selecting the Format menu (Figure 21) and click on the Tabs option which will open the Tabs window (Figure 27). In this window you can change the size of the tab and the alignment.

An alternative approach is to select the Format menu and click on the Paragraph option. This will reveal the paragraph window (Figure 28) that allows you to set the size of the indent from both margins (i.e. left and right) and see the effects in the Preview window. The Special box provides access to indents for the first line, hanging or none. First line indent will only indent the first line of each paragraph while a hanging indent sets the whole paragraph except the first line to be indented.

For example:

First Line indent

      Aaaaaaaaaaaaaaaaaaaaaaaaaaaaa

Hanging indent

Aaaaaaaaaaaaaaaaaaaaaaaaaaaaaaaaaaaaaaaaaaaaaaaaaaaaaaaaaaaaaaaaaaa
      aaaaaaaaaaaaaaaaaaaaaaaaaaaaaaaaaaaaaaaaaaaaaaaaaaaaaaaaaaaaaaaa
      aaaaaaaaaaaaaaaaaaaaaaaaaaaaaaaaaaaaaaaaaaaaaaaaaaaaaaaaaaaaaaaa
      aaaaaaaaaaaaaaaaaaaaaaaaaaaaaaaaaaaaaaaaaaaaaaaaaaaaaaaaaaaaaaaa

The Paragraph window also allows you to set line spacing and to control pagination.

A third method is to use the ruler at the top of the Word work area. If it is not visible you can reveal it by selecting the View menu and clicking on Ruler. By dragging the stops at the end of the ruler you can create first line and hanging indents. It is possible to change the right indent or tab by dragging the right ruler stop.

Exercise 6

Indents

1. Insert your floppy disk into the drive

2. Open Microsoft Word by clicking on the Start button, highlight Programs and select Microsoft Word option or double click on the Word icon on the Windows desktop.

3. Open the file Solar System by selecting the File menu and the Open option to reveal the Open dialogue window. Change Look in: box to Floppy (A:) using the arrow button at the end of the box. This will reveal the files stored on the floppy in the central area of the window (Figure 14). Double click on the file Solar System or single click to highlight it and then click on the Open button.

4. The document Solar System will appear in the Word work area.

5. Experiment with the three alternative approaches to indenting your text. Try to indent the start of each paragraph and also to create hanging indents. Continue until you are confident you can use the alternative approaches.

6. There is no need to save your efforts.

7. Close Word by selecting the File menu and the Exit option. When you close without saving you will see a window appear asking you if you want to save. In this instance you do not but on other occasions it may stop you making a mistake.

Tables

Word and many other wordprocessors can present information in the form of a table. To insert a table into a document requires selecting the Table menu (Figure 29), highlighting Insert and clicking on the Table option. This will open the Insert Table window (Figure 30).

The Insert Table window allows you to set the number of rows and columns in the table and to set the size of each column. The features (e.g. size of column, number of rows and columns) are altered using the up and down arrows alongside the appropriate boxes. By clicking on the arrows you can change the feature. Once you have set the parameters of the table you can insert the table at the cursor by clicking on the OK button.

Exercise 7

Tables

1. Insert your floppy disk into the drive

2. Open Microsoft Word by clicking on the Start button, highlight Programs and select Microsoft Word option or double click on the Word icon on the Windows desktop.

FIGURE 31
**Solar
System
Table**

3. Open the file Solar System by selecting the File menu and the Open option to reveal the Open dialogue window. Change Look in: box to Floppy (A:) using the arrow button at the end of the box. This will reveal the files stored

Planets	Year Length	Moons	Atmosphere
Mercury	88 days	None	None
Venus	225 days	None	Carbon Dioxide
Earth	365 days	One	Nitrogen and Oxygen
Mars	687 days	Two	Very Thin
Jupiter	12 years	Sixteen	Gas Planet
Saturn	29 years	Eighteen	Gas Planet
Uranus	84 years	Seventeen	Gas Planet
Neptune	165 years	Eight	Gas Planet
Pluto	248 years	One	Thin

on the floppy in the central area of the window (Figure 14). Double click on the file Solar System or single click to highlight it and then click on the Open button.

4. The document Solar System will appear in the Word work area.

5. You are now going to insert the table shown below into this document.

Planet	Year Length	Moons	Atmosphere
Mercury	88 days	None	None
Venus	225 days	None	Carbon Dioxide
Earth	365 days	One	Nitrogen and Oxygen
Mars	687 days	Two	Very Thin
Jupiter	12 years	Sixteen	Gas Planet
Saturn	29 years	Eighteen	Gas Planet
Uranus	84 years	Seventeen	Gas Planet
Neptune	165 years	Eight	Gas Planet
Pluto	248 years	One	Thin

6. Insert this table at the end of your document by selecting the Table menu, highlight Insert option and click on Table to reveal the Insert Table window. Set the table parameters to ten rows and four columns. Text is added by clicking in the respective cells or by using the tab keys to move between the rows and columns. Figure 31 shows the table.

7. Check the accuracy of your table and correct any errors by clicking in the appropriate cell.

FIGURE 32
**Customised
Columns**

8. Enter your floppy disk into the drive and save your document by selecting the File menu and the Save As option. This will reveal the Save As dialogue window. Change the Save in: box to Floppy (A) by using the down arrow at end of the box to show list of options. Save the document as File name: Solar System Table. When

Planets	Year Length	Moons	Atmosphere
Mercury	88 days	None	None
Venus	225 days	None	Carbon Dioxide
Earth	365 days	One	Nitrogen and Oxygen
Mars	687 days	Two	Very Thin
Jupiter	12 years	Sixteen	Gas Planet
Saturn	29 years	Eighteen	Gas Planet
Uranus	84 years	Seventeen	Gas Planet
Neptune	165 years	Eight	Gas Planet
Pluto	248 years	One	Thin

FIGURE 33
Table Properties

Table Properties

Table | Row | Column | Cell

Size

☐ Preferred width: 0 cm   Measure in: Centimeter ▼

Alignment

Left   Center   Right   Indent from left: 0 cm

Text wrapping

None   Around   Positioning...

Borders and Shading...   Options...

OK   Cancel

you are ready click the Save button. You have now saved your document as a file called Solar System Table.

9. If you review the table you will see that columns do not fit the information you have entered. To customise the widths of the columns you must highlight the columns you want to change. In this case highlight them all by clicking in the Planets cell and holding down the mouse button, drag the pointer down to the bottom right hand corner of the table.

10. Select the Table menu, highlight the AutoFit option to reveal a range of options. Consider the different choices. Click on the AutoFit to Contents. You will notice that your table changes (Figure 32).

11. You can change the appearance of the information within the table by highlighting the cells and selecting the option you desire such as font, character size, bold, italics, change alignment (i.e. left, right and centre). Remember your design is governed by the house style (see Exercise 5).

12. Centre and embolden the titles of the columns.

13. Change the font size of the whole table to 12.

14. You can align the table as well as the information it contains by using the Table menu and clicking on the Table Properties option. This will reveal the Table Properties window (Figure 33). The window has a number of tabs which will reveal tools to operate on rows, columns and cells.

15. Table Tab - allows you to align the whole table. Use it to centre the whole table.

16. Save your document again by selecting the File menu and the Save option.

17. The other tabs allow you to change height of rows, width of columns and align text in each cell. Explore the options but do not make any permanent changes (i.e. use the Undo and Redo options in the Edit menu). Continue your experiments until you understand the different options.

18. You can also change the borders and shading of your table by using the Format menu and the Borders and Shading option to reveal the Borders and

Shading window (Figure 34).

19. The Borders and Shading window enables you to change the borders of your table by using the Setting, Style, Color and Width of lines. You can explore the different options since the Preview window shows you what your choices look like.

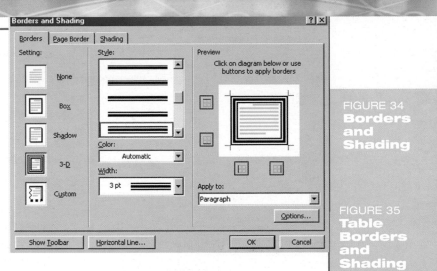

FIGURE 34
Borders and Shading

FIGURE 35
Table Borders and Shading

20. Highlight your table and using the Borders and Shading window select an attractive border.

21. Highlight your table and using the Borders and Shading window and the Shading tab select an appropriate shading colour (e.g. yellow). Figure 35 shows our table.

Planets	Year Length	Moons	Atmosphere
Mercury	88 days	None	None
Venus	225 days	None	Carbon Dioxide
Earth	365 days	One	Nitrogen and Oxygen
Mars	687 days	Two	Very Thin
Jupiter	12 years	Sixteen	Gas Planet
Saturn	29 years	Eighteen	Gas Planet
Uranus	84 years	Seventeen	Gas Planet
Neptune	165 years	Eight	Gas Planet
Pluto	248 years	One	Thin

22. Save your document again by selecting the File menu and the Save option.

23. Print your document by selecting the File menu and Print option.

24. You can now practice using the Find and Replace function available within the Edit menu. Searching from the start of the document, locate the terms Planet and replace them with the word Giant. You should locate the terms times.

25. There is no need to save the amended document since you are simply practising.

26. Close Word by selecting the File menu and the Exit option. When you without saving you will see that a window appears to ask if you want to saveThis is intended to prevent you loosing data. In this case you do not need to save but sometimes you will so always consider the question before making a decision.

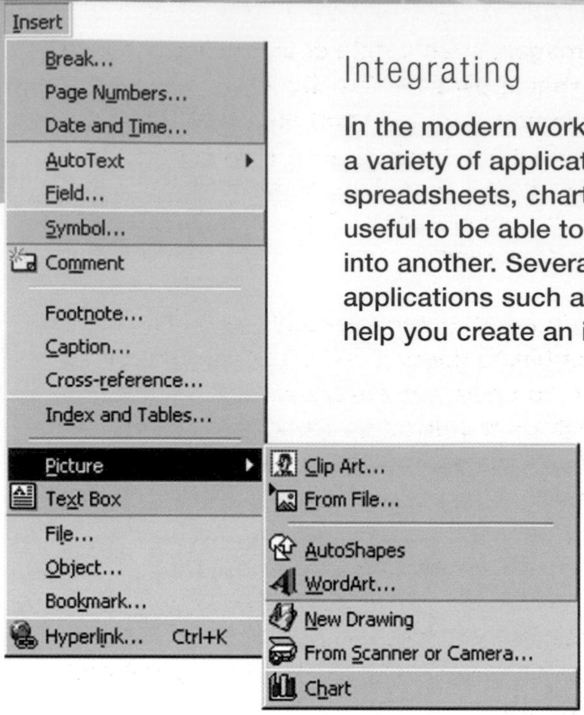

FIGURE 36
**Insert
Menu
Import
Options**

Insert

Break...
Page Numbers...
Date and Time...
AutoText
Field...
Symbol...
Comment
Footnote...
Caption...
Cross-reference...
Index and Tables...
Picture
Text Box
File...
Object...
Bookmark...
Hyperlink...   Ctrl+K

Clip Art...
From File...
AutoShapes
WordArt...
New Drawing
From Scanner or Camera...
Chart

Integrating

In the modern workplace you are often working with a variety of applications such as word processing, spreadsheets, charts and graphs and databases. It is useful to be able to import files from one application into another. Several integrated packages of applications such as Microsoft Office provide tools to help you create an integrated document.

Microsoft Word allows you to import files from other Office applications, to insert images from clip art collections and to add images you have created yourself. If you consider the options within the Insert menu (Figure 36) you will see a variety of tools to import files into your document. In addition you can simply use the Copy, Cut and Paste functions (i.e. Edit menu) to copy or move an image from one Office application and paste it into another.

The Picture option provides access to a range of functions to import images into your documents including clip art, images stored as a file, WordArt, pictures scanned or photographed with a digital camera and charts produced in Excel.

Using the File option you can insert a file from another application to produce an integrated document. In many cases Word will convert the file format into one with which it is compatible. However, some formats will not be accepted and you may see a warning message the first time you attempt to import a file telling you that you need to install the file conversion software.

Warning Message

"Microsoft Word can't import the specified format. This feature is not currently installed. Would you like to install it now?"

To install the conversion program you need to insert the Microsoft Office CD-ROM and click on the OK button and then follow the instructions off the screen.

Nevertheless, the Copy, Cut and Paste options are perhaps the most straightforward way of transfering resources between applications. You can copy a database table, spreadsheet or image and paste its contents into Word in the same way you can within an application.

The general process of importing images, charts, data or text using copy and paste is straightforward. In the original application (e.g. Excel, Access etc) highlight the sheet, table or data that you want to import and copy it using the Copy function which is often available in the Edit menus. Now move to Word or the application in which you are creating the integrated document and using the paste function insert the copied object. The copied image will appear at the cursor position in the document.

The different elements that you are integrating together have probably been created without any intention of combining them. It is therefore important to be clear about how they need to be combined. If you have a specification then it is important to present the integrated document as it is specified. This will ensure that the desired outcome is achieved. If you do not follow the specification the required outcome will not be achieved.

The different components are therefore likely to employ different fonts, character sizes and other layout features so that you may have to make changes so that the integrated document is effectively presented. In order to change the format of imported text or data then you need to highlight it and select the desired font and character size.

Images and charts will often need to be resized to fit into the combined document since they will have been produced for other purposes. In changing the size of an image or chart you need to ensure that its original proportions are maintained or the quality of the image will be reduced. When you import an image or chart it will appear in a rectangle with small rectangles at each corner and at the midpoint of each side. If it does not a single click on the image will enclose the image. This is the equivalent of highlighting it. If you place your mouse pointer on the enclosing small rectangles the mouse pointer will change to become a double-headed arrow. If you hold down the mouse button you can reshape the image or chart by dragging the edge. In changing the shape you need to make sure that the proportions and quality of the image are maintained. You can also move the image or chart by placing the pointer in the centre of the image and holding down the mouse button then dragging the whole image or chart to a new location.

When you import an Excel spreadsheet into Word it will have a small rectangle with a star inside at the left hand top corner. If you place your pointer on this square it will change shape to a star and by holding down the mouse button you can move the sheet to the location of your choice. At the bottom right hand corner is a matching small square which if you place your pointer on changes its shape to a double-headed arrow. By holding down the mouse button you can resize the sheet.

Generic Text and Data Files

Generic text and data files are ones which can be accessed by the majority of applications without their format needing to change. Earlier we discussed how to use the File option to import files into Word which involves the conversion of the file format. Generic files do not normally need to have their files converted since they can be read by a large number of applications (e.g. word processors). A generic text file will often have the extension .txt.

A generic file can be imported using the File option within the Insert menu. When it appears its format will often need to be amended (e.g. sentences broken up, extra spacings and gaps in the text). This is due to the limited formatting instructions contained in a generic file to make it compatible with many applications. Data files will sometimes be split across more than one page due to the position they are imported to. It is good practice to present data on a single page so that it is easier for the reader to understand the data.

When you are initially creating an integrated document you could begin by simply basing it on a generic text file. Word will open a generic text file in the same way it opens a word file. That is, select the File menu and the Open option. This will open the Open window. At the bottom of this window is a box called Files of type with a down arrow button which if clicked provides a list of file formats. This should be All Files or Text Files so that the system can locate text files. When a text file is located you can open it by either highlighting it and clicking on the Open button or by doubling clicking the file. It will open within Word.

Printing Integrated Document

The process of printing an integrated document is identical to printing any document. However, there is probably a greater need to check the appearance of the printed document since you are combining a number of resources into a single document. To preview a document prior to printing in Word you need to select the File menu and the Print Preview option. This will reveal the Print Preview window and show you how your integrated document will appear when printed. If you are satisfied then you can close the window and select the File menu and the Print option to reveal the Print window. The document will be printed if you click on the OK button using the printers default settings.

Exercise 8

Integrated Documents

1. Open Microsoft Word by clicking on the Start button, highlight Programs and select Microsoft Word option or double click on Word icon on the Windows desktop. A blank page will appear

2. Enter the following text:

This is an example of a document combining different resources.
This should be in accordance with house style (see Exercise 5)

3. Leave three blank lines. Select the Insert menu and click on the File option to reveal the Insert File window. Using the down arrow button alongside the Look in: change the folder to read your floppy disk. The files stored on the floppy disk will be shown in the central area. Figure 36A shows this window.

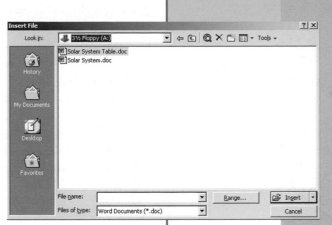

4. Double click on the Solar System.doc and it will be inserted into your new document.

5. Leave a blank line and again select the Insert menu, highlight the Picture item and click on the Clip Art option to reveal the Insert Clipart window. You will be presented with a variety of categories of images. If you click on one then a range of images will be provided. The image can be selected by clicking on it to reveal a pop up menu (Figure 36B). If the Insert clip icon is clicked on then the chosen image will be inserted into the document. Select an image and insert it into your integrated document.

6. You may be presented with messages asking you to insert the Microsoft Office installation disks if the Clip Art has not be installed on your computer.

7. Using the Insert menu and the File option practise adding other resources to your document (e.g. Excel spreadsheet files). You may see messages that indicate you have to install extra facilities to convert the format of files. In order to do this you will need the installation disks for Microsoft Office. If you are not confident about carrying out this task then seek help before going on.

8. Save your document by selecting the File menu and the Save option. Name your file Integrated.

9. Preview your document in order to check its appearance when printed by selecting the File menu and the Print Preview option. Close the Print Preview window and either amend your document to correct any errors or print your document by selecting the File menu and the Print option.

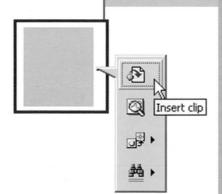

10. Open a new blank document so that you can now practise importing text and data files, images and charts.

Select the Insert menu and the File option. This will open the Insert File window. In any order that you prefer select text files, data files, charts and images import them into your blank document. Continue to import until you are confident that you understand the process. Importing these files and images also provides an opportunity to format the integrated document. Practice your formatting skills until you are again confident. There is no need to save your changes.

11. Close Word by selecting the File menu and the Exit option. When you close without saving you will see that a window appears to ask if you want to save. This is intended to prevent you losing data. In this case you do not need to save but sometimes you will so always consider the question before making a decision.

House Style

Exercise 9 should be undertaken in accordance with a house style. The house style is:

Margins (Left, right, top and bottom)	3 cm
Portrait Orientation	
Header	Text Centred
Footer	your name and centre, centred

Single line spacing

Heading Text	Arial and size 12, Bold and Left Justified
Body Text	Arial and size 10, left justified
Bullet Text	Arial and size 10, left justified
Tables	Arial, size 10, left justified
	Column Headings, Arial, size 12, Bold and Centred
	With Gridlines

Exercise 9

More Practice

1. Open Microsoft Word by clicking on the Start button, highlight Programs and select Microsoft Word option or double click on the Word icon on the Windows desktop.

2. Enter the text below:

House Prices

The price of houses has risen rapidly in the town but spectacularly in the surrounding countryside. In local villages two bedroom cottages have been sold for in excess of £150,000 while detached farmhouses are selling for over £450,000. Local Estate Agents claim that there is a serious shortage of properties for sale. This is driving the prices up. The main demand is for:

• Victorian Terrace Houses in the town
• Cottages with gardens in local villages
• Detached Farmhouses
• Converted building (e.g. Mills)

Table 1 shows the raise in prices since 1990.

Table 1   Price Rises

Type	1990	1995	2000	Now
Cottage	45,000	65,000	90,000	150,000
Semi-detached	70,000	92,000	145,000	250,000
Detached	100,000	140,000	260,000	450,000

3. Centre and embolden your headings. Centre the table and select a suitable border.

4. Insert a header – House Prices

5. Insert a footer – your name, centre

6. Save your document by selecting the File menu and the Save option. Name your file Price.

7. Print your document by selecting the File menu and the Print option.

8. Close Word by selecting the File menu and the Exit option.

Summary

1. Files and Folders

All information stored on a computer is held in a file. Each file has an individual name and they are often stored within folders. Folders can also be stored in other folders. Folders are sometimes called directories.

2. Open Files

Files can be opened by double clicking on them with the mouse pointer. The files will only open if an application which is able to read the file is present on the computer system. If the application is not present Windows will display a message window asking you to locate the appropriate application since the operating system cannot find it.

3. Windows Explorer

Windows Explorer provides you with the tools to create new folders and delete, rename, move, copy and save files and folders. These functions are available on the File menu and toolbar.

4. Types of Files

There are many different types of files. File names normally end with a full stop and three letters (e.g. .doc). This indicates the type of file and helps you to distinguish between them. In addition the icons show the type of file.

5. Printing Windows

Press the ALT key and then the Print Screen (sometimes Print Scrn) key. Paste the windows image into a document (e.g. Word) and print the document using the normal functions of the application.

To capture the contents of the whole display you only need to press the Print Screen key and then paste the image into a document.

6. Spell and Grammar Checkers

In Microsoft Word spell and grammar checkers are available in the Tools menu as the Spelling and Grammar option.

7. Save

Select the File menu and the Save option. This will reveal the Save As dialogue window which allows to choose where to save your file (e.g. floppy disk) and to name it. After you have saved your file once it will be updated each time you click on Save option.

8. Save As

Select the File menu and Save As option. This will let you save your file under a new name or in a new location.

9. Page Setup
Select the File menu and the Page Setup option. This opens the Page Setup dialogue window. You can choose the layout of your page (e.g. margins, orientation, size of headers and footers).

10. Headers and Footers
Select the View menu and the Header and Footer option which will open a header area on your document and a toolbar which provides extra options for the header. If you scroll down the page you will find the footer area at the bottom of the page with the toolbar.

11. Bullets and Numbering
Select the Format menu and click on the Bullets and Numbering options. This will reveal the Bullets and Numbering Window.

12. Special Symbols
Select the Insert menu and click on the Symbol option. This will open the Symbol window.

13. Search and Replace
Select the Edit menu and click on the Replace option to reveal the Find and Replace window.

14. Indenting Text
here are several ways of indenting text.

- Tab key on the keyboard. You can set the size of the tab by selecting the Format menu and clicking on the Tabs option which will open the Tabs window.

- Select the Format menu and click on the Paragraph option. This will reveal the paragraph window.

- Select the View menu and click on Ruler. By dragging the stops at the end of the ruler you can create first line and hanging indents.

15. Tables
Select the Table menu, highlight the Insert option and click on the Table option. This will open the Insert Table window.

16. Changing Column Widths
Highlight the columns you want to change. Select the Table menu, highlight the AutoFit option to reveal a range of options and click on the AutoFit to Contents.

17. Presentation of Table Contents
Highlight the content of the cells you want to change and select the option you desire such as font, character size, embold, italics, change alignment (i.e. left, right and centre).

18. Table Aligning

Select the Table menu and click on the Table Properties option. This will reveal the Table Properties window which has a number of tabs that will reveal tools to operate on rows, columns and cells.

- Table Tab - allows you to align the whole table

- Other tabs allow you to change height of rows, width of columns and align text in each cell

19. Borders and Shading

Highlight your table then select the Format menu and the Borders and Shading option to reveal the Borders and Shading window. This allows you to change the borders of your table by using the Setting, Style, Color and Width of lines options.

20. Layout and Formatting

Select the Format menu and click on the Paragraph option to open Paragraph window. This allows to change alignment, line spacing, and indentation.

21. Importing charts, images, data and text

Copy, Cut and Paste functions allow you to move charts, images, data and text between Microsoft Office applications.

Alternatively select the Format menu and click on File option or highlight the Picture option to reveal submenu which allows you to choose an image from Clip Art or From File (ie a file stored on the computer).

Spreadsheets and Solutions

This chapter will help you to:

- Enter, edit and manipulate data

- Create formulae and use common functions

- Format and present data

- Link live data from one spreadsheet to another

- Use spreadsheets to solve problems and project results

This chapter covers Units 2 (Spreadsheets) and 10 (Spreadsheet Solutions). The content of these two units overlaps so that you cannot offer both of them as part of CLAIT Plus. However, you are free to offer either unit as part of the qualification or study them as single units. There are no pre-conditions for studying these units. However, their content does assume that you have the skills and understanding which are provided by the OCR Level 1 ICT course New CLAIT (e.g. Unit 4 - Spreadsheets and Unit 1 - Using a Computer).

Assessment

Unit 2 - Spreadsheets

After studying Unit 2 your skills and understanding are assessed during a 3 hour practical assignment. This is set by OCR and marked locally. However, the marking will be externally moderated by OCR. This ensures that the standard is being applied correctly across the many different providers of OCR CLAIT Plus. If you are unsuccessful then you can be re-assessed using a different assignment.

Unit 10 - Spreadsheet Solutions

After studying Unit 10 your skills and understanding are assessed using a locally devised practical assignment. The assignment will be marked locally but externally moderated by OCR. This ensures that the standard is being applied correctly across the many different providers of OCR CLAIT Plus. If you are unsuccessful then you can be re-assessed using a different assignment.

The assessment task can be provided by the local tutor or suggested by the individual student. In both cases the task must meet all the assessment objectives of Unit 10 and allow learners to show their understanding. The learner must provide an OCR Evidence Checklist showing where and how the assessment objectives have been met by the completed task.

Comparison

The two units have a great deal in common in terms of the skills, knowledge and understanding that you are required to develop. However, they are not identical and the major difference is that Unit 2 is intended to assist you in using, amending and working with spreadsheets while Unit 10 assumes you want to create a spreadsheet for a distinct purpose. Learners undertaking Unit 10 may be employees of an organisation who need to model part of their business using a spreadsheet. Learners undertaking Unit 2 may have less specific needs. However, these are generalisations and you need to choose which is right for you. The difference in assessment is significant and you should identify which approach you prefer. You will then need to discuss which unit is most appropriate for you with your local tutor or college.

Font Families

Clait Plus uses font families in its assessments rather than font names. In Chapter 1 Font Families are explained and how they relate to font names. As you undertake each exercise consider which font family the font you are using belongs to.

FIGURE 37
Microsoft Excel

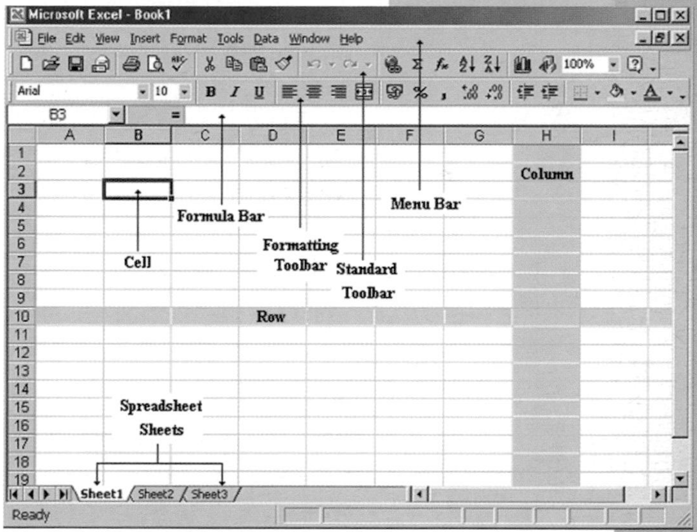

Spreadsheet Applications

This chapter is based on Microsoft Excel 2000, which is a modern spreadsheet package that you can employ to create spreadsheets. Figure 37 shows the Excel application interface. Its main feature is a grid of columns and rows. This is the work area of the spreadsheet. The columns are designated with a letter (e.g. A, B, C etc.) while the rows are numbered (e.g. 1, 2, 3 etc.). The intersection of columns and rows produces a rectangular area called a cell. Each cell is know by the letter and number of its column and row (e.g. A1, B2, C3 etc.).

When you click in a cell it is highlighted. In Figure 37, cell B3 is highlighted. You will also see that the highlighted cell reference is given at the left end of the formula toolbar. At the bottom of the grid in the left hand corner are three tabs called sheets 1, 2 and 3. These allow you to move between three spreadsheets. These three spreadsheets combined are called a workbook. The sheets are often related (e.g. sales figures for three different products).

The work area is surrounded by an interface which is broadly similar to many other Microsoft Office applications. It has a menu bar and a number of toolbars providing access to the many different functions available within Excel to create, amend and manipulate spreadsheets.

The two main ways of loading Microsoft Excel are:

• Click on the Start button in the bottom left hand corner of the Windows desktop. A menu will popup. If you highlight the Programs item a new menu will appear alongside it. If you click on the item shown as Microsoft Excel then the application will load.

• Double click on the Excel icon shown on the desktop.

A variety of exercises are included in this chapter. Their prime purpose is to help you understand how to create and use spreadsheets. They are simplified representations of the world and are not intended to be tutorials on accountancy but explanations of Excel.

The primary purpose of a spreadsheet is to analyse numerical information to assist organisations management. They may consider the sales of a product, wage costs, overheads or many other issues. However, one key factor essential for all spreadsheets is numerical accuracy. Data entered must be correct and calculations need to be checked to ensure they are perfect. When creating a spreadsheet you must devote a lot of time to checking that all data and formulae are accurate.

Modelling

A key role for spreadsheets is to model information and allow you to explore what would be the result of a change.

For example:

You might create a spreadsheet showing the production costs of manufacturing a component. The spreadsheet would allow you to explore what would be the effect of changing the process (e.g. investing in a new machine which allows you to manufacture the component using half the workforce).

You might create a spreadsheet showing the relationship between sales staff and profit. You might explore the effects of increasing or decreasing the number of staff.

You might create a spreadsheet showing the relationship between commission and sales volumes. This would allow you to consider the influence of changing the rates of commission.

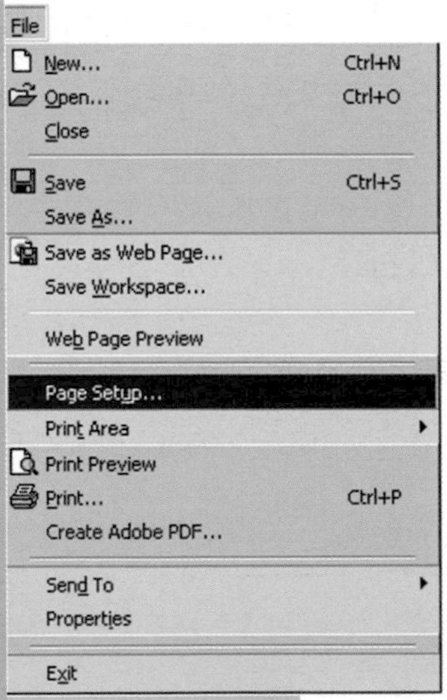

File	
New...	Ctrl+N
Open...	Ctrl+O
Close	
Save	Ctrl+S
Save As...	
Save as Web Page...	
Save Workspace...	
Web Page Preview	
Page Setup...	
Print Area	▶
Print Preview	
Print...	Ctrl+P
Create Adobe PDF...	
Send To	▶
Properties	
Exit	

FIGURE 38
File Menu

Create A Spreadsheet

Unit 10 is assessed by producing a spreadsheet with at least 200 cells and linked to a second sheet. To create a new sheet requires that you understand the nature of the information you are going to model and how you want to present the spreadsheet.

The first step is to establish the structure or layout of the spreadsheet. The layout and structure of a sheet is important in that it will influence the way the information it contains is accepted. Senior managers will only act on the results of a spreadsheet if they are persuaded that it is quality work. A sheet that is well presented with an effective structure will go a long way towards demonstrating it is worth considering. You can start a spreadsheet with an initial structure and then amend it later to improve its appearance.

The structure of a spreadsheet can be established using the Page Setup option which is available from the File menu (Figure 38). If you click on the Page Setup option it will reveal the Page Setup window (Figure 39). This is divided by a series of tabs - Page, Margin, Header/Footer and Sheet.

The Page tab allows you to set the orientation of the sheet (i.e. portrait or landscape). It also provides access to the scaling feature which lets you fit your spreadsheet on to a specified number of pages when you are printing it by scaling the size of the sheet. For both options click on the relevant radio buttons.

The Margins tab provides the means of changing the size of the four margins (i.e. top, bottom, left and right). The window demonstrates the orientation of the sheet and the four margins. Using the up and down arrows near each box you can increase or decrease the margins. The same display also allows you to set the size of the header and footer and finally to centre the sheet on the page either horizontally or vertically. This can improve the appearance of the spreadsheet.

The Header/Footer tab enables you to customise the information which heads and foots the sheet. By clicking on the Custom Header or Custom Footer button you will reveal the Header or Footer window (Figure 42).

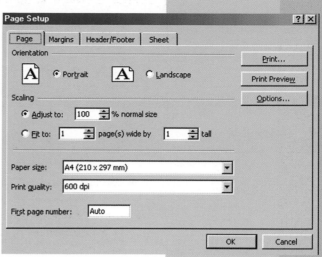

FIGURE 39
Page Setup

FIGURE 40
Margins

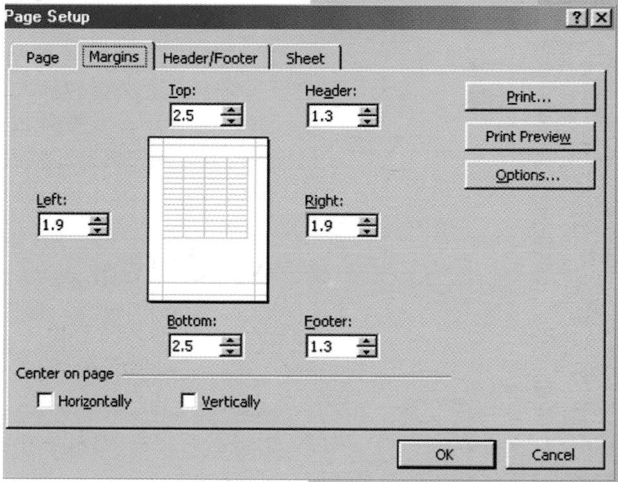

FIGURE 41
Headers and Footers

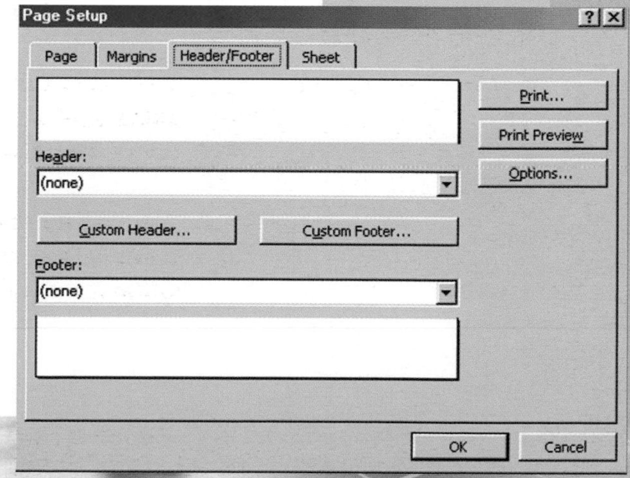

FIGURE 42
Header and Footer Windows

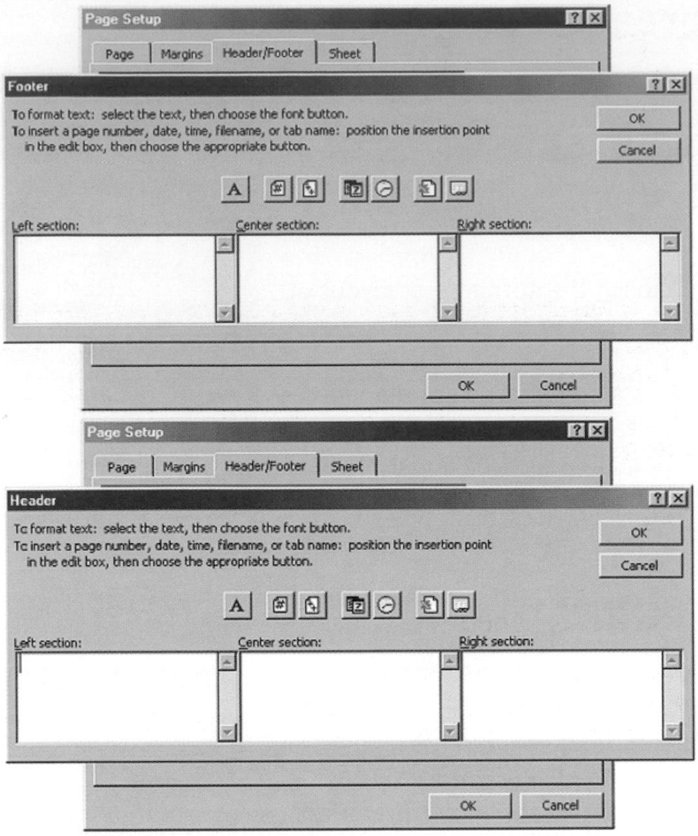

The Header and Footer window allows you to insert text which will appear at the top or bottom of the sheet. In addition you can add a number of automatic fields which will change depending on the sheet when they appear (e.g. number of the page, new date and a change of file name). The font, character size and style of text can be changed using the text button. The other buttons allow automatic fields to be inserted. The text and automatic fields are inserted at the cursor in the left, right or centre of the header or footer.

Figure 42A shows the icons that appear on the Header window (and also on the Footer). Each icon serves a different purpose and these are explained in Figure 42A. The process is to place the cursor in your chosen location or highlight the text and then to click on the icon. The first icon allows you to format the text while the remaining icons provide you with the means of inserting an automatic field into the header or footer.

FIGURE 42A
Header Windows

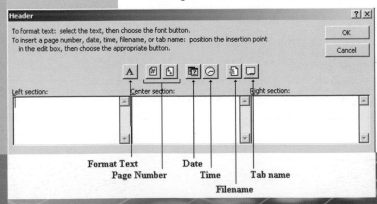

Exercise 10

Create a Spreadsheet Structure

1. Load Microsoft Excel using either the Programs menu or the Excel icon on the desktop.

2. Set the orientation of the sheet to landscape, margins to 2 cm - right and left and 2.5 cm - top and bottom and the header and footer to 1.5 cm (select File menu and Page Setup option)

3. Insert Header to read

Sales Forecast - Arial font and character size 14 embolden - in the centre section

4. Insert automatic fields in the Footer

Filename - left section
Page Number - centre section
Date - right section

5. Enter the table of information below to form your first spreadsheet. Start Item in cell B5

Item	January	February etc (all the 12 months of the year)
Hand Tools		
Power Tools		
Wood		
Metal		
Fastenings		
Paint		
Wallpaper		
Electrical		
Garden		
Kitchen		
Garage		

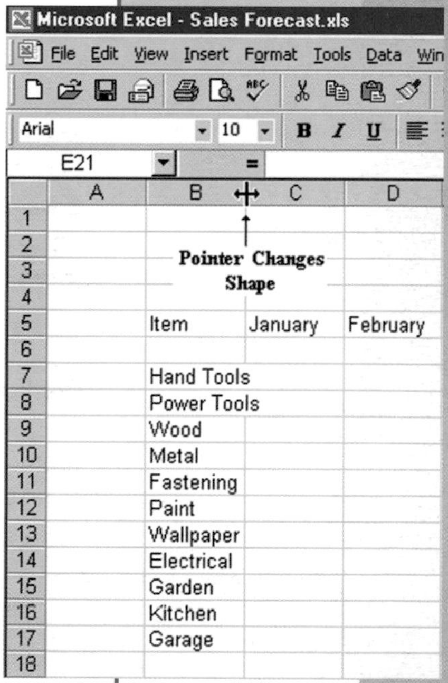

6. Check that you have entered the data accurately and correct any mistakes. If you click in the cell which contains the error you can amend the mistake by pressing the delete key and re-entering. Alternatively the content of a selected cell appears on the formula bar and can be edited if you click on the bar and then use arrow keys and keyboard.

FIGURE 43
Wider Columns

47

7. It is good practice to save your work early and to update the file as you make changes and enhance the spreadsheet. Insert a floppy disk into the A: drive and select the File menu and click on the option Save to reveal the Save As window. Change the Save in: box to select the Floppy disk and add the file name Sales Forecast in the File name box. Click on the Save button. You will probably hear the floppy drive and your spreadsheet will be saved as the file Sales Forecast. The top line of Excel will change to read "Microsoft Excel - Sales Forecast.xls". The ending .xls indicates that you have saved your file as a spreadsheet.

8. You have probably noticed that some of your titles are too large for the cell in which they have been placed (e.g. Hand Tools, Power Tools and September). You can change the size of a column by placing the mouse pointer on the line between the two columns (its appearance will change - Figure 43) and if you hold down the left mouse button you can drag the column wider. Make columns B and K wider.

9. Check the appearance of your spreadsheet as a printed document by selecting the File menu and the Print Preview option. This will show you how the sheet will appear if printed. If the text is too small click on the Zoom button. If it is then too big click on it again. The preview will allow you to check the content and presentation of the header and footer, sheet and margins and orientation. If you click on the Setup button you can see the settings and clicking on the Margins will reveal them. Explore the different options and ensure you have accurately produced the sheet.

10. Save your sheet by selecting the File menu and clicking on the Save option. The Save As window will not appear since the application assumes you simply want to update your file stored on the floppy disk. Figure 44 shows the appearance of the spreadsheet.

11. Close Excel by selecting the File menu item and clicking on the Exit option or by clicking on the close button in the top right hand corner of the application window.

FIGURE 44
Sales Forecast

	A	B	C	D	E	F	G	H	I	J	K	L	M	N
1														
2														
3														
4														
5		Item	January	February	March	April	May	June	July	August	September	October	November	Decembe
6														
7		Hand Tools												
8		Power Tools												
9		Wood												
10		Metal												
11		Fastening												
12		Paint												
13		Wallpaper												
14		Electrical												
15		Garden												
16		Kitchen												
17		Garage												

Saving

When you save a spreadsheet you can choose to save it in a variety of formats. In the Save As window at the bottom is a box called Save as type and there is a down arrow button at the side of this box. If you click on this button then a list of formats that you can save your spreadsheet in appear. They include:

- Microsoft Excel Workbook – current Excel 2000 format
- Web page – your sheet is going to be presented on a website
- Microsoft Excel 4.0 Workbook – older version of Excel
- Other spreadsheet applications

You need to select which format will serve your purpose. Do you want your work to easily read on an earlier version of Excel or on another application, presented on a website or simply used on Excel 2000. The decision has consequences since to save the sheet in the format suitable for an earlier version of Excel you may loose some presentation aspects or other features. If you are in doubt you should save in the format of the current version of Excel (Microsoft Excel Workbook)

Formulae

One of the key features of a spreadsheet is that it can undertake mathematical calculations. It can total columns of figures, add, subtract, multiply and divide the contents of cells. It can carry out complex mathematical operations using formulae which you can devise.

The mathematical operators used in Excel are:

+   add
-   subtract
*   multiply
/   divide
<   less than
<= less than or equal to
>   more than
>= greater than or equal to

Brackets are also important in that they tell Excel to calculate anything in the brackets first before going on with the remaining parts of the calculation. A simple formula could be:

=B2+B3 - this means adding the contents of cell B2 to the contents of cell B3

=B2-B3 - this means subtracting the contents of cell B3 from the contents of cell B2

=B2/B3 - this means dividing the contents of cell B2 by the contents of cell B3

=B2*B3 - this means multiplying the contents of cell B2 by the contents of cell B3

These simple operators can be used to produce more complex formulae and hence carry out complex mathematical actions.
Example:

=(B2+B3)/4 – add the contents of cells B2 and B3 together and divide the total by 4.

=(B2*10)-(B3/B2)-20 – multiply the contents of cell B2 by ten and subtract from it the contents of cell B3 divided by the contents of cell B2 then subtract 20 from the total.

When a formula consists of several arithmetic operators (e.g. add, subtract, multiply, or divide), Excel works them out according to a standard rule. It will work out multiplication and division first, and addition and subtraction second. If the formula contains multiplication and division or addition and subtraction it works out the calculation from left to right. However, also remember that anything enclosed in brackets will be calculated first.

Standard Formula
There are a variety of standard functions available to Excel users. These include:
• SUM – this function totals the contents of a group of cells

• AVERAGE – this function produces the average of a number of values (e.g. a column of figures)

• COUNT – this function counts the number of entries in a groups of cells that contains numbers

• COUNTA – this function counts the number of cells with contents in a given range

• COUNTIF – this function counts the number of cells that are equal to a criteria in a range of cells (eg: M2:M5 holds nails, screws, tacks, screws therefore COUNTIF(M2:M5, "screws")=2).

• MIN – this identifies the minimum value of the contents of a group of cells

• MAX – this identifies the maximum value of the contents of a group of cells

• SQRT – this function calculates the square root of a number (or the contents of a cell)

• IF – this allows you to set a condition so that an action is only carried out if it is satisfied (e.g. IF (G4 >=50, Pass, Fail) - this means that if the contents of cell G4 are equal to or greater than 50 then the word Pass will appear. This could be the outcome of entering examination marks into a spreadsheet. If G4 is less than 50 then the word Fail will appear. The example shows that there are two outcomes of an IF function – one if the condition is true (eg Pass) and one if the condition is false (eg Fail). If you do not specify the false outcome then the world False will appear if the condition is not met. This can be confusing in some situations.

Example:

=SUM(A2:A8) – produces the total of the contents of the cells A2, A3, A4, A5, A6, A7 and A8

=AVERAGE (A2:A5) – produces the average of the contents of the cells A2, A3, A4 and A5 (i.e. (A2+A3+A4+A5)/4)

=COUNT (N11:N17) – counts the number of cells between N11 to N17 inclusively which contains numbers

=COUNTA (N11:N17) – counts the number of cells between N11 to N17 inclusively which hold contact

=COUNTIF (N11:N17, "Car") – counts the number of cells between N11 to N17 inclusively which equal Car

=SQRT(A7) – if A7 is 25 the function produces the square root of 25 which is 5

=IF (A3>40, A3/10) – if the contents of cell A3 is greater than 40 then divide A3 by 10

These functions involve identifying a list of cells. These are called the range of cells and can be selected by highlighting them on the spreadsheet or by writing the first and last cell separated by a colon to designate that all the cells between the two are included. They are enclosed in brackets. At the beginning of the function an equals sign tells Excel to carry out the calculation.

A full list of all the functions can be accessed by clicking on the function button on the Standard toolbar to reveal the Paste Function window (Figure 45). The definition of each function is given at the bottom of the window. Functions serve a wide range of purposes. Some are linked to mathematical operations while others provide the means of testing logic (e.g. IF). The Paste window allows you to insert the function into the sheet but, you can also simply enter the function from the keyboard.

The Paste Function window is divided into two halves. In the left hand side are function categories. If you select one (by single clicking) the functions that relate to it appear in the right hand side of the window. You can select a

FIGURE 45
**Paste
Window**

function by highlighting it with a single click and then clicking on OK. Figure 45 shows the functions for the All category. The logical category provides you with the functions AND, FALSE, IF, NOT, OR AND TRUE while the Statistical category has many functions relating to statistical tests and methods.

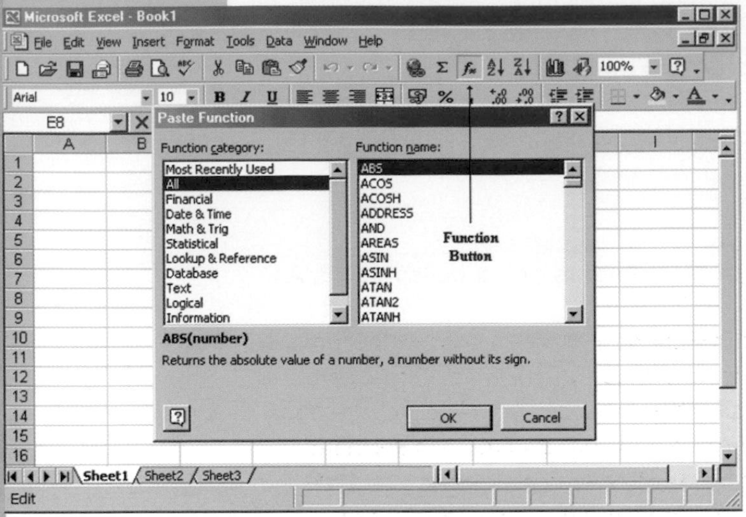

Some of these functions you could design yourself (e.g. SUM (H3:H6) is the same as H3+H4+H5+H6). However, there is always the risk that you will make an error with your own formula, and in many cases they require more information to be entered from the keyboard. The standard functions are a better guarantee of success.

An alternative approach to naming a cell or group of cells is to highlight the cell or cells and then to select the Insert menu and highlight the Name option to reveal a short menu (Figure 45A). Click on the Define option to reveal the Define window (Figure 45A). The highlighted cells reference is shown in the box at the bottom of the window. The name of the cells is entered into the top box. By clicking on the Add button you create the name and you complete the task by clicking on the OK button.

To delete a name select the Insert menu, highlight the Name option to reveal the Define window. A list of the names is shown in the middle box. Highlight the name you want to remove and click on the Delete button.

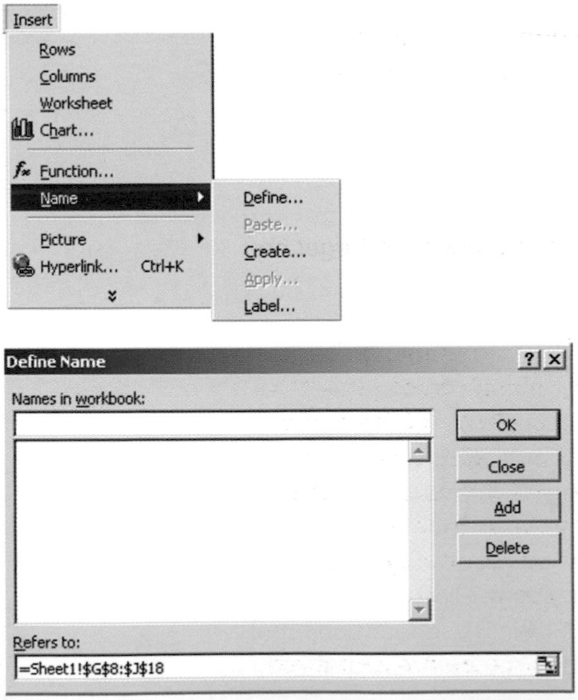

The example below shows the use of functions and their mathematical values for a short column of figures (D6 to D9) in column D of a spreadsheet.
Example
D

6	78	78
7	56	56
8	34	34
9	56	56
10	=AVERAGE(D6:D9)	56
11	=MIN(D6:D9)	34
12	=MAX(D6:D9)	78
13	=SUM(D6:D9)	224
14	=COUNT(D6:D9)	4
15	=COUNTA(D6:D9)	4
16	=COUNTIF(D6:D9,34)	1
17	=SQRT(D9)	7.48

When you select a function from the Paste Function window another window opens to ask you to set the parameters for the function. Figure 45a illustrates the window for the AVERAGE function using references. The window provides a short explanation of what is required. For some functions the requirements are similar to AVERAGE in that a range of cell references is needed. In some cases Excel will offer you a range depending on the cell in which you are inserting the function. However, you should always check if it is correct. The example above provides the parameters for a range of functions. For COUNTIF you need to specify a range of cells for the function to search along with the value you are seeking to equal (e.g. D6:D9, 34 meaning how many times is the value 34 equalled by the contents of any of the cells in the range).

Logical Operators/Functions

Using the IF function you can ask questions of your data. It checks if a defined condition is true and then causes an action to take place. Its format is:

IF (Condition, true, false) - that is, if the condition is correct, then the true statement will take place. If it is not true, then the false statement will take place.

For Example:

You could establish a function so that if a sales person exceeded his target he would receive a bonus

=IF(A10>55, B12*1.20, B12*0.95)– if cell A10 (containing the number of items sold) is greater than 55 (the sales target) then the contents of cell B12 (sales person salary) is multiplied by 1.20 (i.e. salary is increased by 20%). If the content of cell A10 is not greater than 55 then the contents of B12 are multiplied by 0.95 (i.e. salary is reduced by 5%)

The IF function is not the only way of testing conditions. There are also three logical operators. These are:

OR   OR(condition1, condition2) if either of the conditions are correct the true statement is enacted, otherwise the false statement is chosen

For Example:

=OR(C2<120, C2>90), D5*25,"No commission"

This essentially checks that cell C2 is between either 90 and 120. If either is correct then cell D5 is multiplied by 25 to calculate the commission. If neither is true, then No commission is inserted into the cell.

NOT   NOT(condition) if the condition is not correct then the true statement is enacted, otherwise the false statement is chosen

For Example:

=NOT(C5=0), E7=25, E7=10

This means that if C5 is not equal to zero then E7 is set to 25. If C5=0 then cell E7 is set to 10.

AND   AND(condition1 and condition2). If both conditions are correct then the true statement is enacted, otherwise the false statement is chosen

For Example:

=AND(C5>0,D5<100), G6="Within Specification", G6="Out of Specification"

This checks that both conditions are correct (i.e. C5 is greater than zero and D5 less than 100). If they are both correct then the words "Within Specification" are inserted into the cell. If either are incorrect then the words "Out of Specification" are inserted in the cell.

Logical operators can be confusing initially for many people but can be very useful ways of carrying out complex tasks.

An important issue in relation to formula which may seem obvious but is often a source of confusion is that if you change data on a spreadsheet and the data is used within a formula then the value of the formula will also change. In complex spreadsheets with several interdependent formulae a single change in data can lead to a series of changes across the sheet. This is the key advantage of a spreadsheet model in that you can see the effects of changes in data on outcomes. You can therefore explore different options (eg increase in price, a change in transport costs etc).

Error Messages

In any mathematical calculation you can make an error and Excel provides a number of messages to tell you about mistakes. These are:

This occurs when the formula or function produces a number greater than can fit in a cell.

#VALUE   The formula contains a mistake in one of its components (i.e. a cell or mathematical operator).

#DIV0!   This is a common error in that the formula involves being divided by zero. Often you have not entered a value into a cell which is being used to divide another value. You need to check to ensure all the cells have a value.

#NAME?   A meaningless term is included in the formula.

#N/A   This results from a formula requiring data from a cell which does not contain the information at that moment.

#REF!   The formula has an incorrect cell reference.

#NUM!   The formula contains an incorrect number.

#NULL!   The formula has an incorrect cell reference.

In all cases you need to check that the function is correct, you have specified the correct range of cells and that the cells have had the correct contents entered.

It is critical when constructing formulae that they are perfect. Once a spreadsheet is produced its results are assumed to be accurate. An error in a formula will often be overlooked. When a formula is initially developed it should be carefully checked to ensure it is correct. An error in a formula may not be noticed once a spreadsheet is in use and its results may have a considerable influence on business decisions.

References

It is critical in using a spreadsheet to be able to specify which parts of the sheet you want to work on. This can be a single cell which is shown by combining the column letter with row number (e.g. Column Row – A4), or a groups of cells, which is shown by giving the first and last cell separated by a colon. When a cell name or a range of cells is inserted into a formula or function it is called a reference. This means the formula or function is referring to the contents of that cell or range of cells. If the content changes, the value of the formula or function changes.

There are three types of reference:

• Relative
• Absolute
• Mixed

The Relative reference is the normal one you encounter when you use Excel. If you move the cells (e.g. delete or insert rows or columns) then the reference in the formula changes to allow for the new position.

The Absolute reference is one which remains unchanged no matter what happens. You create an absolute reference by using the $ symbol (e.g. SUM (A2:A5) - Relative references while SUM ($A$2:$A$5) - Absolute references).

The mixed reference combines both Relative and Absolute within the same formula or function (e.g. H5+%G$3).

References are especially important when you copy and paste blocks of your sheet. This is called replication and it automatically changes the Relative references to allow for their new position. This is very useful if you want to copy formulae or functions since they will be accurate in their new places. Replication can save a great deal of checking and changing which would be needed if you had to undertake it manually.

When you highlight a cell its reference is shown in the left hand box of the formula bar. You can employ this reference name box to move to any cell of the sheet by entering its reference in the box and pressing enter.

Using the name box you can give an individual cell, or group of cells an individual name. Highlight the cell or area and enter chosen name into the box and then press enter key. If you enter this name into the box in future then the cell or area is selected.

The four types of references can be combined in formula to give you many different options. Named references allow you to specify a particular cell or group of cells within a formula. Relative references allow formula to be replicated therefore saving time and avoiding creating errors while absolute references provide you with the option to fixed an unchanging reference. You can mix different types of reference to maximise the possibilities to solve particular problems or meet different needs.

Spreadsheet solutions requires you to select and use at least three different reference types within your work.

Replication and Accuracy

Replication is the spreadsheet function that allows data and formulae to be copied to new areas of the sheet. If the formula employs relative references then the formula will change itself to conform to its new position. When you replicate formula sometimes zeros will be added to cells that do not contain any data. It is important to remove them to avoid errors when the formulae are calculated such as dividing by zero.

Replication has the advantages of ensuring that the formula and data are accurately entered as well as saving time. Numerical accuracy is vital to spreadsheets in fact perfection is required. Spreadsheets are concerned with modelling numerical data to predict trends, analyse data and identify outcomes. Organisational decisions will often be based on the spreadsheet analysis so if the data is incorrect then the outcomes will also be wrong and will therefore lead to poor decisions. It is therefore critical to the success of spreadsheets that the data is accurately entered. It is good practice to check data at all stages of entering to ensure it is correct.

References and Formulae

The application of relative cell references is not difficult to understand. In that it helps to copy formula accurately from one part of a spreadsheet to another. However, absolute cell references are not so obvious. They are useful when you need to include standard values in formula so that it is important to keep them in a single set of locations. If you were producing a spreadsheet to calculate export prices you might wish to include the exchange rates in a series of cells and then link to them through absolute references. In engineering you are often dealing with mathematical constants (e.g. density of iron), or in statistical calculations there are often constants that need to be used. These could all be placed in cells with absolute references.

Figure 45A illustrates formulae that use both absolute and relative references. The formulae have been replicated to show the changes to the relative references. The spreadsheet shows a simple calculation of the price of an export product. The Euro exchange rate is located in cell D3. Overheads are calculated on the basis of 22.5% of the total cost (i.e. the sum of raw materials, staff, transport and packing costs). The cost in pounds is a simple total while the cost in euros is the cost in pounds divided by the exchange rate.

Figure 45A shows the same calculation but using a named reference instead of an absolute reference and once again it has been replicated to illustrate the changes and the constants. A significant advantage of named references is that you can give them a meaningful name. In this example exchange will have a meaning to the people using the spreadsheet while D3 will not so that if it needs to be amended months or years after being created then it will be easier and chance of making mistakes will be reduced.

FIGURE 46
**Sales
Forecast
Data**

Item	January	February	March	April	May	June	July	August	September	October	November	December
Hand Tools	12,000	13,500	12,120	9,890	10,675	10,950	11,500	10,125	10,975	11,100	10,760	15,600
Power Tools	32,000	27,540	27,895	26,450	26,860	27,125	27,450	26,875	24,800	25,230	25,780	37,800
Wood	15,000	14,760	13,890	12,300	12,860	13,200	12,900	11,500	11,800	12,700	13,500	13,250
Metal	2,300	2,150	1,980	1,875	2,050	2,300	1,550	1,250	2,300	2,100	2,050	1,950
Fastening	4,750	5,050	4,430	3,675	3,980	4,100	3,500	3,250	3,300	3,400	3,050	3,100
Paint	17,800	18,230	16,760	16,980	19,870	22,345	20,125	16,500	17,900	19,500	18,500	17,500
Wallpaper	22,900	23,175	22,980	21,870	20,760	19,650	18,900	17,500	17,900	19,850	20,300	23,500
Electrical	14,500	16,800	15,120	13,870	14,320	13,760	13,750	14,100	13,575	13,900	14,500	16,750
Garden	2,100	1,900	2,700	4,500	5,500	5,700	7,800	4,600	3,800	2,800	1,450	1,900
Kitchen	3,300	3,760	3,560	4,125	4,560	4,875	5,120	4,980	4,570	3,900	4,300	6,700
Garage	7,900	8,800	5,780	6,750	6,890	7,200	7,500	8,000	6,875	6,800	6,500	9,100

Exercise 11

Entering Data and Creating Formulae

1. Insert your floppy disk into the A: drive.

2. Load Microsoft Excel using either the Programs menu or the Excel icon on the desktop. Open the file Sales Forecast by selecting the File menu, then clicking on the Open option to reveal the Open window. Change the Look in:box to select the floppy disk and the file name will appear in the work area. Double click Sales Forecast or single click it and then click the Open button. The spreadsheet will open in Excel.

FIGURE 47
Total

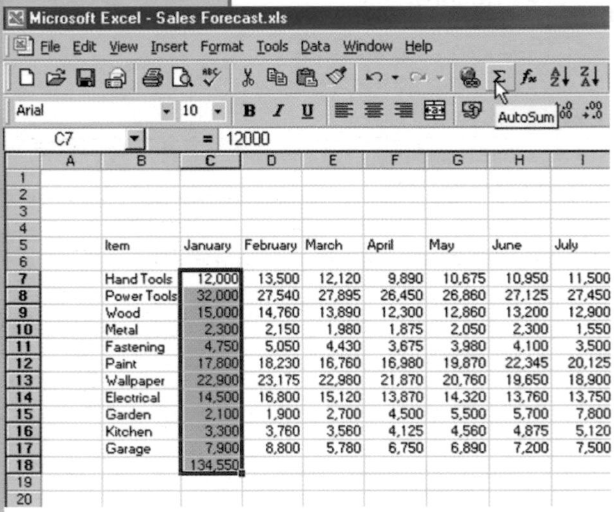

3. Enter the data shown in Figure 46

4. Carefully check the accuracy of your data since you are going to depend on it once you begin to calculate trends and other useful information. The validity of the calculations are totally dependent on the initial correctness of the data. It is worth spending a lot of time checking the entries.

5. Save your sheet by selecting the File menu and clicking on the Save option. It is good practice to save your work every few minutes.

6. You are going to total each monthly column and each item row. There are several ways of doing this but the most straightforward involves using the SUM function on the Standard toolbar. Highlight the column from cell C7 to C18 and then click on the SUM icon on the toolbar (Figure 47) and you will see the total of the column appear - 134,550. Click elsewhere in the sheet to remove the highlighting and then on the total and you will see the formula appear on the formula toolbar - =SUM(A7:C17).

7. Once you have successfully produced the total for the January column then you can replicate it to the other columns. Highlight C18, select the Edit menu and click on the <u>C</u>opy option then <u>P</u>aste the contents to D18. If you highlight D18 you will see the formula =SUM(D7:D17). This shows you that in copying the formula the references have been changed to fit the new position. This is called replication and the references are relative. Repeat this process for the remaining columns.

FIGURE 48
**Print
Preview**

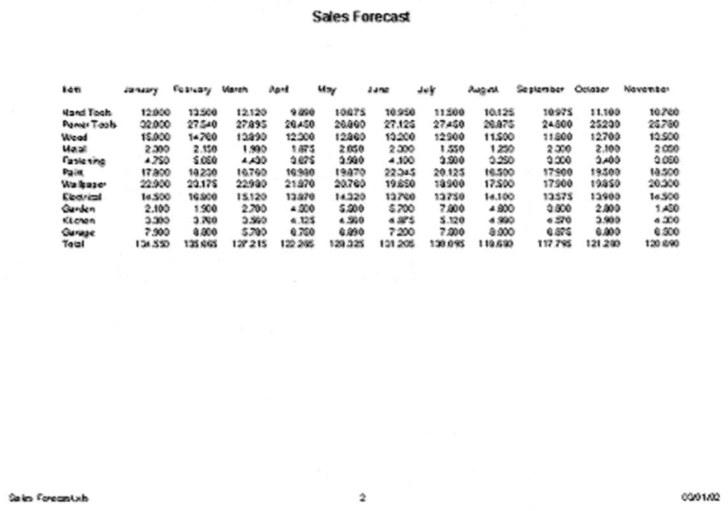

8. Now total the first row (Hand Tools) by highlighting from C7 to O7 and clicking on the SUM icon on the Standard toolbar. This will produce the total 139,195 and the formula =SUM(C7:N7). If you highlight cell O7 then you will see the formula appear on the toolbar. Edit the formula to make the references absolute =SUM($C$7:$N$7). Replicate (copy) this formula to cell O8 and you will notice that the new total is still 139,195 and the formula remains =SUM($C$7:$N$7). The absolute references are not changed by replication. Now use Undo to remove the formula and changes that made cell O7 formula absolute.

9. Replicate the formula =SUM(C7:N7) to O8 and the other rows. Total for Power Tools is 335,805 and formula =SUM(C8:N8).

10. Check the formulae are all correct and then save your sheet by selecting the <u>F</u>ile menu and clicking on the <u>S</u>ave option.

FIGURE 49
**Print
Preview
Gridlines**

11. Now total all the columns in cell O18 – the total is ####### showing that the number is too large to be shown. The formula is =SUM(C18:N18). Insert the name Total in B18 and O5.

12. Print your sheet by selecting the <u>F</u>ile menu and Print Pre<u>v</u>iew. Figure 48 shows the appearance of the printout. It shows that the gridlines, row and column headings are missing and that some of the spreadsheet is absent. This is because it will be printed on a second sheet.

13. To add the gridlines you need to select the <u>S</u>etup button in the Print

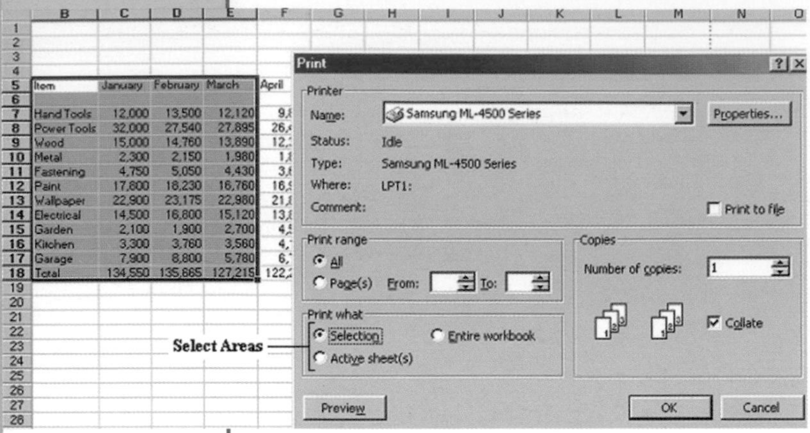

FIGURE 50
Print Selection

Select Areas —

Preview window to reveal the Page Setup window. Select the Sheet tab and click in the Gridlines and Row and column headings boxes so ticks appear. Click on the OK button when you are are finished and you will see the window disappear and a new print preview appear showing gridlines and headings (Figure 49). When you want to print the sheet, click on the Print button. To remove the options, repeat the actions and click in the ticked boxes to see the ticks disappear.

14. Print the sheet without gridlines or row and column headings, and then with them.

15. Save your sheet by selecting the File menu and clicking on the Save option.

16. Close Excel by selecting the File menu item and clicking on the Exit option or by clicking on the close button in the top right hand corner of the application window.

Printing

You can also print parts of a spreadsheet rather than the whole sheet by highlighting the section you require, select the File menu and the Print option. This will reveal the Print window (Figure 50). In the window is a section called Print What with three options:

• Selection – print areas that are highlighted
• Active sheet(s) – print all the sheets you are working on
• Entire workbook – print all the sheets within the workbook

Selection is a useful option if you are seeking to print out to show changes and their effects.

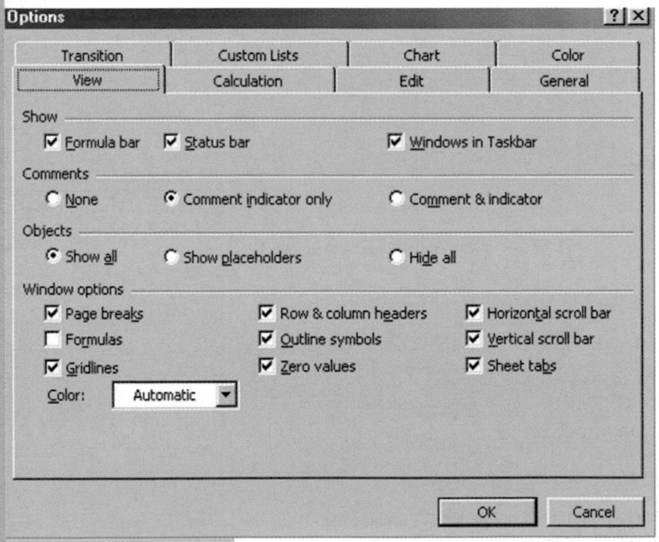

There is a Preview button at the bottom of the window with which you can reveal the Print Preview and access page Setup to allow you to print gridlines and row and column headings. You can print the selection or whole sheet by clicking

FIGURE 51
Options Window

on the print button in the preview window or by clicking the OK button in the Print window.

The printouts that you have considered so far have shown the actual values of calculations. It is also useful to print out the sheet showing the formulae that are being used. This serves several purposes, not least that it is easier to check the accuracy of the formulae on a printout than on the screen.

FIGURE 52
Formatting Toolbar

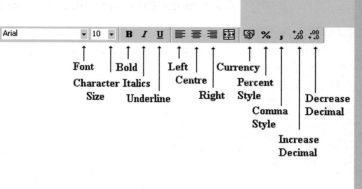

To print the formulae you must select the Tools menu and the Options option. This will reveal the Options window (Figure 51). In the View tab is a section called Window options. You can select to print the formulae by clicking in the Formulas box. This is also an alternative way of selecting Gridlines and Rows and Column headings. When you have made your choices you click on the OK button to enact them.

FIGURE 53
Borders Tool

The formulae are now shown instead of their values and if you now select the Print Preview option you will see the spreadsheet showing them. It is useful when printing formulae to also print the rows and column headers since these allow you to interpret the references within the formulae.

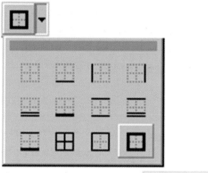

Thick Box Border

Change Format

The Formatting toolbar (Figure 52) provides a variety of tools to enhance the format of your spreadsheet. They all operate in a similar way. You highlight the cell or cells you need to change and select the appropriate tool from the toolbar. You can:

- Change the font
- Alter the character size
- Embolden the entry
- Change to italics
- Underline the entry
- Align the cell or cells contents to the left, right or centre
- Present the numbers as currency (e.g. £100,000.00)
- Present the numbers as a percentage (e.g. 100000%)
- Present the numbers in a comma style (e.g. 100,000.00)
- Increase or decrease the number of decimal places (e.g. 100,000 increased by two places becomes 100,000.00)

FIGURE 54
Amended Spread-sheet

	B	C	D	E	F	G	H
5							
6	**Item**	**January**	**February**	**March**	**April**	**May**	**June**
7							
8	**Hand Tools**	12,000	13,500	12,120	9,890	10,675	10,950
9	**Power Tools**	32,000	27,540	27,895	26,450	26,860	27,125
10	**Wood**	15,000	14,760	13,890	12,300	12,860	13,200
11	**Metal**	2,300	2,150	1,980	1,875	2,050	2,300
12	**Fastening**	4,750	5,050	4,430	3,675	3,960	4,100
13	**Paint**	17,800	18,230	16,760	16,980	19,870	22,345
14	**Wallpaper**	22,900	23,175	22,980	21,870	20,760	19,650
15	**Electrical**	14,500	16,800	15,120	13,870	14,320	13,760
16	**Garden**	2,100	1,900	2,700	4,500	5,500	5,700
17	**Kitchen**	3,300	3,760	3,560	4,125	4,560	4,875
18	**Garage**	7,900	8,800	5,780	6,750	6,890	7,200
19	**Total**	£ 134,550.00	£ 135,665.00	£ 127,215.00	£ 122,285.00	£ 126,325.00	£ 131,205.0

Spreadsheets are heavily concerned with numerical data and provide you with a variety of ways of formatting data (e.g. percentage, date, time, negative, currency, scientific and general). To select a particular format you must initially highlight the cell or cells you want to change and then select the specific icon from the toolbar (Figure 52). Spreadsheet Solutions require you to demonstrate that you can employ three different cell content formats. Formats are important since formula will be designed to calculate values based on the format of the data. An important issue is that the format will control the appearance of the cell contents but they do not change their actual values which are used in calculations.

Example

If a format has been chosen that limits decimal places to two then 12.346 will be presented as 12.35 while when it is part of a calculation its actual value will be used so if the cell is multiplied by 10 it's presented and actual value will be 123.46. However, this will appear to be wrong in that 12.35 multiplied by 10 equals 123.50. This confuses many spreadsheet users.

If you enter a date or time in the correct way Excel recognises them automatically as dates or times. Date formats that Excel accepts are shown by selecting the Format menu and the Cells option to reveal the Format Cells window. In the Number tab and the date or time options you will see a list of accepted formats (e.g.12/12/2002 or 12 December 2002). Excel treats time as a number so it is important to enter it correctly. Time can be entered in a 12 or 24-hour format. If you enter a 12 hour number it must be followed by an a or p to show if it is am or pm, respectively.

Example

12 hour clock   -3.00p

24 hour clock   -15.00

Excel can calculate time if the data is entered correctly. Date and times can be entered in a single cell providing they are separated by a space.

FIGURE 55
Average

P	P
Average	**Average**
£ 11,599.58	=AVERAGE(C8:N8)
£ 27,983.75	=AVERAGE(C9:N9)
£ 13,138.33	=AVERAGE(C10:N10)
£ 1,987.92	=AVERAGE(C11:N11)
£ 3,798.75	=AVERAGE(C12:N12)
£ 18,500.83	=AVERAGE(C13:N13)
£ 20,773.75	=AVERAGE(C14:N14)
£ 14,578.75	=AVERAGE(C15:N15)
£ 3,729.17	=AVERAGE(C16:N16)
£ 4,479.17	=AVERAGE(C17:N17)
£ 7,341.25	=AVERAGE(C18:N18)
£127,911.25	=AVERAGE(C19:N19)

Different formats serve different purposes. Percentages are useful to compare information, currency allows you to consider money which is always relevant to a business, negative values allows you to consider the full range of possibilities, scientific functions extend spreadsheets into the world of research and development and general numerical formats complete the range. The general format is the default one.

FIGURE 56
**Format
Menu**

Spreadsheet Solutions Unit requires that you use at least four different display features.

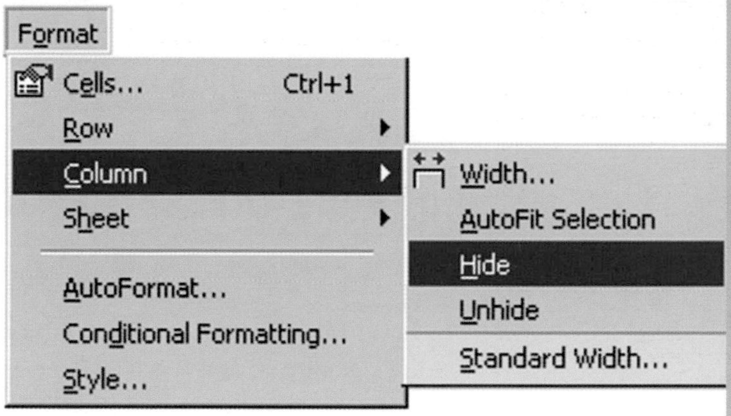

Borders

The appearance of a spreadsheet can be important in persuading people (e.g. senior managers) to accept its value as a useful business tool. To enhance the spreadsheet's appearance you have a variety of tools including the Borders tool with which you can enclose an individual cell, a selection of cells or the whole sheet within a border. Figure 53 shows the Borders tool options, available within the Formatting toolbar. When the icon is clicked a small window of options appears. By clicking on an option you will add it to the cell, selection or whole sheet that you have highlighted.

FIGURE 57
**Format
Cells**

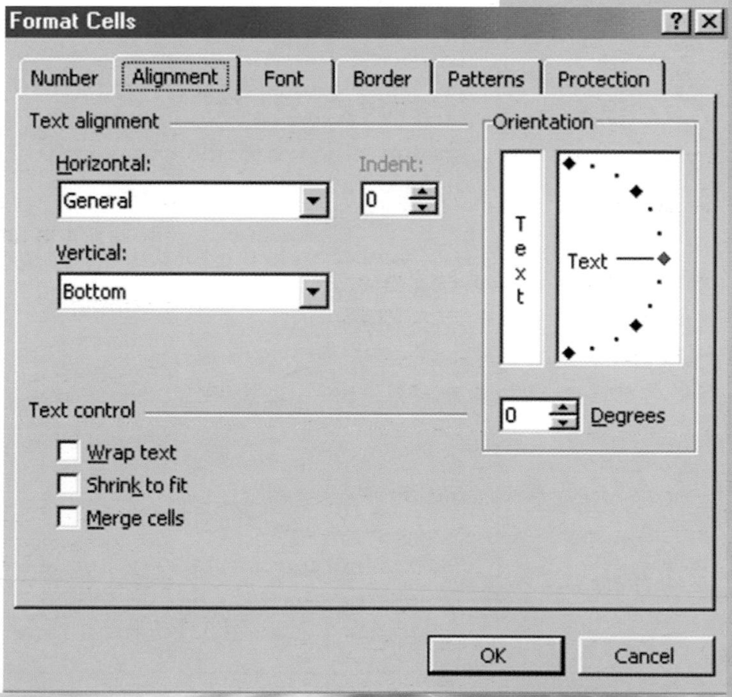

FIGURE 58
Standard Toolbar

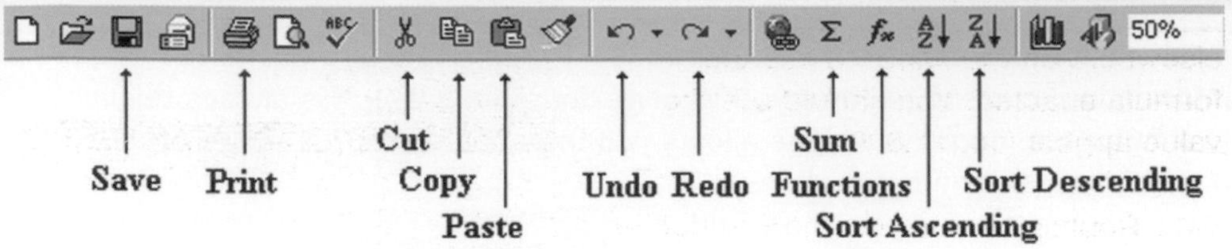

50%

Save   Print   Cut   Copy   Paste   Undo   Redo   Sum Functions   Sort Descending   Sort Ascending

Exercise 12

Enhance the Spreadsheet

1. Insert your floppy disk into the A: drive.

2. Load Microsoft Excel using either the Programs menu or the Excel icon on the desktop. Open the file Sales Forecast by selecting the File menu, clicking on the Open option to reveal the Open window. Change the Look in:box to select the floppy disk and the file name will appear in the work area. Double click Sales Forecast or single click it and then click the Open button. The spreadsheet will open in Excel.

3. You can insert additional rows and collumns. Click on row 4 heading and you will see entire row is highlighted. Click on the Insert menu and select Rows option. A new row will be inserted and the spreadsheet will change position.

4. Now change the character size of the columns headings (e.g. January, February etc.) to 14, centre and embolden them. Highlight the cells and click on the Formatting toolbar options required. You will notice that they change in size and are too large for the column widths. Adjust the widths so that the headings are visible (i.e. January, February, August, September, October, November and December).

5. Now change the character size of the row headings (Items, Hand Tools etc.) to 14 and embolden them. You will notice that they change in size and are too large for the column width. Adjust the width so that the headings are visible.

6. Now change the total row and column to currency (e.g. £ 100,000.00). Again the change may be too large for the column width and you will need to make changes.

7. Now change the data by centring all the figures except the totals.

8. Save your sheet by selecting the File menu and clicking on the Save option. Figure 54 shows the appearance of the spreadsheet.

9. You are now going to calculate the monthly average for each item. In cell P8 insert =Average(C8:N8) - that is, the Average function and the range C8:N8 which are the monthly figures for Hand Tools. When you are finished click elsewhere on the sheet to see the formula enacted. You should see the value appear (i.e. 11,600).

10. Replicate the formula for the other items and change their format to currency. You will need to change the column width to ensure everything is visible. In P6 enter the heading Average in character size 14 and embolden. Figure 55 shows the Average formula and values.

11. Print the whole spreadsheet initially showing the actual values of the calculations using the File menu and the Print option and then showing the formulae in full using the Tools Menu, Options option, View tab and Formulas box (Figure 51).

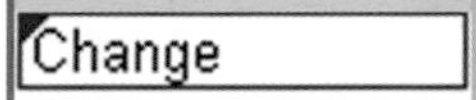

12. Highlight the headings across the top of your sheet (i.e. row 6). Select the border icon on the toolbar and click on the All borders option (if you place your pointer over the options they will be named) and the row will be enclosed in a border.

13. Save your sheet by selecting the File menu and clicking on the Save option.

14. Print using the Selection option in the Print window the headings enclosed in their border to show the changes you have made. You will need to highlight the headings.

15. An important thing to consider with any spreadsheet is the effect of changing some of the assumptions. If in our spreadsheet we decide to have a marketing campaign on selected products at Christmas, how would that impact on our national averages? Our Public Relations company has suggested the following new sales figures for December:

Power Tools - 65,000
Electrical - 38,000
Kitchen - 18,500

Enter these new values in the spreadsheet and see the averages and totals change. Are the changes significant? You could consider other predicted amounts. You might want to be more or less optimistic than the Public Relations

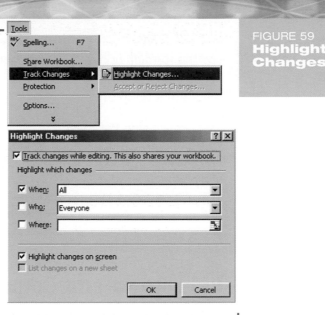

FIGURE 59
Highlight Changes

FIGURE 60
Track Changes

FIGURE 61
Open Window

company. When you enter the new data and click elsewhere then you should see the formula updated. If this does not happen, click on the equals sign on the Formula taskbar and on the OK button in the window that appears. This will update the formula.

16. Print using the Selection option in the Print window the outcomes of your changes. You will need to highlight the new sales figures for December and the new averages and totals.

17. Close Excel by selecting the File menu item and clicking on the Exit option or by clicking on the close button in the top right hand corner of the application window.

Hide Rows and Columns

Within the Format menu (Figure 56) are a number of functions which operate on cells, rows, columns and sheet. The Row and Column options reveal options to change the width of a column or the height of a row and to hide or unhide rows or columns.

It may not seem sensible to hide a row or column but it is useful if, say, you want to show a customer the costs of a project without revealing confidential information.

Column Widths

In earlier exercises you have adjusted the width of columns by using the mouse pointer to drag them. However, Excel provides you with the means to set exact column widths. To set widths select the Format menu and click on Column to reveal a submenu (Figure 56) with the option Width. Clicking on the Width option opens to reveal the Column Width window. To change widths you enter a figure and then click the OK button. The function operates on the column or area of the sheet you have highlighted.

Orientation of Text

When you enter text into a spreadsheet it is normally left justified. To change its orientation select the Format menu and click on the Cells option to reveal the Format Cells window (Figure 57). The Alignment tab provides options to:

• Align the text both horizontally and vertically (the options are available by clicking on the down arrow buttons at the end of the boxes)

• Wrap text - this allows you to enter multiple lines of text in a cell

• Shrink to fit - this reduces the size of text so that it fits into a cell

• Merge Cells - this turns two or more cells in a single larger cell

These functions work in the normal way (i.e. highlight your chosen cells and choose the desired options).

The other tabs provide extra functions. The Border tab provides an alternative way of selecting borders. The Numbers tab allow you to select the format of the figures and the Font tab to choose different fonts, character sizes and the other functions available on the toolbar.

It is important to align spreadsheet data (i.e. columns of figures are normally shown perfectly aligned) so that readers can understand the information presented. Spreadsheet Solutions requires learners to show they can use at least two alignment formats and four display features. Even small differences in alignment of numbers can make it difficult to understand a sheet of numbers. Often important organisational decisions are based on spreadsheet analysis (e.g. signing contracts, setting prices, agreeing pay rises etc.) certainly part of the decision is influenced by being persuaded that the analysis is accurate. This is certainly affected by the presentation. If a sheet is a mess will not persuaded managers to take key decisions. One that presents a quality image will assist managers to accept the information it is offering. Excel provides the means to align data both vertically and horizontally so that you can produce high quality presentations.

Another useful presentation device that is offered within the Format Cells window is the ability to merge cells. This is useful when you want a title or label to cover more than one column or row. Again this is useful to develop a quality presentation of your information. The importance of a quality product should not be underestimated.

Sort Data

There are occasions when you want to sort your data into order and Excel provides you with a straightforward way of sorting a column of data into either ascending or descending order. This function also operates on text in that the list is sorted alphabetically.

The sort functions are available on the Data menu or the Standard toolbar (Figure 58). The sort function on the toolbar allows you to sort on one column while the function available from the Data menu allows you to sort on more than one column of data. Select the Data menu and click on the Sort option to reveal the Sort window (Figure 58a). This allows you to select a series of columns to sort by and to choose either ascending or descending sorts.

Track Changes

In many organisations people work in teams and a spreadsheet may be used by a variety of people. A very useful feature of Excel and other modern spreadsheets is the ability to show changes that have been made. This is available by selecting the Tools menu and highlighting the Track Changes options to reveal the Highlight changes options which when clicked will open the Highlight Changes Window (Figure 59).

You select the options by clicking in the boxes and a tick appears. When you then edit the spreadsheet the changes are shown by the cells being enclosed by a coloured border. This allows you to identify what has been changed. Figure 60 shows a cell which has been changed.

If the spreadsheet is printed then the changes are also shown.

Import Files

There are several ways of importing or opening information/data from other applications within Excel. The most straightforward is to use the Copy and Paste functions which are available in all Microsoft Office functions. An alternative is to use the Open option within the File menu. The file formats which can be imported into Excel are shown in the Files of type box (Figure 61). It is often puzzling when you see files in a range of formats. Why are they in different formats? Format depends on the application software used to create it. This determines its purpose and what it is compatible with. Some generic file formats are designed to allow the file to be opened by a wide range of applications. An example of a generic file format is a text file shown by the extension .txt.The file you want to import is located using the Look in box to identify the floppy disk, drive or folder. The files and folders are shown in the work area and are selected by either highlighting the file with a single click and then clicking on the Open button, or by double clicking on the file.

The chosen file needs to be converted into Excel format. To undertake this task you are helped by an Excel Wizard. This is shown in Figures 62, 63 and 64. The Wizard opens automatically when you try to import a file. If the file you have selected is not one of those which Excel can import you will see an error message appear. This will say that the file format is not valid. A valid file will open the Wizard but you may have to select the correct file in the Files of type box for the file you are importing.

FIGURE 62
Import Wizard 1

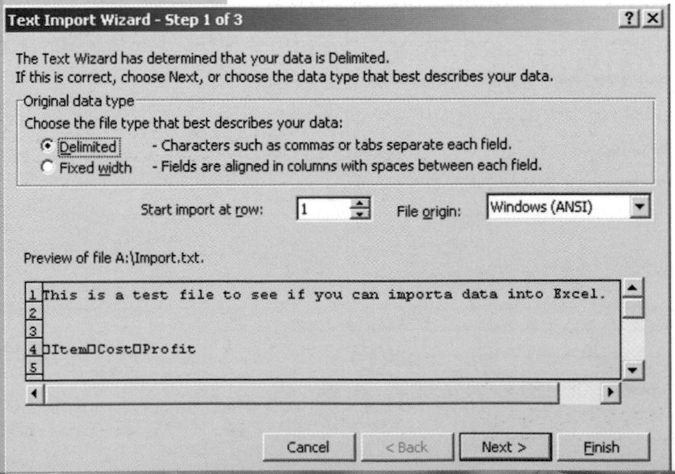

Figure 62 shows the initial Wizard window and this asks you to select if the file you are importing is delimited or fixed column width. The file can be seen in the scroll box for you to check. A delimited file is one in which the data is separated by commas or by tabbing while a fixed width is one where the data is aligned into columns. When you have made your selection you click on the Next button to move to step 2 of the Wizard (Figure 63).

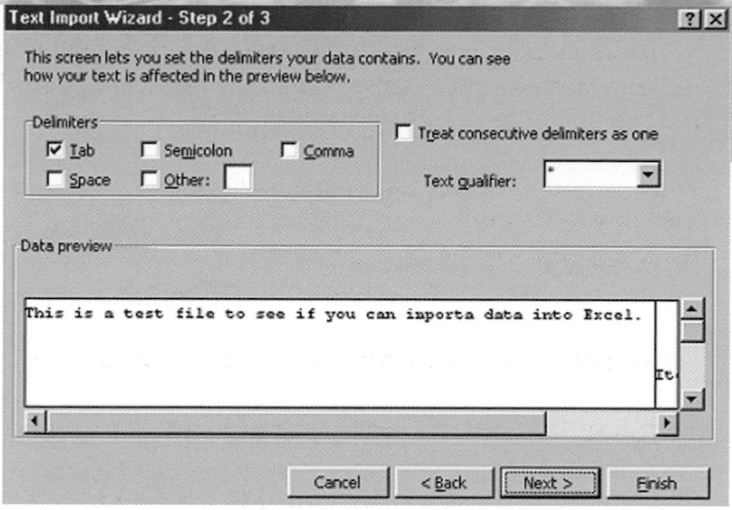

FIGURE 63
**Import
Wizard 2**

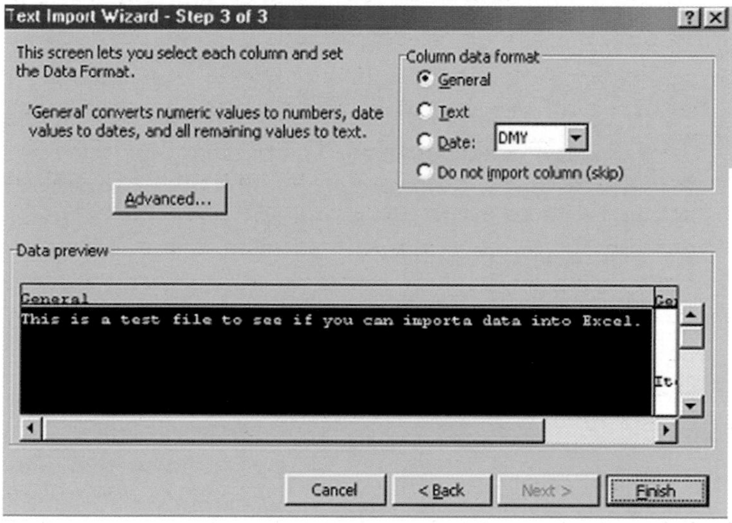

FIGURE 64
**Import
Wizard 3**

Figure 63 illustrates how you define the delimiter used if your file is of this type. You click on the Next button when you have finished. Step 3 (final step) of the Wizard gives you the opportunity to adjust the width of a fixed column width file (Figure 64).

By using the scroll box you can see the changes to the data and check how it will appear in a spreadsheet.

FIGURE 65
**Notepad
Test Data
File**

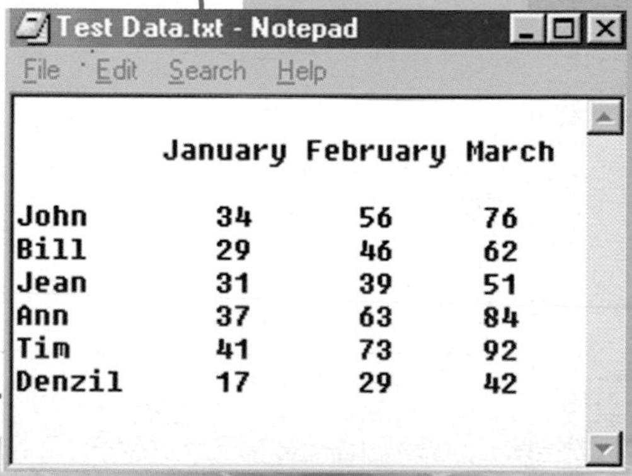

Exercise 13

Importing Data

1. Insert your floppy disk into the computer's drive.

2. Create a data file (Figure 65) using the Notepad application (Start, Programs, Accessories and Notepad). Save the file as

	January	February	March
John	34	56	76
Bill	29	46	62
Jean	31	39	51
Ann	37	63	84
Tim	41	73	92
Denzil	17	29	42

FIGURE 66
**Open
Window**

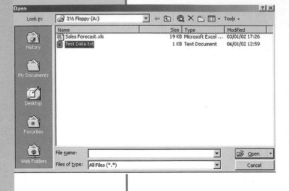

Test Data on to your floppy disk. It will appear as Test Data.txt to show it is a text file (In the CLAIT Plus assessment you will be provided with data files to import and will not need to create them).

3. Load Microsoft Excel using either the Programs menu or the Excel icon on the desktop.

4. Select the File menu and the option Open (Figure 66). Change the Look in box to choose floppy disk and you should see your files. If you do not then it is likely that you need to change the Files of types box to read All Files. Double click on Test Data.txt file and the Wizard Step 1 will appear. The file is delimited so click on the Next button. Figure 67 shows the appearance of the data.

5. The Data is not correctly laid out. You will need to adjust its presentation by using the different delimiters. Experiment with different combinations if you do not know what was used. The best is a combination of tab and space but you may find it is space or tab on their own if this was the way you created the file. Figure 68 shows you the Wizard view of the data once the correct delimiters were selected.

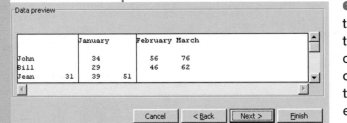

6. Click on Next in Steps 2 and 3 to import the file into the spreadsheet. Figure 69 shows the result of importing the file. The process is complex so you may need to practise this operation several times. Create new files of test data using different delimiters and experiment with the method until you are confident that you import a data file.

FIGURE 67
**Wizard
Step 2
Data
Appearance**

7. Close Excel by selecting the File menu item and clicking on the Exit option or by clicking on the close button in the top right hand corner of the application window.

FIGURE 68
**Wizard
Step 2
Tab and
Space**

House Styles

In many organisations spreadsheets are widely used with large numbers of staff using them. In order to ensure the quality of their presentation and use many organisations have produced standards which are called House Styles. Excel provides the means of establishing styles using the Format menu and the Style option.

	A	B	C	D	E
1					
2		January	February	March	
3					
4	John	34	56	76	
5	Bill	29	46	62	
6	Jean	31	39	51	
7	Ann	37	63	84	
8	Tim	41	73	92	
9	Denzil	17	29	42	
10					

FIGURE 69
Imported File Spreadsheet

This allows you to set a style covering factors such as:

• Number formats
• Fonts
• Alignment
• Borders
• Patterns

When you select the F<u>o</u>rmat menu and click on the <u>S</u>tyle option you open the Style window. This is shown in Figure 70. If you click on the <u>M</u>odify button then the Format Cell window is opened which allows you to choose different formats for your style.

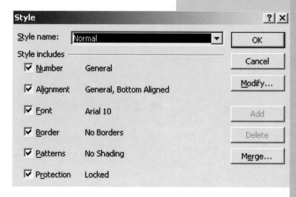

FIGURE 70
Style Window

A new style is applied by highlighting the spreadsheet, selecting the style and clicking the OK button. There is obviously an alternative way of applying a house style which is simply to follow the standard as you create the spreadsheet or by amending each element one by one. Creating a style helps you automate the process and reduce the potential for errors.

	A	B	C	D	E	F	G
1							
2							
3							
4			Factory A	Factory B	Factory C	Factory D	Total
5							
6		Staff	2500	3000	3450	4500	13450
7		Materials	12000	14000	13500	12000	51500
8		Transport	1500	2300	1200	3500	8500
9		Other	2300	1800	340	1450	5890
10		Total	18300	21100	18490	21450	79340

FIGURE 71
Linked Spreadsheet 1

Link Spreadsheets

In many cases you will have a number of inter-related spreadsheets dealing with the same area of work. You may need a sheet showing the manufacturing costs, one of transport costs and one indicating the costs of staff. If you study each of these separately then you will obviously benefit in that you can take more informed decisions. However, each of these areas depends on the others so that ideally they should be directly linked so that a change in one will have immediate effects on the others. In this way you can see what are the consequences of any change.

FIGURE 72
Linked Spreadsheet 2

	A	B	C	D	E	F
1						
2						
3			Factory A			
4						
5			January	February	March	Total
6		Office	450	425	400	1275
7		Production	1000	1100	900	3000
8		Stores	450	400	350	1200
9		Transport	350	390	425	1165
10		Maintenance	250	300	225	775
11		Total	2500	2615	2300	7415

The linked data can be included in formula so that it can be used to solve problems, identify trends or any of the many other uses of formula. In Exercise

14 you will link two sheets. The link is between a cell in which a formula has totalled a column of figures to a cell in another sheet. This cell is in turn part of a column which totalled by a formula. This ability to include links into formula is very useful in developing more complex relationships within spreadsheets.

Exercise 14

Linking Spreadsheets

1. Insert a floppy disk into the computer's drive

2 Load Microsoft Excel using either the Programs menu or the Excel icon on the desktop.

3 Set the orientation of the sheet to portrait, margins to 3 cm - right and left and 2 cm - top and bottom and header and footer to 1.5 cm (select File menu and Page Setup option)

4 Enter the spreadsheet in Figure 71. Use the SUM function to total rows and columns. This spreadsheet shows the costs of each Factory in January.

5. Select the File menu and click on the option Save to reveal the Save As window. Change the Save in: box to select the Floppy disk and add the file name First in the File name box. Click on the Save button. The top line of Excel will change to read "Microsoft Excel - First.xls".

6. Select the File menu and click on the New option to reveal New window. Select the workbook and click on the OK button. A new blank spreadsheet will appear. Enter the spreadsheet in Figure 72. Use the SUM function to total rows and columns. This spreadsheet represents the staff costs of each factory.

7. Select the File menu and click on the option Save to reveal the Save As window. Change the Save in: box to select the Floppy disk and add the file name Second in the File name box. Click on the Save button. The top line of Excel will change to read "Microsoft Excel - Second.xls".

8. Inspection of the two spreadsheets shows that cell C6 of First should equal cell C11 of Second spreadsheet (i.e. staff costs of Factory A in January). You could of course manually transfer the information but it is very straightforward to link the two cells.

9. In cell C6 of First spreadsheet insert [Second.xls]sheet 1!C11. To make the new formula calculate click on the equals sign on the formula toolbar and on the OK button in the window which will appear and you will see the value 2500 appear. Change the values in Second and see how the link operates.

10. To link two cells you simply enter the workbook name, sheet number, an exclamation mark and the cell reference. Practice making more links between the worksheets until you are satisfied that you understand the process.

11. Save the spreadsheets.

12. Close Excel by selecting the File menu item and clicking on the Exit option or by clicking on the close button in the top right hand corner of the application window.

Exercise 15

More Practice 1

1. Insert a floppy disk into the computer's drive

2. Load Microsoft Excel using either the Programs menu or the Excel icon on the desktop.

3. Set the orientation of the sheet to landscape, margins to 2.5 cm - right and left and 2.5 cm - top and bottom and header and footer to 2 cm (select File menu and Page Setup option)

4. Insert Header to read
Sports Results - Arial font and character size 14 embolden - in the centre section

5. Insert automatic fields in the Footer

Filename - left section
Page Number - centre section
Date - right section

6. Enter the table of information shown in Figure 72A to form your first spreadsheet of the average performances of sport club members during the last six months.

7. Check that you have entered the data accurately and correct any mistakes. If you click in the cell which contains the error you can amend the mistake.

8. Select the File menu and click on the option Save to reveal the Save As window. Change the Save in: box to select the Floppy disk and add the file name Sports in the File name box. Click on the Save button. The top line of Excel will change to read "Microsoft Excel - Sports.xls".

FIGURE 73
**BUSH
Scores**

9. Change the size of the columns so that you can clearly see the contents. Use the AVERAGE function to average the columns.

	A	B	C	D	E	F	G
1							
2							
3		BUSH					
4							
5							
6		Attempts	1	2	3	4	Average
7							
8		Gym Test	78	69	84	74	76.25
9		100 metres	15.97	15.15	16.65	15.95	15.93
10		Swimming	69.35	73.85	68.55	69.65	70.35

10. Check the appearance of your spreadsheet as a printed document by selecting the File menu and the Print Preview option.

11. Enter the table of information below (Figure 73) to form a second spreadsheet. Click on sheet 2 to create a new spreadsheet. This shows BUSH's last four scores at the three disciplines.

12. Change the size of the columns so that you can clearly see the contents. Use the AVERAGE function to average the rows.

13. Link the three BUSH averages to the Sports spreadsheet (i.e. sheet2!G8, sheet2!G9 and sheet2!G10).

14. Save your sheet by selecting the File menu and clicking on the Save option.

15. Return to sheet 1 and in column H create an IF function to decide if the individual member is fit or unfit depending on their Gym Test score. Fitness is determined by scoring more than 60 (=IF(E5>60,"Fit","Unfit"). Insert a column heading Fitness.

16. Adjust all the figures in sheet 1 so they are to two decimal places. Change the font to Arial and character size to 12. Embolden all the headings and centre all the data. You will need to adjust the column widths accordingly.

17. Figure 74 shows the new sheet.

18. Print the sheet without gridlines and Rows and column headings and then with them.

19. Print the sheet showing the formula.

20. Save your sheet by selecting the File menu and clicking on the Save option.

21. Close Excel by selecting the File menu item and clicking on the Exit option or by clicking on the close button in the top right hand corner of the application window.

FIGURE 74
Sheet 1

	A	B	C	D	E	F	G	H
1								
2								
3		Person	Age	Group	Gym Test	100 metres	Swimming	Fitness
4								
5		Bush	32	D	76.25	15.93	70.35	Fit
6		Kitchen	43	E	46	16.74	75.35	Unfit
7		Bury	49	G	38	15.94	78.95	Unfit
8		River	27	C	86	13.45	62.55	Fit
9		Wall	53	B	41	17.34	81.55	Unfit
10		Peters	29	E	81	13.75	65.85	Fit
11		Soil	35	A	65	14.15	67.35	Fit
12		Pony	38	C	62	15.15	68.15	Fit
13		Denzil	40	F	59	15.65	72.55	Unfit
14		Chester	46	C	55	16.35	75.85	Unfit
15		Average	39.20		60.93	15.45	71.85	

Exercise 16

More Practice 2

1. Insert your floppy disk into the computer's drive.

2. Create a data file (Figure 75) using the Notepad application (Start, Programs, Accessories and Notepad). Save the file as Import Data (In the CLAIT Plus assessment you will be provided with data files to import and will not need to create them).

3. Load Microsoft Excel using either the Programs menu or the Excel icon on the desktop.

4. Import the file Import Data. The delimiter is a comma. Figure 76 shows the spreadsheet.

5. Enter a formula to total the columns B, C and D and for rows 2, 3, 4, 5, 6 and 7. Enter the formula once for a row and a column and then replicate it.

6. Enter a new column heading in F1 called commission and devise a formula which is based on dividing the February monthly sales figures by 600 and multiplying the product by 50. Enter the formula.

7. Change the format of the commission column to currency.

8. Enclose the Column headings in a border of your choosing.

9. Select the File menu and click on the option Save to reveal the Save As window. Change the Save in: box to select the Floppy disk and add the file name Import Data in the File name box. Click on the Save button. The top line of Excel will change to read "Microsoft Excel - Import Data.xls".

10. Change the font of the whole spreadsheet except the column headings to Times New Roman and a character size 12.

11. Insert a new sheet by selecting Insert menu and clicking on the Worksheet option. A sheet 1 will appear alongside the Import Data sheet. Click on the Sheet 1 tab and enter the sheet shown in Figure 77. This sheet shows the sales performance of Squires who is also featured in the Import Data spreadsheet.

FIGURE 75
Import Data

```
Import Data.txt - Notepad
File  Edit  Search  Help
Staff,January,February,March
Squires,300,700,1200
Johnson,100,300,500
Singh,300,1200,2100
Patel,150,340,800
Gordon,230,560,600
Davies,270,450,560
```

FIGURE 76
Import Data Spreadsheet

	A	B	C	D
1	Staff	January	February	March
2	Squires	300	700	1200
3	Johnson	100	300	500
4	Singh	300	1200	2100
5	Patel	150	340	800
6	Gordon	230	560	600
7	Davies	270	450	560

	A	B	C	D	E	F
1		Squire Performance				
2						
3		Months	Tyres	Brakes	Oil	Filters
4		January	75	125	50	50
5		February	125	200	150	225
6		March	350	250	350	250

FIGURE 77
Squires Performance

12. Total each monthly row using a standard function.

13. The month totals for Squires are the same as the content of each entry in the Import Data sheet (i.e. cells B2, C2 and D2) therefore link the two sheets. Click on the equals sign on the formula toolbar and then on the OK button to calculate the formula.

14. Print the sheet without gridlines and Rows and column headings and then with them.

15. Print the sheet showing the formula.

16. Save your sheet by selecting the File menu and clicking on the Save option.

17. Close Excel by selecting the File menu item and clicking on the Exit option or by clicking on the close button in the top right hand corner of the application window.

Summary

1. Open Microsoft Excel

There are several ways of loading an application in Windows. These include:

• Clicking on the Start button, highlighting the Programs item and clicking on Microsoft Excel option

• Double clicking on the Excel icon on the desktop

2. Page Layout

Select the File menu and click on the Page Setup option to reveal the Page Setup window. There are four tabs:

• Page - to set the orientation of the sheet (portrait and landscape) and scale your spreadsheet on to a specified number of pages when you are printing it

• Margin - set the size of all four margins (i.e. left, right, top and bottom) and header and footer

• Header/Footer - to insert the content including automatic fields

• Sheet

3. Adjusting Column Width

Change the width of a column by placing the mouse pointer on the line between the two columns. The pointer's appearance will change (Figure 43) and you can drag the column wider.

Alternative way

Select the Format menu and click on either the Row or Column option revealing options to change the width of a column or the height of a row.

4. Save

Select the File menu and click on the option Save to reveal the Save As window. Change the Save in: box to select the Floppy disk or other drive/folder and add the file name in the File name box. Click on the Save button.

5. Close

Select the File menu item and click on the Exit option or click on the close button in the top right hand corner of the application window.

6. Mathematical Operators

The mathematical operators used in Excel are:

+	add
-	subtract
*	multiply
/	divide
<	less than
<=	less than or equal to
>	more than
>=	greater than or equal to

7. Mathematical Rules

When a formula consists of several arithmetic operators they are worked out in a standard way. Everything enclosed in brackets is calculated first, then multiplication and division and finally addition and subtraction. If a formula contains multiplication and division or addition and subtraction it works out the calculation from left to right.

8. Standard Formula

Excel provides a number of standard functions. These include: SUM, AVERAGE, COUNT, MIN, SQRT, MAX and IF. A list of all the functions can be accessed by clicking on the function button on the Standard toolbar to reveal the Paste window. The definition of each function is given at the bottom of the window.

9. References

The cell reference is given by combining the column letter with row number (e.g. Column Row - A4). There are three types of reference:

• Relative
• Absolute
• Mixed

The Relative reference is the normal one you encounter when you use Excel. If you move the cells (e.g. delete or insert rows or columns) then the reference in the formula changes to allow for the new position.

The Absolute reference is one which remains unchanged no matter what happens. You create an absolute reference by using the $ symbol (e.g. SUM (A2:A5) - Relative references while SUM ($A$2:$A$5) - Absolute references).

The mixed reference combines both Relative and Absolute within the same formula or function (e.g. H5+%G$3).

Named cell reference is created by highlighting a cell or area and entering its name in the left hand box of the formula bar.

10. Printing
Select the File menu and click on the Print option

11. Print Preview
Select the File menu and click on the Print Preview option to reveal the Print Preview window

12. Print Gridlines, Row and Column Headings
Select the File menu, click on the Print Preview option to reveal the Print Preview window. Click on the Setup button to reveal Page Setup window. Select the Sheet tab and click in the Gridlines and Row and column headings boxes so ticks appear. Click on the OK button when you are finished and you will see the window disappear and a new Print Preview appear showing gridlines and headings.

13. Print Options
Select the File menu and click on the Print option to reveal the Print window. In the window is a section called Print What with three options:

• Selection - print areas that are highlighted
• Active sheet(s) - print all the sheets you are working on
• Entire workbook - print all the sheets within the workbook

14. Print Formulae
Select the Tools menu and click on the Options option to reveal the Options window. The View tab shows a section called Window options. Clicking on the Formulas box will print the formulas. There are also boxes to select the Gridlines and Rows and Column headings. When choices have been made they are enacted by clicking on the OK button.

15. Change Format

The Formatting toolbar provides you with a variety of tools to enhance the format of your spreadsheet (e.g. fonts, character sizes, bold, italics, underline and change alignment). They are selected by highlighting the cell or cells and selecting the appropriate tool from the toolbar.

16. Borders

Click on the borders icon on the Formatting toolbar to reveal a small window of options.

17. Hide Rows and Columns

Select the Format menu and click on either Row or Column options revealing the options to change to hide or unhide rows or columns.

18. Orientation of Text

Select the Format menu and click on the Cells option to reveal the Format Cells window. The Alignment tab provides options to:

• Align the text both horizontally and vertically
• Wrap text
• Shrink to fit
• Merge Cells

19. Sort Data

Select the Data menu and click on the Sort option

Or select either of the two sort icons on the Standard toolbar.

20. Track Changes

Select the Tools menu and highlight the Track Changes options to reveal the Highlight changes options which when clicked will open the Highlight Changes Window.

21. Import Files

Straightforward Way

Use the Copy and Paste functions which are available in all Microsoft Office functions.

Alternative

Select the File menu and click on the Open option. Select the file you want to import. A Wizard will help you convert your file into the Excel format. It opens automatically when you try to import the file.

22. Logical Operators/Functions

The three logical operators are:

OR – OR(condition1, condition2) if either of the conditions are correct the true statement is enacted, otherwise the false statement is chosen

NOT – NOT(condition) if the condition is not correct then the true statement is enacted, otherwise the false statement is chosen

AND – AND(condition1 and condition2) if both conditions are correct then the true statement is enacted, otherwise the false statement is chosen

23. Linking Spreadsheets

To link two cells you simply enter the sheet number, an exclamation mark and the cell reference.

For Example:

Sheet1!A12   Sheet number!cell reference

24. Style

Select the Format menu and click on Style options to reveal the Style window. Clicking on the Modify button open the Format Cell window to select format options.

Databases and Solutions

This chapter will help you to:

- Create a database file, set up fields and enter test data

- Import and interrogate data using complex search criteria

- Present data in various report formats including lists and labels

- Format and present reports

This chapter covers Units 3 (Databases) and 11 (Database Solutions). The content of these two units overlaps so that you cannot offer both of them as part of CLAIT Plus. However, you are free to offer either unit as part of the qualification or study them as single units. There are no pre-conditions for studying these units. However, their content does assume that you have the skills and understanding which are provided by the OCR Level 1 ICT course New CLAIT (e.g. Unit 5 - Databases and Unit 1 - Using a Computer).

Assessment

Unit 3 - Databases

After studying Unit 3 your skills and understanding are assessed during a 3 hour practical assignment. This is set by OCR and marked locally. However, the marking will be externally moderated by OCR. This ensures that the standard is being applied correctly across the many different providers of OCR CLAIT Plus. If you are unsuccessful then you can be re-assessed using a different assignment.

Unit 11 - Database Solutions

After studying Unit 11 your skills and understanding are assessed using a locally devised practical assignment. The assignment will be marked locally but externally moderated by OCR. This ensures that the standard is being applied correctly across the many different providers of OCR CLAIT Plus. If you are unsuccessful then you can be re-assessed using a different assignment.

The assessment task can be provided by the local tutor or suggested by the individual student. In both cases the task must meet all the assessment objectives of Unit 11 and allow learners to show their understanding.

Font Families

Clait Plus uses font families in its assessments rather than font names. In Chapter 1 font families are explained and how they relate to font names. As you undertake each exercise consider which font family the font you are using belongs to.

Databases

Databases are extensively used but are also often invisible to individuals who can be unaware when they make contact with them. When you telephone your bank, the staff member dealing with your enquiry is looking at your records stored on a database. This is equally true of almost any financial transaction (e.g. building society, insurance and credit cards). Many organisations keep records on a database of customers details, preferences, order patterns, contacts etc. Supermarkets will maintain a database of their stock while your employer is likely to hold information about your salary, working hours, rates of pay and holidays on a database.

Databases are extremely useful in organising information. They allow you to manipulate the data to compare difference pieces of information and extract any combination of records to aid decision-making. Managers can see the relevant information before they decide what to do.

FIGURE 78
Access Database

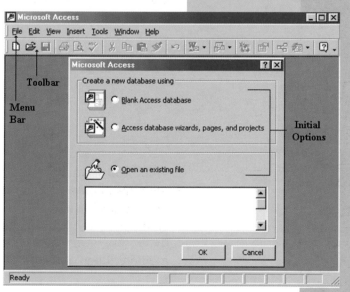

Database Applications

This chapter is based on Microsoft Access 2000 which is a modern package that you can employ to create databases. Figure 78 shows the Access application interface. When the application initially loads, there is an overlaid window which provides you with three options. These are:

• Create a new blank database
• Create a new database using the database wizard
• Open an existing database

New Database

With any application it is always tempting to rush ahead and begin to construct something immediately. Modern software applications provide many powerful tools to edit and enhance the outcome and allow you to start straight away. However, this can produce poorly designed and structured databases. It is not easy to restructure or amend a database once you have constructed it. It is good practice to plan your database before trying to develop it and a few minutes planning will save you many problems later.

We are going to develop a database for a sports club showing the performance of some of the members. We will need to consider what information the database will hold. There are three terms that it is important to remember:

1. Field - this is an individual piece of information or data (e.g. surname)

2. Record - a group of fields with a common purpose (e.g. information about a single individual)

3. Table - a set of records (e.g. information about all the club's sprint runners)

The normal process is to consult the people who are going to use the database in order to identify what information it should contain and how it should be structured. This consultation has taken place and we have been requested to construct a database containing the following information. This is:

• Club membership number, date of membership, fees paid, title, first name, surname, street, town and postcode

• Event

• Career Best performance

When you have identified the information, you need to decide what sort of data it is (e.g. numbers or text). This is vital because the database needs to be able to sort and manipulate the information so it must be sure what form the data takes. Access needs to know the type of data and how large it is so that it can reserve enough space to hold the information. Access allows you to define nine types of data. They are:

• Text -   a text field can hold up to 256 characters which can be letters, numbers or special characters.

• Memo –   this allows you to store items such as sales reports, customer details, product information etc.

• Numbers –   an Access database can store numbers and also carry out calculations (e.g. calculate salary based on hours worked and pay rates)

• Date/time –   a standard format is provided for dates and times

- Currency – this is a special number type designed for currency

- Autonumber – creates a unique number type so that records can be numbered

- Yes/No – a simple type of data that can only be yes or no (e.g. Invoice paid yes/no)

- OLE Object – provides the means of including in the database other windows objects (e.g. graphic image, spreadsheets and word files). When you click on the object, the appropriate application is opened and you can view that object

- Hyperlink – provides the means to link the database to a website. For our sports database we need to decide the data type of each field. Table 1 shows the types of each piece of data.

Table 1   Sport Data Types

Field Name	Data Type
Club membership number	Autonumber – this field will automatically be incremented for each new member
Date of membership	Date
Fees paid	Yes/No
First name	Text – twenty characters
Lastname	Text – fifty characters
Event	Text – fifty characters
Career Best performance	Number

The Database Solution Unit specifies that students be able to create a database with at least six fields, and including four data types. The Sports database exceeds these requirements (i.e. seven fields and five data types).

In addition to deciding on the data types you would also consider querying the data (i.e asking the database questions – how many members ran the 100 metres faster than 12 seconds), designing standard reports that the people using the database will need, and also input forms to provide an efficient data entry process. We will consider these issues later.

A key name to the usefulness of any database is an obvious one but sometimes overlooked. The information contained in a database must be accurate. Potentially many errors are inserted into a database during data entry. It is essentially that data is accurately entered. It takes far longer to correct an error than any time gained by rushed entry. Inaccurate data can produce misleading reports and queries and lead to poor decisions.

FIGURE 79
Sports Database Window

Exercise 17

Creating A Database

1. Load Microsoft Access by selecting Start, highlighting the Programs menu and clicking on the Microsoft Access item or click on the Access icon on the desktop.

2. Microsoft Access application will load (Figure 78). Select Blank Access database by clicking in the radio button. The File New Database opens to enable you to save your new database. Save the database as a file called Sports on a floppy disk.

The Sports Database window (Figure 79) shows three options with the Table object on the left-hand side selected:

• Create a table in Design view
• Create a table by using wizard
• Create a table by entering data

3. Double click on Create a table in Design view and the table window opens.

4. You need to insert your field names and their types. If you enter Club membership in Field Name box and click in the corresponding Data Type box, a small down arrow will appear revealing a list of types. Select autonumber and click in the next Field Name box then enter Date of Membership. Complete the table, as shown in Figure 80.

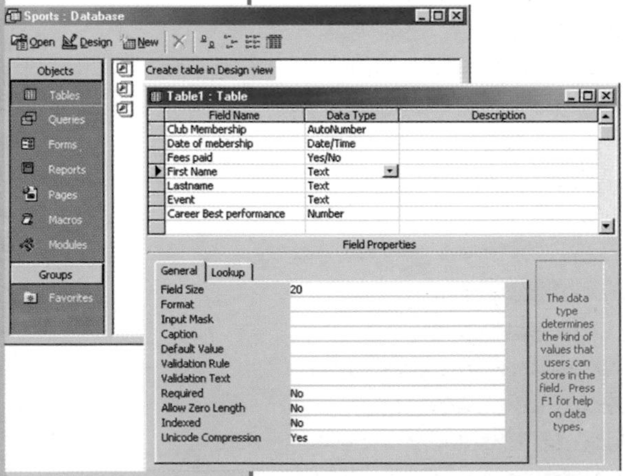

5. When you enter a type, you should observe that in field size a value (e.g. 50) will appear with a text type and Long Integer with a number type. The value 50 indicates the number of characters that the field can store while a Long Integer is a whole number (i.e. no decimal places). Change First Name to 20 characters but leave the other text items at 50 characters. If you wanted to show real numbers (i.e. with decimal places) then you would need to click in the Long Integer box to produce a down arrow which if clicked, gives you other options. In this case Career Best performance needs to include decimal places, so select the decimal option and insert 2 in the Scale

FIGURE 80
Create a Table

and Decimals places fields. This will allow data containing two decimal places to be entered (e.g. minutes and seconds).

6. You need to save your table. If you select the File menu and the Save As option, the Save As window appears. Enter Membership and click on the OK button.

7. A warning message will now appear asking you if you need a primary key. In this case you do not need to define one so click on the No button. A primary key is a unique number which allows different tables to relate to each other. The table window reappears and you should close it by clicking on the close button in the top right hand corner of the table window. You can now see the Sports Database window but with an extra item now added – Membership.

8. Double clicking on Membership allows you to begin entering the data. We will return to this table to enter the data later. Close the window by clicking on the close button in the top right hand corner of the Sports Database window.

9. Unless you wish to immediately carry on with the next exercise, close Access by clicking on the close button in the top right hand corner of the main application window or select the File menu and the Exit option.

Entering Data

The Database Solutions Unit places considerable emphasis on your showing that you can input data. One of the assessment objectives requires that you can input a minimum of 40 records. This is not required as part of the Database Unit. However, both units stress the importance of entering data accurately so that it is probably worth learners who are studying either unit to attempt the exercise on inputting data. The value of a database is based on its contents being accurate. Data errors considerably reduced the value of a database and can lead to wrong conclusions being reached and to poor business decisions. Correcting a single error takes considerably longer than entering many items of data so accuracy is probably more important than speed of entry.

Table 2 shows the records of 40 members of the club. The event column shows a two-letter code rather than the full name of the event (e.g. MA – Marathon). This type of encoding is frequently used to save time during data input. Only a few seconds are saved for each entry but when you are inputting hundreds or even thousands of records then the saving is significant. Errors are also reduced since less needs to be entered. However, this is only half the story in that databases are also concerned with presenting, comparing and contrasting information. A code is little benefit if it is not understood by the database users. An effective code is one that users recognise and can convert to the full terms. This also helps users enter the data since they are easily able to recognise errors and it is always easier to enter meaningful data than a meaningless set of numbers and letters. A set of random numbers is unlikely to be helpful unless users have a reason to memorise them (e.g. product codes widely used in the company). Database reports that contain encoded information need to be meaningful to the reader or its value will be diminished by the need to translate them into the actual terms. The example in table 2 shows encoding based on an attempt to use the first two letters of the event name or something relating to the name (e.g. 100 and 200 metres SP or sprint, SH – Shot, 1500 metres – metric mile MI and 5000 metres – middle distance MD). They are therefore shorter and reasonably meaningful to a sport club user.

Once you have created a database, which reflects your needs then it is important that your data is aligned with the types of data you have specified. If the data is different then you will waste time and perhaps produce confusing results. An example of potential confusion is that there are several alternative ways of showing dates (e.g. American – month, day and year). It is important to present dates in the format that your users understand. In the case of Great Britain this is day, month and year. Often users will wish to search for data relating for a particular date this will seriously be influenced if dates have been entered in the wrong format. An America format 2/09/02 can mean 9th February 2002 in the English format. It is therefore vital that dates are entered correctly. This type of error is difficult to detect and so it is important to ensure accurate and correct input.

Table 2
Data Input

Date of membership	Fees paid	First name	Last name	Event	Career Best performance
12/01/89	Yes	Michael	Doherty	MA	183.56
15/03/89	Yes	Brian	Dowling	SH	6.4
23/05/89	Yes	Hari	Ghorbani	SP	12.95
30/10/89	Yes	John	Gibbins	TW	120.50
12/12/89	Yes	Clive	Groom	HI	1.80
08/01/90	Yes	Peter	Hanson	SP	12.56
26/02/90	No	Hazel	Hill	TR	13.55
14/05/90	Yes	Jane	Hopwood	MA	200.85
17/09/90	No	Bill	Johnson	MD	14.05
09/12/90	Yes	Latia	Rannie	LO	6.25
03/01/91	Yes	Alice	Luckhurst	MD	16.15
22/02/91	Yes	Cheryl	Ludden	SP	15.75
11/04/91	Yes	Mark	Ludlow	SP	12.15
16/05/91	Yes	Asghar	Malik	HI	1.82
27/07/91	Yes	Christine	Morris	TR	13.10
14/11/91	Yes	Kevin	Steele	TW	118.55
12/01/92	Yes	Gary	Newhouse	MA	175.75
02/02/92	No	James	Night	MA	177.55
07/06/92	Yes	Richard	Palmer	SP	12.68

10/08/92	Yes	Julie	Pandey	MA	203.45
11/10/92	Yes	Pannu	Rasmussen	SP	12.10
04/01/93	Yes	Steven	Salt	TW	110.45
05/03/93	Yes	Rao	Palk	LO	5.95
17/05/93	Yes	Mathew	Peek	SP	12.85
19/07/93	Yes	Paula	Pitman	HI	1.56
23/09/93	No	Paul	Pecan	TW	122.85
30/11/93	Yes	Karl	Polkowski	MA	165.85
05/02/94	No	Oliver	Randall	TW	118.65
09/05/94	Yes	Alan	Rider	TR	15.65
13/07/94	Yes	Linda	Rose	LO	6.05
20/09/94	Yes	Fred	Scrim	SP	13.05
12/02/95	Yes	Kate	Scott	MD	15.35
25/07/95	Yes	Murray	Smith	TW	117.50
29/08/95	Yes	Ben	Sibley	TR	16.05
03/01/96	No	Peter	Swain	MI	3.58
16/05/96	Yes	John	Sutton	JA	55.34
21/09/96	Yes	Susan	Taylor	SH	5.6
22/10/97	Yes	Tom	Turner	HU	18.95
17/03/98	Yes	Dorothy	West	SP	15.65
18/06/98	Yes	Tim	Wilson	LA	52.35

FIGURE 81
Access Options

FIGURE 82
Sports Database Window

The event column codes are:

1. 100 and 200 metres – SP
2. 110 and 400 metres hurdles – HU
3. 400 metres – LA
4. 800 metres – TW
5. 1500 metres – MI
6. 5000 metres – MD
7. Marathon - MA
8. Shot – SH
9. Javelin – JA
10. Discus – DI
11. Long Jump – LO
12. Triple Jump – TR
13. High Jump - HI

FIGURE 83
Completed Table

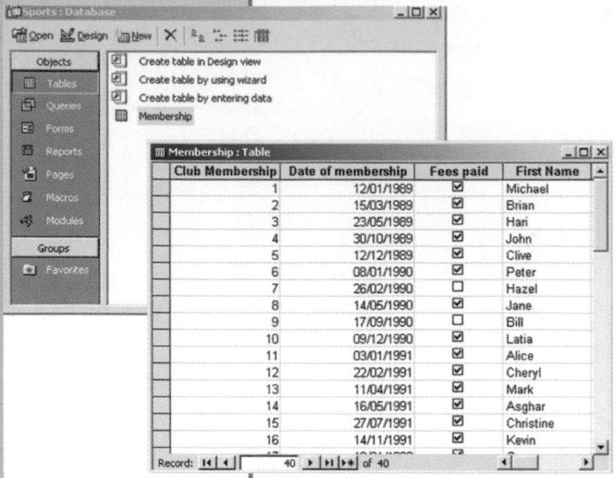

Exercise 18

Entering Data

1. Load Microsoft Access by selecting Start, highlighting the Programs menu and clicking on the Microsoft Access item or click on the Access icon on the desktop. Insert your floppy disk into the drive.

2. The overlaid window (Figure 81) offers you the choice of:

- Creating a Blank Access database
- Creating Access database wizards, pages and projects
- Open an existing database

FIGURE 84
Report Options

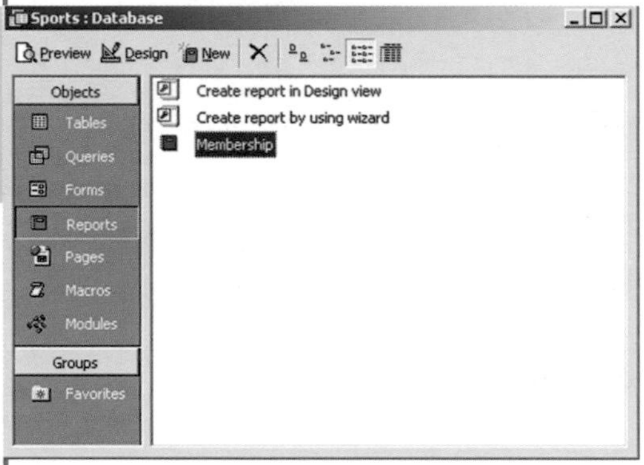

If you have only recently created the Sports database (see previous exercise) then you should see it listed in the area below Open an existing database. If not, select the Open an existing database, highlight Sports and click on the OK button.

3. The Sports: Database window should open (Figure 82). By double clicking on the Membership table item, it will open for data entry.

4. Some of the columns are too small to show the whole title. You can adjust the size by placing your mouse pointer over the line separating the columns and it will change shape to form a double arrow. If you hold down the mouse button you can drag the column line to widen it. Change the column widths so that their titles can be seen.

FIGURE 85
Membership Report

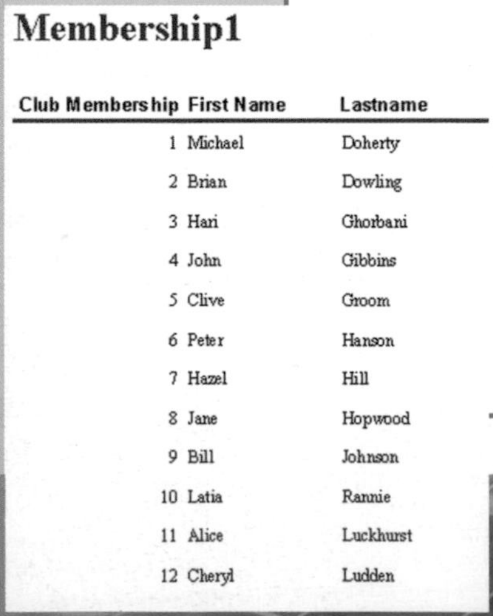

5. Enter the data shown in Table 2. Remember that the membership number is entered automatically by Access. Click in the field Date of Membership and enter the date. You can enter data into any field providing you click into that field first. The Fees paid field shows a small rectangle that you click in to indicate that the fees have been paid. It is left blank if the fees have not been paid.

6. Figure 83 shows the completed table. It is very important to

Membership1

Club Membership	First Name	Lastname
1	Michael	Doherty
2	Brian	Dowling
3	Hari	Ghorbani
4	John	Gibbins
5	Clive	Groom
6	Peter	Hanson
7	Hazel	Hill
8	Jane	Hopwood
9	Bill	Johnson
10	Latia	Rannie
11	Alice	Luckhurst
12	Cheryl	Ludden

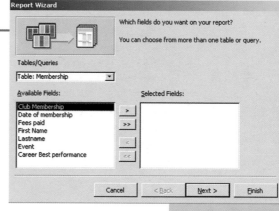

FIGURE 86
**Reports
Window**

check that each record has been entered accurately. If you find a mistake, click on the appropriate field and enter your correction.

7. Save your data by selecting the File menu and the Save option.

8. Close the Membership: Table window by clicking on the close button in the top right hand corner of the window.

9. Close Access by clicking on close button in top right hand corner of the main application window or select the File menu and the Exit option.

Reports

The information stored in a database is only part of the story. The real value of databases lies in accessing the information in a form that is useful to you. This involves designing reports which are the means of presenting selected data in the form that is most useful to you. Access provides two ways of helping you extract information in the form of a report. They are:

• Using the Access wizard to assist your design
• Developing the report manually

If you look at the Sports Database window you will see that down the left hand side are a series of buttons. If you select Reports, then Figure 84 will appear showing you the two approaches to creating reports.

Figure 85 is an example of a simple report simply listing all the members of the Sports Club in order of their membership number.

Reports are intended to present information to users. It is therefore important that the information is effectively shown so that it is easy to understand. This means that you need to control the alignment of the data and how it is presented. The presentation and alignment of a report can be

FIGURE 87
**Report
Wizard**

FIGURE 88
**Selecting
Fields**

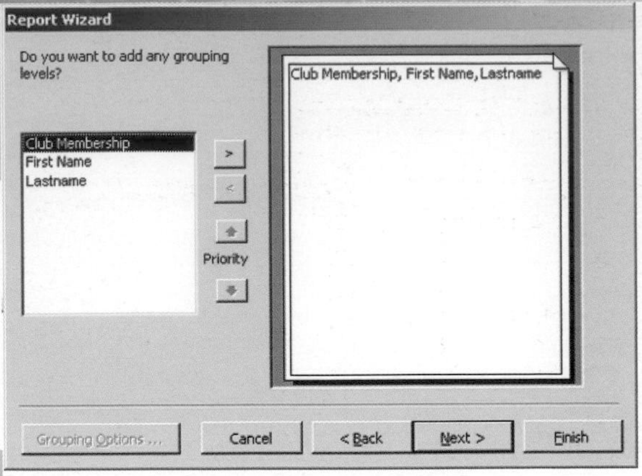

FIGURE 89
Grouping

FIGURE 90
Sorting

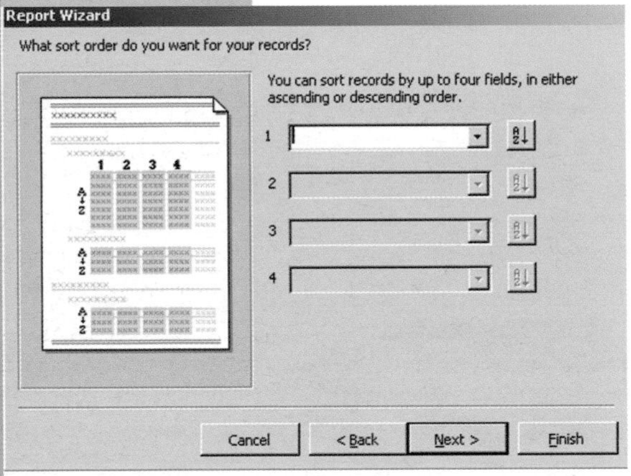

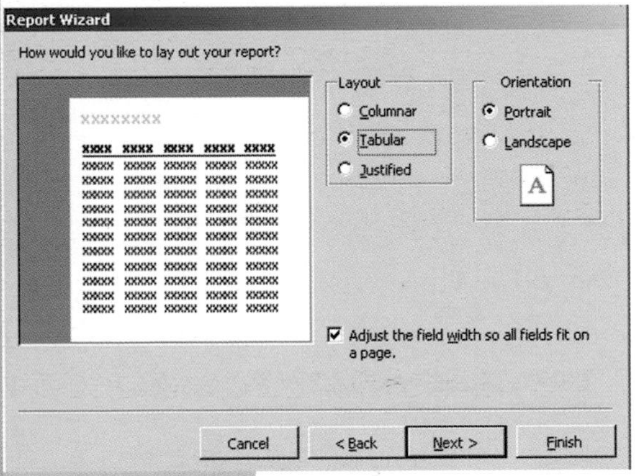

FIGURE 91
Layout and Orientation

changed by highlighting the report you wish to amend and click on the Design icon on the toolbar. This will open the report showing the structure (Figure 98). If you click on the text boxes and headers you will see they are enclosed in a frame with small rectangles these allow you to resize and move them. You can also use the Format menu Align option to align the text (i.e. left, right, top, bottom and to grid).

When you print or review a report on the screen you will sometimes notice that the fields are not printed or shown in full. This is sometimes the result of different text boxes overlapping so that you need to move and resize them. This is important because:

• It avoids confusing readers of the report who may be mislead by shortened title or data. This is important if decisions are being taken on the basis of the information

• Presentation of a report will help convince managers that they need to act on the information it contains. A poorly presented report will not help to persuade managers to treat the information with the importance it deserves

An important approach to presenting a report is to group records together within some common characteristic. This could be the year when the members joined the sports club or any other characteristic (i.e. a specific field). Using the Report Wizard you offered the opportunity to group your information by a specific field. Figure 89 shows the window.

Example

Comparing the presentation of grouped with list of the same information

Orders Grouped by Year   List of Orders

1999 Order ABC

1999
2001 Order BHK

2000 Order DGH
Order ABC
2000 Order HJY
Order JCF
1999 Order JCF

2001 Order JKY
2000

Order DGH
Order HJY

2001

Order JKY
Order BHK

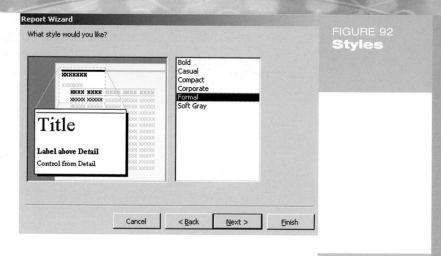

FIGURE 92
Styles

The order of presentation of the information is selected during the Report Wizard process. Figure 87 shows the window in which you select the order of fields. While Figure 91 allows you to select the presentation from three options Columnar, Tabular and Justified. The layouts associated with each presentation type is shown in the window. This window also provides you with the option to select the orientation of the report (i.e. portrait or landscape) and adjust the field widths so they all appear on the page.

FIGURE 93
Title

In creating a report you are provided with the option of basing it on a table or an existing query you have developed so that the results of a search can be reported on. Figure 87 shows a box Tables/Queries that allows you to select particular tables or queries on which to base the report.

FIGURE 94
New Report

Printing

You will often need to print a report or a table of information in order to provide the information to a wider audience than those who have direct access to the database. Presentation of the information is important so you should preview the document before you print it to check it. The Print Preview option is available from the File menu and operates in the same way that it does in other Microsoft Office applications. You are presented with an image of the report or table as it will appear when printed. Sometimes because of

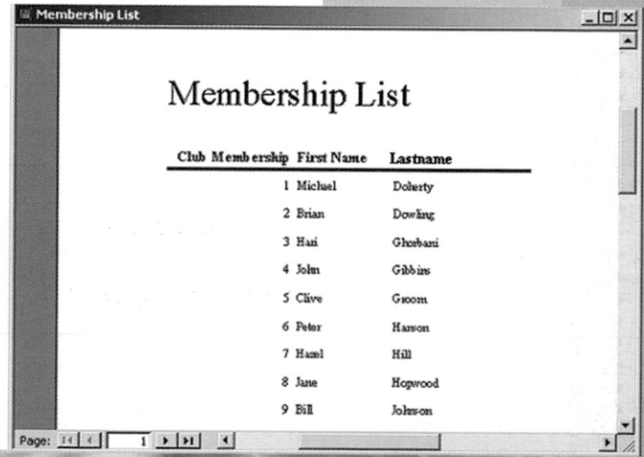

FIGURE 95
Membership List

FIGURE 96
Page Setup

FIGURE 97
Margin and Orientation Changes

the density of the information you will need to use the zoom function (i.e. a magnifying glass) on the toolbar to see the detail.

If the preview is acceptable then you can either print it directly from the preview window by selecting the Print icon on the toolbar or close the window and select the File menu and then the Print option to reveal the Print window. By clicking on the OK button the report or table will be printed. If the preview is not satisfactory you may need to select the File menu and Page Setup to change the margins, orientation and column settings. If you are printing a report you may have to use the Design option to move and resize the boxes.

Exercise 19

Reports

1. Load Microsoft Access by selecting the Start button, highlighting the Programs option and clicking on the Microsoft Access item or click on the Access icon on the desktop. Insert your floppy disk into the drive.

2. The application will open with the overlaid window offering three choices. Select the Open an existing database option and you should see the Sports database listed. Highlight Sports and click on the OK button. The Sports database window will open.

3. If the Reports button is not pressed then click on it (Figure 86) to show you the two options to creating a report.

4. Select Create report by using a wizard and the Report Wizard window (Figure 87) will appear. This shows the Table that the report will be based on in the box below the Tables/Queries title. It allows you to change the table or to select a query on which to base your report. The process is the same in both cases. This window allows you to select which fields you wish to include in your report. You select a field by highlighting it and clicking on the single arrow button pointing towards the right hand box. If you click on the double arrow button you will select all the fields. If you accidentally select a field by mistake you can correct it by highlighting it and using the left pointing arrow button.

5. Select Club Membership, First name and Lastname to produce a report which is essentially a list of the members (Figure 88).

6. When you have successfully selected your fields click on the Next button to reveal the next window (Figure 89) that allows you to group your information by again highlighting the item and using the arrow button. Experiment with different groupings. However, return to the original state when you have finished and click on the Next button. You should note that there is a Back button that lets you to return to the previous window if you have made an error.

7. The next window (Figure 90) enables you to sort your records into ascending or descending order. In this example we do not wish to sort the records so simply click on the Next button to reveal Figure 91. This window allows you change the orientation of the report from portrait to landscape as well as selecting the layout of the report – Columnar, Tabular and Justified. You can explore these options since this window provides you with a preview facility. Select Portrait and Tabular and click on the Next button.

8. The next window (Figure 92) offers you a choice of styles and you can explore the options by watching the preview area. Select Formal and click on the Next button.

9. You are now approaching the end of the wizard process and by using the window you can choose the title of your report – enter Membership List. You can preview your report or modify its design. Click on the Finish button. The report will now appear (Figure 94).

10. Select the File menu and the Print Preview option to check the report. Print the report by selecting the File menu, click on the Print option

FIGURE 98
Design of Report

FIGURE 99
Frame

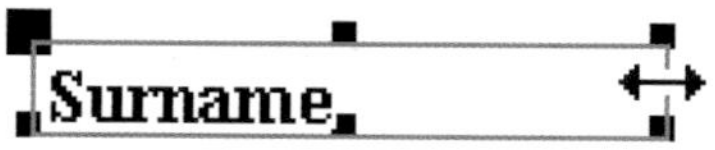

FIGURE 100
Double-Headed Arrow

FIGURE 101
Forms

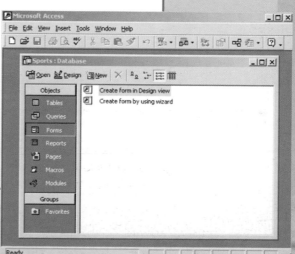

FIGURE 102
Form Wizard

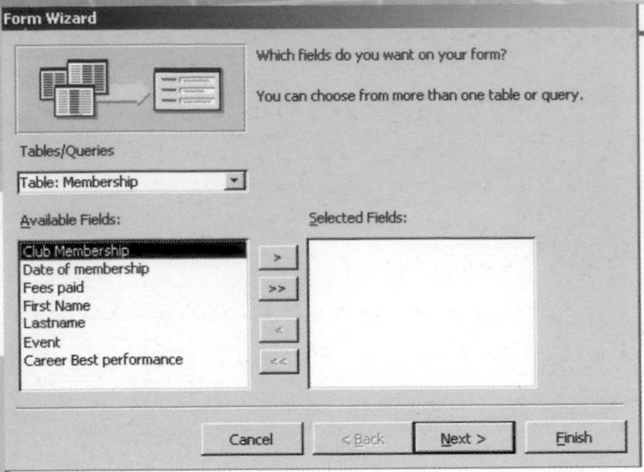

Form Wizard

Which fields do you want on your form?

You can choose from more than one table or query.

Tables/Queries

Table: Membership

Available Fields:

Club Membership
Date of membership
Fees paid
First Name
Lastname
Event
Career Best performance

Selected Fields:

Cancel   < Back   Next >   Finish

FIGURE 103
Selecting Fields

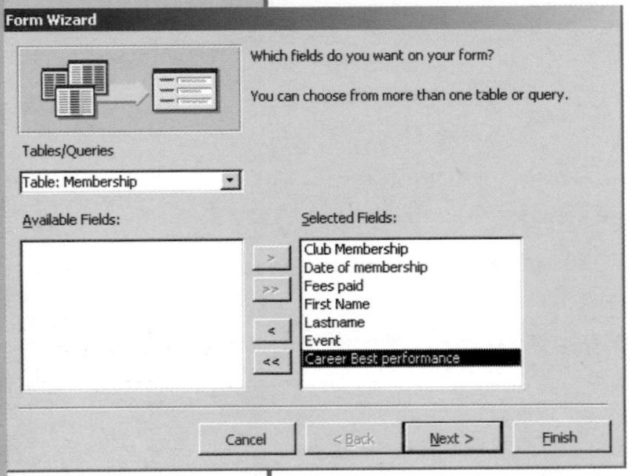

Form Wizard

Which fields do you want on your form?

You can choose from more than one table or query.

Tables/Queries

Table: Membership

Available Fields:

Selected Fields:

Club Membership
Date of membership
Fees paid
First Name
Lastname
Event
Career Best performance

Cancel   < Back   Next >   Finish

FIGURE 104
Layout

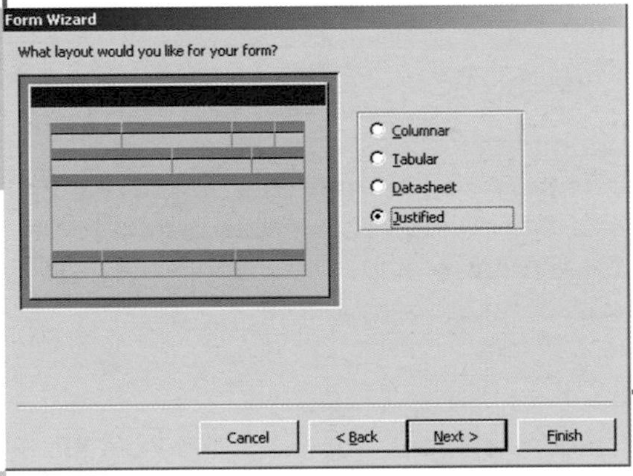

Form Wizard

What layout would you like for your form?

○ Columnar
○ Tabular
○ Datasheet
● Justified

Cancel   < Back   Next >   Finish

FIGURE 105
Styles

Form Wizard

What style would you like?

Blends
Blueprint
Expedition
Industrial
International
Ricepaper
SandStone
Standard
Stone
Sumi Painting

Label   Data

Cancel   < Back   Next >   Finish

and then click on the OK button to print with the default settings or select the printer icon in the Print Preview window. Before you print, check that the printer is switched on and has paper.

11. Close the report window using the control buttons in the top right hand corner of the window. You will now see the Sports database window with the new report, Membership List, included (Figure 95).

12. If you wish to stop now, close the Sports: Database window using the close button in the top right hand corner of the window to move to the next exercise ignore this step.

13. Close Access by clicking on the close button in the top right hand corner of the main application window or select the File menu and the Exit option.

Although you have created a report using the Wizard it is possible to make changes to the layout and presentation. You can alter the report's:

• Margins (i.e. left, right, top and bottom)
• Orientation (i.e. portrait or landscape)
• Headers and Footers
• Automatic fields (i.e. date, page and filename)

Exercise 20

Amending the Report

1. Load Microsoft Access by selecting the Start button, highlighting the Programs option and clicking on the Microsoft Access item or click on the Access icon on the desktop. Insert your floppy disk into the drive.

2. The application will open with the overlaid window offering three choices. Select the Open an existing database option and you should see the Sports database listed below. Highlight Sports and click on the OK button. The Sports database window will open.

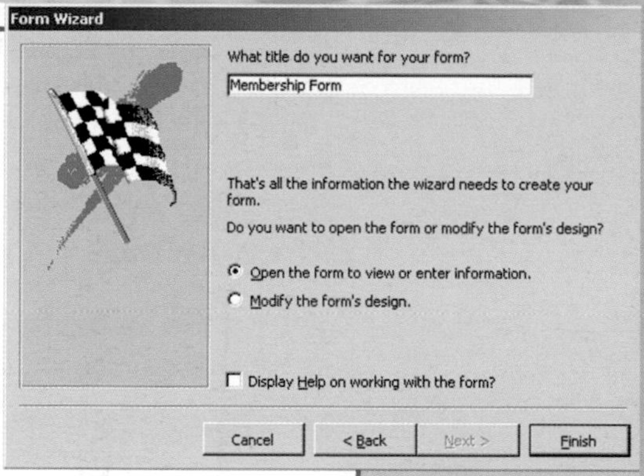

3. If the Reports button is not pressed then click on it to show the Membership List report. Click on Membership List to reveal the report. Investigate the report – scroll down to bottom of page 1 and you should notice that the date is shown and page 1 of 2. These are produced by automatic fields inserted into the report by the Wizard that calculate the date and page length.

4. It is straightforward to change the report's margins and orientation by selecting the File menu and the Page Setup option. This will open the Page Setup window (Figure 96), allowing you to change the margins and if you select the Page tab, you can alter the orientation.

5. Change all four margins to 34.99 mm and the orientation to landscape. Figure 97 shows the result of these changes. Close the report window using the control buttons in the top right hand corner of the window.

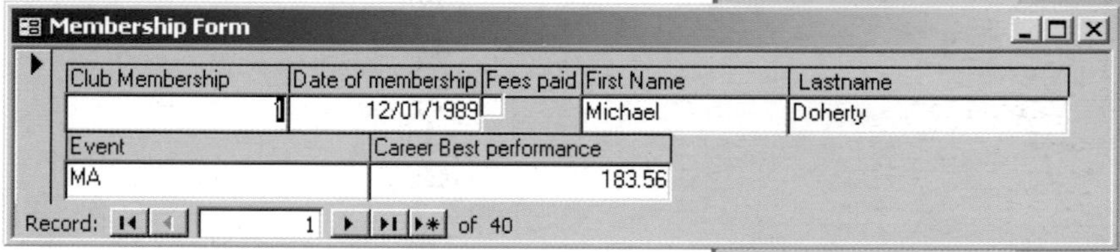

6. Access also provides tools to alter the details of the report. If you highlight Membership List and click on the Design icon on the toolbar, the structure of the report is revealed (Figure 98). You can now manipulate the various elements of the report. Investigate changing the structure by resizing and moving the boxes and use the Align option in the Format menu to change alignment. For example resize the Membership List text box so it fills the whole width and explore different alignments. Continue until you are confident.

7. If you click on the element Membership List you will see that the title is enclosed in a frame (Figure 99). This is the equivalent of highlighting it. You can drag the frame and its contents – the mouse pointer changes to a small hand and you can move the frame by holding down the mouse button and dragging it. Move the title Membership List to the centre of the report.

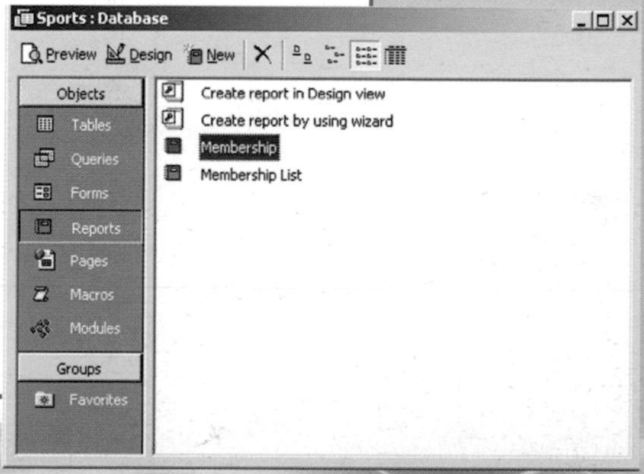

FIGURE 106
Finish

FIGURE 107
Membership Form

FIGURE 108
Blank Form

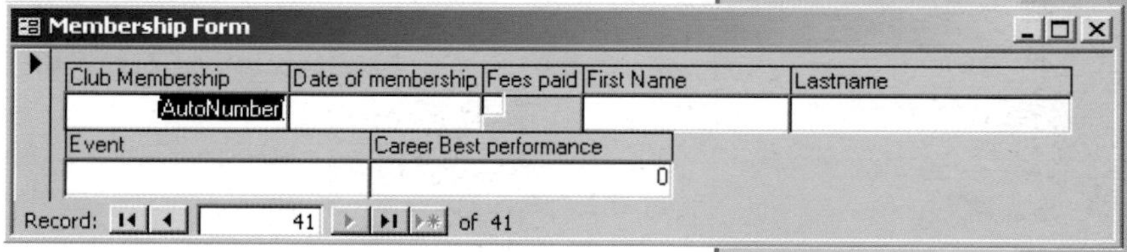

FIGURE 109
Sports: Database Report

FIGURE 110
New Report

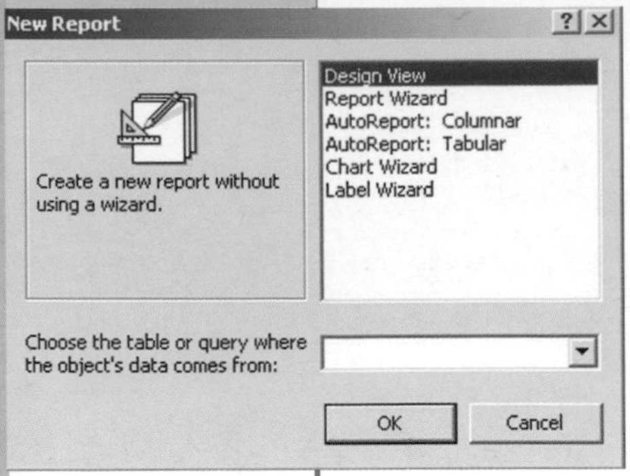

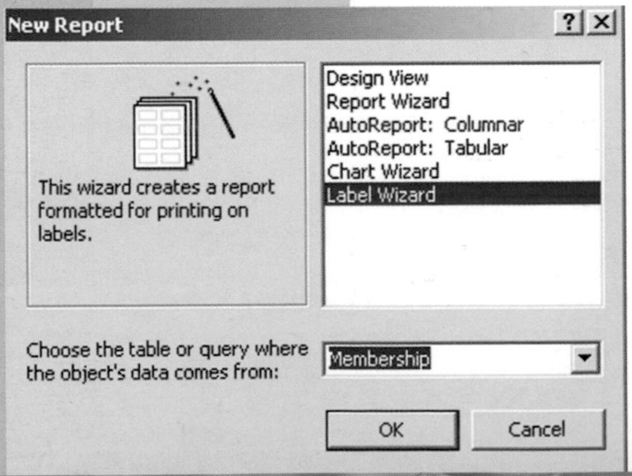

8. With the Membership List enclosed in a frame you can also change the font and character size. Change the font to Arial and character size to 28 using the toolbar. You will need to adjust the size of the frame to this by placing the pointer on the frame edge and it will change to a double-headed arrow (Figure 100). If you hold down the left mouse button you can drag the frame edge to make it larger.

9. Now change the character size of the sub-heading (Page Header) to 12. You will need to rearrange the three headings. In order to align the information you will also need to align the detail to the Page Header sub-titles.

10. If you consider the Page Footer you will see:

=Now() – this is the date automatic field
="Page "& [Page] & "of" & [Pages] – this is the page automatic field

These are inserted using the Insert menu and either the Page Numbers or Date and Time option. Explore the options and you will notice that you can alter the presentation of the date and pages.

11. When you have finished you can close the Design view of the report using the control buttons in the right hand corner of the window. You will be presented with a message window asking you if you would like to save the changes you have made. Click on the Yes button.

12. Close the Sports: Database window using the close button in the top right hand corner of the window.

13. Close Access by clicking on the close button in the top right hand corner of the main application window or select the File menu and the Exit option.

FIGURE 111
Label
Wizard

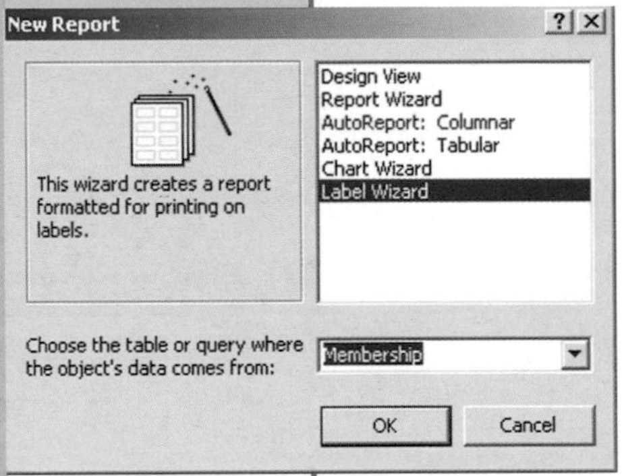

FIGURE 112
Type of
Labels

Forms

When entering information into a database, it is important that the source of the data is designed to make data entry as easy as possible. The source is normally some type of form. In the example we have been using of a Sports Club, the source document could be the membership application form. A common problem is that the membership form's layout does not correspond to the database table. This is often made worse by the use of abbreviations in the database so that mistakes can easily be made.

Access allows you to design a data entry form that resembles the source document to avoid errors and to make the process efficient. Figure 101 shows Sports: Database in forms view (i.e. the Forms button has been clicked) and the two ways that Access provides of creating forms. These are:

- Create a form in Design view
- Create a form by using wizard

By printing out the data entry form you have created a form which serves both as an input document and also as a membership application form. This will minimise errors and reduce the need to transfer data between documents.

Exercise 21

Data Entry Form

1. Load Microsoft Access by selecting the Start button, highlighting the Programs option and clicking on the Microsoft Access item or click on the Access icon on the desktop. Insert your floppy disk into the drive.

2. The application will open with the overlaid window offering three choices. Select the Open an existing database option and you should see the Sports database listed below. Highlight Sports and click on the OK button. The Sports database window will open.

3. Click on the Forms button on the left-hand side of the window and you will reveal two options to create a form. This is shown in Figure 101. Click on the Create form by using wizard to open the

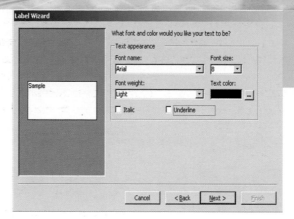

FIGURE 113
Label Characteristics

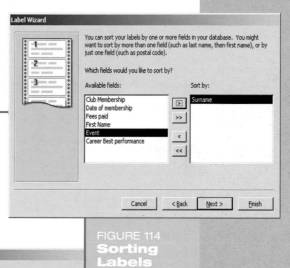

FIGURE 114
Sorting Labels

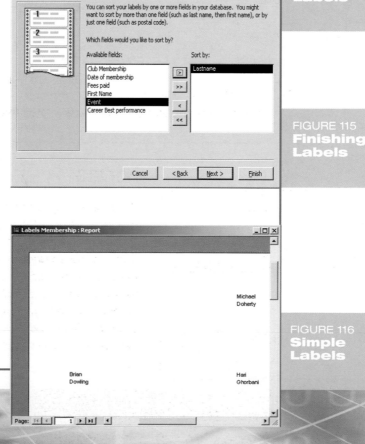

FIGURE 115
Finishing Labels

FIGURE 116
Simple Labels

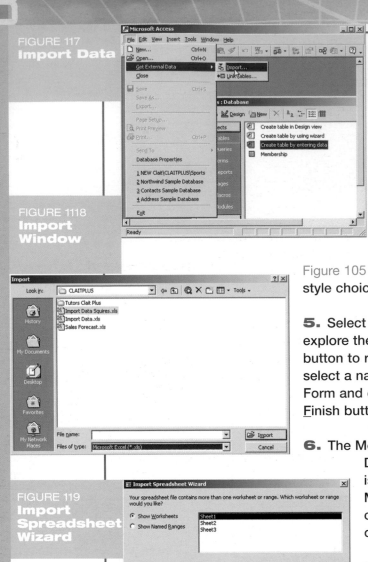

FIGURE 117
Import Data

FIGURE 1118
Import Window

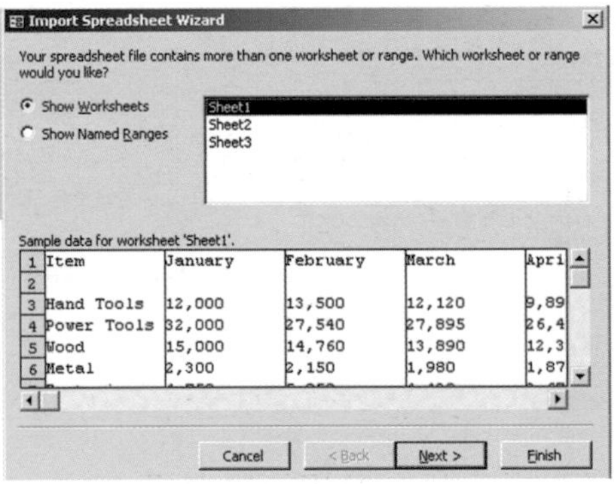

FIGURE 119
Import Spreadsheet Wizard

FIGURE 120
Selecting Fields

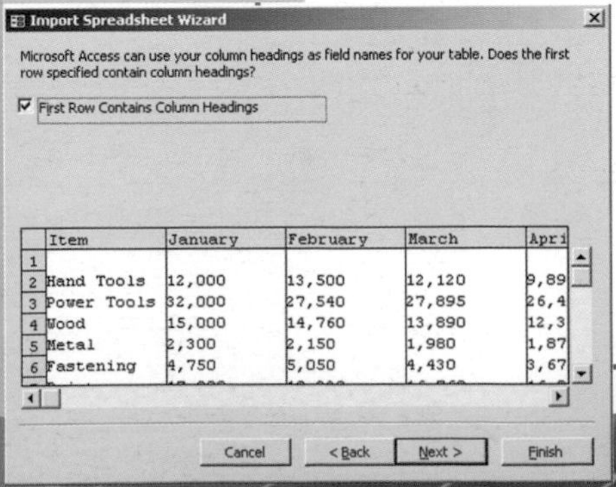

Form Wizard window (Figure 102). The fields to include in the form are chosen using highlighting the field and clicking on the single arrow keys. If the double arrow is selected all the fields are included. In this case select all the fields (Figure 103).

4. Click on the Next button to move to the next stage of the wizard (Figure 104). This gives you a choice of four layouts. In this case select Justified and click on the Next button to reveal Figure 105 which provides you with a variety of style choices.

5. Select the Standard style but you should also explore the different options. Click on the Next button to reveal Figure 106. This allows you to select a name for your form. Enter Membership Form and complete the process by clicking on Finish button.

6. The Membership Form is shown in the Sports Database window when the Forms button is pressed. By double clicking on Membership Form you can see the completed form showing the first record of the membership table (Figure 107).

7. The forms for all members can be printed out by selecting the File menu, the Print option and the OK button. All the records will be printed in the form layout. Print the data forms. The printout can help administer the Sports Club by allowing you to work manually on the membership list (e.g. copies can be provided for all members of the management team).

8. A blank form can be produced by selecting the Arrow Star button on the bottom line of the form. Figure 108 shows the blank form ready to enrol a new member.

9. Close the Sports: Database window using the close button in top right hand corner of the window.

10. Close Access by clicking on the close button in the top right hand corner of the main application window or select the <u>F</u>ile menu and the E<u>x</u>it option.

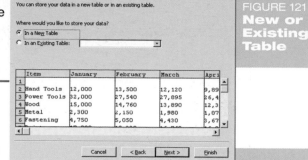

FIGURE 121
New or Existing Table

Presentation of Data

You have already investigated some of the possibilities of presenting the information contained in a database so that it is more useful to you. Reports and forms allow you to extract data in a way that meets your needs. You can group information, present it as a table, in a column or in justified form. One way that is often required is extracting information in order to produce address labels.

FIGURE 122
Modify Fields

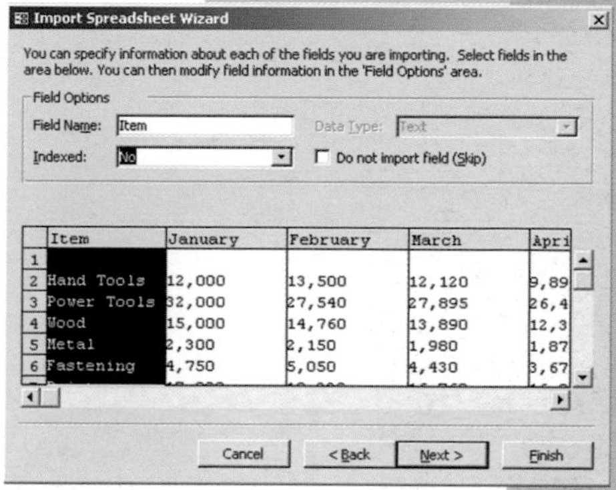

Figure 109 shows the Sports: Database window with the Reports button selected. If you click on <u>N</u>ew on the toolbar then a new window will appear called New Report (Figure 110). This provides access to the Label Wizard which will assist you to design a label.

In order to use the Label Wizard you need to select a table from which to supply the information. The table can be inserted in the New Report window or selected from the list available if the down arrow button at the end of the box is clicked.

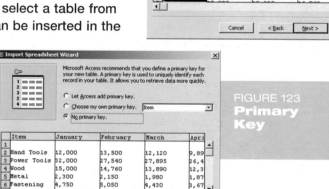

Figures 111 to 117 show the sequence of steps to produce the label.

The assessment for Unit 3 Database requires that you import a file in .CSV format which will be supplied to you.

FIGURE 123
Primary Key

Reports can be designed to present data in many forms such as particular field order, table/list/group format and summaries. During the Report Wizard process you select the order of presentation of the fields (Figure 87), Figure 91 provides you with the options to present your data in table form (tabular) or columns (columnar) while Figure 89 allows you to group the data.

FIGURE 124
Final Step

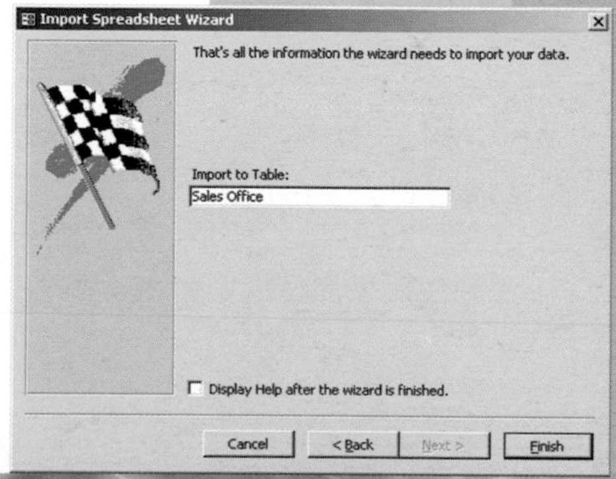

Queries can also be designed to present the data in your chosen order by using the Query Wizards (i.e. Simple and Crosstab Query Wizard) in a similar way to producing a report. If you produce a query in Design View the order of presentation is determined by the order in which you select the fields (Figure 132).

FIGURE 125
Sales Office Table

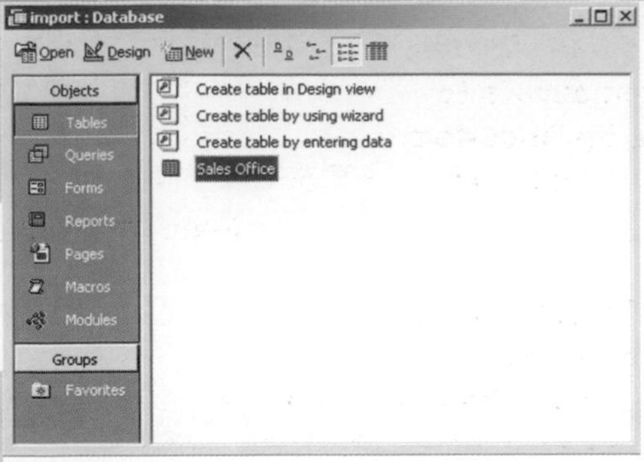

FIGURE 126
Sales Office Table

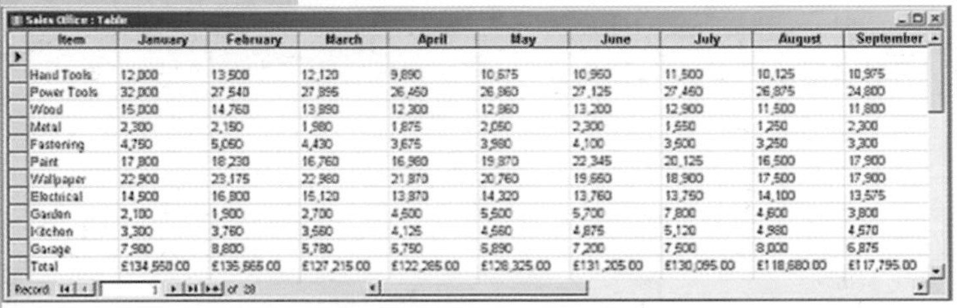

Sales Office : Table

Item	January	February	March	April	May	June	July	August	September
Hand Tools	12,000	13,500	12,120	9,890	10,675	10,960	11,500	10,125	10,975
Power Tools	32,000	27,540	27,895	26,450	26,860	27,125	27,450	26,875	24,800
Wood	15,000	14,760	13,890	12,300	12,860	13,200	12,900	11,500	11,800
Metal	2,300	2,150	1,980	1,875	2,050	2,300	1,550	1,250	2,300
Fastening	4,750	5,050	4,430	3,675	3,980	4,100	3,500	3,250	3,300
Paint	17,800	18,230	16,760	16,980	19,870	22,345	20,125	16,500	17,900
Wallpaper	22,900	23,175	22,980	21,870	20,760	19,650	18,900	17,500	17,900
Electrical	14,500	16,800	15,120	13,870	14,320	13,760	13,750	14,100	13,575
Garden	2,100	1,900	2,700	4,500	5,500	5,700	7,800	4,600	3,800
Kitchen	3,300	3,760	3,560	4,125	4,560	4,875	5,120	4,980	4,570
Garage	7,900	8,800	5,780	6,750	6,890	7,200	7,500	8,000	6,875
Total	£134,550.00	£135,665.00	£127,215.00	£122,265.00	£128,325.00	£131,205.00	£130,095.00	£118,680.00	£117,795.00

Record: 1 of 28

Importing a Data file

The Databases unit requires that you are able to import or open a data file in Access. The Solutions unit does not include this requirement.

Access provides a standard approach to importing data using the File menu, highlighting the Get External Data and clicking the Import option (Figure 117). The option is only available when a database window is open so you will need to create a new database or open an existing one.

FIGURE 127
Deleting a Column

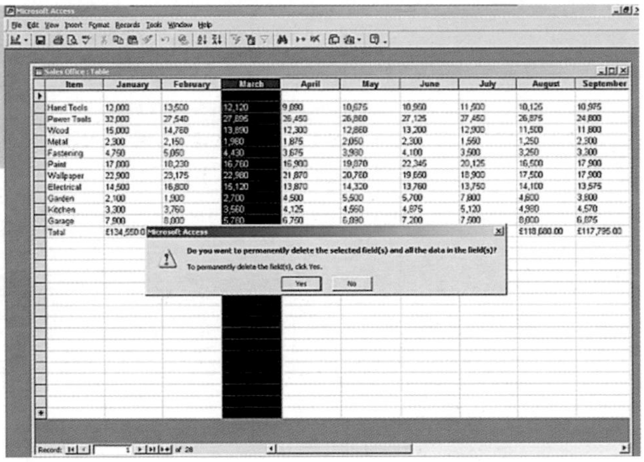

The Import option opens a window in which you can select files that can be imported into an Access database. Figure 118 shows the spreadsheet files created Chapter 2 that can now be imported into Access. The file is selected by double clicking on it or by single clicking on the file and then on Import button. Access will then guide you through the process of converting the data into a database format.

FIGURE 128
Find and Replace

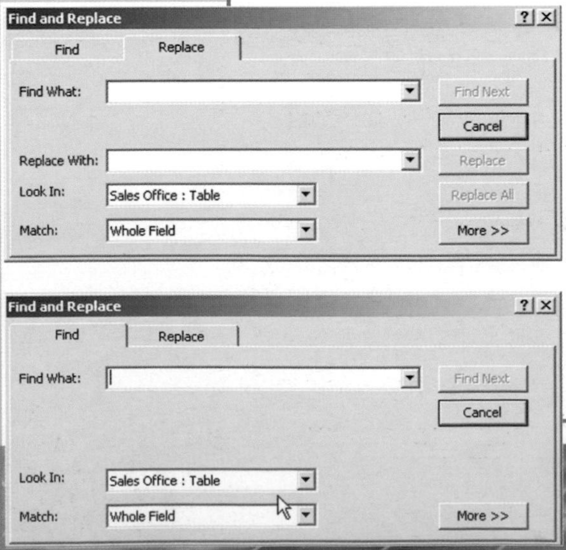

Exercise 22

Importing a Data File

1. Load Microsoft Access by selecting the Start button, highlighting the Programs option and clicking on the Microsoft Access item or clicking on the Access icon on the desktop. Insert your floppy disk into the drive.

2. The application will open with the overlaid window offering three choices. Select Blank Access database by clicking in the radio button.

The File New Database opens. Save the database as a file called Import on a floppy disk. An alternative is to open an existing database, in which case the imported data is saved either in a new table or combined in an existing table.

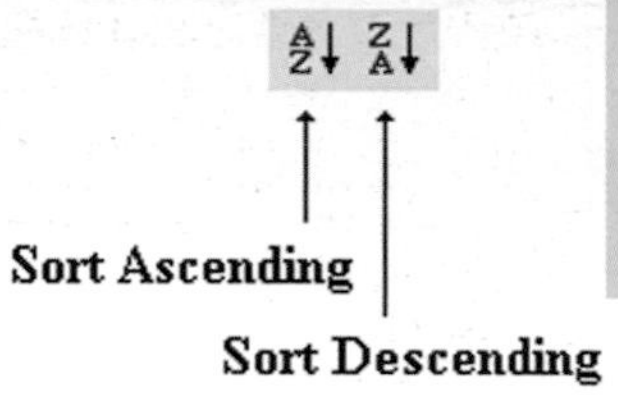

3. Click on the File menu, highlight Get External Data to reveal the Import option. Click on Import to show the Import Window (Figure 118). You are going to import one of the spreadsheets you created in Chapter 2 – Sales Forecast - so you need to adjust the Look in box to the location you saved the spreadsheet (e.g. floppy disk). When Sales Forecast is in the window, double click on the file to load it into Access.

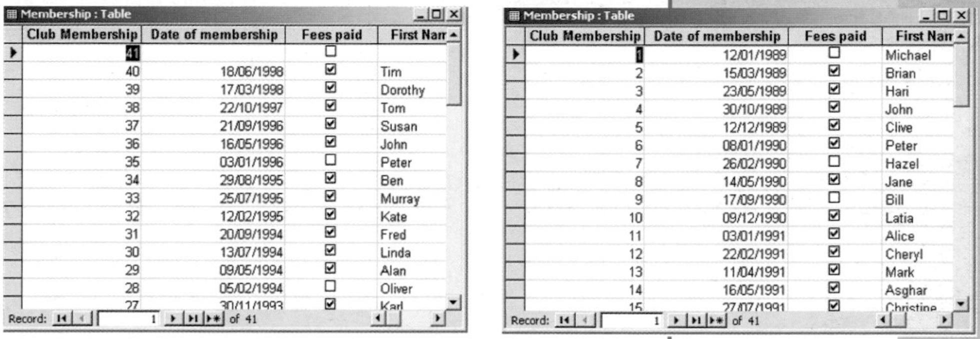

4. The Import Spreadsheet Wizard will appear with the contents of Sales Forecast within the window (Figure 119). The display shows each spreadsheet sheet. In this case you want to select sheet 1. Click the Next button to open the next window which will ask you to select the database fields (Figure 120). In this case the spreadsheet columns headings are suitable for the title of the database fields so click in the radio button – First Row Contains Column Headings and then on Next button.

6. The next window to appear (Figure 121) asks you to choose between storing the imported information into a new table or an existing one. In this case, select a new table and click on the Next button..

7. The new window (Figure 122) that is shown offers you the opportunity to modify the fields in the database table. You select the column of the field by clicking in it. Experiment with moving between the columns but do not make any changes. Click on the Next button.

8. The next step is revealed (Figure 123). Now you can add a

FIGURE 129
Sort Functions

FIGURE 130
Sorting

FIGURE 131
Query

FIGURE 132
Query Window

Sort Ascending

Sort Descending

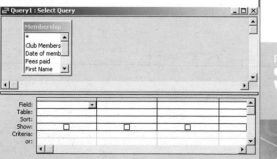

FIGURE 133
Part Completed Query

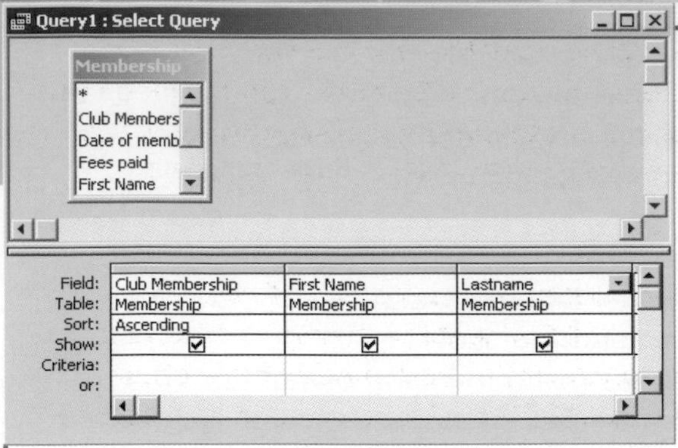
Query1 : Select Query
Membership
*
Club Members
Date of memb
Fees paid
First Name
Field: Club Membership | First Name | Lastname
Table: Membership | Membership | Membership
Sort: Ascending
Show:
Criteria:
or:

primary key which is essentially a unique record identifier. However, in this case you do not need a primary key. Select, No primary key by clicking in the radio button and then click on the Next button.

9. The Final step (Figure 124) is then shown which allows you to complete the process of importing data by clicking on the Finish button. However, you need to first of all name your new table, so enter Sales Office in the Import to Table: box in the centre of the window and then click Finish. An information window will appear to tell you have finished importing the file. Click the OK button on the information window after you have read it.

FIGURE 134
Save Query

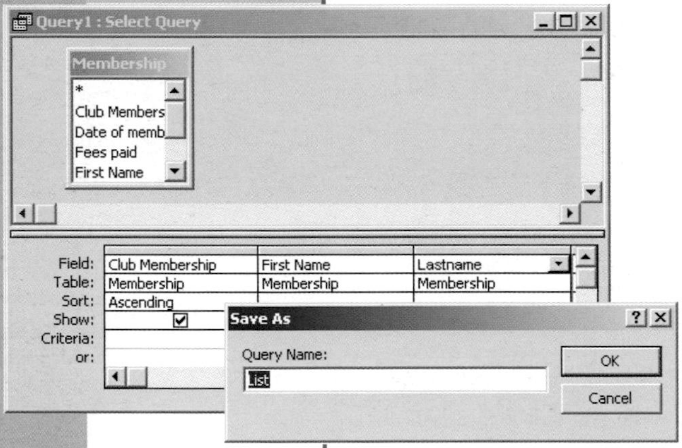
Query1 : Select Query
Membership
*
Club Members
Date of memb
Fees paid
First Name
Field: Club Membership | First Name | Lastname
Table: Membership | Membership | Membership
Sort: Ascending
Show:
Criteria:
or:
Save As
Query Name:
List
OK
Cancel

10. You will now see your new table has been listed in the database window you originally created. In this case this was the Import Database.

11. In Figure 125 you can see the table you have created by importing the spreadsheet data.

12. If you double click on the file Sales Office the table will open and you can see the new data (Figure 126).

13. Close the window by clicking on the close button in the top right hand corner of the Sales Office window.

14. Close Access by clicking on the close button in the top right hand corner of the main application window or select the File menu and the Exit option.

FIGURE 135
List Query

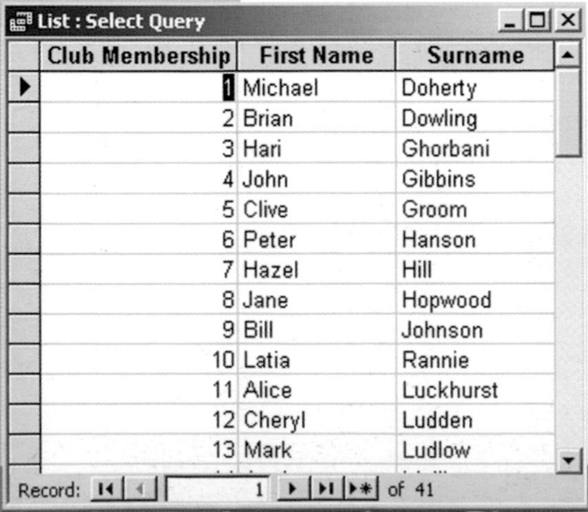
List : Select Query
Club Membership | First Name | Surname
1 Michael Doherty
2 Brian Dowling
3 Hari Ghorbani
4 John Gibbins
5 Clive Groom
6 Peter Hanson
7 Hazel Hill
8 Jane Hopwood
9 Bill Johnson
10 Latia Rannie
11 Alice Luckhurst
12 Cheryl Ludden
13 Mark Ludlow
Record: 1 of 41

Maintenance

The maintenance of any database requires that occasionally you need to add, amend and delete records and fields. To amend a field is a straightforward task in that you need to click in it, delete the contents and enter the new data. It is also possible to delete an entire column (i.e. remove a field from all records) or an individual row (i.e. an individual record). By placing your pointer over the column or row heading you will see it change shape to become a thick black arrow. If you click now, the whole column or row is highlighted. To delete the row or column select the Edit menu and click on the Delete option. Before the row or column is removed a message window will appear to ask you to confirm that you want the record or field deleted permanently (Figure 127).

This type of approach is effective if you want to change an individual data item or delete a record or entire field but if you want to change a recurring piece of the information, then Access provides a more productive method called Find and Replace. If you select the Edit menu and click on Replace, then the Find and Replace window will appear (Figure 128). This window provides two different functions. It can simply search your data to locate a particular piece of information or it can locate an item and then replace it. The latter is very useful when you have to change an item which occurs in several places in your database. The functions allow you select a particular table to search and specify the degree of match you are seeking (i.e. any part of the field, the whole field or the start of a field).

FIGURE 136
New Query

Sorting

Access provides a number of ways of presenting information. One of the most straightforward is sorting. Information can be ordered alphabetically or numerically so that it is ascending (i.e. lowest to highest) or descending (i.e. highest to lowest). The sort functions are available on the toolbar (Figure 129).

Figure 130 and Figure 130a show the results of sorting the membership table by ascending and descending numbers, alphabetically and by date. Compare the effects on the other data of the different types of sorting.

Access provides a number of ways presenting information. One of the most straightforward is sorting. Information can be ordered alphabetically or numerically so that it is ascending (i.e. lowest to highest) or descending (i.e. highest to lowest). The sort functions are available on the toolbar (Figure 129).

Figure 130 shows the results of sorting the membership table.

FIGURE 137
Fees Query

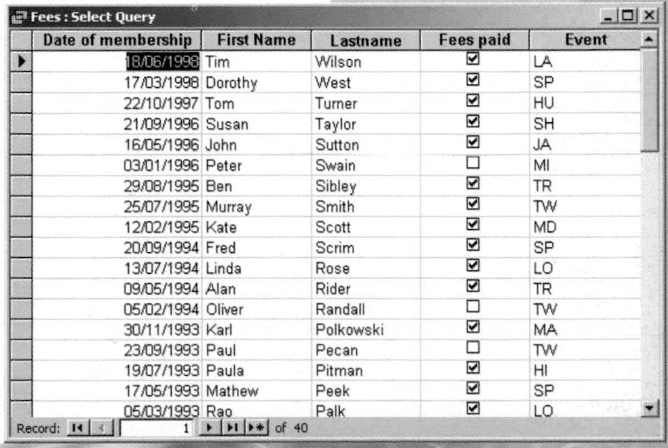

Queries

A major requirement of any database is the ability to extract the information that it contains. Access enables you to find out what information is held within the database in any form or combination you require. Extracting data is called querying the database. The starting point for producing a query is the database window. Figure 131 shows the two ways of producing a query which are available once you have selected

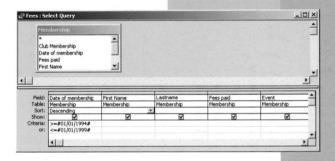

Fees : Select Query				
Date of membership	First Name	Lastname	Fees paid	Event
18/06/1998	Tim	Wilson	☑	LA
17/03/1998	Dorothy	West	☑	SP
22/10/1997	Tom	Turner	☑	HU
21/09/1996	Susan	Taylor	☑	SH
16/05/1996	John	Sutton	☑	JA
29/08/1995	Ben	Sibley	☑	TR
25/07/1995	Murray	Smith	☑	TW
12/02/1995	Kate	Scott	☑	MD
20/09/1994	Fred	Scrim	☑	SP
13/07/1994	Linda	Rose	☑	LO
09/05/1994	Alan	Rider	☑	TR
30/11/1993	Karl	Polkowski	☑	MA
19/07/1993	Paula	Pitman	☑	HI
17/05/1993	Mathew	Peek	☑	SP

Record: 1 of 33

the Queries button on the left-hand side of window.

The FIND and Replace function ensures that you locate every item that you are seeking to locate or to replace A manual search is likely to miss items so the function is a method of guaranteeing a perfect result. It is also considerably quicker.

Exercise 23

Query

1. Load Microsoft Access by selecting the Start button, highlighting the Programs option and clicking on the Microsoft Access item or clicking on the Access icon on the desktop. Insert your floppy disk into the drive.

2. The application will open with the overlaid window offering three choices. Select the Open an existing database option and you should see the Sports database listed below. Highlight Sports and click on the OK button. The Sports database window will open. Click on the Queries button to reveal Figure 131.

3. Select Create query in Design view and you will see an overlaid window Show Table appear. Click on the Add button and you will notice a small window called Membership. Now click on the Close button in Show Table to reveal Figure 132.

4. The cursor will be flashing in the Field box and if you click on the down arrow all the Membership table fields are available for you to select from. Select the Club Membership item by clicking on it and you will see it appear in Field box. Now click in the Sort box and you will see another down arrow button appear that provides access to sorting functions. Select the Ascending option.

5. Now click in the next column and select First Name in the Field box. Repeat this action in the third column selecting Lastname. Figure 133 shows the result you should have obtained.

6. Now Close the window using the buttons in the top right hand corner. A message window will appear asking you if you want to save the

Fees : Select Query				
Date of membership	First Name	Lastname	Fees paid	Event
21/09/1996	Susan	Taylor	☑	SH
15/03/1989	Brian	Dowling	☑	SH
			☐	

Record: 1 of 2

query as Query1. Click on the Yes button and another window (dialogue) box will appear (Figure 134) to offer you the opportunity to name your query. Change the name to List. And click on the OK button. You will see your query appear in the Sports: database window (assuming the Queries button has been selected).

7. You have created a straightforward query to produce a list of member's names and their membership numbers (i.e. only the fields you have selected will appear in your query). If you double click on the query (List) you will see the results of the query appear (Figure 135).

8. If you need to change your query because, for example, it is producing incorrect results you need to select the Design icon on the toolbar with List highlighted.

9. Highlight List and click on the Design icon to reveal Figure 133. You are now going to change the list to select only those members who have not paid their membership fees.

9. Select the fourth column and in the Field box insert Fees Paid Field. Now click in the Criteria row and enter =No. You are telling Access only to present records of members who have a value equal to No (i.e. not paid) in this field. Fees Paid can only have two values Yes or No. Close the window and you will be asked if you want to save your changes. Click on the Yes button to return to the Sports: Database window with List showing. Double click on List to see your new query (Figure 137).

10. Close Access by clicking on the close button in the top right hand corner of the main application window or select the File menu and the Exit option.

Fees : Select Query				
Date of membership	First Name	Surname	Fees paid	Event
18/06/1998	Tim	Wilson	☑	LA
17/03/1998	Dorothy	West	☑	SP
22/10/1997	Tom	Turner	☑	HU
21/09/1996	Susan	Taylor	☑	SH
16/05/1996	John	Sutton	☑	JA
03/01/1996	Peter	Swain	☐	MI
29/08/1995	Ben	Sibley	☑	TR
25/07/1995	Murray	Smith	☑	TW
12/02/1995	Kate	Scott	☑	MD
20/09/1994	Fred	Scrim	☑	SP
13/07/1994	Linda	Rose	☑	LO
09/05/1994	Alan	Rider	☑	TR
05/02/1994	Oliver	Randall	☐	TW
30/11/1993	Karl	Polkowski	☑	MA
23/09/1993	Paul	Pecan	☐	TW
19/07/1993	Paula	Pitman	☑	HI
17/05/1993	Mathew	Peek	☑	SP
05/03/1993	Rao	Palk	☑	LO

Record: 1 of 40

Fees : Select Query				
Date of membership	First Name	Surname	Fees paid	Event
18/06/1998	Tim	Wilson	☑	LA
17/03/1998	Dorothy	West	☑	SP
22/10/1997	Tom	Turner	☑	HU
21/09/1996	Susan	Taylor	☑	SH
16/05/1996	John	Sutton	☑	JA
29/08/1995	Ben	Sibley	☑	TR
25/07/1995	Murray	Smith	☑	TW
12/02/1995	Kate	Scott	☑	MD
20/09/1994	Fred	Scrim	☑	SP
13/07/1994	Linda	Rose	☑	LO
09/05/1994	Alan	Rider	☑	TR
*			☐	

Record: 1 of 11

FIGURE 140
AND OR Comparison

Criteria

In the previous exercise you had your first experience of using a criterion to select information. This is relatively simple but you can use a variety of symbols to be more precise. These are:

- > greater than
- < less than
- >= greater than or equal to
- <= less than or equal to
- <> not equal to

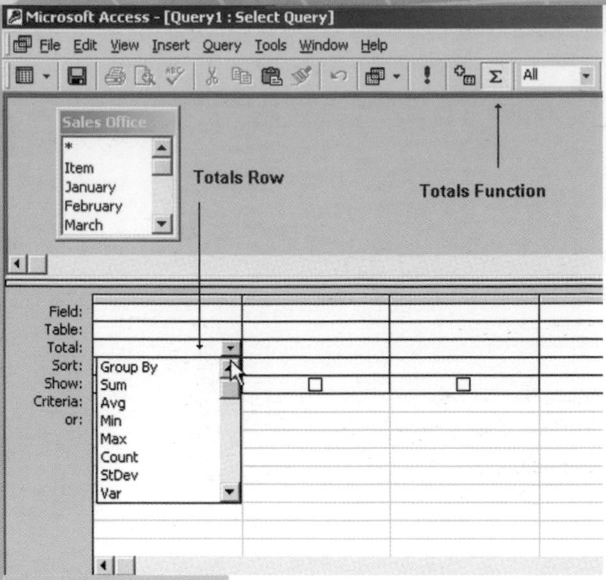

These symbols are available on the keyboard.

>   greater than (Hold the shift key down and then the full stop key)

<   less than   (Hold the shift key down and then the comma key)

>= greater than or equal to (Hold the shift key down and then the full stop key, release the keys and press the equal key)

<= less than or equal to (Hold the shift key down and then the comma key, release the keys and press the equal key)

<> not equal to (Hold the shift key down, press the comma key and then the full stop key)

FIGURE 140A
Calculations

In addition to these symbols are the logical operators:

• AND
• OR

AND combines two different criteria, both of which must be correct before the action can be undertaken.

Example:

Club Membership >=10 AND <=20

This selects records of members who have a membership number greater than or equal to 10 and also less than or equal to 20 (i.e. records for Club Members 10 to 20 inclusive).

OR allows two criteria to be selected so that if either are true then the action can take place.

Example:

Fees Paid = No OR Date of Membership <01/01/90

This selects the records of members who have not paid their fees or were members before 01/01/1990. In this example notice that we are linking two different fields together. Both AND and OR can be used within a single field and also combining fields.

Exercise 24

Queries and Criteria

1. Load Microsoft Access by selecting the Start button, highlighting the Programs option and clicking on the Microsoft Access item or click on the Access icon on the desktop. Insert your floppy disk into the drive.

2. The application will open with the overlaid window offering three choices. Select the Open an existing database option and you should see the Sports database listed below. Highlight Sports and click on the OK button. The Sports database window will open. Click on Queries button to reveal Figure 131.

3. Select Create query in Design view and you will see an overlaid window Show Table appear. Click on the Add button and you will notice a small window called Membership appearing. Now click on the Close button in Show Table to reveal Figure 132.

4. The cursor will be flashing in the Field box and if you click on the down arrow all the Membership table fields are available for you to select from. Select the Date of Membership. Click in the Sort box and you will see another down arrow button appear that provides access to sorting functions. Select the Descending option.

5. Now click in the criteria row and enter >=01/01/94. You are selecting all members who joined the club on or after 1st January 1994.

6. Now click in the OR row and enter <= 01/01/99. You are adding an extra alternative condition to select members who joined on or before 1st January 1999. If the criteria are too long press the Shift and F2 keys together with the cursor in the criteria box. This opens a Zoom window to let you see the whole criteria. Try it.

7. Now click in the next column and select First Name in the Field box. Repeat this action selecting Lastname in the third column, Fees Paid in the fourth and Events in the fifth. Figure 136 shows the result you should have obtained.

8. Now close the window using the button in the top right hand corner. A message window will appear asking you if you want to save the query as Query1. Click on the Yes button and another window (dialogue) box will appear offering you the opportunity to name your query. Change the name to Fees then click on the OK button. You will see your query appear in the Sports: database window (assuming Queries button has been selected).

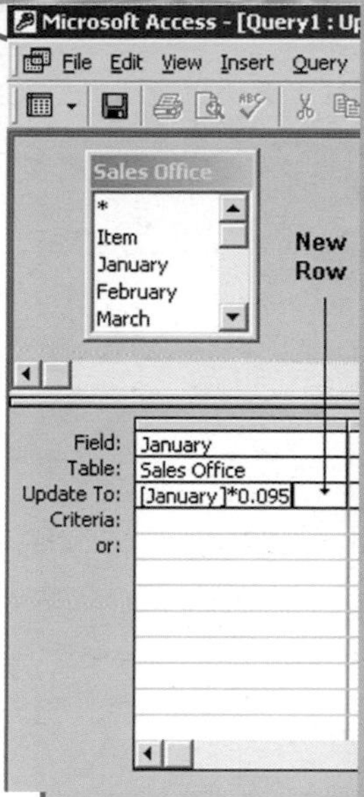

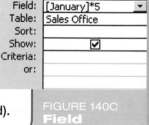

FIGURE 140B
Update Query

FIGURE 140C
Field Calculation

FIGURE 141
June Query

May : Select Query		
Item	**June**	
Hand Tools	10,950	
Power Tools	27,125	
Wood	13,200	
Metal	2,300	
Fastening	4,100	
Paint	22,345	
Wallpaper	19,650	
Electrical	13,760	
Garden	5,700	
Kitchen	4,875	
Garage	7,200	
Total	£131,205.00	

Record: 1

9. You have created a straightforward query producing a list of members with a particular range of membership dates. If you double click on the query (Fees) you will see the results of the query appear (Figure 137). Print the query you have created.

10. You are now going to change this query by highlighting Fees and clicking on the Design icon on the toolbar. You want to select those members who have paid their membership fees, so in the criteria row of the Fees Paid column enter =Yes.

11. Close the window and save the query. Double click on Fees to see the result of your change (Figure 138). Notice the change in the number of records now selected (i.e. changes from 40 to 33). Print out the new query.

12. We will now change the query by adding an extra criterion to the Events column. Enter =SH (i.e. Shot putting). The results of the new query are shown in Figure 139.

Extra Exercises

13. Amend Date of Membership column criteria to read >=01/01/94 AND <=01/01/99 and remove the criteria from Events column. Compare the result with the OR criteria. Figure 140 shows the comparison. This shows the different effects of AND or OR. Experiment with the logical operators until you are a confident user of them.

14. Close Access by clicking on the close button in top right hand corner of the main application window or select the File menu and the Exit option.

Wild Cards

When designing criteria to search, it is possible to use a device called a wild card. This is useful when you only know part of a name or title. Say you wanted to list all the members in our database beginning with the letter S. This would be shown as S*, the * indicating any combination of letters is acceptable. * is the wild card.

Calculations

It is possible to insert calculations into a query by adding an extra row to the Design view grid. With the Design view grid open you can add the Total row by clicking on the Total icon on the toolbar (Figure 140a). The down arrow button in the Total row gives access to a range of standard mathematical functions. These allow you to average, sum and count a field as well as identifying the minimum and maximum amounts.

It is also possible to add another type of extra row called an update which will produce a query which will automatically update the values in a given field. This is useful if you have a price rise or a change in costs which affect the overall profit. You can design an update query which will change the values in your table. With the Design view grid open, select the Query menu and click on the Update Query option. A new row called Update to: will appear in the grid (Figure 140b).

You can also carry out customised calculations by inserting a calculation into an empty field within the Design View grid.

For example

[January]*5-   this multiplies the value of the January field by five

[January]/[February] -   this divides the value of the January field by the value of the February field

This allows you to undertake any calculation within a query. Figure 140c illustrates a field calculation.

It is often useful to print calculation fields since they can represent important data and a printout allows the information to be more widely shared.

Summaries

There are many occasions when you want to summarise the information that is held in a database table and Access provides you with a straightforward way of summarizing data using a Query. If you select the Create query using wizard and the Simple Query Wizard you will reveal the Simple Query Wizard (Figure 140d)

The wizard allows you to select the fields you want to include in the query by highlighting the field and click the arrow button and the field will be moved to the Selected Fields area. When you have completed your selection you can move forward by clicking on the Next button. As you move through the wizard you will be offered the choice of displaying the details of the fields or a summary. If you select Summary and Summary Options then Figure 140f will appear offering you the options to display the Sum, Average, Minimum and Maximun values of the fields. Figure 140g shows the outcome of a query that selected the Collection Number, First Edition and Value of a database with average, minimum and maximum values. This is just an example.

More Practice

1. New Database

Create a new database called Equipment Orders based on Table 3.

Table 3	Equipment Orders
Field Name	Data Type
Customer Reference	Autonumber – this field will automatically be incremented for each new member Number
First Order	Date
Name	Text
Address	Text
Equipment Ordered	Text
Cost	Decimal number
Credit Customer	Yes/No

2. Enter the data in Table 4 into the Equipment Orders database. The Database Solutions unit requires learners to input 40 or more records. This is not a requirement of the Database unit but entering data is useful practice for anyone using databases. The equipment ordered is coded to improve speed of input.

Table 4   Data Input

First Order	Name	Address	Equipment Ordered	Cost	Credit Customer
01/02/86	Brown	Liverpool	A12	1110	Yes
03/02/87	Clare	Manchester	B67	650	No
06/08/83	Davies	London	K17	230	Yes
11/09/95	Edwards	Brighton	P11	345	Yes
15/05/92	Frame	Leicester	N45	890	Yes
10/04/93	Gornski	Newcastle	A12	1110	No
02/05/89	Davies	Stoke	B34	120	No
21/07/93	Smith	Bristol	A09	560	No
31/01/95	Rao	Poole	B67	650	Yes
18/03/90	Weatherall	Exeter	P11	345	Yes
12/04/99	Weston	London	N45	890	No
16/02/92	Hunter	Manchester	A09	560	Yes
22/07/97	Merlow	Stoke	K17	230	No
18/10/98	Marmo	Preston	P11	345	Yes
07/08/97	Palul	Liverpool	P11	345	Yes
08/12/00	Polkey	Dover	B34	120	Yes
14/11/96	Sutcliffe	London	B67	650	Yes
16/09/95	Suter	Bristol	N45	890	Yes
18/06/94	Sunter	Leeds	B34	120	Yes
24/01/95	Johnson	Halifax	A12	1110	Yes
28/06/99	Jehaya	Bradford	A09	560	No
13/03/90	Godson	Leeds	B67	650	Yes
19/10/91	Churchill	Manchester	P11	345	Yes
23/11/91	Chloek	Liverpool	P11	345	Yes
12/05/93	Churm	London	N45	890	Yes
15/06/94	Cheng	Exeter	K17	230	Yes
18/04/95	Bailey	Poole	B67	650	Yes
12/05/96	Safe	Bristol	A09	560	No
09/09/90	Land	Cardiff	B67	650	No
17/05/97	Crystal	Glasgow	B67	650	No

12/04/99	Dacks	Leeds	A09	560	Yes
18/07/97	Stein	Bolton	K17	230	Yes
11/09/93	Barford	London	N45	890	Yes
09/05/98	Canton	Dover	A09	560	No
12/03/01	Caress	Bristol	B67	650	Yes
01/08/00	Henderson	Manchester	A09	560	Yes
04/07/94	Kilborne	Stoke	K17	230	No
27/10/00	Marlowe	Bury	A09	560	No
15/04/96	Parnham	Bradford	B67	650	Yes
14/09/99	Ruffle	York	N45	890	Yes

3. Amend your table by:

Add these new records

13/02/99	Giles	Bury	A12	1110	Yes
25/08/98	Singh	Halifax	B34	120	Yes
03/11/01	Harris	Manchester	N45	890	No

Delete this record:

| 04/07/94 | Kilbourne | Stoke | K17 | 230 | No |

Change Credit Customer to No:

| 12/04/99 | Dacks | | Leeds | A09 | 560 | Yes |

Change Date of First Order to 12/05/00:

| 14/09/99 | Ruffle | | York | N45 | 890 | Yes |

4. Reports

Using the Sales Office Database create reports which show:

• a list of items and sales in April, May and June
• a list of items and total sales

In both cases explore columnar, tabular and justified layouts.

5. Queries

Using the Sales Office Database create queries that:

• present a list of the items and sales in June (Figure 141)
• present a list of items than sold more than 30,000 and less than 100,000 in Total (Figure 142)

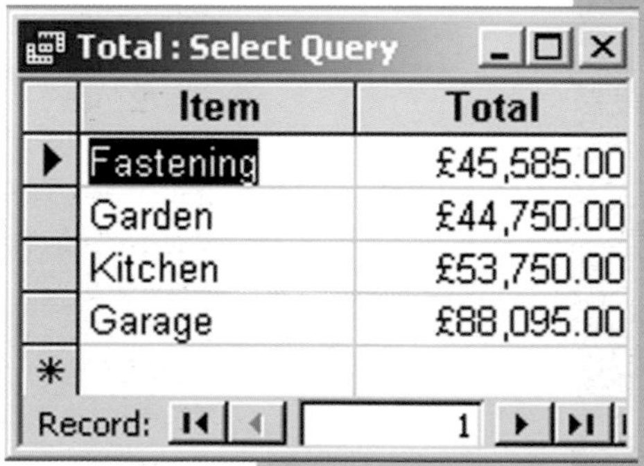

Total : Select Query

Item	Total
▶ Fastening	£45,585.00
Garden	£44,750.00
Kitchen	£53,750.00
Garage	£88,095.00
*	

Record: |◀ ◀ | 1 | ▶ | ▶| |

FIGURE 142
Total Query

Summary

1. Open Microsoft Access

There are several ways of loading an application in Windows. These include:

• Clicking on the Start button, highlighting the Programs item and clicking on Microsoft Access option

• Double clicking on the Access icon on the desktop

2. Create a blank database

Microsoft Access application will load and reveal three options:

• Create a new blank database
• Create a new database using the database wizard
• Open an existing database

Select Create a new blank database by clicking in the radio and OK buttons. The File New Database will open to enable you to save your new database. Save the database as a file.

3. Open an existing database

Microsoft Access application will load and reveal three options:

• Create a new blank database
• Create a new database using the database wizard
• Open an existing database

If you have only recently created the database then you should see it listed in the area below Open an existing database. Alternatively, select Open an existing database, highlight the database and click on the OK button.

4. Create a New Table

Once you have saved your new database, the Database window will open to show three options with the Table object on the left hand side selected:

• Create a table in Design view
• Create a table by using wizard
• Create a table by entering data

Double click on Create a table in Design view and the table window opens Insert your field names and their types. If you enter a name in the Field Name box and click in the corresponding Data Type box, a small down arrow will appear revealing a list of types. Select the appropriate type and so on to complete the table.

Save your table by selecting the File menu and the Save As option. The Save As window appears. Enter the table name and click on the OK button.

5. Types of Access Data

Access allows you to define nine types of data. They are text, memo, numbers, date/time, currency, autonumber, yes/no, OLE Object and hyperlink.

6. Entering Data in a Table

Double click on the table in the Database window and it will open. If it is a new table then the columns may be too small to show the whole field name. Adjust the size by placing your mouse pointer over the line separating the columns and it will change shape to form a double arrow. If you hold down the mouse button, you can drag the column line to widen it.

Click in the fields and enter the data. It is very important to check that each record has been entered accurately. If you find a mistake, click on the appropriate field and enter your correction.

7. Reports

In the Database window, click on the reports button (left hand side of window) and the two ways of producing a report will be revealed. These are:

• Create report in Design view
• Create report using wizard

Reports can be based on tables or queries.

8. Page Setup

Select the File menu and the Page Setup. This will open the Page Setup window. Margins can be adjusted and orientation changed by additionally selecting the Page tab.

9. Amend Report Layout

Highlight the report and click on the Design icon on the toolbar. The structure of the report will be revealed. Clicking on an element will enclose it in a frame. The frame and its contents can be manipulated using the mouse pointer (i.e. pointer changes to a small hand). Items enclosed in a frame can also have their font and character size changed.

10. Forms

From the Database window select the Forms button on the left hand side of the window and the two options to create a form will be revealed. Click on Create a form using the wizard. This will help you through the process of producing a form.

11. Labels

From the Database window with the Reports button selected, click on New on the toolbar and a new window will appear called New Report. This allows you to choose the Label Wizard which will assist you in designing a label.

12. Importing a Data file

Select the File menu, highlight the Get External Data item and click the Import option. The option is only available when a database window is open so you need to create a new database or open an existing one.

13. Query

Select the Queries button in Database window and click on the Create query in Design view option.

Alternatively you can select the Create query by using wizard. This allows you to create a summary query.

14. Delete Records and Fields

Highlight your chosen row or column. Select the Edit menu and click on the Delete option. Before the row or column is removed, a message window will appear to ask you to confirm whether you want the record or field deleted permanently.

15. Find and Replace

Select the Edit menu and click on Replace. The Find and Replace window will appear.

16. Total

With the Design view grid open you can add the Total row by clicking on the Total icon on the toolbar. Click on the down arrow button in the Total row to access a range of standard mathematical functions (e.g. average, sum and count).

17. Update

With the Design view grid open select the Query menu and click on the Update Query option.

18. Customised calculations

Insert a calculation into an empty field within the Design View grid (e.g. [March]*7 to multiply the value of the March field by seven and [High]/[Low] to divide the value of the High field by the value of the Low field

19. Sort

The SORT function is available on the toolbar and allows you to sort data into ascending or descending order. It sorts on numerical, alphabetical and chronological information.

20. Add calculated Field in query

With Design view grid open add the Total row by clicking on the Total icon on the toolbar. The down arrow button in the Total row gives access to a range of standard mathematical functions.

Customised calculations can be inserted into an empty field within Design View grid.

This chapter will help you to:

• Set up a master page/template and style sheet according to the design brief

• Import and manipulate text and image files

• Amend publication content using proof correction symbols

• Prepare a publication for press

This chapter covers Units 4 (Desktop Publishing) and 12 (Desktop Publishing Solutions). The content of these two units overlaps so that you cannot offer both of them as part of CLAIT Plus. However, you are free to offer either unit as part of the qualification or study them as single units. There are no pre-conditions for studying these units. However, their content does assume that you have the skills and understanding which are provided by the OCR Level 1 ICT course New CLAIT (e.g. Unit 6 - Desktop Publishing, Unit 1 - Using a Computer and Unit 2 - Word processing).

Assessment

Unit 4 - Desktop Publishing

After studying Unit 4 your skills and understanding are assessed during a 3 hour practical assignment. This is set by OCR and marked locally. However, the marking will be externally moderated by OCR. This ensures that the standard is being applied correctly across the many different providers of OCR CLAIT Plus. If you are unsuccessful then you can be re-assessed using a different assignment.

Unit 12 - Desktop Publishing Solutions

After studying Unit 12 your skills and understanding are assessed using a locally devised practical assignment. The assignment will be marked locally but externally moderated by OCR. This ensures that the standard is being applied correctly across the many different providers of OCR CLAIT Plus. If you are unsuccessful then you can be re-assessed using a different assignment.

The assessment task can be provided by the local tutor or suggested by the individual student. In both cases the task must meet all the assessment objectives of Unit 12 and allow learners to show their understanding.

Desktop Publishing

Desktop Publishing is an exciting and motivating application. It provides, for example, a means of using your creativity to produce interesting publications in a wide variety of forms. You can design newsletters for your organization or group or combine illustrations with text to produce publicity material. In a sense desktop publishing allows you to become your own design studio and printer while not leaving your workplace.

The danger is that the facilities offered to you are so rich in possibilities that you design publications which use too many of the facilities and produce documents that overpower your readers. Good practice suggests that publications should be kept simple and straightforward. This means:

• Do not use too many colours

• Do not use too many fonts or different character sizes (e.g. each should be used for a distinct purpose – different types of heading). Fonts are sometimes called typefaces.

• Illustrations should complement the text

• White (blank) space aids readability so leave plenty around your text and illustrations – line spacing can aid/improve readability

• Present a visually balanced publication

• Ensure consistent presentation

Font Families

Clait Plus uses font families rather than font names. Chapter 1 explains font families and gives examples of the fonts that link to them. This chapter will employ font families:

Examples

Serif - Courier New and Times New Roman

Sans Serif – Tahoma and Arial

House Styles

Desktop Publishing provides you a wide range of choices in designing publications. This is a major advantage but is accompanied by the risk that each document produced will be so different that readers will be confused. In order to provide a consistent appearance to their publications many

FIGURE 143
Microsoft Publisher

organisations have developed standards for documents. These are called House Styles.

House styles will often include:

• Size of paper
• Orientation (Portrait or Landscape)
• Size of Margins
• Gutter
• Header and Footer
• Font Family (eg. Serif)
• Character Size (eg. 12)
• Different fonts and character sizes for heading and the main body of text
• Line spacing (eg. double)

You may find it useful to identify if your employer or another organisation you are involved in have a house style. Consider what it includes.

Microsoft Publisher

This chapter is based around the Desktop Publishing application Microsoft Publisher. Figure 143 shows the opening display of Publisher. The main application is overlaid with the Microsoft Publisher Catalog which provides you with a variety of initial designs giving you the choice of a wide range of publication designs such as:

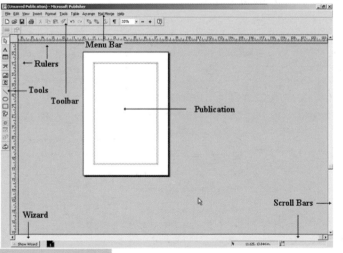

• Newsletters
• Brochures
• Catalogues
• Publicity Flyers
• Postcards
• Invitations

Within many of these options are sub-categories offering an even wider choice.

If you are developing a newsletter for your company or community then it is likely to be issued many times (e.g. every month) so it is important to present a consistent image to your readers. It is therefore useful to design a master or template for your publication as this provides a standard layout for your content. It will also save time since you can use the master over and over again.

FIGURE 144
Microsoft Publisher Work Area

The other technique to ensure that your publications are consistent is to define text styles. These are combinations of text characteristics (e.g. font, character size etc.) that you can apply to your content so that it takes on the style. This is a quick way of formatting your text and providing a consistent look and feel to the document. This technique helps to improve your productivity while maintaining the quality of your publication. Over time you will build up a range of masters and styles.

These standards (i.e. a combination of master document and text style) sometimes represents the organisations house styles.

Figure 144 shows the work area of Microsoft Publisher. This is another Microsoft Office application so has the familiar layout and structure that you will probably be aware of. The main difference from applications such as Microsoft Word are:

• The outline of a document in the work area – this shows you the shape and orientation of your publication (e.g. rectangle in landscape orientation)

• A row of drawing tools down the left hand side of the application window

• Rulers down the left hand side and across the top of the work area – these help you position your text and images in your publication

Layout

There are a number of functions and options that you need to be aware of in order to use Publisher effectively. These are:

• Page size – Publisher allows you to select both standard and non-standard pages

• Columns – a page can be divided into columns so that text flows up and down them (Figure 145)

• Gutter – there is a small gap between columns which is called a gutter (Figure 145)

• Margins – normally text does not start and

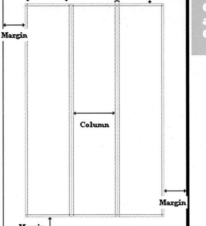

FIGURE 145
Columns and Gutters

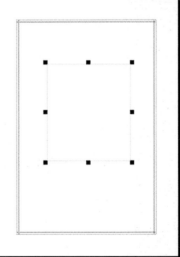

FIGURE 146
Frames

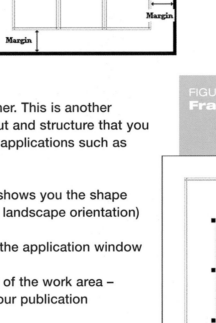

FIGURE 147
Headers and Footers

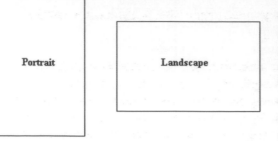

FIGURE 148
Orientation

Portrait Landscape

stop at the edge of thepage. To improve presentation a margin (gap) is left along right and left edges. Margins are also left at the top and bottom of the page (Figure 145). You can set margins using the Layout Guides in the Arrange menu.

- Text frames – to enter text into publisher you must first create a text frame. All text has to be placed within a frame (Figure 146).

- Picture frames – in a similar way to text frames, you can create a picture frame in order to place an image precisely in your publication (Figure 146). It is also possible to insert a picture directly into your publication.

FIGURE 148A
Layout Guides

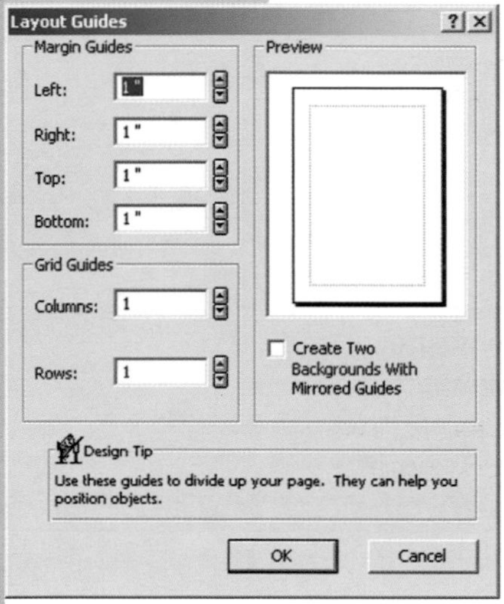

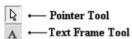

- Headers and Footers (Figure 147) – these are special areas at the top (header) and bottom (footer) of the page in which you can place information which will appear on every page (e.g. copyright statements, author, organisation etc.)

- Orientation – pages can be aligned in landscape or portrait orientation

People sometimes become confused between page and text frame margins since you can adjust both of these different margins. The difference is that a page margin applies to the whole page while a text frame applies only to the frame. Figure 145 shows page margins.

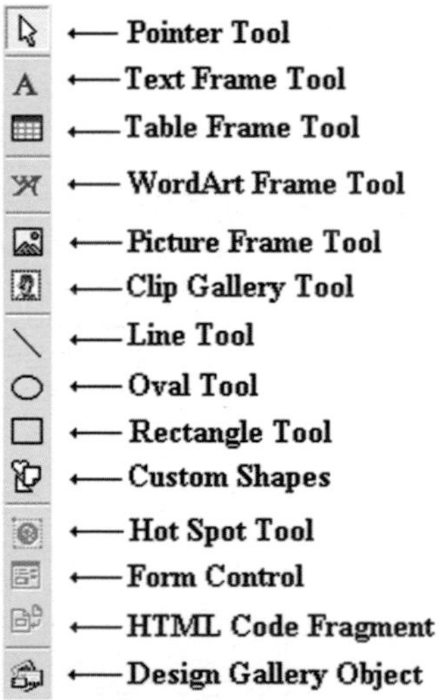

You can choose your document size by selecting the File menu and clicking on Page Setup option. The Page Setup window will appear. Select the Special Size radio button and window will change to show Choose a Publication Size area. This allows you to select from a list revealed by clicking on down arrow button or to enter width and height directly. The selections are applied when you click the OK button and publication shown in work area.

⌖ ← Pointer Tool
A ← Text Frame Tool
▦ ← Table Frame Tool
✴ ← WordArt Frame Tool
🖼 ← Picture Frame Tool
🖾 ← Clip Gallery Tool
╲ ← Line Tool
○ ← Oval Tool
□ ← Rectangle Tool
🖒 ← Custom Shapes
◉ ← Hot Spot Tool
▤ ← Form Control
⬚ ← HTML Code Fragment
⬚ ← Design Gallery Object

Layout Guides

To ensure consistency Publisher provides you with layout guide lines that appear on the screen but do not print out. These are rather like pencil marks that act as guides and are then rubbed out when you have finished. You can set margins, columns and rows and even allow for printing facing pages (i.e. like a book) using the Layout Guides. It is usually the first step in designing a publication to provide yourself with guidelines (e.g. for page margins). It is

FIGURE 149
Tools

important to remember than these are only guide lines indicating where to insert text, pictures and tables.

To establish some guidelines, select the Arrange menu and click on Layout Guides to reveal the Layout Guide window (Figure 148a). You can set margins or divide the page with columns and rows to help you layout the design. They are shown as pink and blue lines. The pink lines show the exact division of the page in terms of the precise sizes of margins, columns etc. while the blue lines allows a small gap from the exact measurements. This gap is called the gutter. When you are positioning text frames and images you can place them anywhere but that ignores the value of guidelines. Good practice is to place objects on the blue lines so that you take advantage of the safety margin of the gutter.

A text frame can have its own margins so that if you place a frame next to the page margin then effectively you are increasing the size of the margin to become the sum of the two margins. To ensure that the page margin is accurate you need to reduce the text frame margin to zero.

Background and Foreground

It is useful to understand the nature of foreground and background. Background can be considered as part of the paper so if you have a watermark in the paper, you can add text on top of it. The text would be foreground while the watermark is background. When you create headers and footers they are in the background while columns, pictures and text which form the content of the publication are mainly in the foreground.

Tool Bar

A key feature of Publisher is the tool bar (Figure 149) down the left hand side of the application, offering a range of tools to create text and picture frames and to draw objects. The tools are accessed by clicking on them. This changes the shape of the pointer (e.g. cross hair).

Entering Text

You can enter text into a text frame from the keyboard. You must first click in the frame and the text will appear at the cursor. Since the publication is shown reduced in size to fit into the work area it is sometimes means that text is too small to see and you need to use the zoom function.

FIGURE 150
Text Frame Properties

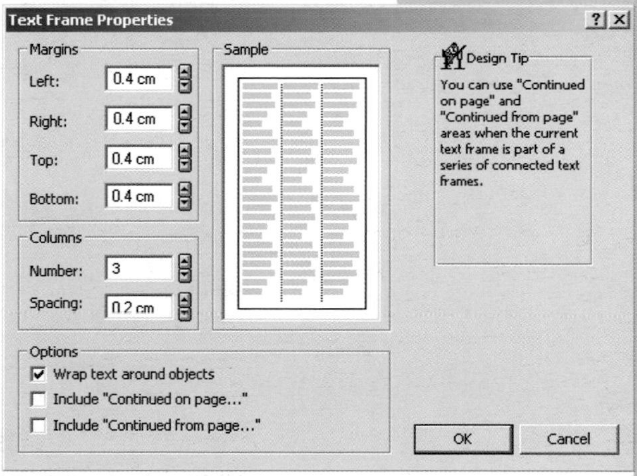

FIGURE 151
**Header
and Footer**

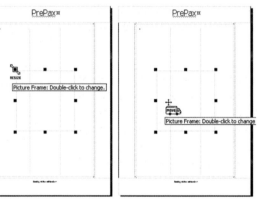

The other option is to import a text file into the frame. Both options are included in the later exercises. Desktop Publishing Solutions requires that you enter at least 20 words from the keyboards as one of its assessment objectives.

FIGURE 152
**Changing
Pointers**

Exercise 25

Master Newsletter

FIGURE 153
**Save As
Window**

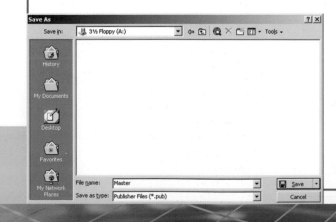

1. During this exercise you are going to create a master publication for a newsletter for your company. The newsletter must conform to this design brief. It will be printed on A4 paper in portrait orientation with the default margins (ie. the ones automatically provided by selecting the Full page option). It should have a header and footer in the top and bottom page margins. The header should show the name of the company (i.e. PrePax) and the footer give page numbers and date of publication in the centre of the page. The body of the newsletter should be divided into three equal columns with a 0.2 cm gutter and 0.4 cm margins (i.e. left, right, top and bottom of text frame – remember these are the frame margins not the page margins). The middle of the page should contain a picture overlapping the three columns. Text should wrap around the picture.

2. Load Microsoft Publisher by selecting Start, highlighting the Programs menu and clicking on the Microsoft Publisher item or click on the Publisher icon on the desktop.

3. The catalog overlay will appear. Select the Blank publication tab, the Full Page option and click on create. The overlay will disappear and a rectangular document will appear in the middle of the work area.

4. Down the left-hand side of the work area the wizard may be visible. If it is, then click on the Hide Wizard button at the bottom and the wizard will be removed. Select the Arrange menu and click on the Layout Guides then identify the margins which have already been set by selecting the Full Page option. You should see that they are all set for 2.54 cm. You could change them but in this case we are content with the default settings.

5. Select the Text Frame tool from the toolbar and the pointer will turn into a cross hair. Position it in the top left-hand corner of the page and then, holding down the mouse button, drag the pointer to the bottom right hand corner and then release the button. A text frame needs to be in place before you can divide it into columns.

6. The text frame should be highlighted (i.e. frame is visible). Click on the frame if it is not highlighted. Select the Format menu and click on Text Frame Properties to reveal the window

FIGURE 154
Master Publication

PrePax¤

FIGURE 155
Layout Guides

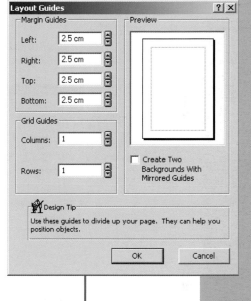

FIGURE 156
Format Menu

125

FIGURE 157
**Text Style
Window**

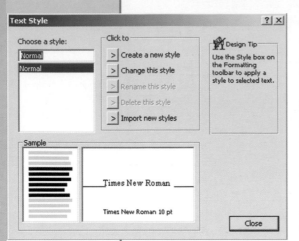

(Figure 150) which allows you to adjust the margins, set the number of columns and set the gutter spacing for the text frame. You click on the small up and down arrows or click in the relevant box and enter the new value. The sample area will change to show you the effect of your new value. If it does not change, then click your pointer out of the box and you should see the change enacted.

7. Set the number of columns to 3 and spacing to 0.2 cm, select the Wrap text around objects option, left and right margins to 0.4 cm and top and bottom margins to 0.14 cm. Click on the OK button when you have completed your changes.

8. The next step is to insert headers and footers in the area forming the top and bottom margins. To create a header or footer, you need to change the view of the page to background by selecting the View menu and click on the Go to Background option. You will see the page return to a simple outline. Now select the Text frame tool and insert a text frame at the top and bottom of the page in the area formed by the page margins. Figure 151 shows the frames.

FIGURE 158
**Create a
new style**

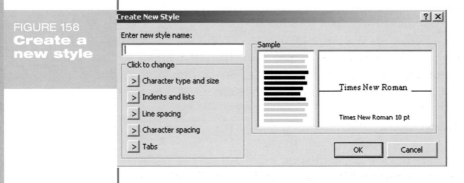

9. Click on the footer to highlight the text frame. Select the Insert menu and click on the Page Numbers option. A symbol will appear in the bottom left-hand corner of the footer. Click on the centre icon on the toolbar to move the page number to the middle of the footer. The symbol will automatically number the pages of the publication. Select the Insert menu and click on the Date and Time option. You will be presented with various choices of layout for the date. Select one that appeals to you. Your footer now has two automatic fields embedded within it which will automatically number the page and date the publication.

Now click in the header to highlight it. Change the font to Tahoma and character size to 36 using the toolbar, select the centre option and enter PrePax.

FIGURE 159
Font

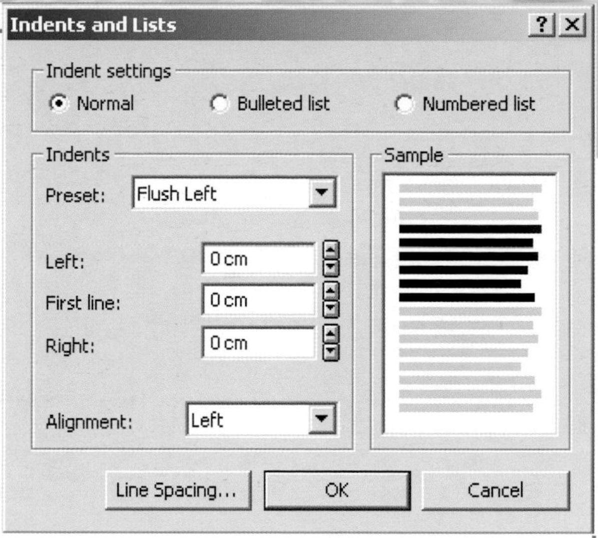

10. When your frames are placed and text is entered then select the <u>V</u>iew menu and click on G<u>o</u> to Foreground.

11. The final step to create the master document is to then insert a picture frame in the middle of the text frame. Click on the Picture Frame Tool and the pointer will change to a cross hair to allow you to select the top left-hand corner of the picture. Hold down the left mouse button and drag the pointer to the bottom right-hand corner. A frame will appear in the middle of the frame. The rulers will help you position the frame and you can move it using the pointer. The pointer changes shape when moved over the frame (Figure 152) to allow you to resize or move your frame.

12. Now save your master document. Insert a floppy disk into the computer's drive. Select the <u>F</u>ile menu and click on <u>S</u>ave option. The Save window will appear. Change the Save <u>i</u>n: box to floppy disk (Figure 153), name the file as Master in the File <u>n</u>ame box and click on the <u>S</u>ave button.

13. The Master publication is shown in Figure 154. If you select the <u>F</u>ile menu and the <u>P</u>rint option you will reveal the Print window. Click on the OK button and your publication will be printed (assuming your computer is connected to a printer). You should see a blank page produced with only the header text shown (i.e. PrePax) and the page number and date in the footer.

14. Close the application by either selecting the <u>F</u>ile menu and click on <u>E</u>xit option or click on the Close button in the top right-hand corner of the application window.

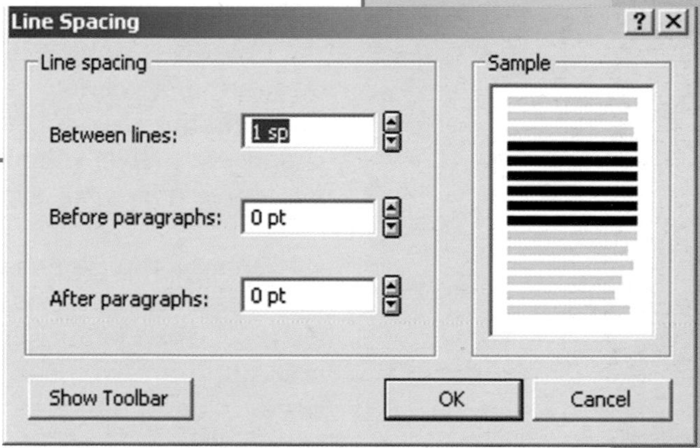

Layout Guides

The precise positioning of text and pictures is vital in order to create high quality images. Publisher provides functions to aid positioning. By selecting the <u>A</u>rrange menu and clicking on the <u>L</u>ayout Guides you reveal the window that will allow you to create guidelines for your publications. Figure 155 shows the Layout Guide window. The guidelines help you place your objects (i.e. text and pictures) accurately. However, they are the equivalent of placing

FIGURE 160
**Indents
and Lists**

FIGURE 161
**Line
Spacing**

pencil marks on a page which you later rub out so they only guide and are not physically present.

Text Styles

FIGURE 162
Layering

New text styles can be created by selecting the Format menu (Figure 156) and clicking on the Text Style option to reveal the Styles window shown in Figure 157. Different options appear in the Format menu depending on whether a text frame is highlighted or not. Figure 156 shows the differences.

Exercise 26

Text Style

1. Insert your floppy disk into the computer's drive

2. Load Microsoft Publisher by selecting Start, highlighting the Programs menu and clicking on the Microsoft Publisher item or click on the Publisher icon on the desktop. Click on the Exit Catalog button to close the catalog overlay. Select the File menu and click on the Open option to reveal the Open Publication window. Change the Look in: box to Floppy Disk and the Master publication should appear. You can open the publication by double clicking on the file.

If you have recently completed Exercise 25 you may see Master listed at the bottom of the File menu and you can load it directly from the list by clicking the file. You will see the Master appear in the work area.

3. Select the Format menu and click on the Text Styles option. The window (Figure 157) will appear. Click on the Create a new style button and a further window will be revealed (Figure 158).

4. Enter News in the new style name box and click on Character type and size. Another window called Font will open (Figure 159). Change the font to Ariel and the size to 12 then click on the OK button. You will then return to the Create New Style window (Figure 158). Click on the Indents and Lists and another window will appear (Figure 160).

5. Change the alignment to Justified and click on the OK button to return to the Create New Style window. Select Line spacing to reveal a (Figure 161) new window. Change the spacing between lines to 1.5, before paragraphs to 1pt and after paragraphs to 1 pt. Click on the OK button when the changes have been made to return to the Create New Style window. In the sample area of the display you should see the style you have created. Click on the OK button to create the style and you will see the News style appear in the Text Style window list. Click on the Close button to remove the window.

6. On the left hand side of the Format toolbar is the text style box which will probably be reading Normal. If you click on the down arrow button you will see the News style listed. News is the text style of the main body of text that will form the newsletter. You could now go on to create other styles such as main headings, sub-headings, lists, etc. Each would have a different name, providing you with the means of creating newsletters consistently.

7. Save the Master publication on to your floppy disk.

8. Close the application by either selecting the <u>F</u>ile menu and clicking on the E<u>x</u>it option or clicking on the Close button in the top right hand corner of the application window. Alternatively, proceed to the next exercise.

Exercise 27

Apply Text Styles

1. Insert your floppy disk into the computer's drive

2. Load Microsoft Publisher by selecting Start, highlighting the Programs menu and clicking on the Microsoft Publisher item or click on the Publisher icon on the desktop. Click on the Exit Catalog button to close the catalog overlay. Select the <u>F</u>ile menu and click on the <u>O</u>pen option to reveal the Open Publication window. Change the Look <u>i</u>n: box to Floppy Disk and the Master publication should appear. You can open the publication by double clicking on the file.

If you have recently completed Exercise 26 then you may see Master listed at the bottom of the <u>F</u>ile menu and you can load it directly from the list by clicking the file. You will see the Master appear in the work area.

This is an opportunity to practise applying styles. You do not need to save your work so refuse if the application offers you the opportunity to save the file.

3. The Format Toolbar is only revealed in full when a text frame is highlighted, so click on a Master publication text frame. Click on the Style box down arrow and select News from the list. Everything you now enter into the frame will follow the News style. The Format Toolbar font and size will have changed to show Arial and character size 12.

FIGURE 163
Drop Cap Window

4. Enter:

This is the first Newsletter of the PrePax Organisation and is intended to help communication between the different departments by explaining new developments, changes in the organisation and presenting news items.

The Newsletter will be published every month and employees are invited to submit ideas for stories or comments on the publication to John Reynolds, Newsletter Editor.

If you cannot see the text change the Zoom percentage (Standard Toolbar).

Desktop Publications Solutions unit requires that you enter at least twenty words of text.

5. If you click anywhere within an individual paragraph and then select a style, the style of the paragraph will change. Select the second paragraph by clicking within it then change the style to Normal and you will see the paragraph change. Now select News and watch the style change back to News.

6. Experiment with changing the styles until you are confident.

7. Close the application by either selecting the <u>F</u>ile menu and clicking on the Exit option or click on the Close button in the top right hand corner of the application window. There is no need to save your practice so when you are prompted to save the file, decline by clicking on the No button.

Layering

An interesting function of Publisher is that it lets you overlap pictures and text. This is called layering and it is similar placing objects on top of each other (Figure 162). If you are able to layer pictures and text in an effective way you can produce very eye catching and professional publications.

Background

FIGURE 164
Import Text File

It is possible to move images from the foreground of a publication to the background. The image appears to disappear but is simply in the background. It may not be obvious why you would want to place an image in background but it useful when you want to create another layer without being distracted by the image. To send an image to background, highlight it and select the <u>V</u>iew menu and click on the G<u>o</u> to Background option. The image will disappear. To make the image reappear select the <u>V</u>iew menu and click on the G<u>o</u> to Foreground. The image will now reappear.

FIGURE 165
Newsletter Pages

Figure 162a illustrates the process of sending and returning an image from background. The steps are:

1. Insert an image into a publication
2. Send image to background (image disappears)
3. Create a text frame
4. Return image to foreground shows the image is now placed on top of the text frame. This demonstrates using the process as part of a layering effect.

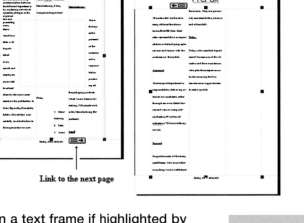

Dropped Capital

Another way of enhancing the appearance of text is to use a technique called Dropped Capitals.
This is available from the Format menu when a text frame if highlighted by clicking on the Drop Cap option. This reveals the Drop Cap window (Figure 163) which allows you to choose a fancy first letter (Capital letter) and draw the reader's attention. If you are not happy with any of the standard dropped capitals then you can create your own by clicking on the tab (Custom Drop Cap) in the Drop Cap window.

FIGURE 166
Importing an Image File

Resources

Normally when you are creating a desktop publication, you will already have produced the text and pictures that will form the content of the document. It is possible to enter text from the keyboard into a publication but it is better to use a word processed document and assemble it using Publisher.

In order to practise importing text and pictures into a publication, you need access to a word-processed document and one is provided below to use with our master document. You should either create this as a word-processed document (save the file as Newsletteron1.doc on to your floppy disk) or use some other resources of your own. During your assessment the imported text files and images will be provided.

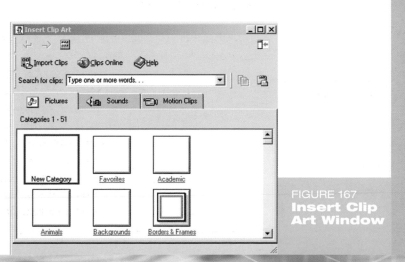

FIGURE 167
Insert Clip Art Window

FIGURE 168
Insert Clip Art

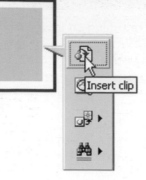

Newsletter One

This is the first Newsletter of the PrePax Organisation and is intended to help communication between the different departments by explaining new developments, changes in the organisation and presenting news items.

The Newsletter will be published every month and employees are invited to submit ideas for stories or comments on the publication to John Reynolds, Newsletter Editor. This edition is essentially an introduction to the organization for new staff.

There are five departments within PrePax. These are Manufacturing, Sales, Transport, Support and Policy:

- Manufacturing
- Sales
- Transport
- Support
- Policy

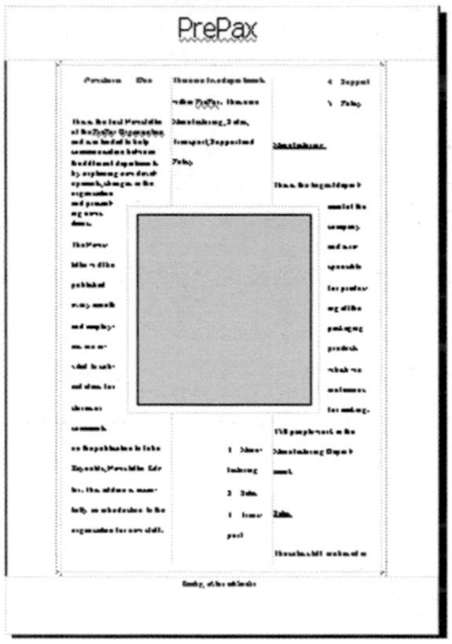

Manufacturing

This is the largest department of the company and is responsible for producing all the packaging products which we are famous for making. 350 people work in the Manufacturing Department.

Sales

The sales staff are based in many different locations across Great Britain. Each sales representative is responsible for a distinct geographical area and liaison with the customers in that patch.

Transport

The transport department is responsible for delivering orders to our customers either through our own fleet of lorries and vans or using sub-contractors. We offer all customers a 72 hours delivery service.

Support

Support consists of the many small teams who ensure that everything works well behind the scenes. They are personnel, accommodation, finance and office staff.

FIGURE 169
Newsletter

FIGURE 170
Widows and Orphans

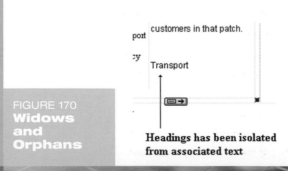

Headings has been isolated from associated text

Policy

Policy is the smallest department. It comprises of the directors and their assistances who plan the company's activities ensuring that we maximize our opportunities to make a profit.

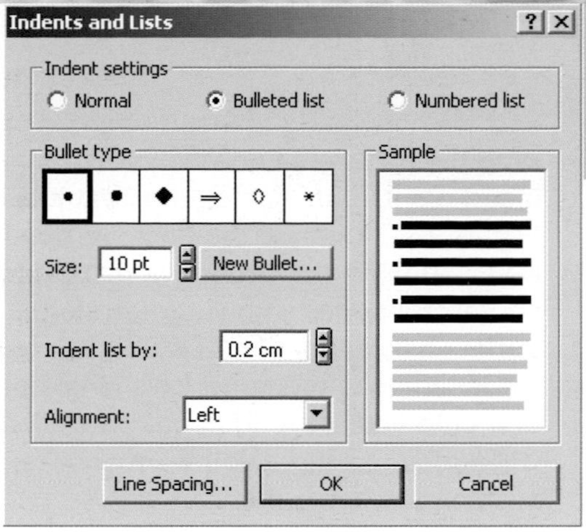

FIGURE 171
Indents and Lists Window

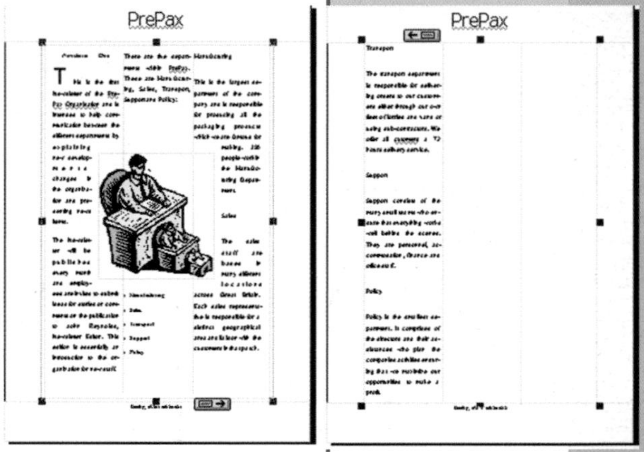

FIGURE 172
Revised Newsletter

Exercise 28

Manipulating Text and Image Files

1. Insert your floppy disk into the computer's drive

2. Load Microsoft Publisher by selecting Start, highlighting the Programs menu and clicking on the Microsoft Publisher item or click on the Publisher icon on the desktop. Click on the Exit Catolog button to close the catalog overlay. Select the File menu and click on the Open option to reveal the Open Publication window. Change the Look in: box to Floppy Disk and the Master publication should appear. You can open the publication by double clicking on the file.

FIGURE 173
Proof Correction Symbols

3. The PrePax master document should be visible in the Publisher's work area. You are now going to insert your file Newsletteron1.doc into the publication. This text file contains more text than will fit onto a single page. You need to create an extra page and there are two different ways of producing a new page. You can choose to insert a second page before inserting the text file by selecting the Insert menu and the Page option to reveal the Insert Page window (Figure 163a). You need to insert a one new page, after the current page and to duplicate all objects on the page (i.e. you are copying the master pages layout onto the new page). In the bottom left hand corner of the Publisher display you will see the number 1 and 2 with 2 highlighted. To move to the first page click on the figure one and one will be highlighted.

	Document Mark	Margin
New Paragraph	⌐	⌐
Change	the green text	red
Delete	men and and women	♂
Insert	select/File menu	the ∧
Indent	⌈This is the way	⌈1
Punctuation	Sentences must finish with a full stop ∧	⊙
Return to original	Stet	Stet
Close up	⌣	⌣
Capitalisation	england	≡
Transpose	way the	⌐⌐

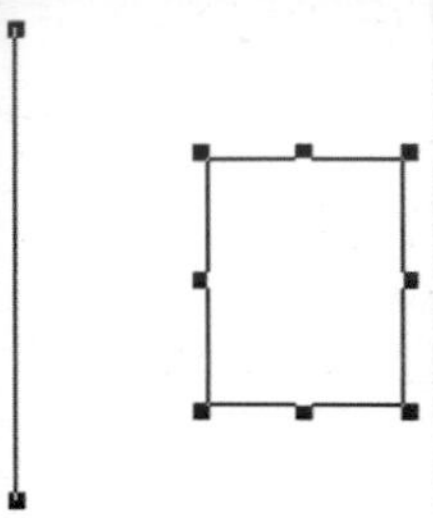

FIGURE 174
Lines and Boxes

FIGURE 175
Cropping an Image Tools

Crop Picture

FIGURE 176
Cropping

Picture Frame: Double-click to chan

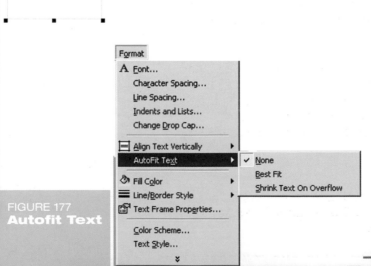

FIGURE 177
Autofit Text

You are now going to insert your file Newsletteron1.doc into the publication. With the text frame in which you are inserting text highlighted, select the Insert menu and click on the Text File option to open the Insert Text window (Figure 164). Change the Look in: box to select your floppy disk. The file Newsletteron1.doc should appear. Double click on the file and you will see its contents inserted into your newsletter. However, a message window will appear asking you if you would like to use autoflow. This means the text you are inserting is too large for a single page and Publisher wants to place some of it onto your second page. So click on the Yes button. A second message will appear asking if you want your text to flow into existing frames. Again click on the Yes button.

4. The text will now cover parts of two pages and will flow around the two picture frames. There is no need for the picture frame on the second page so click on it to highlight the frame and press the delete key. The frame will be removed.

5. Save your newsletter as the file PrePax on to your floppy disk by selecting the File menu and clicking on the Save option.

6. An alternative to creating a new page is to insert your text into the single page and again you will be presented with a warning message giving you the choice of using autoflow and then a new message asking if you want Publisher to create new text frames and pages. Click on the Yes button. A final message may appear telling you that Publisher has created a new page and you are now looking at page two. Click on the OK button.

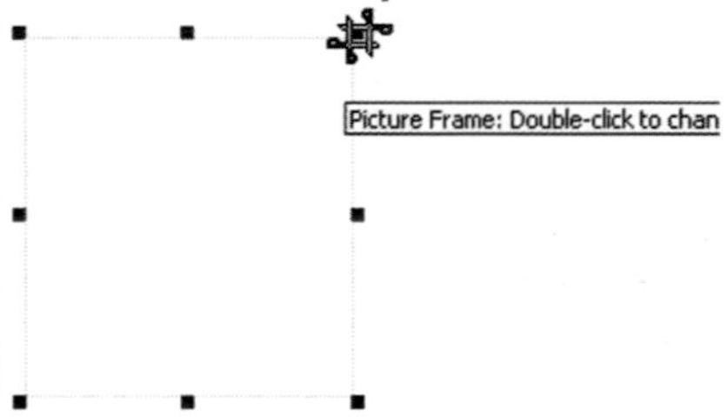

7. Figure 165 shows the two pages of your newsletter. At the top of the second page is a button with an arrow which, if clicked, returns you to the first page. The first page has a similar button at the bottom of the page linking you to the second page. Notice that the text you have imported has flowed up and down the columns and around your picture frame.

8. You are now going to insert a picture into the newsletter. Move to the first page and click on the image (picture) frame to highlight it. Select the Insert menu and highlight Pictures to reveal a sub-menu (Figure 166). This provides options to import a Clip Art image, a picture stored in another folder or an image captured by a camera or scanner. Click on the Clip Art option to reveal the Insert Clip Art window (Figure 167). Select an appropriate clip art image and insert the image into the publication (Figure 168).

9. Save the newsletter by selecting the <u>F</u>ile menu and the <u>S</u>ave option. In this case the Save window does not appear since you have already selected a folder to store the publication. It simply updates the saved file.

FIGURE 178
Create Table Window

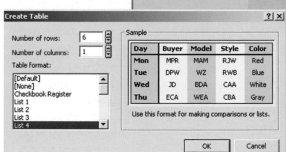

10. Figure 169 shows the newsletter after the text and image files have been inserted. Publisher reduces the size of the publication so that it is easier to see the whole layout. You can increase the size of the image using the zoom function on the Standard toolbar. Experiment with different sizes to check the presentation of your newsletter. Use the News text style to change the text. Adjust the text and image so that your publication is effectively presented. You may need to reduce the size of the image so that the text flows around the picture without leaving large gaps or adjust line spacing so that you achieve the required layout. Explore the different ways of adjusting your publication until you are confident that you can achieve the desired results.

FIGURE 179
Hyphenation

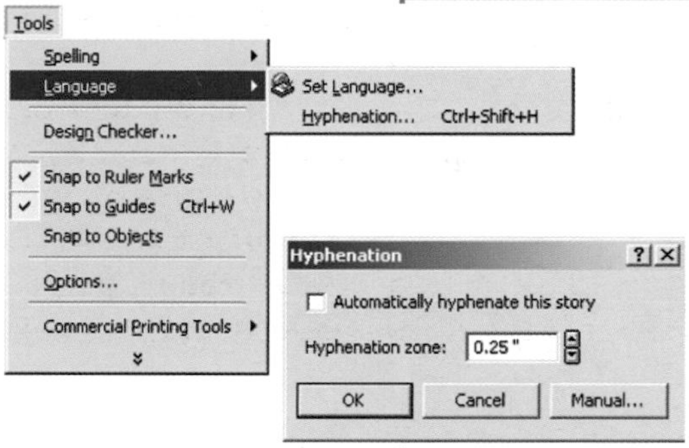

11. During your inspection of the publication you will notice 'widows and orphans'. These are examples of a single words being left behind on a page (or column) or pushed on to a new page or column (e.g. a single word on a new page). Figure 170 shows an example that needs to be removed to ensure a quality document. When you make a change to your publication you need to check you have not created widows or orphans. There are various ways of removing them such as changing line spacing, increasing white space, etc.

12. Select an appropriate Drop Capital for your publication.

FIGURE 180
Condensed or Expanded Text

13. The bullet points are not well presented because indenting is excessive. Highlight the bullets then select the <u>F</u>ormat menu and click on the <u>I</u>ndents and Lists option to reveal the Indents and Lists window (Figure 171). This will allow you to select a new indent if you click in the Bulleted list radio button. Change the Indent list by box to 0.1.

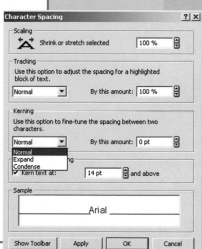

14. When you are happy with the presentation, select the File menu and click on the Print option then on the OK button in the Print window. This will print the newsletter with the printers default settings. Figure 172 shows my efforts. The printout is another means of checking your publication to see if the results are what you desire.

15. Save your publication again.

16. Close the application by either selecting the <u>F</u>ile menu and clicking on the <u>E</u>xit option or click on the Close button in the top right hand corner of the application window.

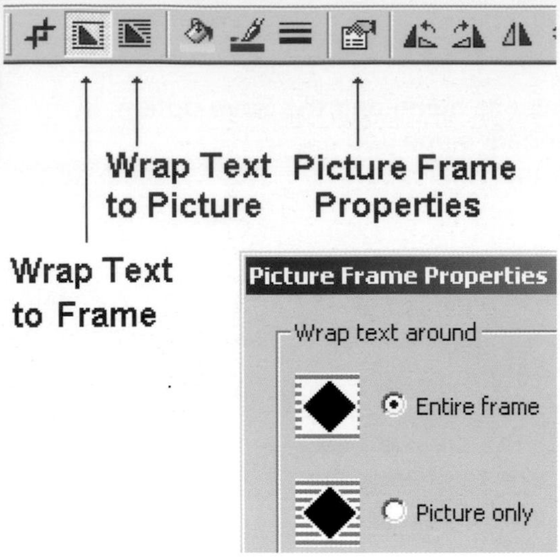

FIGURE 181
Text Wrap Functions

Wrap Text to Picture

Picture Frame Properties

Wrap Text to Frame

Picture Frame Properties

─ Wrap text around ─

◉ Entire frame

○ Picture only

FIGURE 182
Edit Irregular Wrap

Edit Irregular Wrap

FIGURE 183
Print Setup

FIGURE 184
Crop Marks

Crop Mark

Correcting a proof

Although you can amend a publication on a screen it is sensible to print your document and check the paper copy. These are called proof copies while they are being developed. There are a number of standard symbols which are used to show changes that need to be made. Figure 173 shows the correction symbols.

Using the printout of PrePax newsletter check the document and use the symbols to record the changes that are needed.

Lines and boxes

The tools (Figure 144) provide you with the means of adding lines and boxes to different parts of the desktop publications. You could:

• Add lines to emphasise the columns
• Add a line to separate the Header from the rest of the document
• Enclose headings in a box

A line or box is drawn by clicking on the icon in the tool bar which changes the pointer to a cross hair that allows you to position the start of your line or the corner of the box. By holding down the left mouse button and dragging the line or box you can form it. It is shown enclosed in small black boxes (Figure 174). In this mode, it can be mauipulated (e.g. moved, dragged etc.).

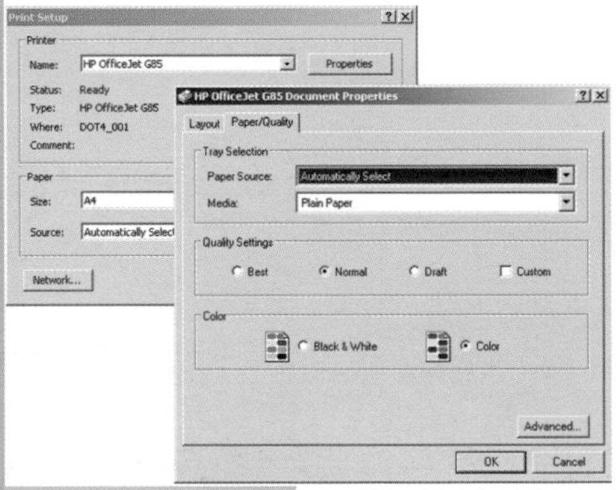

Crop an Image

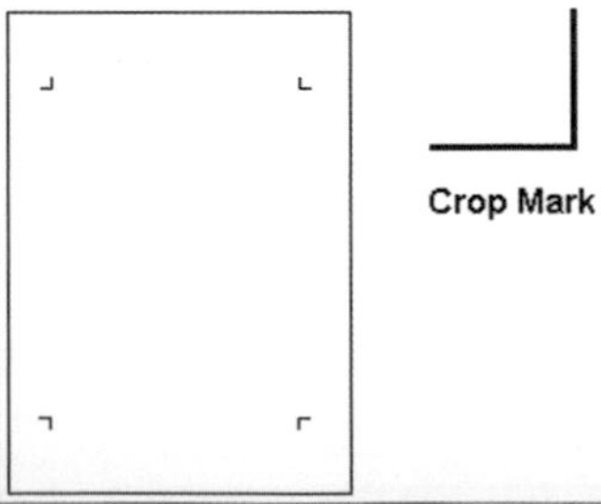

It is a straightforward task to insert a picture file into a publication but frequently you need to change the size of the image, move it or alter its appearance. Earlier we saw how to change the size, location and shape of an image by using the pointer (Figure 152). This is often called resizing the image. When you resize an image you can change its proportions and therefore reduce its quality (i.e. it becomes distorted). However, you do not lose any of the content of the image which you do with other methods. There are two other methods which can be used. These are:

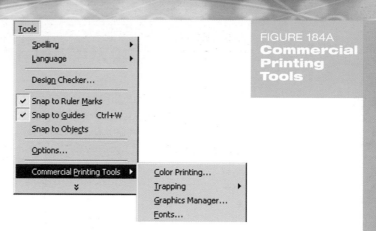

• Masking – that is, covering part of the image with another picture or text frame. In effect you are hiding some of the image behind the other frame. This can be effective since there is no risk of reducing the quality of the image which resizing can bring. However, masking is probably only suitable if you want to hide one edge of an image since it can be difficult to mask several different parts of a picture. If you later want to edit the publication masking can make this more complex

• Cropping – that is, cutting part of the image to remove an unnecessary element. This is an effective method if the image contains elements that you would like to permanently remove. The image is made smaller and the quality of the remaining image if not changed

Resizing is best when you need to change the size of an image without loosing any content, masking allows you hide a small part of an image without resizing and risking any change in quality and cropping allows you to remove content that is not required.

To crop a picture you need initially to highlight the image frame which reveals functions on the format toolbar (Figure 175). Clicking on the Crop Picture icon produces a new pointer (i.e. crossed scissors) when it is positioned over the edge of the image frame (Figure 176). If the mouse button is held down the pointer can be dragged to cut the image, allowing you to remove parts not needed for the publication.

FIGURE 185
Insert Table

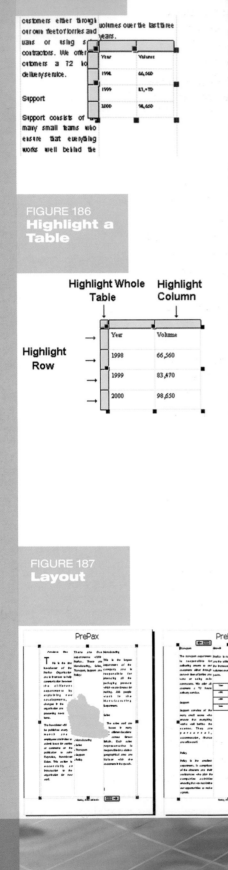

FIGURE 186
Highlight a Table

FIGURE 187
Layout

Copyfitting Techniques

Copyfitting is a means of fitting text into a particular space. If a headline needs to fit onto a single line then copyfitting will reduce the character size until it does fit into the space. You can set Publisher so that copyfitting is automatic. The Autofit functions are available from the F*o*rmat menu within the Autofit Te*x*t option which opens a sub-menu of choices (Figure 177) when the text frame is highlighted.

Create a Table

Another type of frame is the Table Frame. This is accessed from the tools area in the same way as the Text and Picture Frame Tools. The frame is inserted into the publications in exactly the same manner. As soon as you have created the frame, the Create Table window opens (Figure 178) to allow you to set the number of rows and columns that make up the table.

The window gives you access to a range of different table formats which you can explore, since a sample of them is shown each time you highlight one.

Hyphenation

Publisher will automatically insert hyphens so you may find that hyphens appear in places that you would not have inserted them. At the end of a line, Publisher may split a word using hyphens so that gaps do not appear.

For Example:

With Automatic Hyphenation

This is the first Newsletter of the Pre-
Pax Organisation and is intended to help communication

Without Automatic Hyphenation

This is the first Newsletter of the PrePax Organisation and is intended to help communication

To switch automatic hyphenation on or off you need to highlight the text frame or table and then select the Tools menu, highlighting the Language option and clicking on the Hyphenation option. Figure 179 shows the hyphenation choices. By clicking in the radio button the automatic hypenation feature can be switched on or off.

Condensed and Expanded Text

Good presentation of text in desktop publishing is vital. Publisher lets you adjust the space between letters so that you have the freedom to condense or expand text to fit precise spaces. This is available on the Format menu when a text frame or table is highlighted. Click on the Character Spacing option and the condensed or expand options are available under Kerning. When you select one of the options you can adjust the spacing using the box alongside the option, your choice being illustrated in the Sample area at the bottom of the window.

Text Wrap

In Publisher you can insert pictures, tables and other objects. Once your publication contains an object you have the choice of wrapping text around the object or not. In the PrePax newsletter you wrapped text around the image frame. It is also possible to wrap text around the actual picture (i.e. not the frame). The image wrapping functions are available on the Format toolbar when a picture frame is highlighted. Figure 181 shows the different options.

You can select icons that will wrap text around the picture frame or around the picture, (One of these, the Picture Frame Properties icon) also offers these functions but with the additional function of setting the margins around the image. If you select one of these options a new function appears on the format toolbar – Edit Irregular wrap (Figure 182). This allows you to manipulate how the text flows around the image. The image is enclosed in an outline with several small black squares that can be dragged by the mouse to change the text wrap.

Rotate and Reverse Text

Microsoft Publisher provides you with a variety of means to add interest to your publications by rotating the text or reversing the text foreground and background colours.

To rotate text you need to highlight the text frame and select the Arrange menu and the Rotate and Flip option to reveal a submenu with three options Custom Rotate, Rotate Left and Rotate Right. The options are also available on the toolbar. The Rotate Left and Right allow you to move the text through 90 degrees. Selecting the Custom Rotate option reveals a window (Figure 182a). This allows you to rotate left or right using the two rotational buttons. You can use the buttons multiple times to experiment with the look of the text. When you are content you click on the Apply button.

Another straightforward way of enhancing or emphasising text is to reverse the colours of the text foreground and background colours (e.g. instead of black text on a white background reverse the colours to show white text on a black background). To reverse the colours highlight the text frame and select the Font Color icon on the toolbar and change font colour to white. Next select the Fill Color icon and select black. The text colours will be reversed. Figure 182b provides an example.

Printing

The whole purpose of desktop publishing is to produce a printed document. There are a range of printing choices. These include:

- Printing in colour
- Printing a spot colour
- Printing in black and white
- Printing on a local printer
- Using a commercial printer

Publisher supports all of these different options. The most straightforward way of printing your document is to employ your own printer. You need to check its settings to ensure that it is going to produce a good copy of the publication. These are available if you select the File menu, click on the Print Setup to reveal the Print Setup window. Figure 183 shows the window. The actual printer setup window depends on the printer that you are using.

It is always useful to print a single copy to check the appearance of the publication. What shows on the screen is not always reproduced on paper. This check copy is called a proof copy and a commercial printer will send you a proof before printing the remainder. It is very important to systematically check the publication. You may have to alter the design (e.g. colours are sometimes unsuitable when you see them printed) to ensure that text is legible or adjust the layout to achieve a balanced image. It is normal to show changes using the correction symbols.

If your publication is smaller than the paper it is being printed on, the printer will produce crop marks on the publication. These show what needs to be cut off to produce the correct sized document (Figure 184).

Commercial Printing

Publisher helps you set up your publication so that it is suitable for commercial printing. There are three choices:

- Print in black and white
- Print as process colours
- Print as spot colours

These options are available by selecting the Tools menu and highlighting the Commercial Printing Tools to reveal a menu of options (Figure 184a).

The Color printing option provides access to Colour Printing window (Figure 184b). There are three options:

- Composite RGB – this sets up the publication for commercial process-colour printing – it is important to check the proofs to ensure the colours are the ones you want to use

- Spot Colours – Change Spot Color button reveals a dialogue window which allows you to choose between Black and White only and Black plus one or two different colours (Figure 184c)

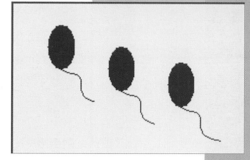

FIGURE 187A
Image 1

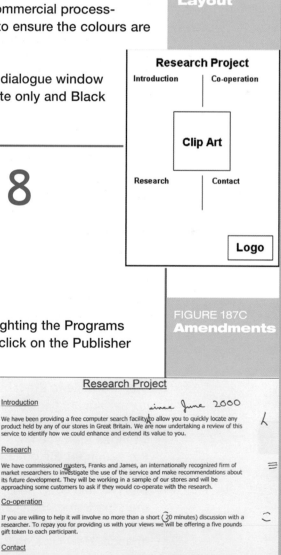

FIGURE 187B
Layout

Exercise 28

Inserting Tables, Cropping and Printing

1. Insert your floppy disk into the computer's drive

2. Load Microsoft Publisher by selecting Start, highlighting the Programs menu and clicking on the Microsoft Publisher item or click on the Publisher icon on the desktop. Click on the Exit Catalog button to close the catalog overlay. Select the File menu and click on the Open option to reveal the Open Publication window. Change the Look in: box to Floppy Disk and the PrePax publication should appear. You can open the publication by double clicking on the file.

3. Insert a new section at the end of your publication:

FIGURE 187C
Amendments

Growth

PrePax is rapidly growing and the table below shows the increase in our sales volumes over the last three years.

4. You are going to insert a table into your newsletter. The table shows the sales figures for the last three years and illustrate the success of the business:

Year	Volume
1998	66,560
1999	83,470
2000	98,650

5. Select the Table Frame tool and insert a frame below your new text approximately the width of a column with four rows and two columns. Complete the table with the information shown above (Figure 185). When you have finished, click in another part of the publication to remove the table surround.

You can adjust the size and shape of the table in the same way as with a picture. Consider adding a border to your table using the Format menu and the Line/Borders Styles. Remember that your table must be highlighted (i.e. enclosed).

6. Often you need to crop the images that you insert into publications. Crop the bottom part of the clip art picture. Highlight the image. The Cropping icon will appear on the toolbar. Click on the Cropping icon and place the mouse pointer over the bottom left hand corner of the picture. The pointer will change shape (i.e. cross scissors). Hold down the mouse button and move the pointer up the image. When you release the button the picture will be cut to remove the area you have dragged the pointer over. Practise cropping the image using the undo button to start again until you are confident you can crop a picture.

7. Create a new text style for the table. Name your style Table. It should employ the Times New Roman font, size 10, bold and centre the text. Apply the new style to the table by highlighting the whole table, clicking on the corner square (Figure 186) and then on the Table style (i.e. toolbar style box). You should see the whole table change. If only one cell, column or row changes then you have only highlighted part of the table and need to repeat the action for the other parts.

8. The text wrap needs to change so that it wraps around the picture rather than the frame. Highlight the picture frame by clicking on it then click on the Wrap Text to Picture icon on the toolbar. Watch the text around the image change. Now click on the Edit Irregular Wrap icon on the toolbar. The picture's enclosure will now alter to show a surround of small black rectangles. You can adjust the wrap by dragging these rectangles with your mouse. Experiment with changing the wrap. You can undo changes by clicking on the undo icon.

9. Consider the presentation of your publication and balance the display. Your changes will have altered the layout. You may have widows and orphans. Adjust the layout to produce an effective publication. Figure 187 shows our layout. Try to improve on it.

10. Print your newsletter as a composite proof and in red spot colour only.

11. Save your publication again.

12. Close the application by either selecting the File menu and click on Exit option or click on the Close button in the top right hand corner of the application window.

Review

It is always important to review your publication so consider the appearance of the newsletter you have created and if it is an effective publication. You might wish to consider issues such as:

• Should it be presented in three columns perhaps two or even one would be better?

• Consider the image – is it suitable – is it positioned in the most useful place?

• Should the columns be separated by a line or a wider gutter?

• Is the text style the best choice?

• Is the table in the correct place or should it appear earlier?

You should systematically consider all the possibilities.

More Practice

1. Master Publication

Create a master publication for a publicity flyer for your organisation. The flyer must conform to this design brief. It should be:

a) A4 document presented in portrait orientation

b) Page size – width 12 cm and height 20 cm

c) Margins – Top 1.5 cm
Bottom 1.5 cm
Left 1 cm
Right 1 cm

d) Gutter – 1 cm

e) Header – Right align your name
– Centre today's date using the automatic field in the format dd/mm/yy
– Left align your centre number

f) Footer – Centre the page number beginning with 1
– Left align the filename

2. Create a New Text Style

Create new text styles:

Feature	Font	Size	Style	Alignment (Justification)
Heading	Arial	24	Bold	Centred
Sub-headings	Arial	12	Underlined	Left
Body	Tahoma	10		Left
Bullet	Tahoma	10		Left
Table	Tahoma	10		Left

3. Content

The flyer is intended to inform people about a research project that your organisation is undertaking to investigate the use of a computer search facility you provide in each of your shops. Normally during the assessment text and image files are provided so that you can concentrate on the design aspects of desktop publishing without the extra burden of creating the resources.

The text for the flyer is:

Research Project

Introduction

We have been providing a free computer search facility to allow you to quickly locate any product held by any of our stores in Great Britain. We are now undertaking a review of this service to identify how we could enhance and extend its value to you.

Research

We have commissioned masters, Franks and James, an internationally recognized firm of market researchers to investigate the use of the service and make recommendations about its future development. They will be working in a sample of our stores and will be approaching some customers to ask if they would co-operate with the research.

Co-operation

If you are willing to help it will involve no more than a short (20 minutes) discussion with a researcher. To repay you for providing us with your views we will be offering a five pounds gift token to each participant.

Contact

If you are interested in volunteering to help please speak to the sales assistant wearing the yellow jacket in the store.

In addition to the text of the flyer you will need to include two images. Image 1 is shown in Figure 187A and is the logo of your organization while you should select an appropriate image from the Clip Art provided with Microsoft Office to add to the flyer.

The layout of the flyer is shown in Figure 187B

4. Directions

In designing the flyer you will need to:

• Save your master page
• Check your text file and make amends shown in Figure 187C
• Import text and image files
• Apply house text style
• Save and print your flyer

5. Add Drop Capitals after each sub-heading

6. Double space your body text

7. Insert the additional section and table below using the house style:

Visits

The researchers will be visiting the following stores:

Date	Store
12 July	Barrow
18 July	Leeds
20 July	Newcastle
21 July	Manchester
23 July	Bristol

8. Change your style sheet:

Heading	26 character size
Body Text	Justified

9. Save your flyer and print it

Summary

1. Load Microsoft Publisher

Load Microsoft Publisher by selecting Start, highlighting the Programs menu and clicking on the Microsoft Publisher item or click on the Publisher icon on the desktop.

2. New Blank Publication

Select the Blank publication tab on the catalog overlay and one of the options. Click on create to open the option in the work area.

3. Save

Select the File menu and click on Save option. The Save window will appear. Change the Save in: box to the location of your choice (e.g. floppy disk), name the file in the File name box and click on the Save button.

4. Text Frame

Select the Text Frame tool from the toolbar and the pointer will turn into a cross hair with which you can position the top left-hand corner of the frame and then, holding down the mouse button, drag the pointer to the bottom right-hand corner and then release the button.

5. Columns

A text frame needs to be in place before you can divide it into columns. Highlight the text frame by clicking on it. Select the Format menu and click on Text Frame Properties to reveal the window. This window allows you to adjust the margins, set the number of columns and set the gutter spacing for the text frame.

6. Header and Footer

Change the view of the page to background by selecting the View menu and click on Go to Background option. Select the Text frame tool and insert a text frame at the top and bottom of the page.

7. Layout Guides

Select the Arrange menu and click on the Layout Guides to reveal the Layout Guide window.

8. New Text Styles

Select the Format menu and click on the Text Style option to reveal the New Styles window.

9. Format Toolbar

The Format Toolbar is only revealed in full when a text frame is highlighted. To highlight a text frame simply click within it.

10. Applying a Text Style

Click on the Style box down arrow and select the Style from the list. Everything you now enter into the frame will follow this style.

Alternatively

An alternative approach is to click anywhere within an individual paragraph and then select a style. The style of the paragraph will change.

11. Create a Table

Another type of frame is the Table Frame which is available from the tools area. Insert the Table frame into the publications. When you have created the frame the Create Table window opens to allow you to set the number of rows and columns that make up the table.

12. Lines and Boxes

A line or box is drawn by clicking on the icon in the tool bar which changes the pointer to a cross hair. This allows you to position the start of your line or the corner of the box. By holding down the left mouse button and dragging the line or box you can form the object. While the object (i.e. line or box) is enclosed by the small black boxes it can be manipulated (e.g. moved, dragged etc.).

13. Crop an Image

Highlight the image frame which reveals functions on the format toolbar. Clicking on the Crop Picture icon produces a new pointer (i.e. crossed scissors) when it is positioned over the edge of the image frame. When the mouse button is held down the pointer can be dragged to cut the image.

14. Copyfitting Techniques

With the text frame highlighted select the Format menu, highlight the Autofit Text option to reveal a sub-menu of choices.

15. Hyphenation

Highlight the text frame or table and then select the Tools menu, highlighting the Language option, and clicking on the Hyphenation option.

16. Condensed and Expanded Text

Highlight the text or table frame. Select the Format menu, click on the Character Spacing option and the condensed or expand options are available under Kerning.

17. Text Wrap

Highlight the picture frame and select the functions from the format toolbar. You have the option of wrapping text around the picture frame or the actual picture. You can edit the irregular text wrap produced by selecting the Picture wrap option using the function Edit Irregular Wrap on the toolbar.

18. Printing

Select the File menu, click on the Print Setup to reveal the Print Setup window. This will allow you to adjust the print out depending on your printer.

19. Commercial Printing

Select the Tools menu and highlight the Commercial Printing Tools to reveal a menu of options. Select the Color printing option to reveal the Color Printing window.

20. Rotate text

Highlight the text frame and select the Arrange menu and the Rotate and Flip option to reveal submenu.

21. Reverse text colours

Highlight the text frame and select the Font Colour icon then choose the reverse colour. Select the Fill Colour icon and choose reverse colour.

22. Document Size

Select the File menu and click on the Page Setup option to reveal a window. Select the Special Size radio button,

23. Background

Highlight the image, select the View menu and click on Go to Background. Image will seem to disappear. To make image reappear select the View menu and click on Go to Foreground.

24. Line Spacing (Leading)

Click in the text frame you wish to alter (ie highlight it). Select the Format menu and click on the Line Spacing option to reveal the Line Spacing window. To change the spacing between the lines enter the value in the Between lines box. Click on OK button to make change.

Presentation Graphics and Solutions

This chapter will help you to:

- Create a presentation

- Set up a master slide

- Insert and manipulate data

- Control a presentation

- Support a presentation

This chapter covers Units 5 (Presentation Graphics) and 13 (Presentation Graphics Solutions). The content of these two units overlaps so that you cannot offer both of them as part of CLAIT Plus. However, you are free to offer either unit as part of the qualification or study them as single units. There are no pre-conditions for studying these units. However, their content does assume that you have the skills and understanding which are provided by the OCR Level 1 ICT course New CLAIT (e.g. Unit 10 - Presentation Graphics and Unit 1 – Using a Computer).

Assessment

Unit 5 – Presentation Graphics

After studying Unit 5 your skills and understanding are assessed during a 3-hour practical assignment. This is set by OCR and marked locally. However, the marking will be externally moderated by OCR. This ensures that the standard is being applied correctly across the many different providers of OCR CLAIT Plus. If you are unsuccessful then you can be re-assessed using a different assignment.

You are supplied with a variety of resources such as an image file, speakers notes in a text file and slide text file so that you can concentrate on creating the presentation rather than the resources.

You will be provided with two text files which you will have to import for the slide and speaker notes.

Unit 13 – Presentation Graphic Solutions

After studying Unit 13 your skills and understanding are assessed using a locally devised practical assignment. The assignment will be marked locally but externally moderated by OCR. This ensures that the standard is being applied correctly across the many different providers of OCR CLAIT Plus. If you are unsuccessful then you can be re-assessed using a different assignment.

The assessment task can be provided by the local tutor or suggested by the individual student. In both cases the task must meet all the assessment objectives of Unit 13 and allow learners to show their understanding.

Presentation Graphics

Over recent years there has been a large increase in the use of Presentation Graphics to support business meetings, conferences and teaching. They allow individuals to create a set of slides and handouts quickly to illustrate and support their presentations. These can be projected from the computer through a video (data) projector or printed on to transparencies for use with an overhead projector. In either case, high quality visual aids can be straightforwardly produced.

Microsoft PowerPoint is the presentation graphics application on which this chapter is based (Figure 188). It is a modern tool for creating presentations and offers users a wide range of facilities to combine text and graphics. However, it is good practice to develop a consistent format for your slides that does not overuse colour, images or text effects. Many organisations provide their staff with a house style to follow which incorporates standard features such as the organisation's logo. PowerPoint provides you with the means of creating a standard template or master for your presentations.

A master/template will include:

Background colour
Standard Graphics (e.g. logo)
Slide number
Presenters name and date (this will help you manage your presentations when you have several)
Heading Style (i.e. font, size, colour and style)
Bullet Style (i.e. font, size, colour and style)
Sub-bullet Style (i.e. font, size, colour and style)

It will also specify the location of different elements (e.g. pictures, slide numbering and dates) and the use of PowerPoint effects. PowerPoint and other presentation graphic packages allow you to employ animation techniques to add interest to presentations. However, it is good practice not to overuse these effects.

In Exercise 28 you are going to create a Master style. The House Style that you are going to follow is:

Master Slide

Feature	Colour	Style	Position	Comments
Background	none			
Graphic			Left corner of text area	
Number Slides		Bottom right hand corner of the slide		
Text (footer)		Bottom centre the slide		Enter your of name and centre
Date		Bottom right hand corner of the slide		
Timings				Each slide 60 seconds
Transtitions				1 effect on every slide
Builds				1 effect on every slide

Text

Style Name	Typeface	Point Size	Feature	Alignment
Heading	Sans Serif	40	Bold/blue	Centre
Bullet (level 1)	Serif	28	Include bullet character	Left
Sub-bullet (level 2)	Serif	24	Include bullet character	Left
Sub-bullet (level 3)	Serif	20	Include bullet character	Left

Table

Style Name	Typeface	Point Size	Feature	Colour	Alignment
Text	serif	24	No bullet characters	black	Left
Currency					Use decimal tabulation

Typeface (Font)

The House Style sheets use the term typeface which is an alternative to the term font. There are two types of font (or typefaces) called Sans Serif and Serif. A serif type font has small projections on the ends of the characters while a sans serif type font does not. You might say that serif fonts have more fancy characters or that sans serif fonts have plain characters. You need to experiment with your choice of fonts to find the ones that you like.

Examples

Serif

Courier New
Serifa BT
Times New Roman

Sans Serif

Arial
Helvetica

Microsoft PowerPoint

Figure 188 shows the initial view of PowerPoint when it initially loads. The overlay window asks you to select if you want to start with:

- A blank presentation (i.e. you create the presentation)

- An existing presentation (i.e. to amend or add to the presentation)

- Using a wizard to help create a presentation (i.e. provides you with a step-by-step guide to creating a presentation)

- Using design templates to create a presentation (PowerPoint provides a wide range of templates)

Exercise 28

Start a New Presentation Master Slide

1. Insert a floppy disk into the computer's drive.

2. Load Microsoft PowerPoint by selecting Start, highlighting the Programs menu and clicking on the Microsoft PowerPoint item or click on the PowerPoint icon on the desktop.

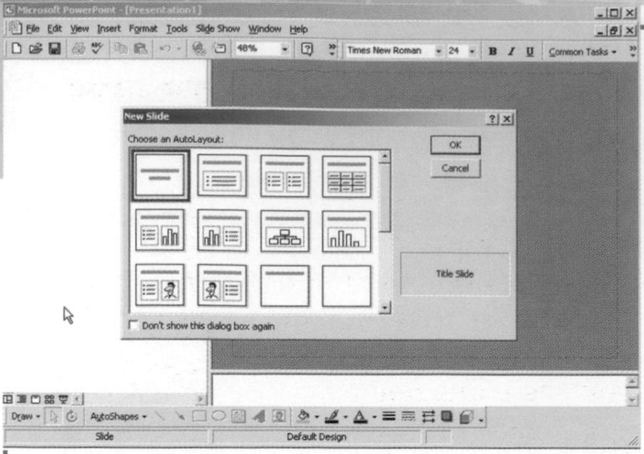

FIGURE 189
New Slide Window

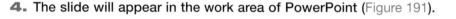

FIGURE 190
Title Slide

FIGURE 191
New Slide

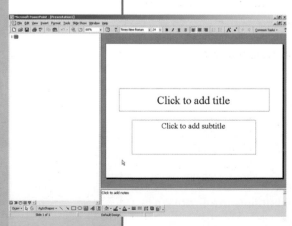

3. Select the Blank Presentation option by clicking in the radio button alongside the option and then on the OK button. The New Slide window will appear overlaying the PowerPoint application (Figure 189). This allows you to select an initial outline slide on which to build your presentation. When you start your second slide you can change the outline etc. In this case choose the title slide (Figure 190) by clicking on the slide to highlight it and then on the OK button. Observe the other outline options (e.g. slides with graphics, flow charts, columns, text/graphics combines etc.).

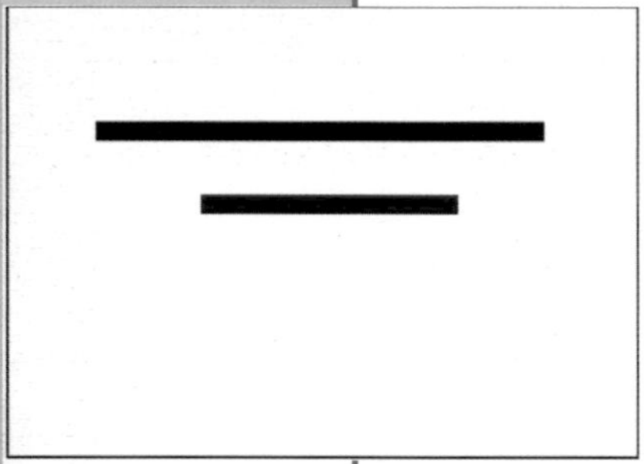

4. The slide will appear in the work area of PowerPoint (Figure 191).

5. You are now going to create a Master slide for this presentation. Select the View menu then highlight the Master option to reveal a sub-menu (Figure 192). Click on the Slide Master option. The Master Slide template will appear in the PowerPoint work area (Figure 193).

6. To edit the Master (i.e. to change the characteristics) you need to click on the different slide features (e.g. Title). However, before you start to change the Master you should decide on the background colour for the slide. Select the Format menu and click on Background option to reveal the Background window (Figure 194). This allows you to choose a background colour for your slides. In this case we will select no colour.

7. Click on the Master Title and from the toolbar choose Tahoma (font), size 40, bold and centred (Figure 195). Click on Master Text Style (i.e. first level bullet point) and choose Times New Roman, size 28 and left justified. Click on Second Level and choose Times New Roman, size 24 and left justified. Click on Third Level and choose Times New Roman, size 20 and left justified. Delete fourth and fifth levels.

8. The bottom left-hand side box contains the date in English format (i.e. dd/mm/yy) and left justified. Click on the box and highlight the Date and Time. Select the Insert menu and click on the Date and Time option to reveal the Date and Time window (Figure 196). Select the layout dd/mm/yy and click the automatic update radio button. You have not changed anything but it gives you the opportunity to practise.

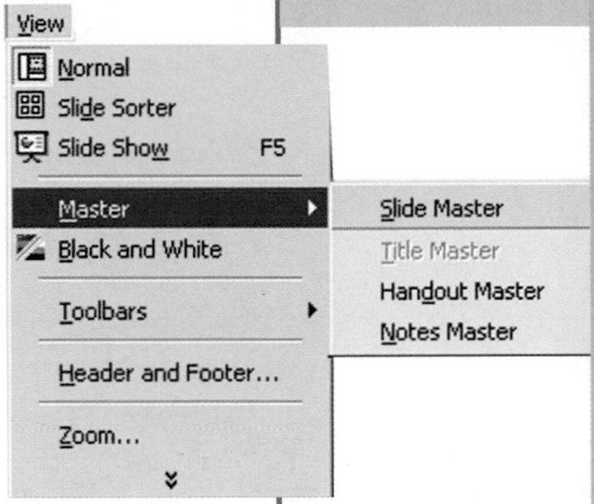

FIGURE 192
**Master
Slide
Function**

9. Click on the Footer to highlight it and enter your name and centre name. Both should be centred.

10. Click on the right-hand box Number Area. Select the Insert Menu and click on Slide Number. A message window appears asking if you want to number just this slide or every one. You want to number all slides so click on the OK button. This will reveal the Header and Footer window (Figure 197). Click in the Footer radio button to show the footer you have created on the slides. Click on the radio button Slide Number and then the Apply to All button.

11. The next step is to select a font colour. The default colour is black which is acceptable except for the Title, so click in the title box and then select the Font colour icon on the Drawing toolbar (Figure 198). Choose blue.

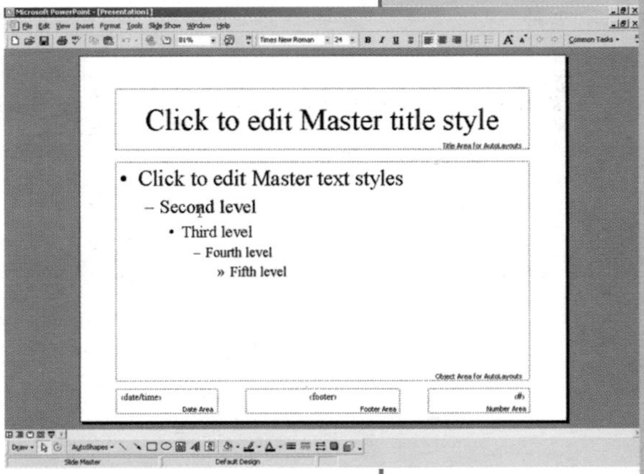

FIGURE 193
**Master
Slide
Template**

12. The last step is to place a graphic image in the bottom right hand corner of the text area. Select the Insert menu, highlight Pictures to reveal the sub-menu (Figure 199) and click on Clip Art. This will open the ClipArt window. Select an image that would be suitable for a business presentation.

13. The clip art image will appear on the slide enclosed in a frame with small rectangles at the corners and centres of the lines. These allow you to change the shape and size of the image. You can move the image by positioning the mouse over the image, holding down the mouse button and dragging the image around. The mouse pointer is shaped like crossed arrows. To resize or change the shape of the image, position your mouse over one of the rectangles and it will change to a double-headed arrow. By holding down the mouse button and dragging, you can change the shape and size of the picture. Experiment but remember that changing its shape and size may distort the image so you need to ensure the images proportions are acceptable when you have finished.

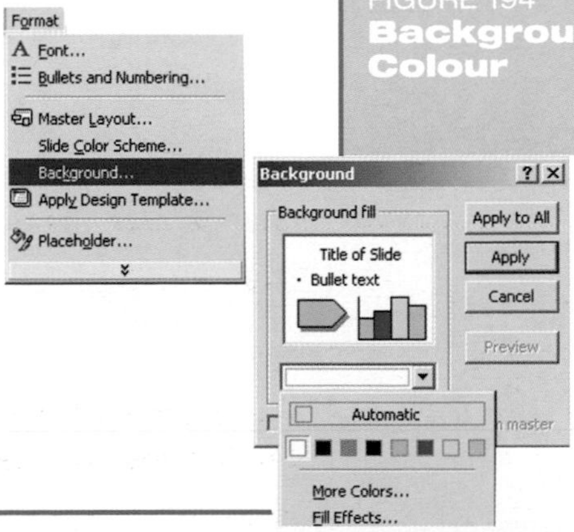

FIGURE 194
**Background
Colour**

14. You have now established your Master and need to save it. Select the File menu and the Save option. The Save As window will appear and save the Master as a file called Presentation1 on to your floppy disk. You will need to change the Save in box to floppy disk and enter the file name in the File name box. Figure 200 shows the window.

15. The Master is shown in Figure 201.

Tahoma   40   **B** *I* U S

Font
Size   Centred

16. Close the application by either selecting the File menu and clicking on the Exit option or click on the Close button in the top right hand corner of the application window.

Transition and Other Effects

A slide show is a presentation of a set of individual slides. PowerPoint allows you to control the change from one slide to the next by using transition effects. For example you can slowly dissolve the closing slide and gradually reveal the next one. These effects can add considerable interest to a standard presentation. Amongst the transition effects is the control of time so that you can display each slide for a set period and then change it. This is very useful for providing a continuous presentation for an exhibition stand or similar function.

Date and Time

Available formats:

17/03/2002
Sunday, 17 March 2002
17 March, 2002
17 March 2002
17-Mar-02
March 02
Mar-02
17/03/2002 18:51
17/03/2002 18:51:03
18:51
18:51:03
6:51 PM
6:51:03 PM

Language:
English (U.K.)

Calendar type:
Western

☑ Update automatically   OK   Cancel

The transitions are available by selecting the Slide Show menu and clicking on the Slide Transition option to reveal the Slide Transition window (Figure 202). This lets you select the type of transition and either have a standard change for the whole presentation or a different transition between each slide.

Header and Footer

Slide | Notes and Handouts

Include on slide
☑ Date and time
  ◉ Update automatically
    17/03/2002
    Language: Calendar type:
    English (U.K.)   Western
  ○ Fixed

☑ Slide number
☐ Footer

☐ Don't show on title slide

Apply to All
Apply
Cancel

Preview

In Figure 202 you will notice that there are buttons that allow you to apply your choice of transition to all slides (i.e. Apply to All) and to individual slides (i.e. Apply). In the bottom left-hand corner of the window you will see an area called Advance. This gives you the choice of moving to the next slide by clicking the mouse button (i.e. manually) or by automatically (i.e. you set the time between each slide).

In addition to these relatively simple transition effects you can add a wide range of others to add interest to your slides such as adding sound effects and animating parts of your presentation. The Slide Transition window allows you to add sound effects to your slide change. Use the Sound box and down arrow to gain access to a list of sounds.

Draw ▾ ⊾ ⟳ AutoShapes ▾ \ ↘ □ ○ ▤ ◢ ⊞ | ⊘ ▾ ✎ ▾ A ▾ ≡ ≡ ⇄ ▤ ⬤ ▾

Colour Fill   Line Style
Line Colour   Font Colour

You can animate the appearance of your message and either control the changes manually through the mouse or automate the process so that you set time delays before each effect. The main effects are available by selecting the Sli<u>d</u>e Show menu and clicking on the Cust<u>om</u> Animation option. This reveals the Custom Animation window (Figure 203).

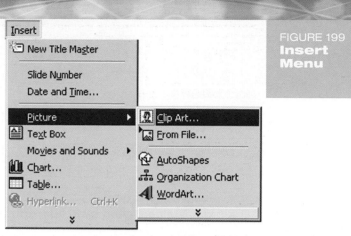

FIGURE 199
**Insert
Menu**

Although PowerPoint provides a wide variety of effects, it is good practice to limit their use since they can distract from your overall message. One or two carefully chosen effects can enhance your presentation while too many can leave your audience confused.

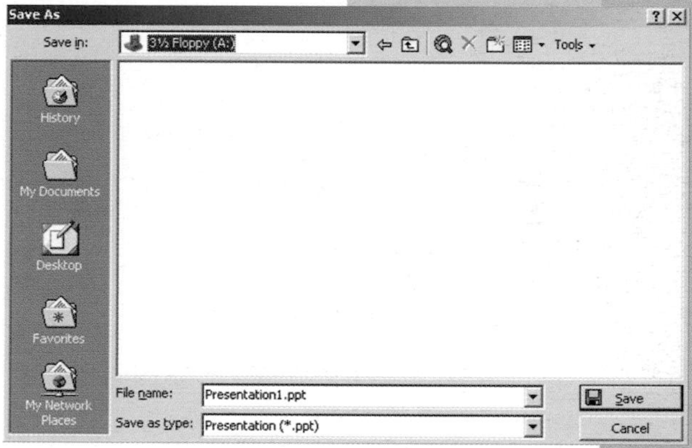

Charts

When starting a new presentation or inserting a new slide you are offered the choice of a variety of different layouts (Figure 189). Amongst the choices are to have slides which are:

FIGURE 200
**Save
Master File**

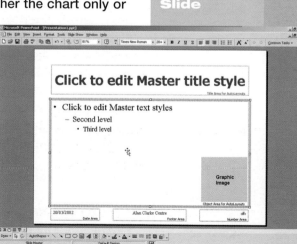

- Text only
- Graphics (picture) only
- Text and Graphics
- Charts only
- Text and Charts
- Organisational charts
- Organisational charts and text

Figure 204 shows some of the main options.

FIGURE 201
**Amended
Master
Slide**

Three of the slide options feature charts. If you select either the chart only or text and chart slides then you will see a chart placeholder which if you doubleclick will reveal a chart with its corresponding data in the form of a datasheet (Figure 204A). The datasheet contains sample information indicating where you can enter your own information to create a new chart. If you enter information then you will see the chart change in a corresponding way. When you have completed entering your data then just click away from the chart or datasheet and you will see the datasheet disappear and the new chart will be inserted into the slide. If you need to amend the chart then doubleclick the chart again to reveal the datasheet.

You can also insert a Microsoft Excel Chart into a slide by selecting the <u>I</u>nsert

FIGURE 202
Slide Transition

FIGURE 203
Custom Animation

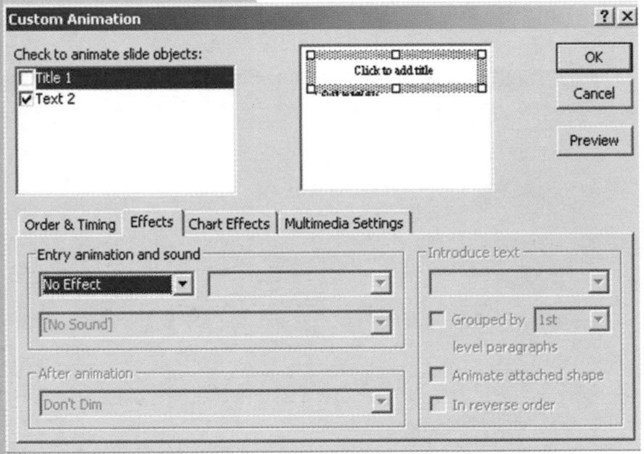

FIGURE 204
Standard Layouts

Title

Text Only

Text in Columns

Text and Chart

Chart only

Organisational Chart

menu and click on the Object option to reveal Insert Object window. This provides you with two choices to create a new slide or to select an existing one.

PowerPoint also provides a special type of chart. This is an organizational chart. If you select the organizational chart slide then you will see an organisational chart placeholder. If you doubleclick on it the Microsoft Organisation Chart window will be revealed (Figure 204B). You can enter your own labels into the chart and then extend it by dragging and dropping the extra elements on the row above the work area. When you have finished select the File menu and click on the Exit and return to PowerPoint option. If you want to revise an organizational chart you have created then double click on it and the Microsoft Organisation Chart window will reappear so you can make changes.

Create a Presentation

You have created a Master slide or a template for your slides. You now need to employ it to guide you through producing a slide show. Your Master can still be amended or adapted. When you have used PowerPoint for a period you will begin to develop a library of presentations and different Master slides to suit different purposes.

You are going to create a presentation for a senior manager who is demonstrating a new product to the company directors. It is always useful to plan your presentations before you rush to create the slides. Outline what you would like to say, what the objectives of the presentation are and how long you plan to speak. People often produce more material than they can fit into the time available. Consider carefully what are the key things you need to say and how best to present them. It is often appropriate to finish early to allow time for questions. Few audiences appreciate speakers who finish late or have to rush their final slides in order to keep to time.

For this presentation the manager wants to:

- Introduce himself (1 slide)
- Explain the new product (2 slides)
- Discuss prices (1 slide)
- Discuss sales approach (1 slide)

- Discuss customers (1 slide)
- Forecast Chart (1 slide)
- Conclude the presentation (1 slide)

Your final presentation will consist of eight slides. These will be based on the Master you have already developed. The requirements of the Presentation Graphics Solutions unit is an eight slide presentation.

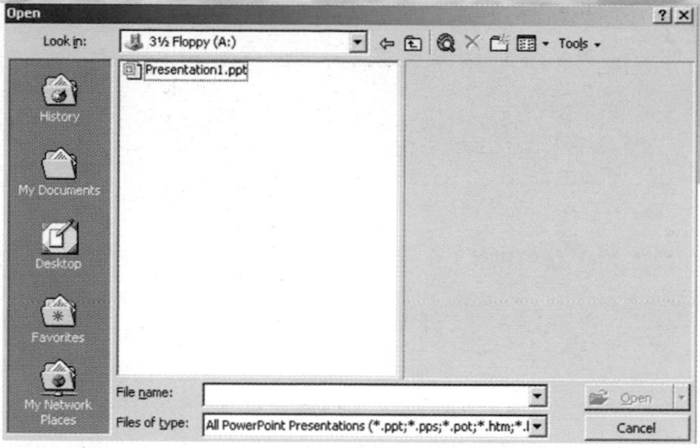

FIGURE 205
Open Window

Exercise 29

Create a Presentation

1. Insert a floppy disk into the computer's drive.

2. Load Microsoft PowerPoint by selecting Start, highlighting the Programs menu and clicking on the Microsoft PowerPoint item or click on the Publisher icon on the desktop.

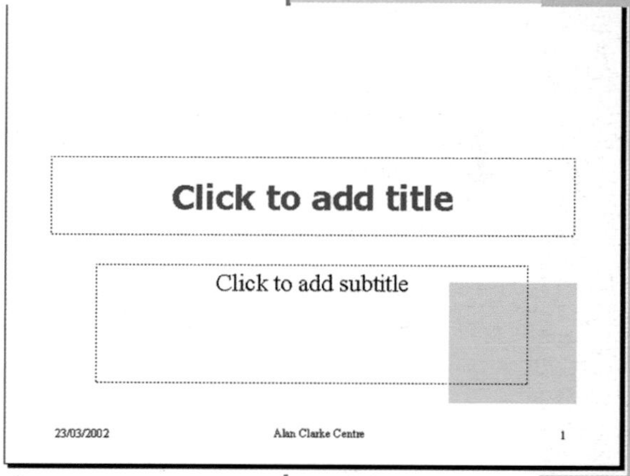

3. Select Open an Existing Presentation. If you have only recently completed Exercise 28 then you may see Presentation1 in the area below the option. If it is there, then you can load it by double clicking it. If it is not visible then click on the OK button to reveal the Open window. Change the Look in: box to Floppy Disk to locate Presentation1. It can be loaded by double clicking the file. Figure 205 shows the Open Window.

FIGURE 206
Title Slide

Click to add title

Click to add subtitle

23/03/2002   Alan Clarke Centre   1

4. The master slide Presentation1 will load into the PowerPoint work area. It is useful now to save the presentation under a new name to avoid overwriting the master slide which you may want to use later for a different presentation. Select the File menu and the Save As option. This will open the Save As window. Change the Save in box to Floppy Disk and enter New Product to File name box and then click on the Save button.

FIGURE 207
Slide

5. You now need to create your presentation. Select the View menu and click on the Normal option. The master slide will be replaced by the Title slide in the master slides style (Figure 206). Enter AMEX STATIONERY in the Click to add title area. In this case

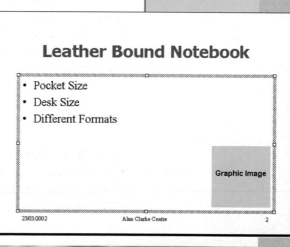

Leather Bound Notebook

- Pocket Size
- Desk Size
- Different Formats

Graphic Image

23/03/2002   Alan Clarke Centre   2

FIGURE 208
New Layout

Leather Bound Notebook

- Pocket Size
- Desk Size
- Different Formats

Graphic Image

23/03/2002   Alan Clarke Centre   2

FIGURE 209
Third Slide

Options

- Lined Paper
- Squared Paper
- Plain Paper

- Address Book
- Diary
- Folder

Graphic Image

23/03/2002   Alan Clarke Centre   3

FIGURE 210
Whole Presentation

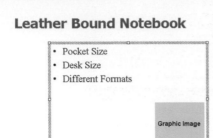

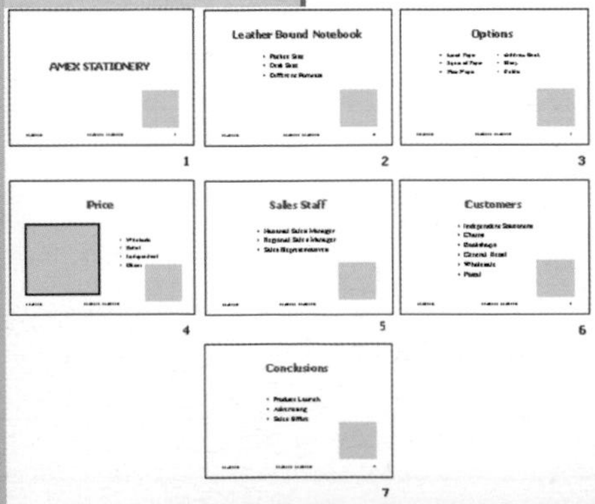

you do not have a sub-title. So select the Insert menu and click on the New Slide option.

6. The New Slide window will appear (Figure 189). Select a text-only layout with a single column (see Figure 204). Click on Click to add title and enter Leather Bound Notebook. Click on Click to add text and insert Pocket Size then press the enter key. The cursor will move to the next line and a new bullet will appear. Enter Desk Size and then press the enter key to move to a new line. Enter Different Formats. Figure 207 shows the result.

7. Figure 207 shows that your bullet point text is presented on the left side of the slide. The text area is enclosed in a box with small squares at the corners and in the centre of each side. These squares allow you to change the shape of the text area and adjust the position of the text. If you place your mouse point on the enclosure lines but not on the squares the pointer changes shape to a star. If you hold down the mouse button while the pointer is in this shape you can move the whole text area. Try to move the text area but return it to its original place when you have finished.

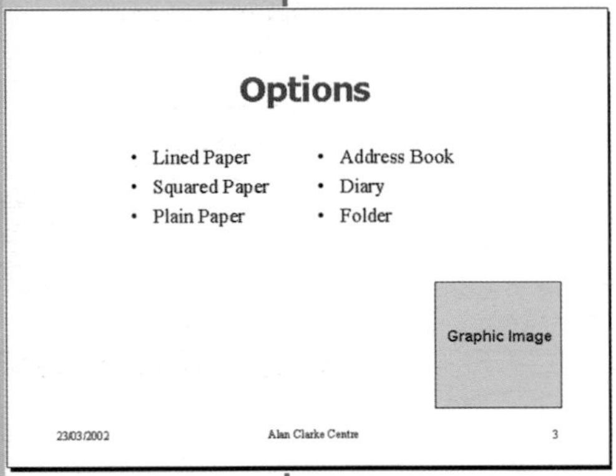

8. If you place your mouse over a square then the mouse pointer changes to a double-headed arrow. If you hold down the button you can drag the text area to change its size and shape. Experiment changing the shape until you are content with the new appearance. Figure 208 shows my efforts.

9. Select the Insert menu and click on the New Slide option. Select the Text in Columns layout and insert the title Options. Insert in the left-hand column – Lined Paper, Squared Paper and Plain Paper and in right hand column – Address Book, Diary and Folder. You will notice that each column is enclosed so that they can be moved, resized or shape adjusted. Change the columns to improve the presentation of the slide. Figure 209 shows the slide.

10. Now create a further four slides:

Slide 4 – Graphics and Text slide – the title of the slide is Price, add a clip art image to represent money and on the text column add Wholesale, Retail, Independent and Chains

When inserting Clip Art you may be asked to insert the Microsoft Office CD-ROM containing the Clip Art if this has not been installed on the hard disk.

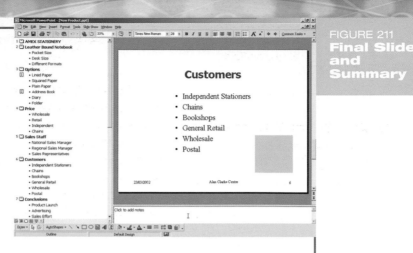

Slide 5 – Text only slide – the title of the slide is Sales Staff, add to text National Sales Manager, Regional Sales Manager and Sales Representatives

Slide 6 – Text only slide – the title of the slide is Customers, add to text Independent Stationers, Chains, Bookshops, General Retail, Wholesale and Postal

Slide 7 – Chart only slide – the title of the slide if Forecast. The data sheet for the slide is:

	1st Quarter	2 nd Quarter	3 rd Quarter	4 th Quarter
Address	15	16	21	23
Diary	27	22	31	26
Folder	8	11	9	12
Notebook	35	34	30	32

Slide 8- Text only slide – the title of the slide is Conclusions, add to text Product Launch, Advertising and Sales Effort

11. Adjust the layout to improve the appearance of all slides. When you are adjusting the shape and size of a graphic there is a danger that you will alter its proportions so that a poor image results. Figure 210 shows the whole presentation.

12. Figure 211 shows a slide alongside a summary of the text within the whole presentation.

13. Save your presentation by selecting the File menu and clicking on Save. No window will appear since the system assumes you are saving in the current location using the same filename.

14. Close the application by either selecting the File menu and clicking on the Exit option or clicking on the Close button in the top right hand corner of the application window.

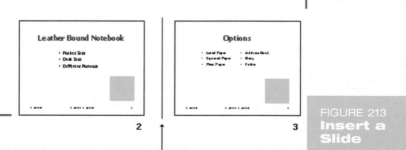

Insert Position

FIGURE 214
**Organisatio
-nal Chart
Slide**

Editing a Presentation

PowerPoint provides functions so you can edit the presentation. You are able to:

• Change the order of the presentation
• Delete slides
• Insert new slides
• Edit individual slides (e.g. text, graphics etc.)
• Hide slides

FIGURE 215
**Microsoft
Organisation
Chart**

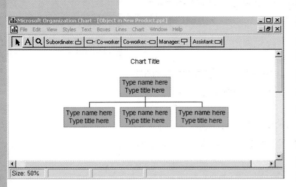

You can gain an overview of the whole presentation by selecting the View menu and clicking on the Slide Sorter option. This reveals a display showing a small (thumbnail) picture of each slide. Slides can be dragged around the presentation by clicking on them to highlight them. A highlighted slide is enclosed in a rectangle. Highlighted slides (Figure 212) can be dragged to new positions in the presentation and deleted by pressing the delete key. New slides can be added by clicking the position (Figure 213) you would like to add a new slide to and then selecting the Insert menu and clicking on the New Slide option.

An alternative approach is to scroll through the slides from the work area. You can return from the Slide Sorter display by selecting the Insert menu and clicking on the Normal option. Slides can be inserted using the Insert menu and clicking on the New Slide or deleted by selecting the Edit menu and clicking on the Delete Slide option.

FIGURE 216
**Sales
Organisation
Chart**

It may seem a little odd that you would want to hide a slide but there are occasions when you want to show different information to different groups. For example you may have created a presentation for internal staff that you later need to show some customers. Hiding slides allows you to quickly change the presentation.

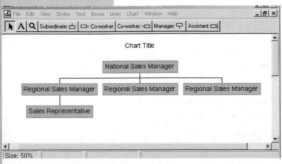

To hide a slide select the View menu and click the Slide Sorter option. Click on the slide you want to hide to highlight it and select the Slide Show menu and click the Hide Slide option. The slide is now hidden. This is indicated by the slide number being crossed. To reverse the process click on the Hide Slide option.

You can create a link from another slide to the hidden one so that by clicking on a word, image or button you can present the hidden slide. The Hyperlinks section explains how to create links to hidden slides.

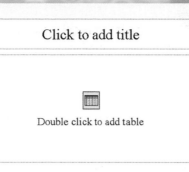

FIGURE 217
Tables

Exercise 30

Editing

1. Insert a floppy disk into the computer's drive.

2. Load Microsoft PowerPoint by selecting Start, highlighting the Programs menu and clicking on the Microsoft PowerPoint item or clicking on the Publisher icon on the desktop.

3. Select Open an Existing Presentation. If you have only recently completed Exercise 29 then you may see New Product in the area below the option. If it is there, then you can load it by double clicking on it. If it is not visible, then click on the OK button to reveal the Open window. Change the Look in: box to Floppy Disk to locate New Product. It can be loaded by double clicking the file.

4. You are going to insert an additional slide between slides 5 and 6 showing the organisation of the sales staff. Select the View menu and click on the Slide Sorter option. You will see all seven slides appear as small images. Click between slides 5 and 6 and you will see a line appear between them.

FIGURE 218
Insert Table

5. Select the Insert menu and click on the New Slide option. This will reveal the New Slide window. Select the organisational chart layout and click the OK button. A new slide will appear in the position you have selected.

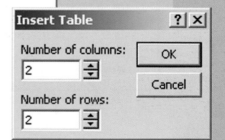

6. Double click on the new slide and you will return to the work area with the new slide occupying the display (Figure 214). The slides are automatically renumbered so that the new slide is now number 6.

7. Double click on the slide to insert the organisational chart. You may be presented with a warning message telling you this feature is not installed and offering you the opportunity to add the feature. This will involve using the Microsoft Office CD-ROM.

8. The Microsoft Organisation Chart window is opened (Figure 215). This

FIGURE 219
Tables and
Borders

Tables and Borders

Table ▾

allows you to create a chart. Click on the Top box of the chart and enter National Sales Manager then delete any text that remains. Now move to the next row down. Enter into each box Regional Sales Manager and delete any remaining text.

9. You now need to create an additional row so click on the Subordinate box and your pointer will change shape to a new small box. Click on the left Regional Sales Manager box and you will see a new element attached to this box appear. Click into this box and enter Sales Representative. Your chart should now look like Figure 216.

10. Select the File menu and click on the Exit and return to New Product.ppt. A message window will appear asking you if you want to update New Product. Click on OK and your chart will appear on the slide.

11. Your organisational chart may have been inserted overlapping the standard graphic image or be poorly placed on the slide. If you click on the chart you will enclose it so that it can be dragged or shape/size changed. Adjust the layout of the slide.

12. Click on the Title and enter Sales Organisation.

13. Save your new presentation by selecting the File menu and clicking on the Save option.

FIGURE 220
Enter
Information
into a Table

14. Select the View menu and click on Slide Sorter. You are going to change the order of the slides by moving slide 4 Price to appear after slide 7 Customers. Click on the Price slide to highlight it (enclose it) and holding down the mouse button drag the slide to the new position. A line will appear in this new position. You can then release the button.

15. Save your new presentation by selecting the File menu and clicking on the Save option.

16. Close the application by either selecting the File menu and clicking on the Exit option or clicking on the Close button in the top right-hand corner of the application window.

Click to add title

Hyperlinks

Hyperlinks are the means by which you can add extra slides to your presentation which only appear if you click on a sensitive area or button on an existing slide. This allows you to customise a presentation to meet the needs of different audiences or to provide more control over the presentation.

Figure 217A shows the connection between the main presentation slides and the hyperlink ones. Hyperlinks can also link your presentation to a document, a website, intranet location or an email address.

To add a hyperlink select the text on the slide and click on the Insert menu and select the Hyperlink option. The Insert Hyperlink window will appear which allows you to link the slide to a chosen location where the other slides or documents are stored. If you are linking to other slides and want to return to the original presentation you must create a second hyperlink to your original slide. The link text will change colour and be underlined to show the hyperlink.

You can add standard hyperlink buttons to a slide by clicking on the Slide Show menu, highlighting the Action buttons option to reveal a small menu of buttons. Click on the button of your choice and the pointer changes to a cross to allow you to position it on the slide. Once it is located the Action Settings window opens to allow you to select the action which will take place when the button is pressed. You can establish buttons to link you to the previous, next, first or last slides. This gives you considerable control over the presentation.

Earlier we discussed the use of Hiding slides to protect confidential information. It is possible to create links to hidden slides so that you can have the option of showing the slide. You need to highlight the text or image and then selected the Insert menu and click on the Hyperlink option. This will reveal the Insert Hyperlink window. Click on

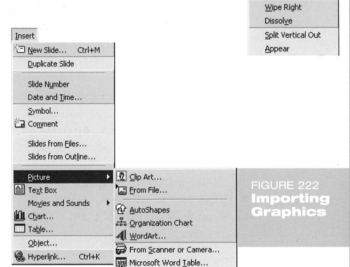

the bookmark button to reveal the Select Place in Document window. To complete the link you need to choose the hidden slide by double clicking on it. The window will close and the hidden slide name will appear in the Type the file or Web page name box. Click the OK button to finish the task.

Using Blank Slides

One of the major difficulties in designing a presentation is to time the slide show. You do not know how many questions you will be asked or if a previous presenter has not arrived and you are given more time than you planned for. One way of maintaining control is to insert blank slides into the presentation.

FIGURE 224
**Spell
Checker**

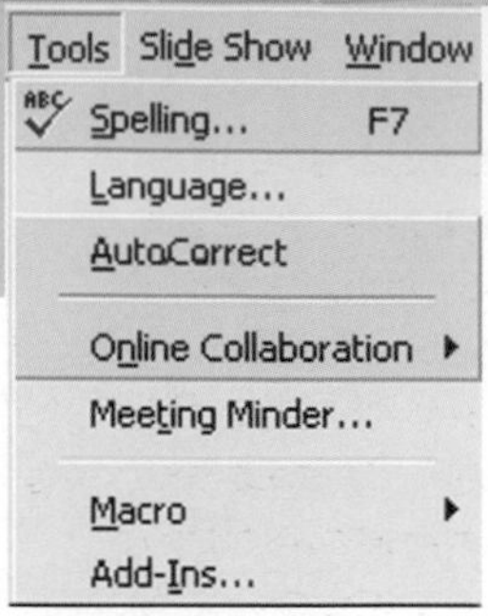

Tools	Slide Show	Window
ABC Spelling...		F7
Language...		
AutoCorrect		
Online Collaboration		▶
Meeting Minder...		
Macro		▶
Add-Ins...		

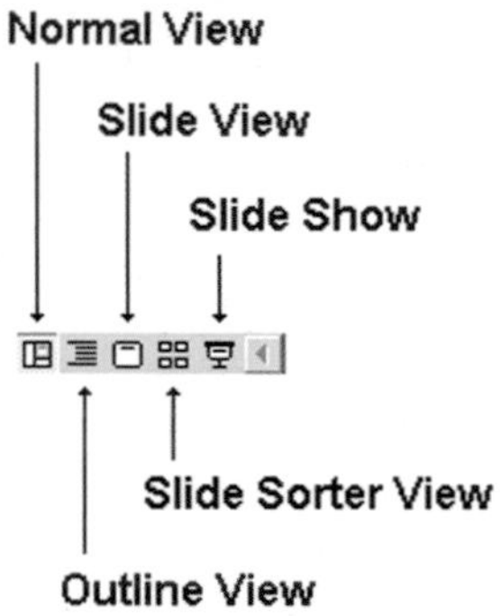

This allows you the opportunity to pause or even stop if time runs out. Blanks should be inserted at logical places to allow you to pause, perhaps to provide an opportunity for questions or comments.

Tables

One of the layout options is a table. You can select this from the New Slide window and a table slide is placed within the presentation (Figure 217). Double clicking on the slide will open the Insert Table window (Figure 218) in which you can choose the number of rows and columns. When you have selected the size of the table and clicked on the OK button you will see the table on the slide and the Tables and Borders window appear. This lets you change the appearance of the table. When you have made your selections you are presented with an empty table in which to enter your information (Figure 220). The mouse pointer appears to be a pen.

FIGURE 225
**Slide Show
Button**

Normal View

Slide View

Slide Show

田 ≡ □ 品 ♀ ◄

Slide Sorter View

Outline View

You also insert a table into an existing slide by selecting the Insert menu and the Table option to reveal the Insert Table window which allows you to set the number of rows and columns. This will produce a table for you to enter text. The table can be resized and moved using the mouse pointer to position it on the slide.

Tables are one means of aligning information on a slide. You can also use the Tab key to align information. The justification icons on the toolbar also allow you to align the text left, right and center in the same way that text is aligned in Word.

Exercise 31

Transitions and Effects

1. Insert a floppy disk into the computer's drive.

2. Load Microsoft PowerPoint by selecting Start, highlighting the Programs menu and clicking on the Microsoft PowerPoint item or click on the Publisher icon on the desktop.

3. Select Open an Existing Presentation. If you have only recently completed Exercise 30 then you may see New Product in the area below the option. If it is there, then you can load it by double clicking on it. If it is not visible, then click on the OK button to reveal the Open window. Change the Look in: box to Floppy Disk to locate New Product. It can be loaded by double clicking the file.

4. You are now going to apply a transition effect between each slide of the presentation. Select the Slide Show menu and click on the Slide <u>T</u>ransition option to reveal the Sli<u>d</u>e Transition window. Click on the down arrow button next to the transition box to display a list of options. Select an option and you will see it demonstrated in the Effects box. Explore the options and choose one you feel is effective. You are also provided with three speeds as transitions (i.e. slow, medium and fast). To select a new speed, click in the appropriate radio button.

5. In the area Advanced you are going to set the presentation to change slides automatically. The House style sets 60 seconds as the time for each slide so click in the automatic box and adjust time to read 60 seconds or 1 minute. Both the On Mouse Click and Automatically after options now have a tick in them so that you can manually change slides or they will change themselves after a minute. Now click on the Apply to All button.

6. You are now going to add effects to each slide. The House style is for one effect for each slide. Scroll through the slides until you reach the title one. Click on the title to highlight it (i.e. enclosed in a frame). Select the Sli<u>d</u>e Show menu and highlight the <u>P</u>reset Animation option to reveal a list of options (Figure 221). Select the <u>C</u>amera option.

7. Repeat the process for each slide.

8. Save your new presentation by selecting the <u>F</u>ile menu and clicking on the <u>S</u>ave option.

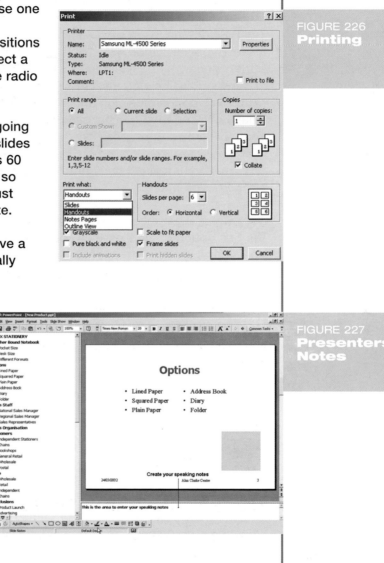

FIGURE 226
Printing

FIGURE 227
Presenters Notes

9. Two other ways of enhancing your presentation are using hyperlinks and hiding slides. You may want to use this presentation for external audiences so that some slides are not appropriate (e.g. Forecasts of Income). Let us hide the Forecast slide. Select the View menu and click on the Slide Sorter option. Thumbnail images of each slide will appear. Click on the Forecast slide to highlight it (i.e. it will be enclosed in a rectangle). Now select Slide Show and click on Hide Slide option. The number of the slide will be crossed.

10. In some cases you may want the choice of showing the hidden slide. This can be achieved by using hyperlinks. Move to the slide prior to the Forecast slide and highlight the text you want to make the link (e.g. Slide Title). Select the Insert menu and click on the Hyperlink option to reveal the Insert Hyperlink window (Figure 221a). Click on the Place in This Document button since you are linking to a slide in this presentation. A box will appear in the window showing a list of slides including a Slide Titles item with a plus sign. Click on the plus sign and a full list of slide names will appear. Doubleclick on the Forecast slide and you will return to slide working area. You have linked the slides.

11. Save your revised presentation by selecting the File menu and clicking on the Save option.

12. Close the application by either selecting the File menu and clicking on the Exit option or click on the Close button in the top right hand corner of the application window.

Importing Text and Graphics

Microsoft Office applications enable you to cut, copy and paste text and graphics between applications. It is possible to cut or copy text from Word and paste it into PowerPoint. You can also send text from Word to PowerPoint directly using the option Send To which is available from the File menu. This reveals a submenu with the option Microsoft PowerPoint. This will change the file into a PowerPoint presentation.

Graphics can be inserted into PowerPoint by selecting the Insert menu and highlighting the Picture option to reveal a submenu of options (Figure 222). This provides you with a series of choices including inserting clip art or selecting a graphic image from a file, a scanner or a digital camera. You can also import a Word table into one of your slides.

Find and Replace

When you need to make changes to a presentation you can either do it manually by locating the slide, delete the text and then inserting the replacement text or you could employ the Replace function available by selecting the Edit menu and clicking on the Replace option to reveal the Replace window (Figure 223). This allows you to search for a word or phrase and replace it throughout the whole presentation.

Spell Checker

One of the most frequent problems with presentations is showing a mis-spelt word to an audience. They will see the error immediately and often you are only aware of it when someone tells you after the presentation. PowerPoint provides a spell checker and it is good practice to check your completed presentation. The spell checker is available by selecting the Tools menu and clicking on the Spelling option.

Showing a Presentation

There are several ways of running a presentation. These are:

1. Select the View menu and click on Slide Show option
2. Select the Slide Show menu and click on the View Show option
3. Click on the Slide Show button in the bottom left hand corner of the display (Figure 225).

Exercise 32

Show Presentation

1. Insert a floppy disk into the computer's drive.

2. Load Microsoft PowerPoint by selecting Start, highlighting the Programs menu and clicking on the Microsoft PowerPoint item or clicking on the Publisher icon on the desktop.

3. Select Open an Existing Presentation. If you have only recently completed Exercise 31 then you may see New Product in the area below the option. If it is there then you can load it by double clicking on it. If it is not visible, then click on the OK button to reveal the Open window. Change the Look in: box to Floppy Disk to locate New Product. It can be loaded by double clicking the file.

4. Run the presentation using one of the options. You will see the slide occupy the whole screen. You may need to click your mouse to see the transition effects. Observe what happens when you move between slides. Try waiting for 60 seconds to see the slides automatically change. The precise change will depend on your previous choice of effects.

FIGURE 228
Current Organisation

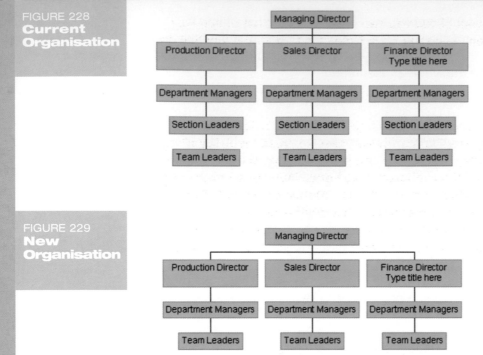

FIGURE 229
New Organisation

5. Run the presentation several times including allowing the automatic presentation to work.

6. Close the application by either selecting the <u>F</u>ile menu and clicking on the <u>E</u>xit option or click on the Close button in the top right hand corner of the application window.

Printing Supporting Documents

As well as producing slides using PowerPoint you can also create a variety of printed documents to support the presentation. The slides themselves can be printed onto transparencies for use with an overhead projector. In addition you can print:

• Copies of individual slides
• A set of notes for the presenter
• Handouts which allow audience to add notes
• A copy of the presentation in outline view

These are all available by selecting the <u>F</u>ile menu and clicking on the <u>P</u>rint option to reveal the Print window (Figure 226). This gives you a variety of options. In the Print What area you can select from a list. The handouts options allows you to print copies of slides as small thumbnail images in a number of different formats (e.g. 6 images to a page). You can also print full size copies of individual slides, groups or the whole presentation using the Print range options.

When you are creating your slides you can also produce a set of speaking notes to accompany them using the Slide Notes area below the working area (Figure 227).

Screen Prints

Windows provides you with the means of capturing the display on the computer screen. To capture the display you need to press the PrtSc (Print Screen button). The display is captured and stored in a special area of the computers memory called the clipboard. If you open Word or another suitable application you can paste the captured display into the document. This is useful in that you can capture the slides as they appear on the screen so you can document the build up of the slide and other special effects. Clait Plus requires that you use Screen Prints as evidence of transitions, builds and hyperlinks.

Exercise 32

Printing

1. Insert a floppy disk into the computer's drive.

2. Load Microsoft PowerPoint by selecting Start, highlighting the Programs menu and clicking on the Microsoft PowerPoint item or click on the Publisher icon on the desktop.

3. Select Open an Existing Presentation. If you have only recently completed Exercise 32 then you may see New Product in the area below the option. If it is there, then you can load it by double clicking on it. If it is not visible, then click on the OK button to reveal the Open window. Change the Look in: box to Floppy Disk to locate New Product. It can be loaded by double clicking the file.

4. Notice that under the slide is an area labelled Click to add notes. Click in this area since you are going to produce a set of speakers notes. In slide 1 enter:

Good morning I am pleased that you were able to find the time in a busy day to attend my presentation. I am sure that you will find its contents beneficial.

In the final slide Conclusions enter:

This is an exciting new product that will potentially generate substantial profits for the company. However, it requires an effort from everyone in this room in order to be successful.

Now enter appropriate text for the other slides to produce a full set of notes.

5. Select the <u>F</u>ile menu and click on the Print option to reveal the <u>P</u>rint window. Print:

a) copies of all slides – full size
b) handouts with six, four and two copies of the slides on each page
c) notes pages
d) outline view

Explore all the options until you are confident that you can produce the desired documents.

6. Now run the presentation and practice capturing the screen displays using the PrtSc key. Paste your captures into Microsoft Word or Windows Paint. Print the resulting document. Continue until you are confident.

7. Close the application by either selecting the <u>F</u>ile menu and clicking on the <u>E</u>xit option or click on the Close button in the top right hand corner of the application window.

More Practice

Master Slide

Feature	Colour	Style	Position	Comments
Background	none			
Graphic			Rightcorner of text area	
Number Slides		Bottom right hand corner of the slide		
Text (footer)		Bottom centre the slide		Enter your of name and centre
Date		Bottom right hand corner of the slide		
Timings				Each slide 30 seconds
Transtitions				1 effect on every slide
Builds				1 effect on every slide

Text

Style Name	Typeface	Point Size	Feature	Alignment
Heading	Sans Serif	44	Bold/red	Centre
Bullet (level 1)	Serif	36	Include bullet character	Left
Sub-bullet (level 2)	Serif	32	Include bullet character	Left

Table

Style Name	Typeface	Point Size	Feature	Colour	Alignment
Text	serif	24	No bullet characters	black	Left
Currency					Use decimal tabulation

For this presentation a manager wants to explain some changes to the employees of a company:

• Introduction (1 slide)
• Explain the changes (3 slides)
• Current Organisation (1 slide)
• New Organisation (1 slide)
• Invite Questions (1 slide)
• Conclude the presentation (1 slide)

Text for the Slides

Slide 1   Kingston Computing Ltd

Slide 2   Changes

                 Global Competition
                 More Efficient Structures
                 Reduce Costs

Slide 3   Changes

                 Flexibility
                 Team Working
                 Learning Organisation

Slide 4   Changes

	Stream Line Organisation
	Reduce Management
	More Delegation

Slide 5   Current Organisation

Slide 6   New Organisation

Slide 7   Questions

                   Please ask any questions

Slide 8   Conclusion

                   Change
                   Co-operation
                   Thank you

Instructions 1

1. Open PowerPoint
2. Create a Master Slide using House Style
3. Create Presentation
4. Save Presentation
5. Add transitions and effects according to House Style
6. Print a copy of slide 4, handout with six slides to the page and outline view
7. Save Slides
8. Print a copy of all slides
9. Close application

Instructions 2

1. Open PowerPoint
2. Open Presentation
3. Alter sequence of slides – move slide 5 to become slide 2
4. Change text in slide Changes to read Changes 1, Changes 2 and Changes 3
5. Insert a new slide 7 between Changes 3 and Questions with a table (3 columns and 3 rows)

Birmingham	Manchester	Brighton
200	340	230
185	295	205

6. Save Revised Presentation

7. Print new slide

8. Close application

Option

Explore using hyperlinks and buttons within the presentation. Hide a slide and use a hyperlink to provide a flexible link to it.

Summary

1. Loading Microsoft PowerPoint

Selecting Start, highlight the Programs option to reveal menu and click on the Microsoft PowerPoint item or click on the PowerPoint icon on the desktop.

2. Save

Select the File menu and the Save option. The Save As window will appear.

3. Blank Presentation

Click in the radio button alongside the Blank Presentation option and then on the OK button. The New Slide window will appear overlaying the PowerPoint application. This allows you to select an initial outline slide on which to build your presentation.

4. Master Slide

Select the View menu, highlight the Master option to reveal a sub-menu. Click on the Slide Master option. The Master Slide template will appear in the PowerPoint work area.

5. Edit Master

To edit the Master (i.e. to change the characteristics) you need to click on the different slide features (e.g. Title) and select the new characteristics (e.g. font, text colour and character size).

6. Background Colour

Select the Format menu and click on the Background option to reveal the Background window. This allows you to choose a background colour for your slides.

7. Date and Time

Select the Insert menu and click on the Date and Time option to reveal the Date and Time window.

8. Page Numbers

Select the Insert Menu and click on the Slide Number option.

9. Font Colour

Select the Font colour icon on the Drawing toolbar and choose your colour.

10. Hyperlinks

Select slide text, click on the Insert menu and select Hyperlink option.

To add hyperlink buttons, click on Slide Show menu, highlight Action buttons option to reveal buttons. Select a button, position it on slide and select action from Action Setting window.

11. Transitions

Select the Slide Show menu and click on the Slide Transition option. This will reveal the Slide Transition window.

12. Animation

Select the Slide Show menu and click on the Custom Animation option. This will reveal the Custom Animation window.

or

Select the Slide Show menu and highlight the Preset Animation option to reveal a list of options.

13. Open An Existing Presentation

Select Open an Existing Presentation option and you may see your presentation in the area below the option. If it is there then you can load it by double clicking on it. If it is not in the area, then click on the OK button to reveal the Open window.

14. New Slide

Select the Insert menu and click on the New Slide option.

15. Manipulate Text and Graphics

The text and graphic areas are enclosed in a box with small squares at the corners and in the centre of each side. These squares allow you to change shape of text area and adjust the position of the text or graphics.

Placing your mouse pointer on the enclosure lines but not on the squares it changes shape to a star. If you hold down the mouse button while the pointer is in this shape you can move the whole text area.

If you place your mouse pointer on the squares it will change shape to a double-headed arrow. If you hold down the mouse button then you can drag the enclosure to change the shape and size of the area.

16. Overview

Select the View menu and click on the Slide Sorter option.

17. Manipulate Slides in Slide Sorter

Highlight the slide to drag it to a new position in the presentation or delete it by pressing the delete key. New slides can be added by clicking the position in which you would like to add a new slide and then selecting the Insert menu and clicking on the New Slide option.

18. Organisation Chart
Select the organisation chart layout from the New Slide window. Double click on the slide to insert the organisational chart. The Microsoft Organisation Chart window will open.

19. Importing Text
Cut or copy text directly between Word and PowerPoint

Send text from Word to PowerPoint directly using the option Send To which is available from the File menu in Word. This reveals a submenu with the option Microsoft PowerPoint. This will change the file into a PowerPoint presentation.

20. Importing Graphics
Select the Insert menu and highlight the Picture option to reveal a submenu of options

21. Find and Replace
Select the Edit menu and click on the Replace option to reveal the Replace window.

22. Spell Checker
Select the Tools menu and click on the Spelling option.

23. Showing a Presentation
Select the View menu and click on Slide Show option.

or

Select the Slide Show menu and click on the View Show option.

or

Click on the Slide Show button in the bottom left hand corner of the display.

24. Printing
Select the File menu and click on the Print option to reveal the Print window.

25. Speakers Notes
When you are creating your slides you can also produce a set of notes using the Slide Notes area below the working area.

26. Close Application
Select the File menu and click on the Exit option or click on the Close button in the top right hand corner of the application window.

27. Chart/Graph

Select a chart slide template and doubleclick on the chart/graph placeholder to reveal a chart and its corresponding datasheet. Enter your data to produce a new chart.

To insert a Microsoft Excel Chart select the Insert menu and click on the Object option to reveal the Insert Object window.

28. Speakers Notes

Click on the area below the slide working area labelled Click to add notes. Enter your notes.

You can print your notes by using the Print option in the File menu. The Print what: allow you to select Notes Pages.

29. House Styles

Many organisations have developed standards for their presentations. This ensures a consistency and quality in the use of them. To ensure standards it is often useful to develop a Master slide. Many organisations provide a master slide. Many organisations provise a master slide to ensure their standards are adhered to. Standards are often called house styles.

Computer Art

This chapter will help you to:

- Create artwork incorporating text and images in layers

- Edit and retouch scanned images

- Use a variety of graphic effects

- Create an animated image for electronic media

- Prepare artwork for print/electronic publication

This chapter covers Unit 6 (Computer Art). There are no pre-conditions for studying this unit. However, its content does assume that you have the skills and understanding which are provided by the OCR Level 1 ICT course New CLAIT (e.g. Unit 8 - Computer Art and Unit 1 – Using a Computer).

Assessment

After studying Unit 6 your skills and understanding are assessed during a 3 hour practical assignment. This is set by OCR and marked locally. However, the marking will be externally moderated by OCR. This ensures that the standard is being applied correctly across the many different providers of OCR CLAIT Plus. If you are unsuccessful then you can be re-assessed using a different assignment.

CorelDRAW

This chapter is based on CorelDRAW 10 which is a vector based graphics package. This means that you can create artwork using a variety of tools. You can produce posters, book covers, web page graphics and animations as well as a variety of other illustrations. CorelDRAW 10 consists of three applications. These are: CorelPHOTO-PAINT 10, CorelDRAW 10 and Corel R.A.V.E. You need to use all three as part of this chapter.

Figure 230 shows the CorelDRAW interface. This resembles many other windows based applications in that it consists of:

- A work area
- A menu bar
- Toolbars (Figures 231and 232)

The major visual difference is that there are toolbars down both edges of the work area. The left edge toolbar consists of a series of drawing tools (Figure 233) while the right toolbar is a colour palette (Figure 234).

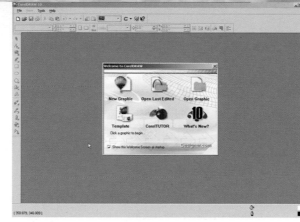

FIGURE 230
CorelDRAW

CorelDRAW allows you to measure precisely the size of artwork that you are creating. Figure 231 shows that you can set the dimensions of the artwork in terms of page sizes (e.g. A4) or in exact measures in a wide variety of units including millimetres, centimetres, inches and pixels. The page size is adjusted using the small down arrow next to the page box

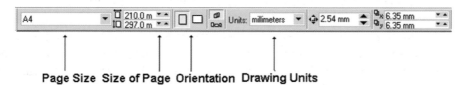

Page Size Size of Page Orientation Drawing Units

FIGURE 231
Toolbars

which reveals a list of options. These are chosen by clicking on them. The dimensions can be adjusted using the up and down arrows which directly change them. The toolbar also allows you to change the orientation of the page between portrait and landscape. This toolbar changes to provide other options when different drawing tools are chosen. Explore the different options when you load the application.

The quality of an image is dependent on its resolution. A high resolution will allow the image to convey fine detail. However, to convey fine detail on paper requires a good printer. The quality of a printer is given in the number of dots per inch (dpi). This is frequently given as 300dpi. There are printers that can produce far higher dots per inch. Clearly the more dots that can be printed, the higher quality the image. However, a high quality printer will not overcome a low resolution image. To produce the best quality requires both a high resolution image and a good printer.

Artwork is not only designed to be displayed on paper but also for web pages. Images for web pages are specified in the form of pixels. The maximum width of an image for a web page is 640 pixels since this allows most users to see it without horizontal scrolling. You can make them far wider but the viewers will need to scroll from side to side to see the whole picture.

Figure 232 shows the standard functions many of which appear on other Windows applications such as new, open, print, cut, copy, paste, undo and redo. In addition you can also import and export images using other tools. A useful function is Help which will provide you with an explanation of the tools purpose.

FIGURE 232
Standard Toolbar

New | Print | Undo
Open | Cut | Redo | Zoom | Help
Save | Copy | Import
Paste | Export

FIGURE 233
Drawing Tools

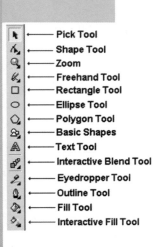

Pick Tool
Shape Tool
Zoom
Freehand Tool
Rectangle Tool
Ellipse Tool
Polygon Tool
Basic Shapes
Text Tool
Interactive Blend Tool
Eyedropper Tool
Outline Tool
Fill Tool
Interactive Fill Tool

Figure 233 shows you the range of drawing tools. CorelDRAW assists you to draw straight and curved lines, rectangles, ellipses, polygons and other shapes. You can add colour to your drawings (e.g. Fill Tool) as well as text. In essence you can do many tasks which would normally require a skilled artist even though you lack many of his skills. The colour palette (Figure 234) is a natural companion to the drawing tools in that you select the colours for your lines and fills from the palette. At the bottom of the palette is a down arrow button that allows you to scroll down the list of colours and a left pointing arrow which will reveal the whole palette as three lines of colours. Again explore these options when you load the application.

CorelPHOTO-PAINT also has a toolbar down the left hand side of the work area and you should explore these when you first encounter it. In both applications some tool icons have an arrow in the bottom right hand corner. This indicates that if you click on the icon then a series of other tools will pop out. These are all relates but it is sometimes puxzzling to locate a tool until you become familiar with the application.

FIGURE 234
Colour Palette

Image Size

Corel Draw allows you to set the size of your artwork in terms of the page size. However, it is also possible to create an image and define its precise size. In order to do this you need to use Corel Photo-Paint 10. When the application loads it displays an overlay window with six choices similar to Corel Draw click on New Image to reveal the Create a New Image window.

The window allows you to define the size of the image using the Width, Height and Resolution boxes. The higher the resolution the more detail that the image can show when it is printed. The image can be copied and pasted into a Corel Draw document.

Design Brief

The creation of artwork is often controlled by a design brief which specifies the nature of the images, layout and structure. Figure 235 shows a simple design brief. This suggests that a background image will provide a foundation

FIGURE 235
Design Brief

on to which two text boxes and an image are placed. All these different objects are part of a single layer. They can be moved around and even stacked on top of each other. More layers can be added to form the artwork. This has the advantage that each individual layer can be edited separately. Complex designs can be created using layers.

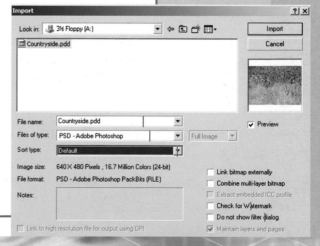

Exercise 33

New Artwork

1. CorelDRAW is opened by either selecting the Start button, highlighting the Programs option, then highlighting the CorelDRAW option to reveal a submenu and clicking on the CorelDRAW 10 item or by double clicking on the CorelDRAW icon on the Windows desktop.

FIGURE 236
New Graphics

2. The initial display is shown in Figure 230 which reveals an overlay with six options in the form of icons. If you place your mouse pointer over the icons a brief explanation of each is displayed. Click on the New Graphic icon since we are going to take the first steps to producing a poster. This will open a page within the working area of the application (Figure 236).

3. Notice that the size of the page is A4 (i.e. 210 x 297 mm). The position of the pointer is shown on the rulers (i.e. across the top and left side of the work area) as a dotted line which moves as the pointer does. This assists you to accurately place objects on the page. Location of the pointer is also indicated by numbers in the bottom left hand corner of the display. This uses an axis similar to a graph with two axes (e.g. x and y).

FIGURE 237
Import Window

4. You are going to create a poster so the size of the page needs to change. Click on the down arrow button alongside the page box (i.e. A4) to reveal a list of

FIGURE 238
**Import
Pointer**

Countryside.pdd

options. Choose A1, which is a poster-sized page. The poster is for a village fete. The background is a photograph taken with a digital camera near to the village.

5. The image can be imported by clicking on the Import icon on the toolbar. This opens the Import window (Figure 237). Change the Look in: box to the folder in which your background image is stored. In my case, the Countryside image is stored on a floppy disk. Observe the nature of the image – it is 640 x 480 pixels and is based on 16.7 million colours. To import the picture into the poster you need to click on the Import button again.

6. The Import window will disappear and the mouse pointer will change as shown as in Figure 238. This allows you to position the image precisely on the page. Place the new pointer in the top left-hand corner and click. The countryside image will appear enclosed in a frame which enables you to drag the edges of the image and thus change its size. Figure 239 shows three

FIGURE 239
**Imported
Image**

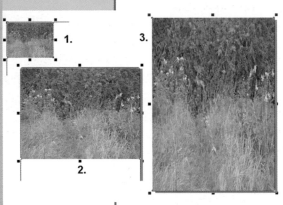

stages in altering the countryside picture. Number one is the initial image. This is expanded by placing the pointer over one of the black squares in the frame. The pointer will change shape to become a double headed arrow. By holding down the mouse button you can drag the image's edge to form a new size filling the top of the page. This is shown in image number two. However, we want the picture to provide a background for the poster so it needs to grow to fill the bottom of the page. This is again achieved using the pointer to drag the bottom edge of the image to produce image number 3.

7. When you drag the image into a shape that is not its natural one (in this case turning a square into a rectangle) the image will distort to some extent. You need to judge the degree of distortion. In this case you are creating a countryside background so it is not important that leaves or other objects in the picture are elongated. The important thing is that a rural image is presented. If the distortion is too great you need to think again about your design.

FIGURE 240
**Save
Drawing**

8. If you place your mouse pointer on the centre of the image (the centre is marked to help you locate it) you will see the pointer change shape to a star. If you hold down the mouse button, you can move the whole image and precisely position it.

9. Save the poster by selecting the File menu and clicking on the Save option. The Save Drawing

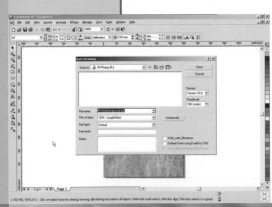

window will appear (Figure 240). You need to change the Save in box to the location you want to store the poster. Enter Posterbackground.cdr into the file name box and then click on the Save button.

10. The design brief asks you to insert an image in the bottom right-hand corner of the poster. This is the logo of the Village Fete committee. The logo can be imported by clicking on the Import icon on the toolbar. This opens the Import window (Figure 237). Change the Look in: box to the folder in which your logo is stored then locate and highlight it. In my case the logo image is stored on a floppy disk. To import the picture into the poster you need to click on the Import button.

FIGURE 241
Logo Position

11. Position the logo in the bottom right hand corner of the poster using the pointer to adjust its size and position (Figure 241).

12. The design brief requires that you place two text boxes on to the poster. The Text Tool is available on the Drawing Toolbar (left hand side of the work area). Click on the Text Tool and the pointer will change to a cross hair and the letter A. The cross hair allows you to position the text box by clicking and holding down the button and dragging the box open. Position the boxes as shown in the design brief (Figure 235).

FIGURE 242
Horizontal Alignment

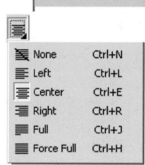

≣ None	Ctrl+N
≣ Left	Ctrl+L
≣ Center	Ctrl+E
≣ Right	Ctrl+R
≣ Full	Ctrl+J
≣ Force Full	Ctrl+H

13. You can now enter text into the boxes. If you place your pointer into the box then it changes shape to a cursor to let you select where to enter text by clicking. A cursor flashes at the chosen position. The text boxes are shown by a broken outline. If you click on the text box then it becomes enclosed in a frame with small black squares. This allows you to reshape and move the text box in the same way you move an image. Select the colour yellow for your text (click on the yellow colour on the palette (right-hand side of work area)), select a font and set the character size to 200. Enter across the top of the poster – Village Fete. Centre the text using the horizontal alignment icon on the toolbar (Figure 242).

FIGURE 243
Poster

14. Now enter the following text into the central text box in yellow, character size 150 using a font of your choice. On separate lines enter

Saturday

17 June

2 to 5pm

FIGURE 244
Layer

Text	Text	Logo
Background		

FIGURE 244A
Object Manager

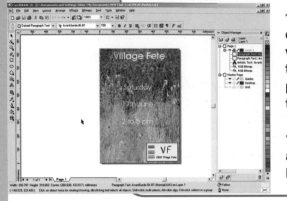

Notice that the lines of text are separated by a blank line. The final poster should look like Figure 243.

15. Save the poster by selecting the File menu and clicking on the Save As option. The Save Drawing window will appear (Figure 240). You need to change the Save in box to the location you want to store the poster and enter Poster.cdr into the file name box, then click on the Save button.

16. Close the application by selecting the File menu and click on the Exit option or click on the close button in the top right hand corner of the application.

Layers

In producing the Village Fete poster you have created a layer. Figure 244 shows the layer and its different objects (e.g. logo).

Objects can be moved over each other and when combined are useful devices to create artwork. Extra layers can be added with varying degrees of transparency so that different things can be seen through from other layers. You might have created your poster with a background layer, a text layer and a logo layer. Each could then be independently edited. This is rather like designing three overhead transparency slides and placing them on top of each other to create complex images.

It is possible to create a master layer containing the images that would appear on every page of a long document (e.g. logo, copyright statements etc.). This would save time and guarantee a consistent image.

Layers can be managed using the Object Manager, available by selecting the Tools menu and clicking on the Object Manager which will open the Object Manager window (Figure 244A).

The Object Manager shows the single layer and the objects associated with it. You can add layers by selecting the new layer icon in the bottom left hand corner (Figure 244B). The Figure displays a blank master layer.

FIGURE 244B
New Layer

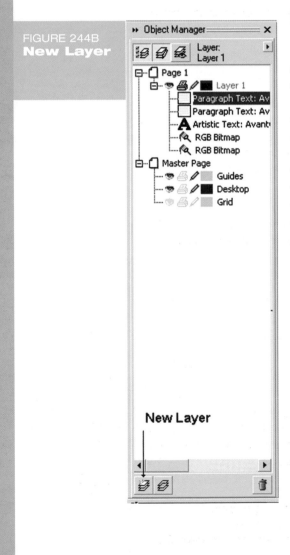

New Layer

Against each layer in the object manager you will notice some icons. If you place your pointer over them you will see that they are labelled. In order, they are visibility, printing, editing and master. You can select to make your layer visible, editable etc.

Mask

Masks is another method like layers than allows you to develop complex and engaging artwork. It lets you hide parts of a layer or allow other layers to be seen. Masks work by varying the degree of transparency across the layer. A mask can have holes in it so that you can edit the visible areas. In some cases you might want to remove a portion of your image. Once you delete an area, it is essentially permanently removed whereas a mask allows you to change your mind or make small adjustments.

If you have a multiple layer image with each layer having an associated mask then you can build up very complex graphics. However, to achieve this level of skills will require a great amount of practice.

There are a number of different types of masks such as:

• Empty masks which cover the whole underlying image

• Selection masks are empty masks with a hole in them so you can see the a part of the underlying image (e.g. you might create a mask with a circular hole through which the image can be seen)

• Image masks are those made from another image so one image will overlay another. You can create complex effects by placing one image on top of another and by employing the transparency tools.

Exercise 34

Stacking and Masking

1. CorelDRAW is opened by either selecting the Start button, highlighting Programs option, then highlighting the CorelDRAW option to reveal a submenu and clicking on CorelDRAW 10 item or by double clicking on the CorelDRAW icon on the Windows desktop.

2. The initial display shows an overlay with six options in the form of icons. If you place your mouse pointer over the icons, a brief explanation of each is displayed. Click on the Open Graphic icon to reveal the

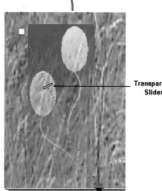

Transparency Slider

FIGURE 244C
New Layer

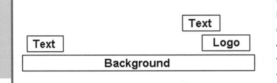

Transparency Type   Starting Transparency

Open Drawing window. Change the folder in the Look in: box to the one in which you stored the Poster artwork. Enter Poster.cdr in the File name: box and click on the Open button.

3. The Poster artwork will appear in the work area of CorelDRAW.

4. Click on the centre of the middle text box (i.e. Saturday). The pointer will change shape to a star and you can move the box by holding down the mouse button. Move the box until it overlays the logo. Notice what happens – you should be able to see through the text box while the text appears to be on top of the logo. This illustrates the stacking effect (Figure 245).

FIGURE 245
New Order

5. Experiment with moving the logo on top of the text box and any other combinations until you are clear about moving images and text boxes and understand the nature of stacking.

6. Do not save the changes.

7. You are now going to practise adding a new layer to the poster by selecting the Tools menu and clicking on the Object Manager option. This will open the object manager window on the right of the work area. Click on your poster to highlight it (i.e. enclose it) then select the New Layer icon in the bottom left-hand corner of the window (Figure 244B). Layer 2 will be added to the window. No obvious change will happen to your poster since the layer is transparent.

8. Next let's import an image of some balloons to the poster in the bottom left hand corner of your new layer. Select the Interactive Transparency Tool and click with it on the top left hand corner of the balloons image. Holding down the mouse button, drag the pointer to the bottom right hand corner. The pointer will change shape to a black square and an arrow and a diagonal line will be drawn across the rectangle. A white bar will be placed across the line and the transparency of the image will have changed. If you click on the bar you can drag it along the diagonal line to increase or reduce transparency and reveal the layer below (Figure 244C). This illustrates the potential of adding layers and masking images.

FIGURE 246
**Selecting a
Source**

9. If you wanted to apply a uniform level of transparency across an image then you need to select the Uniform transparency type from the toolbar (having selected the Interactive Transparency Tool) and the Starting Transparency level (e.g. 50%). Notice that by selecting a tool a new toolbar appears. This is often the case and can be initially confusing. There are a variety of other transparency tools to explore. Try the different options.

10. There is no need to save your revised poster but you are free to save it to another file name.

11. Layers, stacking and masks all require a considerable amount of practice to develop your skill. Experiment with the tools and the poster or another image you have. Add layers, vary the transparency and mask the images. Try to be creative but keep notes of what is effective.

12. Close the application by selecting the File menu and click on the Exit option or click on the close button in the top right hand corner of the application

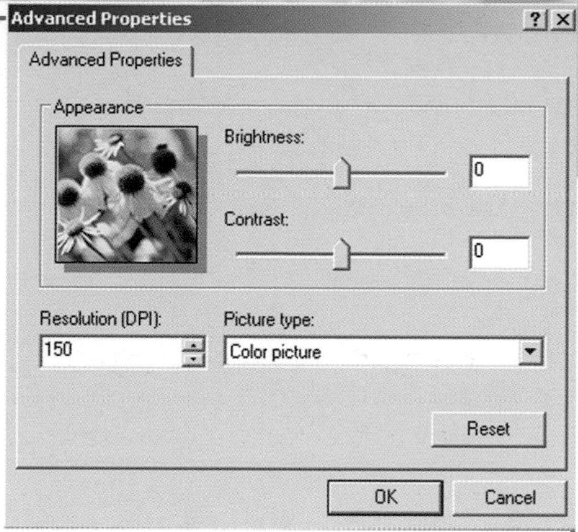

FIGURE 247
Advanced Properties Window

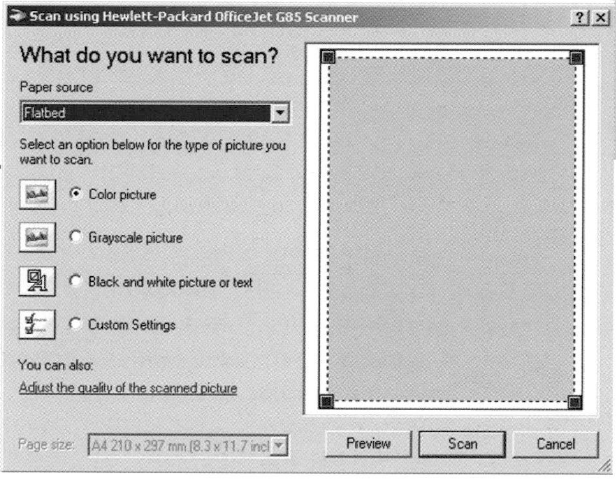

Scanning an Image

CorelDRAW allows you to scan an image if you have a scanner connected to your computer. If you select the File menu and highlight Acquire Image you will reveal

FIGURE 248
Scan Window

a submenu. Click on the Select Source option and a list of sources will appear (Figure 246). You select the option (e.g. scanner) you intend to use.

To import an image from the scanner, next select the File menu, highlight Acquire Image and click on the Acquire option to reveal the Scan using .... (whatever scanner you are linked to). Figure 248 shows my window (Scan using Hewlett-Packard OfficeJet G85 Scanner.

The window provides you with a range of options for scanning different content:
• Colour Pictures
• Greyscale picture
• Black and white picture or text
• Custom settings

Greyscale is a colour picture with each colour shown by a different shade of grey. The options available will depend on the type of scanner that you have attached to your computer.

FIGURE 249
Scanned Image

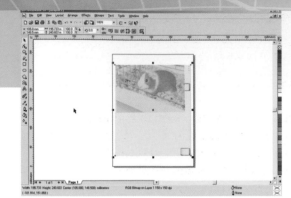

There is also an option to adjust the quality of the scanned image (Figure 247). If you click on this option then Advanced Properties window will appear (Figure 248) in which you can adjust the resolution (dots per inch), brightness and contrast. If you move the sliders then you can see the effects immediately in the Appearance area.

Exercise 35

Scanning an Image

FIGURE 250
Cropping an Image

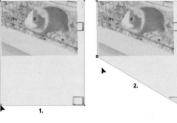

1. CorelDRAW is opened by either selecting the Start button, highlighting the Programs option, then highlighting the CorelDRAW option to reveal a submenu and clicking on CorelDRAW 10 item or by double clicking on the CorelDRAW icon on the Windows desktop.

2. The initial display is shown in Figure 230 which reveals an overlay with six options in the form of icons. Click on the New Graphic icon. This will open a page within the working area of the application (Figure 236). The scanning options are only available when a graphic is being created.

3. Select the File Menu, highlight Acquire Image and click on the Select Source option to reveal the Select Source window. Select the scanner of your choice.

4. Select the File Menu, highlight Acquire Image and click on the Acquire option to reveal the Scan window. If you have a preview option employ it to view your image. Adjust the scan options to produce the image of your choice. Scan the image as a colour picture. You will probably see a variety of messages telling you that data is being transferred.

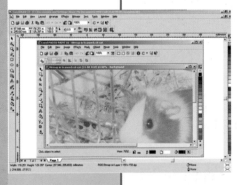

5. When the transfer is completed you will see your scanned images appear on the artwork page (Figure 249).

6. In our case the image of the Guinea Pig includes a large area of blank space which needs to be removed. This is achieved using the Shape Tool by clicking on it. The image will change to show small squares at each corner and the pointer will take the form of an arrow. If you click on the small squares you

FIGURE 251
Bitmap Editor

can move them to new positions, cropping the image. Figure 250 shows the steps.

Dust and Scratch

Threshold: |_____| 0   Radius: |_____| 3

Reset   OK   Cancel   Help

FIGURE 252
Dust Scratches

7. Save the scanned image by selecting the File menu and clicking on the Save option. The Save Drawing window will appear. You need to change the Save in box to the location you want to store the picture and enter Scanned.cdr into the file name box then click on the Save button.

8. The image can be edited by selecting the Bitmaps menu and clicking on the Edit Bitmap. This opens the editing window (Figure 251). This is within Corel PHOTO-PAINT 10 and provides access to more tools and effects.

9. When you scan old pictures they are often scratched and/or dusty. Corel PHOTO-PAINT provides the means to remove them. Select the Effects menu, highlight the Noise item and click on Dust and Scratches to reveal the Dust and Scratch window (Figure 252). The window asks you to set two variables - threshold and radius. These are interactive settings so

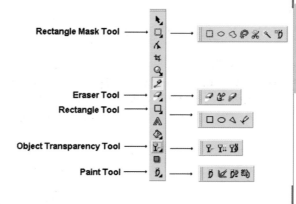

FIGURE 253
Corel PHOTO-PAINT 10 Tools

Rectangle Mask Tool →
Eraser Tool →
Rectangle Tool →
Object Transparency Tool →
Paint Tool →

that as you move the slider with the mouse you can see the effects on the picture below the window. Experiment with the two controls. There is a slight delay between moving the sliders and seeing the change. In my case the best setting for radius is 1 and threshold is 0.

10. Many photographs show red eye (i.e. light reflected from the person or animals eyes make them look red). You can remove this by replacing the red with another colour. Select the Effects menu, highlight the Color Transform item and click on Red Eye Removal and a warning message will tell you that you need a mask which is an area of the image that you have designated. You can select the whole image as a mask from the Mask menu and the Select All option or identify an area using the Rectangle Mask Tool which provides a variety other ways of defining an area. This tool is on the left hand toolbar (Figure 253).

11. Several of the tools have a small diagonal arrow head that tells you a range of other options are available if you place your pointer on the icon and hold down the button (Figure 253).

12. Explore the different tools (if you place your pointer over each tool it will be labelled). Try to add colour using the different paint brushes, experiment with the transparency tools and the mask tools. The Effects brush is

FIGURE 253A
Color Transparency Tool

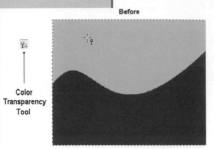

Before

Color Transparency Tool

After

FIGURE 254
Hue/ Saturation/ Lightness

particularly interesting while the Clone brush is also worth exploring. Use the undo and redo tools on the toolbar to correct any errors. There are a wide range of tools so systematically consider what happens with each tool. You can apply colour by clicking on the palette and then the brush or fill tool. When you select a tool you will notice that the horizontal toolbar changes providing even more options. Those associated with the Paint Tools are also worth exploring (e.g. many different paint effects).

13. Explore the different colour effects within the Effects menu and Color Transform option.

14. Explore the other options within the Effects menu

15. It is often necessary to remove the background from pictures. Corel Photo-Paint provides a variety of methods to undertake this task. One useful tool is the Color Transparency Tool which samples a colour and replaces it any where in the picture with transparency. This tool does not require that you click and drag. Simply to click on the colour you want to replace. You can use the tool multiple times to turn several colours transparent. Experiment with this tool on an image with a background (e.g. lots of sky). Create a new image and import a suitable picture into it.

16. A colour consists of three components – hue, saturation and lightness. With CorelPHOTO-PAINT you can alter each of them. Select the Image menu and highlight Adjust then click on Hue/Saturation/Lightness to reveal the Hue/Saturation/Lightness window (Figure 254). As you move the three sliders you can see the changes both in the Before and After images and also in the scanned image. Experiment with the different combinations.

17. You can correct colours (i.e. change a colour) using the Image menu, Adjust and then options such as Color Tone, Color Hue and Replace Colors. Explore – Hue and Tone allow you to experiment.

18. There are many different tools and options to try so experiment until you are confident that you are able to locate each tool and understand its purpose. If you create any impressive images save them and keep notes of your experiments.

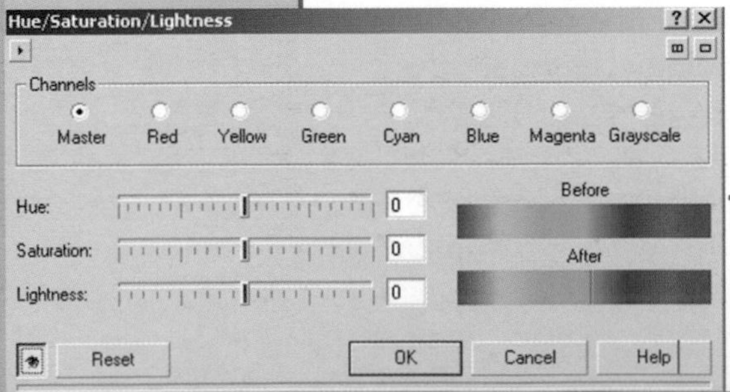

19. Close the application by selecting the File menu and click on the Exit option or click on the close button in the top right hand corner of the application.

Hue/Saturation/Lightness

Channels
Master   Red   Yellow   Green   Cyan   Blue   Magenta   Grayscale

Hue: 0

Saturation: 0

Lightness: 0

Before

After

Reset   OK   Cancel   Help

Format Text (Colour and Shape)

You have already seen that you can enter text in a wide variety of fonts, character sizes and colours. In addition you can rotate, sketch, skew and transform text.

FIGURE 255
Text

Exercise 36

Text

1. CorelDRAW is opened by either selecting the Start button, highlighting Programs option, then highlighting the CorelDRAW option to reveal a submenu and clicking on CorelDRAW 10 item or by double clicking on the CorelDRAW icon on the Windows desktop.

FIGURE 256
Rotating the Text

2. The initial display is shown in Figure 230 which reveals an overlay with six options in the form of icons. Click on the New Graphic icon. A new page will be inserted within the working area of the application.

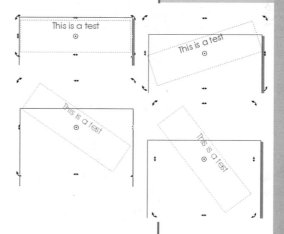

3. Click on the Text Tool and create a text frame across the top of the page occupying about a quarter of the page. Select a font and set character size to 48. Enter This is a test. Highlight the text and select the colour red from the palette – you will see your text change colour. Centre the text using the Horizontal Alignment tool (Figure 255).

4. You can rotate text by selecting the Pick Tool and clicking with it on to the text frame. The text frame will now be enclosed with arrows at the corners showing how to rotate the box by dragging with the mouse – the pointer changes to a circle. Figure 256 shows the box being rotated.

FIGURE 257
Skewing

5. There are also double-headed arrows in the middle of the top and bottom lines of the text box with these you can skew the text using the mouse – the pointer changes to two opposed arrows. Figure 257 show the effect. By combining rotating and skewing you can produce interesting effects.

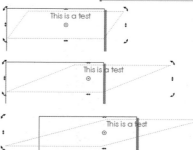

6. You can also transform your text by selecting the <u>A</u>rrange menu and highlight <u>T</u>ransformations to reveal a submenu of options (Figure 258).

7. Explore the options.

FIGURE 258
Arrange Menu

Arrange		
Transformations	▶	Position Alt+F7
🔄 Clear Transformations		Rotate Alt+F8
⊟ Align and Distribute...		Scale Alt+F9
Order	▶	Size Alt+F10
🌟 Group	Ctrl+G	Skew
🔀 Ungroup	Ctrl+U	
×🔀 Ungroup All		
🔳 Combine	Ctrl+L	
🔳 Break Paragraph Text: AvantGarde Bk BT (Normal) (UK) Apart	Ctrl+K	
🔒 Lock Object		
🔓 Unlock Object		
🔓 Unlock All Objects		
Shaping	▶	
○ Convert To Curves	Ctrl+Q	
◇ Convert Outline To Object	Ctrl+Shift+Q	

8. Continue to experiment until you are confident that you can rotate, skew and transform text.

9. You can also enter text using the Freehand Tool. Essentially you are sketching with an electronic pen. This can be very effective if you adjust the width of the tools nib (i.e. outline width tool on the horizontal toolbar or use the Artistic Media Tool – Figure 259). Explore the options until you are satisfied you can draw text this way.

10. Close the application by selecting the File menu and click on Exit or click on the close button in the top right hand corner of the application.

Artistic Text

FIGURE 259
Sketching

CorelDRAW also contains another form of text called Artistic Text. Select the Text Tool and simply click within the drawing area and enter your text. A cursor like a line will appear to show you where the text will be entered. This is called an insertion marker. Once you have finished entering text it will be enclosed in a frame. This allows you to move, rotate and skew your text in the normal way. If you drag artistic text you can produce remarkable effects.

Freehand Tool

Artistic Media Tool

Changing Width of Tool

You can change the two types into each other by clicking on the text with the Pick tool and selecting the Text menu then the Convert to Paragraph Text or Convert to Artistic Text.

You can apply special effects to artistic text. One of the most interesting is extruding text with which you can turn 2 D text into what appears to be 3 D. To extrude text you need to select the Interactive Extrude Tool. You click and drag on the text and you will see the text extend (Figure 259a).

FIGURE 259A
Extruding Text

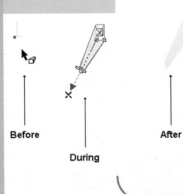

Before

During

After

Exercise 37

Graphic Effects

1. CorelDRAW is opened by either selecting the Start button, highlighting Programs option, then highlighting the CorelDRAW option to reveal a submenu and clicking on CorelDRAW 10 item or by double clicking on the CorelDRAW icon on the Windows desktop.

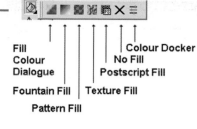

FIGURE 260
Fill Options

2. The initial display reveals an overlay with six options in the form of icons. Click on the New Graphic icon. A new page will be inserted within the working area of the application.

3. Set the size of the page to 120 x 100 mm using the toolbar controls.

4. Click on the Rectangle Drawing tool and draw a rectangle covering the whole area of the page. Ensure that it is enclosed in a frame (i.e. highlighted so the fill tool can operate on the rectangle). Click on a colour in the palette and you will see the rectangle fill with the chosen colour. Remove the colour using the undo icon on the toolbar.

FIGURE 261
**Fill
Patterns**

5. Click on the Fill Tool and hold down the mouse button. You will see a number of different Fill options (Figure 260). Select the Pattern fill option and you will reveal Pattern Fill window (Figure 261) which provides a variety of patterns to fill the rectangle. Pick one and click on the OK button. The rectangle will fill with that pattern. Undo this fill using the undo icon and explore the other options.

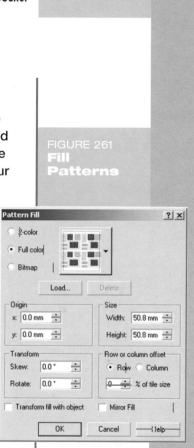

6. Finally, fill the rectangle with a solid colour. Now select the <u>B</u>itmaps menu and click on Convert to Bitmaps to reveal a small window Convert to Bitmap. Click on the OK button, select <u>B</u>itmaps menu and click on <u>E</u>dit Bitmap. The Corel PHOTO-PAINT will open. Maximise the windows to fill the display.

7. Select the Rectangle tool and draw a small rectangle in the middle of your image. Enclose it in a frame (i.e. highlight). Now select the Object Transparency Tool. The pointer will change to a cross hair with a small wine glass. Place the pointer in one corner of the new rectangle and holding down the button, drag the pointer to the opposite diagonal corner. Right click your mouse button and a menu will appear. Click on Apply. You will see that your rectangle now has different degrees of transparency across the diagonal (Figure 262). This is essentially a masking technique.

8. Close Corel PHOTO-PAINT (select the <u>F</u>ile menu and the E<u>x</u>it option) to return to CorelDRAW.

FIGURE 262
Transparency

9. There are various other effects. One of the most used is Drop Shadow. If you open a new page (select the <u>F</u>ile menu and click on the <u>N</u>ew option) a blank page will appear in the middle of the work area. Set the size of the page to 100 x 100 mm.

10. Click on the ellipse tool and draw a circle in the top left hand corner of the page. With the circle

FIGURE 263
**Drop
Shadow**

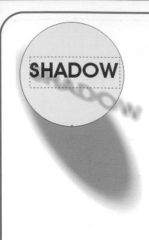

highlighted (i.e. enclosed in a frame) click on the yellow colour and the circle will fill with yellow. Now select the Text Tool and draw a rectangular text box across the circle. Enter the word SHADOW in a font and size that will fit the box. Embolden your text if it looks better.

11. With the text box highlighted (i.e. enclosed in a frame) select the Interactive Drop Shadow Tool. The pointer changes to a large arrow and rectangle. Click on the left hand corner of the text box and holding down the mouse button, drag the pointer down and diagonally. This will produce the shadow of the text and allow you to change the angle to produce the effect you desire. Experiment and see what you can create. If you are not happy remember that you can use undo to start again.

FIGURE 264
**Corel
R.A.V.E**

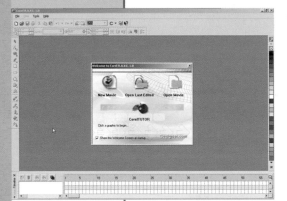

12. You can also form shadows of objects other than text. Click on the circle to enclose it in a frame. Select the Interactive Drop Shadow Tool. Click on the edge of the circle, hold down the button and drag the pointer away to produce a circle shadow. Figure 263 shows my efforts.

13. Save the image by selecting the File menu and clicking on the Save option. The Save Drawing window will appear. You need to change the Save in box to the location you want to store the picture and enter Effects.cdr into the file name box then click on the Save button.

14. Experiment with the different effects until you are confident.

15. Close CorelDRAW (select the File menu and the Exit option)

Animation

CorelDRAW has an additional feature to allow you to create animations using the Corel R.A.V.E (Real Animated Vector Effects) tool. Figure 264 shows the application. It is almost identical to the CorelDRAW application except that at the bottom of the application window is the timeline which you can control the speed of the animation.

FIGURE 265
**Animation
Frames**

Animations are composed of a series of individual frames (i.e. images) which are quickly changed so that a movement effect is produced. The aim is to produce an attractive and eye catching display. They are often placed on websites to advertise features or products. Figure 265 shows a series of frames.

Exercise 38

Simple Animation

1. Corel R.A.V.E is opened by either selecting the Start button, highlighting Programs option, then highlighting the CorelDRAW option to reveal a submenu and clicking on Corel R.A.V.E 1.0 item. Alternatively, load CorelDRAW and select the Application Launcher (Figure 266) to reveal the Corel family of applications. Click on Corel R.A.V.E.

2. The initial display reveals an overlay with four options in the form of icons. Click on the New Movie icon. This will open a page within the working area of the application.

3. Set the size of the frame to 500 x 500 pixels.

4. CLAIT Plus does not require you to produce the graphics and text that you will use to create individual frames. They will be provided for the assessment along with a design brief for you to follow. However, in this exercise you will be producing some simple frames around which to develop the animation.

5. Select the Rectangle tool and draw a rectangle covering the whole frame and click on the yellow colour to fill it (remember that the rectangle must be highlighted – enclosed in its frame).

6. Now observe the timeline at the bottom of the display. You will see a rectangle has been added to the left of the timeline and a black circle to the timeline items. Figure 267 shows the before and after effect on the timeline of creating the first frame.

7. Now click on the black spot which represents the yellow rectangle and drag it to the fifth line. This makes the yellow rectangle the background for the other frames.

8. To create the second frame click on the next line

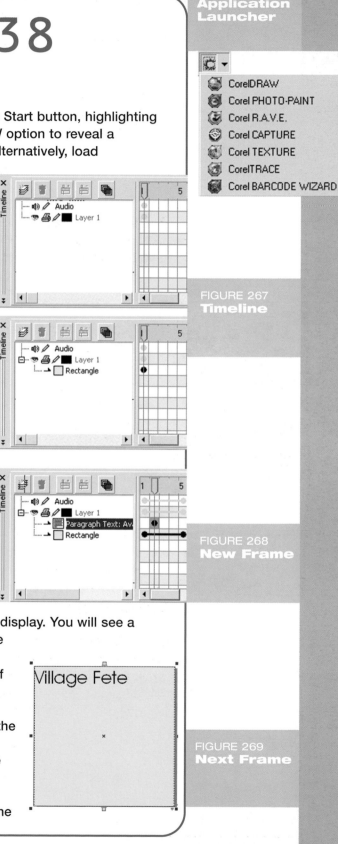

FIGURE 266
Application Launcher

FIGURE 267
Timeline

FIGURE 268
New Frame

FIGURE 269
Next Frame

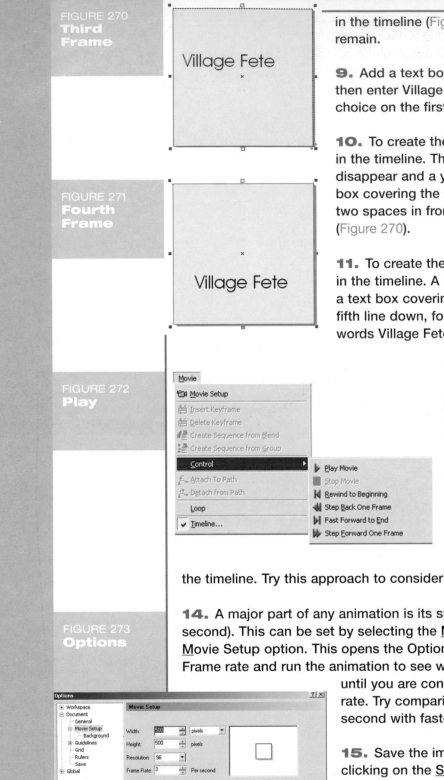

FIGURE 270
Third Frame

Village Fete

FIGURE 271
Fourth Frame

Village Fete

FIGURE 272
Play

Movie

- Movie Setup
- Insert Keyframe
- Delete Keyframe
- Create Sequence from Blend
- Create Sequence from Group
- Control ▶
  - ▶ Play Movie
  - Stop Movie
  - Rewind to Beginning
  - Step Back One Frame
  - Fast Forward to End
  - Step Forward One Frame
- Attach To Path
- Detach from Path
- Loop
- ✓ Timeline...

FIGURE 273
Options

Options

- Workspace
- Document
  - General
  - Movie Setup
    - Background
  - Guidelines
  - Grid
  - Rulers
  - Save
- Global

Movie Setup

Width: 500 | pixels
Height: 500 | pixels
Resolution: 96
Frame Rate: 3 | Per second

Set From Document

OK   Cancel   Help

in the timeline (Figure 268). The yellow rectangle will remain.

9. Add a text box covering the whole frame and then enter Village Fete in a font and size of your choice on the first line (Figure 269).

10. To create the third frame click on the next line in the timeline. The yellow Village Fete rectangle will disappear and a yellow frame will appear. Add a text box covering the whole frame. Enter on the third line, two spaces in from the edge, the words Village Fete (Figure 270).

11. To create the fourth frame click on the next line in the timeline. A blank yellow frame will appear. Add a text box covering the whole frame. Enter on the fifth line down, four spaces in from the edge, the words Village Fete (Figure 271).

12. To play your animation select the Movie menu, highlight the Control option and click on Play Movie (Figure 272). Observe what happens with the frames and timeline. You can stop the animation by selecting the Movie menu, highlight Control and click on Stop Movie

13. Page through the animation frames by clicking on each line of the timeline. Try this approach to consider each frame.

14. A major part of any animation is its speed (i.e. number of frames per second). This can be set by selecting the Movie menu and clicking on the Movie Setup option. This opens the Options window (Figure 273). Change the Frame rate and run the animation to see what happens. Keep experimenting until you are confident that you can adjust the frame rate. Try comparing slow rates (i.e. 3 frames per second with faster rates (i.e. 20 frames per second).

15. Save the image by selecting the File menu and clicking on the Save option. The Save Drawing window will appear. You need to change the Save in box to the location you want to store the picture and enter VillageFeteMovie.clk into the file name box then click on the Save button.

FIGURE 274
Background

16. There is an alternative to creating a background frame. It requires you to open the Option window (Figure 273) and click on Background (left hand side of the display) to open another element of the Options window (Figure 274). You can set the background as a solid colour or as a bitmap image.

17. Close Corel R.A.V.E and CorelDRAW by selecting the File menu and the Exit option for each application.

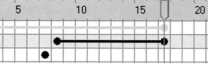

Timing of the Display

Using Corel R.A.V.E allows you can set the frame rate of the animation.

For example:

10 frames per second means that each frame is shown for 0.1 second. You can increase this display time for an individual frame by dragging the frame across several time lines since each one represents 0.1 second. If you drag the frame across ten lines it will display for a second (Figure 275). You are actually creating ten identical frames but it has the same overall effect.

FIGURE 275
Timeline

The display time of each line depends on the frame rate you have set.

For example:

2 frames per second – each line is 0.5 seconds
5 frame per second – each line is 0.2 seconds
10 frames per second – each line is 0.1 seconds

The bitmaps used in Exercise 39 were drawn using Windows Paint.

FIGURE 276
Importing

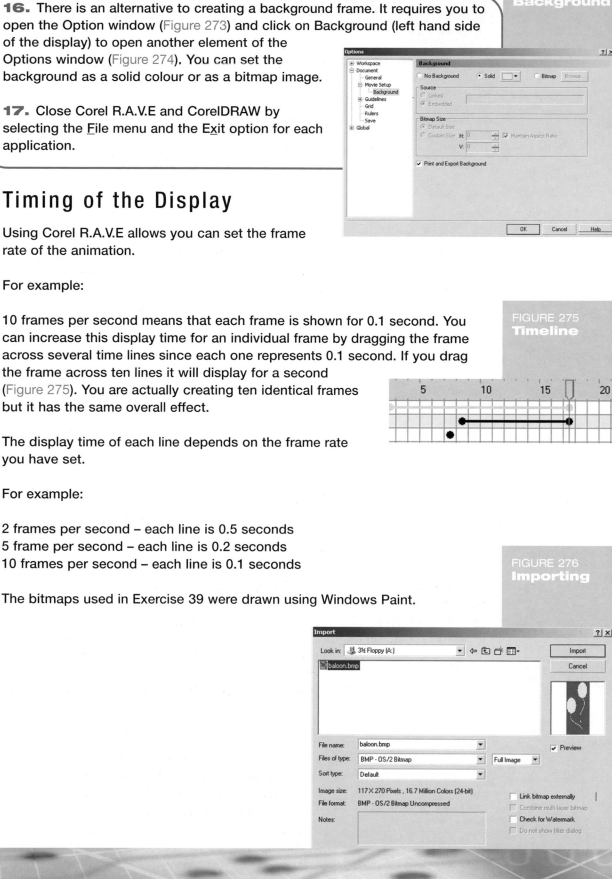

FIGURE 277
**Imported
Image**

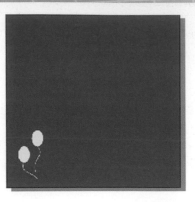

FIGURE 278
**Balloon
Animation**

Exercise 39

Importing Images

1. Corel R.A.V.E is opened by either selecting the Start button, highlighting Programs option, then highlighting the CorelDRAW option to reveal a submenu and clicking on Corel R.A.V.E 1.0 item. Alternatively, load CorelDRAW and select the Application Launcher to reveal the Corel family of applications. Click on Corel R.A.V.E.

2. The initial display reveals an overlay with four options in the form of icons. Click on the New Movie icon. This will open a page within the working area of the application.

3. Select the Movie menu and the Movie Setup option. Set the frame rate to 6 per second. Click on Background and Solid. Select red for the background colour and click on the OK button.

4. Click on the second line of the timeline then on the Import icon to reveal the Import window. Change the Look in: box to the folder in which the graphic image is stored. In my case it is a floppy disk (Figure 276). Highlight the file you want to import and click on the Import button. The pointer will change shape to a set-square with the file name. Click to insert the graphic and change the shape of the graphic so that a suitable size (Figure 277).

5. Click on the graphic (i.e. balloon) to enclose it in a frame and copy the image using the Edit menu and the Copy option. Now click on the next line of the timeline and a blank red frame will remain. Paste the graphic onto the frame slightly above the original position. You are going to create an animation of balloons rising up the edge of the frame.

6. Repeat creating three more frames. Figure 278 shows the whole sequence.

7. Insert a seventh frame and create a text frame in the middle. Enter Balloon Festival 2002 in a font and size of your choice. Centre the text and adjust it to appear in the centre of the frame. You want this frame to stay on the display for 1 second so drag the black dot across the next six lines.

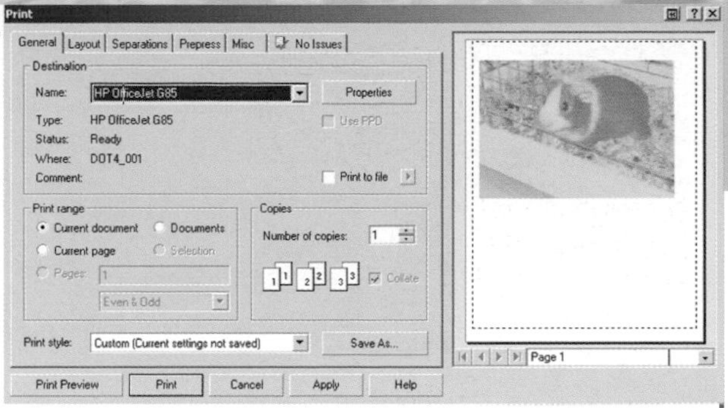

8. Save the image by selecting the File menu and clicking on the Save option. The Save Drawing window will appear. You need to change the Save in box to the location you want to store the picture and enter BalloonFestivalMovie.clk into the file name box then click on the Save button.

9. Close Corel R.A.V.E and CorelDRAW by selecting the File menu and the Exit option for each application.

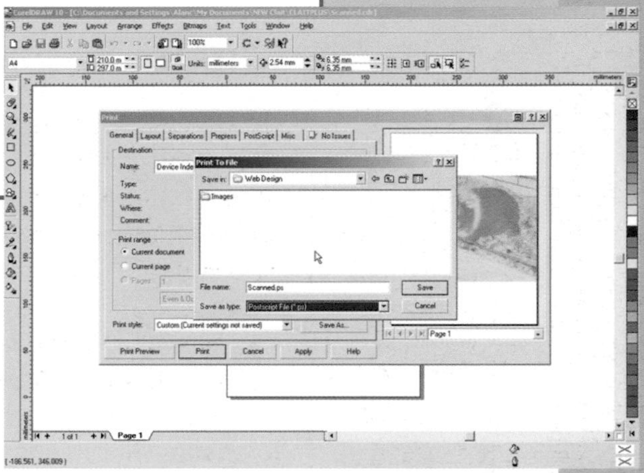

FIGURE 279
Printing

FIGURE 280
Print to File Window

Publishing

CorelDRAW prints both vector drawings and bitmap images as a series of dots. A high resolution image does not guarantee a good quality printout since the quality of the printed artwork depends on the printer. An inkjet printer's quality is probably limited to 300 to 600 dpi (dots per inch). Printing on a higher quality printer will produce clearer and better quality artwork. To print your artwork select the File menu and the Print option to reveal the Print window (Figure 279). This allows you preview your work and to select the wide range of options available to you.

The simplest way of printing your document is to accept the default settings and click on the Print button. Your work will be produced as the preview shows you.

In many cases you may want to access a high quality external printer. This will require you to convert your file to encapsulated postscript (.eps) format. In order to do this you need to print to a file rather than to a printer. Essentially you prepare your document for printing but send the file to storage rather than the printer. You can then send your file to the external printer. However, you need to be connected to a

FIGURE 281
Proofing Options

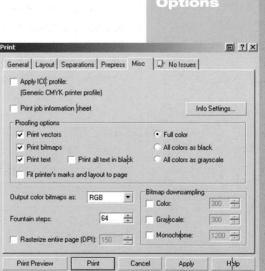

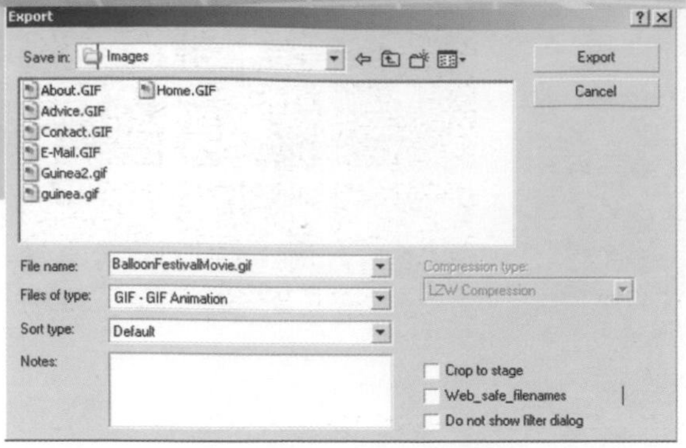

FIGURE 282
**Export
Animation**

FIGURE 282
**Export
Animation**

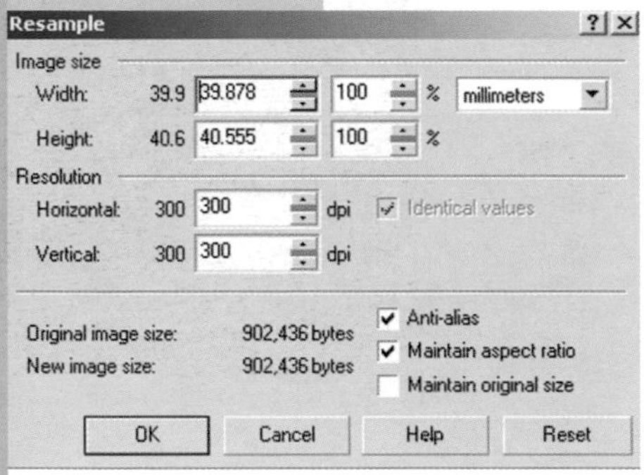

FIGURE 283
**Resample
Window**

Postscript printer to generate the file or to the Device Independent Postscript File. If you do not have a postscript printer or file you will need to ask your printer for advice.

To generate an encapsulated postscript file click in the Print to file radio button in the general tab and choose a postscript printer or Device Independent Postscript File. Click on the Print button to reveal the Print to File window (Figure 280) and select which folder to save your file to.

Often when you are printing artwork you want to examine its quality and the normal approach is to produce full colour proofs. To determine what appears on your proofs select the Misc tab (Figure 281) which contains a proofing options area where you can choose what appears on the proofs. The options allow you to print vectors, bitmaps and text as well as producing full colour proofs.

Outside the proofing options area is one called Rasterize entire page (DPI) with a box alongside letting you to adjust the dots per inch of the printed image. Rasterize means that you have converted a vector image into a bitmap. It is now displayed as pixels.

To ensure that the final document is presented accurately, select the Crop/Fold marks in the Prepress Tab which will print marks on the page to indicate where the paper should be cut or folded to produce the finished document.

Exporting Animations

You can export the animations created within Corel R.A.V.E in a variety of formats such as:

• Macromedia Flash – often forms part of a website
• Animated Gif – often a way of producing an animation for a website
• Video for Windows
• Quicktime Movie

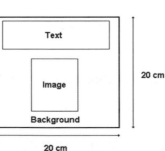

FIGURE 284
**Design
Brief**

To export your animation, select the Export icon on the toolbar to open the Export window (Figure 282). You will be able to select the file format and folder to export your work to.

Resolution

To change the resolution of your images, you need to be in Corel PHOTO-PAINT (i.e. Edit Bitmap from CorelDRAW). Select the Image file and the Resample option to reveal the Resample window (Figure 283). You can change the resolution of an image while maintaining its original dimensions if the Identical Values radio button is ticked. This is useful should you need to reduce the storage size of an image but wish to keep to the physical design brief size of the artwork. The Anti-alias button smoothes the edges of the image. If you select the maintain original size button this maintains the storage size while adjusting the resolution so that the physical dimensions of the image may alter.

FIGURE 285
Dice Animation

FIGURE 286
Unicorn Casino

Unicorn Casino

Screen Print

If you need to capture what appears on the screen, press the Print Scrn key then a copy of your screen display is made and stored on the Windows clipboard. You can then Paste the image into an application of your choice such as Windows Paint from where you can print the display. If you want to copy only the contents of the active window, press the Alt and Print Scrn keys together.

More Practice 1

Figure 284 shows the design brief for some artwork. Create the document following the instructions below:

1. Produce a new artwork with the design brief dimensions (i.e. 20 cm x 20 cm)

2. Save your new work as file called Practice

3. Scan an image of your choice to form the background of the artwork. You will need to change its size and shape to fill the area

4. Remove any scratches, dust and red eye from the image if appropriate

5. Make any changes to the image to improve its appearance

6. Add a new layer and import another image and position it according to the design brief

7. Add a new layer and enter More Practice in a font and character size that suits you

8. Change the transparency of the image to 50%

9. Print a full colour proof of the artwork complete with crop marks

More Practice 2

Animation

Create an animation showing a set of dice (Figure 285)

Frame 1 – Blue background
Frame 2 – Number 1 Dice
Frame 3 - Number 2 Dice
Frame 4 - Number 3 Dice
Frame 5 - Number 4 Dice
Frame 6 – Number 5 Dice
Frame 7 - Number 6 Dice
Frame 8 – Unicorn Casino (centred) Figure 286

Frame rate 6 per second except that Unicorn should display for 1 second.

Summary

1. Load Application

Select the Start button, highlight the Programs option, then highlight the CorelDRAW option to reveal a submenu and click on CorelDRAW 10 item or double click on the CorelDRAW icon on the Windows desktop.

2. Save

Select the File menu and click on the Save option to reveal the Save Drawing window.

3. Size

Click on the down arrow button alongside the page box to reveal a list of options. Choose the desired option.

or

To set the size, select the units by clicking on the down arrow next to the Units box then click on the up and down arrows alongside the size boxes.

4. Import an Image

Click on the Import icon on the toolbar to open the Import window.

5 Resize or Move Images

Click on the image to enclose it in a frame. The edges of the image can be dragged using the mouse pointer.

The image can be moved by placing the pointer on its centre. The pointer will change shape (star) allowing you to drag the whole image by holding down the mouse button.

6. Text Box

Click on the Text Tool and the pointer will change to cross hairs and the letter A. The cross hairs enable you to position the text box by clicking and holding down the mouse button and dragging the box open.

7. Enter Text

Place your pointer into the text box and the cursor will change shape. Select the location where you want to enter text by clicking. The cursor will flash at the chosen position.

8. Resize and Move Text Box

Click on the Text Box to enclose it in a frame with small black squares. Placing your mouse on the edges will change the shape of the pointer. Hold down the mouse button in order to drag the edges to resize and reshape the box.

The Text Box can be moved by placing the pointer on its centre where the pointer will change shape (star) allowing you to drag the whole box by holding down the mouse button.

9. Scanning an Image

Select the File menu and highlight Acquire Image to reveal a submenu. Click on the Select Source option and a list of sources will appear. Select the option (e.g. scanner) you intend to use.

Select the File menu and highlight Acquire Image to reveal a submenu. Click on the Acquire option

10. Crop a Scanned Image

Click on the Shape Tool. The image will change to show small squares at each corner and the pointer will take the form of an arrow. Click on the small squares and move them to new positions cropping the image.

11. Edit Bitmapped Image

Select the Bitmaps menu and click on the Edit Bitmap(Corel PHOTO-PAINT will open)

12. Dust and Scratches (Corel PHOTO-PAINT)

Select the Effects menu, highlight the Noise item and click on Dust and Scratch to reveal the Dust and Scratch window.

13. Red Eye (Corel PHOTO-PAINT)

Select the Effects menu, highlight the Color Transform item and click on Red Eye Removal. A warning message will tell you that you need a mask. A mask is an area of the image that you have designated. You can select the whole image as a mask from the Mask menu and the Select All option or identify an area using the Rectangle Mask Tool which provides a variety other ways of defining an area. This tool is on the left hand toolbar.

14. Adjust Colours

Select the Image menu and highlight Adjust then click on Hue/Saturation/Lightness to reveal the Hue/Saturation/Lightness window.

15. Rotate and Skew Text

Select the Pick Tool. Clicking with it on the text box will enclose the frame with arrows at the corners. You can rotate the box by dragging with the mouse. The pointer changes to a circle.

There are double-headed arrows in the middle of the top and bottom lines of the text box use them to skew the text by dragging with the mouse (pointer changes to two opposed arrows).

alternatively

Select the Arrange menu and highlight Transformations to reveal a submenu of options

16. Artistic Text

Select the Text Tool and simply click within the drawing area then enter your text. A cursor like a line will appear to show you where the text will be entered. This is called an insertion marker. Once you have finished entering text it will be enclosed in the normal way. This means you can move, rotate and skew your text in the normal way.

17. Convert Text Types

Select the text with the Pick tool then select the Text menu and the Convert to Paragraph Text or Convert to Artistic Text.

18. Extruded Text

Select the Interactive Extrude Tool and click and drag on the text to see it extrude.

19. Sketching/Draw Text

Click on the Freehand Tool. Adjust the width of the tool's nib using the outline width tool on the horizontal toolbar and draw your text.

20. Fill

Click on the Fill Tool to reveal a number of different Fill options. Select your chosen option.

21. Bitmap Editor

Select the Bitmaps menu and click on Edit Bitmap. The Corel PHOTO-PAINT will open.

22. Layer

Select the Tools menu and click on the Object Manager option to reveal the Object Manager window on the right of the work area. Select the new layer icon in the bottom left hand corner of the window.

23. Masking - Transparency

When importing or drawing an image select the Interactive Transparency Tool and click with it on or near the image. Holding down the mouse button, drag the pointer to the chosen location. The pointer will change shape to a black square and arrow and a line will be drawn across the image. A white bar will be placed across the line and the transparency of the image will have changed. The bar can be moved to increase or reduce transparency.

24. Shadow
Select the Interactive Drop Shadow Tool. The pointer changes to a large arrow and a rectangle. Click on the edge of the object frame and holding down the mouse button, drag the pointer to the chosen position.

25. Open Corel R.A.V.E
Select the Start button, highlight the Programs option, highlight the CorelDRAW option to reveal a submenu and click on the Corel R.A.V.E 1.0 item. Alternatively, load CorelDRAW and select the Application Launcher to reveal the Corel family of applications. Click on the Corel R.A.V.E option.

26. Form Animation Background
After creating a background frame, click on the black spot on the timeline and drag it to the chosen position.

alternatively

Select the Movie menu and click on the Movie Setup option to reveal the Options window. Click on the Background option.

27. Play Animation
Select the Movie menu, highlight the Control option and click on the Play Movie option.

28. Speed of Display
Select the Movie menu and click on the Movie Setup option to open the Options window.

29. Import Images
Click on the Import icon to reveal the Import window.

Web Page Creation

This chapter will help you to:

- Create a web page from unformatted source material

- Use standard images and formatting to create a consistent house style

- Create and format tables, frames and forms

- Use Meta tags to define content

- Set dimensions, alignments and other attributes of page items

This chapter covers Unit 7 (Web Page Creation). There are no pre-conditions for studying this unit. However, its content does assume that you have the skills and understanding which are provided by the OCR Level 1 ICT course New CLAIT (e.g. Unit 9 - Web Page Creation, Unit 3 Electronic Communication and Unit 1 - Using a Computer).

Assessment

After studying Unit 7 your skills and understanding are assessed during a 3 hour practical assignment. This is set by OCR and marked locally. However, the marking will be externally moderated by OCR. This ensures that the standard is being applied correctly across the many different providers of OCR CLAIT Plus. If you are unsuccessful then you can be re-assessed using a different assignment.

Resources

The exercises included in this chapter require text files and images which are provided within the tutor pack. However, if you do not have access to the pack please use other available text files and images so that you can practise the techniques discussed in the chapter. During the CLAIT Plus assessment the resources required are provided for your use as part of the process.

Microsoft FrontPage

Web pages can be created using a variety of tools and systems. Microsoft FrontPage is an application that provides you with a straightforward way of doing this without having to understand HTML (Hypertext Mark Up Language) which is used to produce them. HTML provides instructions for the structure, presentation and content of the page. These instructions are called tags. FrontPage automatically converts your design into HTML and as well as how it appears as a web page.

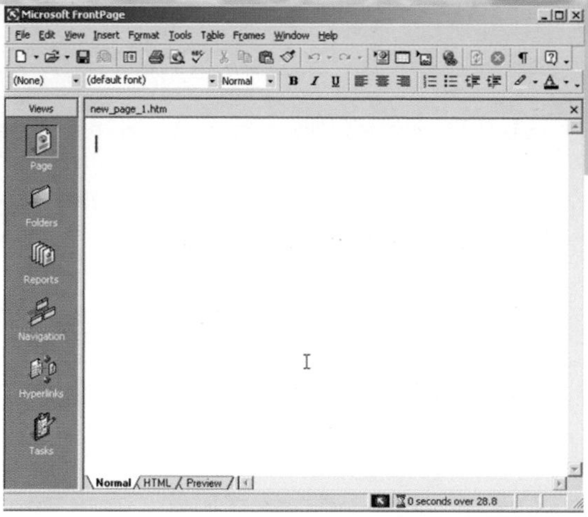

If you understand HTML you can obviously edit the language yourself using FrontPage's HTML view. However, this is not required to produce quality pages since FrontPage provides templates for a variety of different types of page to improve your productivity and quality.

FIGURE 287
Microsoft FrontPage

Figure 287 shows the Microsoft FrontPage interface. It is similar to other Microsoft Office applications in that it has a work area where you design your pages, toolbars containing a number of tools that other applications employ (e.g. Cut. Copy and Paste) and a menu bar. The two main visual differences are:

FIGURE 288
Basic HTML

• A toolbar down the left hand side of the display called Views

• Three different views of the page in the bottom left hand corner of the display (i.e. Normal, HTML and Preview)

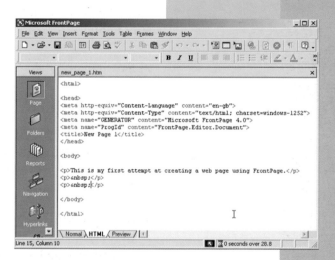

The Normal view is used to design your page, the HTML view allows you to see the language and Preview to test your page (i.e. what does it look like on a website). However, it is critical to test your pages using a browser rather than rely only on Preview. It is essential to test your pages in the real environment.

HTML Tags

Although you do not need to know HTML to use FrontPage it is useful to have a basic understanding of tags. This forms part of the new CLAIT Plus qualification. Figure 288 shows some basic HTML language.

Figure 288 **shows some HTML tags:**

<html> marks the start of the HTML commands

</html> marks the end of the HTML commands

\<head\> marks the beginning of the HTML introduction

\</head\> marks the end of the HTML introduction

\<meta\> marks information about the page itself (e.g. author, authoring tool – FrontPage etc.)

\<title\> marks the start of the title of the page

\</title\> marks the end of the title of the page (i.e. title appears between the two tags – New Page 1)

\<body\> shows the start of the main body (i.e. content of the page)

\</body\> shows the end of the main body (i.e. end of the content)

\<p\> start of a paragraph of text
\</p\> end of a paragraph

Other Tags include:

\<u\> and \</u\> underline
\<b\> and \</b\> bold
\<a\> and \<a/\> hypertext links.

If you consider the HTML in Figure 288 you will see that there is a definite pattern of tags.

Creating a web page

FrontPage and HTML gives you a great deal of freedom in designing web pages. However, some basic good practice is:

• Consistency – many users of the web complain of getting lost, confused and distracted by the structure and design of websites and pages. You should be consistent in the layout and presentation of the pages that make up a website. It is important to create standard features that appear on every page such as navigation bars. This not only aids the use of the site but also improves the productivity of designing pages in that you have a standard structure to build on.

• Length of a page – there is no limit to how long a web page can be. However, long pages are often difficult to use (i.e. locating information) so good practice suggests that a maximum length is approximately three A4 pages.

- Users often want to find information quickly and will abandon a site if they cannot immediately find the content they are seeking. It is therefore important to present information in a clear and concise way (i.e. short sentences, lists and illustrations).

- Most users will complain if a page takes too long to download. This is a feature often associated with the use of illustrations, sound and video content. It is always good practice to minimise the size of a page and reduce the download time. One way to do this is to use repetitive content since after it is downloaded, it is available to the other pages and thus effectively reduces their size.

A fundamental component of any website are the hyperlinks between the different pages. In later exercises you will have the opportunity to create links but a fundamental issue is the nature of a link. These are two types:

- relative
- absolute

A relative link is one which will change if the website is moved from where it was created to a new location (ie. the last). This is the normal process as it is important that links are relative (ie. they change to allow for site to be moved).

An absolute link is one which is fixed and will not change. This should only be used if the site will never be moved otherwise links may fail.

Many organisations have tried to embody a consistent approach in a house style which they ask their web page designers to follow. This is normally accompanied by a Design Brief which provides the content for each page.

Character Sizes

In most Microsoft Office application the character sizes are shown as 10 pts, 12 pts, 24pts etc. HTML has a different size classification. FrontPage shows both sizes to make it easier to transfer your understanding from other applications.

The sizes are:

1	8 pts
2	10 pts
3	12 pts
4	14 pts
5	18 pts
6	24 pts

Table

To insert a table into a webpage you need to select the Table menu and highlight the Insert option to reveal a sub menu. Click on the Table option. This will open the Insert Table window (Figure 293). You can insert the number of rows and columns, align the contents of the cells (left, right, center and justify), border size and width of table either in pixels or as a percentage of page width.

Once you have created a table you can amend it using the options within the Table menu. These allow you to insert or delete extra rows and columns, split or merge cells and change the properties of a cell. The first step is to highlight the row, column, cell or table and then select the desired option. If you highlight the Properties option you will reveal a submenu. Click on the Cells option to reveal the Cell Properties window. This allows you to change many features of the cell or cells including changing the alignment.

For example

Horizontal – left, right, center and justify

Vertical – top, middle, baseline and bottom

File Formats

Creating web pages involves using a variety of resources so it is important that you are able to recognise the different file types. Most files have an extension made up of three/four letters which indicates their type. Some of the most frequently encountered are:

.txt	- text file
.doc	- Word file
.rtf	- rich text file
.gif	- a graphic file
.bmp	- bitmap graphic file
.jpg (jpeg)	- a graphic file
.htm	- web page
.html	- web page
.pdf	- Acrobat document file
.xls	- Excel spreadsheet
.mdb	- Access database file

Example House Style

Site Structure

- all files must be saved to Web Design folder
- all image files should be stored in sub-folder of Web Design called Images

• all links to files and images on website should be relative, not absolute

Standard Page Properties

• Title – specified in Design Brief
• Background Colour - #00FFFF (Hexadecimal code of the colour Aqua)

Standard Text Properties

• Text Colour - #000000 (Hexadecimal code of the colour Black)
• Link Colour – #0000FF (Hexadecimal code of the colour Blue)
• Visited Link Colour – #800080 (Hexadecimal code of the colour Purple)
• Active Link Colour - #0000FF (Hexadecimal code of the colour Red)
• Typeface (font) – sans serif
• Text Size:

- Main Heading – HTML size 6 (24 pt)
- Subheading – HTML size 4 (14 pts)
- Body Text – HTML size 3 (12 pts)

Image Properties

• Image height and width must be accurately specified
• Image borders set to zero
• Alt (alternative) text specified by Design Brief

Design Brief - Standard

This is the design brief for the standard layout page on which all the pages will be based.

Meta Tags

Each page should have the following meta tag information:

Name	Content
Author	Your name and centre number
Keywords	guinea, pigs, hotel, holiday
Description	see individual page design brief

Navigation Table

Table of navigation icons must be placed at the top of each page

Width 400, Height 48, columns 5, Rows 1, Centred, Cellspacing 0, Cellpadding 0 and Border 0

Home	Contact	Advice	E-Mail	About

FIGURE 289
Format Menu

Format
A Font...
Paragraph...
:= Bullets and Numbering...
Borders and Shading...
Dynamic HTML Effects
AA Style...
Theme...
Background...
Properties...   Alt+Enter
≫

The images are all width 80 and height 48.

Image	Alt Text	Link
Home	Home Page	Home.htm
Contact	Contact us	Contact.htm
Advice	Practical Assistance	
Advice.htm		
E-Mail	Messages	E-mail link to guineaPIGS@Farmhalt.co.uk
About	Background	About.htm

Copyright Notice

Each Page should have this notice at the bottom:

Copyright © GuineaPIGS 2002, centred, body text size and linked to
guineaPIGS@Farmhalt.co.uk

Exercise 42

Creating a Standard Page

FIGURE 290
Page Properties Window

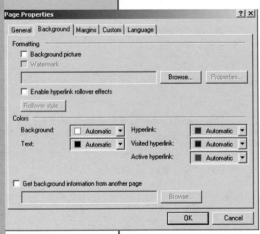

1. FrontPage is opened by either selecting the Start button, highlighting the Programs option and clicking on the FrontPage option or by double clicking on the FrontPage icon on the Windows desktop.

2. The application will open (Figure 287) with a new page in the work area. If the window is not maximised then use the standard buttons in the top right hand corner of the window to display it filling the screen.

3. The first step is to set the background colour to the one specified in the house style. Select the Format menu and click on the Background option (Figure 289) to reveal the Page Properties window (Figure 290). In the Background tab you will see the Background box with automatic inserted in it. Click on the down arrow alongside the box and a small palette of colours will appear. Select aqua by clicking on it.

4. This window also allows you to choose the text colour, in this case, the default colour is black which is also the house style colour so you do not need to change it.

FIGURE 291
HTML Tags

```
<body bgcolor="#00FFFF" text="#000000" link="#0000FF" vlink="#800080">
```
Background Colour   Text Colour   Link Colour   Visited Link Colour

5. In addition, you can select the colours for

hyperlinks. The House style gives the link colour as blue (#0000FF) and visited link as purple (#800080). Set these colours in the same way as you chose the background and body text. Click on the OK button to confirm your choices.

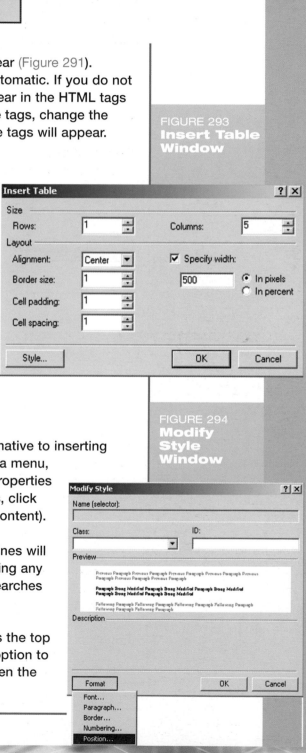

FIGURE 292
Table Menu

6. The web page should now have changed colour to aqua. Click on the HTML tab at the bottom left hand corner and the corresponding HTML tags for the page will appear (Figure 291). FrontPage offers default settings which are shown as automatic. If you do not change these settings then they will sometimes not appear in the HTML tags which may puzzle you. If you do need to see them in the tags, change the colour to a different one then back to the default and the tags will appear.

FIGURE 293
Insert Table Window

7. Observe that the background colour is shown as <body bgcolor "#00FFFF">. If you delete the code and insert #008080 then return to the Normal view then you will see that the background colour has changed to teal. This is an alternative way to set the colours. Return to the HTML tags, delete #008080 and replace it with #00FFFF. Your background should now be aqua again.

8. Insert two extra meta tag lines reading:

<meta name="Author" content= "Your name and centre number">
<meta name="Keywords" content=" guinea, pigs, hotel, holiday ">

FIGURE 294
Modify Style Window

This complies with the Design Brief, but there is an alternative to inserting directly into the HTML. Right click on the page to reveal a menu, click on the Page Properties option to reveal the Page Properties window. Select the Custom tab and in the User variables, click the Add button. You can now add Name and Value (i.e. content).

The keywords are especially important since search engines will identify the page based on these words. A search including any of these words is going to locate the page while other searches will miss it.

9. The next step is to create the navigation table across the top of the page. Select the Table menu, highlight the Insert option to reveal the Table option (Figure 292). Click on Table to open the Insert Table window (Figure 293).

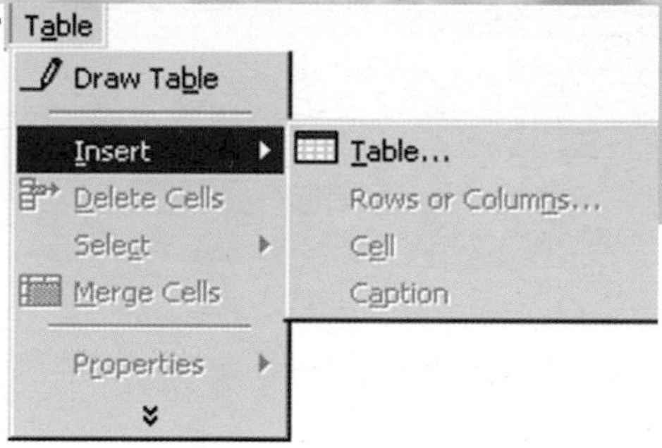

FIGURE 295
Position

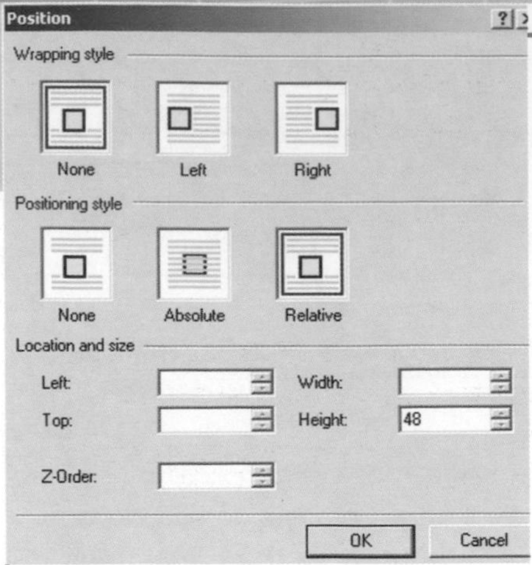

Position

Wrapping style

None   Left   Right

Positioning style

None   Absolute   Relative

Location and size

Left: Width:
Top: Height: 48
Z-Order:

OK   Cancel

FIGURE 296
Insert Menu

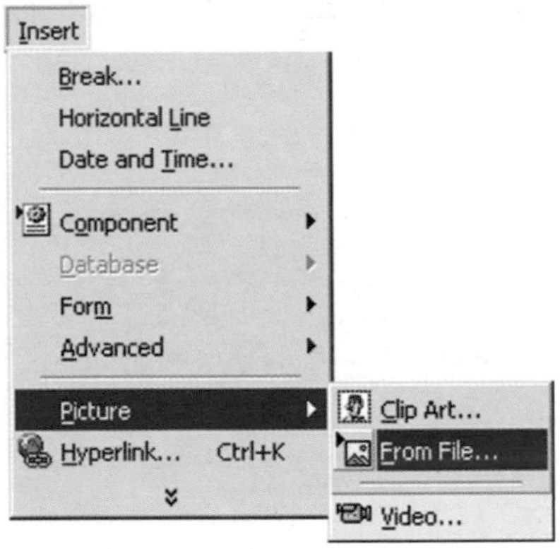

Insert

Break...
Horizontal Line
Date and Time...
Component   ▶
Database   ▶
Form   ▶
Advanced   ▶
Picture   ▶   Clip Art...
Hyperlink... Ctrl+K   From File...
                           Video...

FIGURE 297
Select File

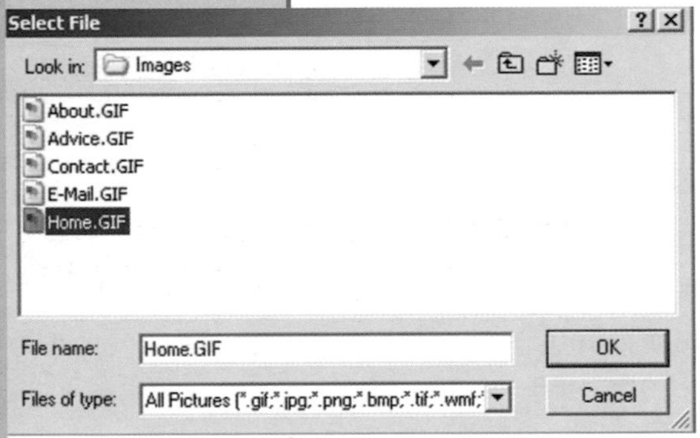

Select File   ? X

Look in: Images   ▼ ← 🖿 🖆 📰▾

About.GIF
Advice.GIF
Contact.GIF
E-Mail.GIF
Home.GIF

File name: Home.GIF   OK
Files of type: All Pictures (*.gif;*.jpg;*.png;*.bmp;*.tif;*.wmf; ▼   Cancel

FIGURE 298
Importing Images

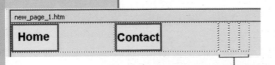

Next Cells

10. Insert the information about the table from the Design Brief into the window. Click on the Style button to reveal the Modify Style window (Figure 294) and click on the Format button to open the drop down menu. Click on Position to reveal the Position window (Figure 295) which allows you to choose between absolute and relative. Absolute position is one that is fixed in relation to the top left hand corner of the page while relative position is one determined in relation to other elements in the text flow. The navigation table is always at the top of the page and is thus a relative position so click in the Relative box and insert 48 in the height box. Click on the OK buttons in each window. The table will appear across the top of the page.

11. In each cell of the table you are going to insert a graphic. Click in the left hand cell to place the cursor and then select the Insert menu, highlight the Picture option and click on the From File option (Figure 296) to reveal the Select File window. Change the Look in: box to show the Images subfolder of the Web Design folder which is specified in the Design Brief (Figure 297). Double click on Home.gif and it will be inserted into the left hand cell. Repeat the action for Contact.gif, Advice.gif, E-Mail.gif and About.gif. The table may distort during this process but place the next image in the next cell (Figure 298).

12. When you have inserted all five images the navigation should look like Figure 299.

13. Right click on each image in turn to reveal a menu and click on the Page Properties option to open the Picture Properties window. In the general tab there is a box called Alternative representations text. Enter the Alt text appropriate to the image (Design Brief Standard) – e.g. Home image – Home Page.

14. Save the Standard page by selecting the File menu and clicking on the Save option to reveal the Save As window. Change the Save in box to read

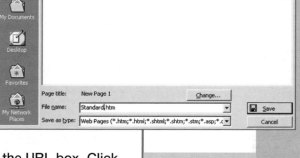

Web Design folder since the House Style requires us to save all files to this folder. Enter the File name: Standard.htm in the box and click on the Save button (Figure 300).

15. At the bottom of each page there should appear a copyright statement. So click towards the bottom of the display page to place the cursor. The length of pages will vary so the position of the statement is relative to the other contents of the page so precise positioning is not relevant.

16. Enter in Arial (i.e. a sans serif font), character size 3 (HTML) and centred - Copyright © GuineaPIGS 2002.

17. Both the Copyright statement and the E-Mail navigation button are linked to an e-mail account. Click on the E-Mail button. It will be highlighted by being enclosed in a frame. Select the Insert menu and click on the Hyperlink option to reveal the Create Hyperlink window. There are four small buttons alongside the URL box. Click on the third button (i.e. an envelope) to open Create E-mail Hyperlink (Figure 301). Enter the e-mail address guineaPIGS@Farmhalt.co.uk and click on the OK button. The address will appear in the URL box – mailto:guineaPIGS@Farmhalt.co.uk. Click on the OK button.

18. Now repeat the operation for the copyright statement. Remember that you must highlight the statement first before setting up the link.

19. Save the Standard page by selecting the File menu and clicking on the Save option.

20. Close the application by selecting the File menu and the Exit option or click on the application close button in top right hand corner.

FIGURE 299
Navigation Table

FIGURE 300
Save As Window

FIGURE 301
Create Hyperlink

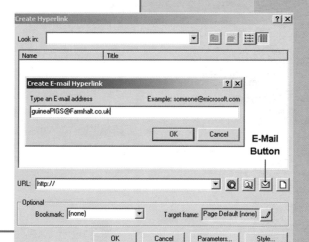

File Names

In creating web pages and sites you will be using a variety of resources in the form of graphic images and files. FrontPage keeps track of these resources. However,

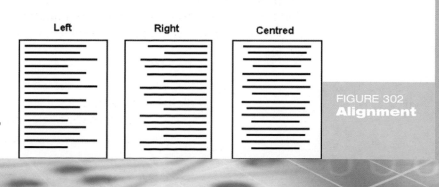

FIGURE 302
Alignment

FIGURE 303
Formatting Toolbar

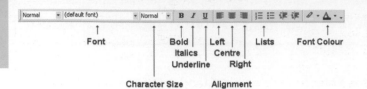

Font · Bold · Italics · Underline · Character Size · Left · Centre · Right · Alignment · Lists · Font Colour

if you change a file name or move resources to a new folder then when the site is operating it will often be unable to locate them so it is important to retain the original names of files and graphics, as well as the linked resources and it is good practice to save everything to the same folder or floppy disk. When saving your pages you will often be prompted to save the embedded files. This is a function of FrontPage to help you retain all the data required for the web page.

Downloading Files

Often you will seek to download files from websites. On the OCR website (http://www.ocr.org.uk) are a number of files which are available for users to download. If you would like to practice downloading files then select one of the files with the extension .zip on the OCR website to download. Downloading is initiated by double clicking the file. A window will appear to offer you the choice of opening the file or save it. To open the file requires that you have a compatible application on your computer. In many cases you will want to save the file initially before opening it. If you select the save option then the Save As window will appear. You need to select the folder in which to save the file in the Save in box. The filename is normally supplied by the website but you are free to change it. It is always important to select meaningful names but do not change the file extension since this allows you to identify the type of file. When you are ready to save the file you click on the Save button. The window will close and a new window becomes visible which shows you the speed at which the file is being downloaded. The speed of downloading depends on the nature of your connection. When the download has been completed a message will appear in the window. You are then presented with the options to open the file or to end the process by closing the window.

Text Formatting

You can precisely control the appearance of the text on your web pages. It can be aligned (Figure 302), emphasised (e.g. emboldened, underlined and in italics) and its size altered. Underline is normally not used on web pages since to underline a word or phrase is a standard way of showing a hyperlink.

The FrontPage formatting toolbar provides the tools to select fonts, character sizes, emphasise text and align it. Figure 303 shows the toolbar.

Sans Serif   Serif

FIGURE 304
Serif and Sans Serif

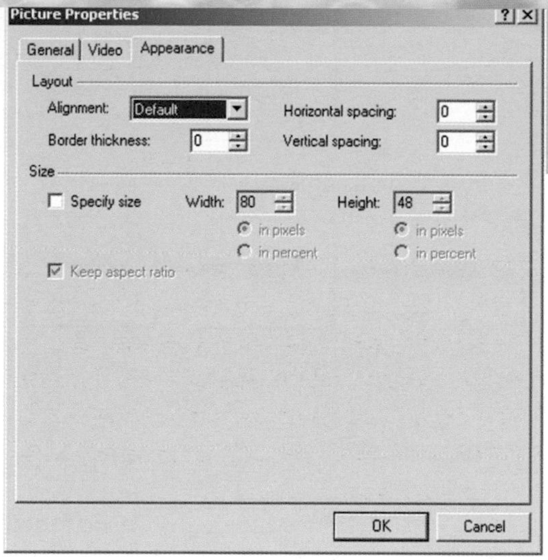

Font sizes are shown using HTML as 1, 2, 3 etc. These are called absolute values but you can also designate relative sizes. The relativity is to the default value (which is 3) so if you set a value of +2, then the size is two size levels above the default, −1 is one size level less than the default.

In HTML it would read <FONT=5> </FONT> - set size to absolute size 5 or in relative terms <FONT=+2></FONT> - set size to two levels above the default value.

FIGURE 305
Picture Properties

There are two types of fonts (typefaces). These are called serif and sans serif. Serif fonts are those with small appendages to the characters while sans serif are plain. Figure 304 shows the difference.

You can change the colour of the font by highlighting the text and selecting the Font Colour icon to reveal a palette of colours. Click on the colour you want for your highlighted text.

Finally you can insert special symbols into your text by selecting the Insert menu and click on the Symbol option to reveal a window of special symbols, They are selected by highlighting them and clicking on the Insert button. The symbol is inserted at the cursor.

Lists

A useful way of displaying information on a web page is a list. Lists are easy and quick to read, often key factors for users of the web. There are two types of lists – ordered and unordered. An unordered list is a simple one showing all the items equally indented while an ordered list uses indents to show the relationship between items.

Examples:

Ordered

• Savings
  - Building Society
  - Bank
  - Coins

• Salary
• Interest

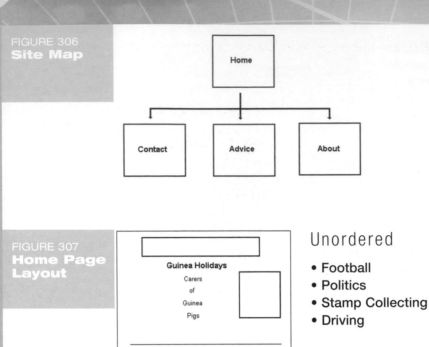

FIGURE 306
Site Map

FIGURE 307
Home Page Layout

Unordered

• Football
• Politics
• Stamp Collecting
• Driving

In the ordered list the indentation tells you that building society, bank and coins are all forms of saving. In the unordered list there is no obvious relationship between the items. In both types of lists a wide variety of different bullets are available, including numbers and symbols. Bullets can be inserted from the Formatting Toolbar or from the Format menu and Bullets and Numbering option.

Image Attributes

Like text, images have characteristics such as size, font and alignment. They are equally as important because you are designing a precise page in which you need to know the exact size of the image. This can be changed and adjusted by adding a border and its alignment altered (e.g. right, left and centred). If you right click on an image then a menu appears. Click on the Picture Properties option to reveal the Picture Properties window. The Appearance tab (Figure 305) opens a window which allows you to change alignment, border thickness and size. If you are changing the size of an image, it is important to specify Keep aspect ratio to avoid distorting the picture. Different styles of borders are also available from the General tab display by selecting the Style button, clicking on the Format button and selecting a Border from drop down list.

All forms of graphical images and pictures can enhance simple text displays. However, for someone who is visually impaired the pictures are meaningless and if your page relies on them to convey understanding of the content, you have effectively created a barrier for the user. HTML offers you a way to overcome this barrier using the alt tag. This allows you to add a text description of the image which a text only browser can read which are typically used by a visually impaired person. Text only browsers read the text to the user. They are presented with a message rather than a meaningless image.

FIGURE 308
Open File

Example (alt tag)

1. Before

<td><img border="0" src="Images/Contact.GIF" width="80" height="48"></td>

2. After

<td><img border="0" src="Images/Contact.GIF" width="80" height="48" alt="[navigation link to the contact page]" ></td>

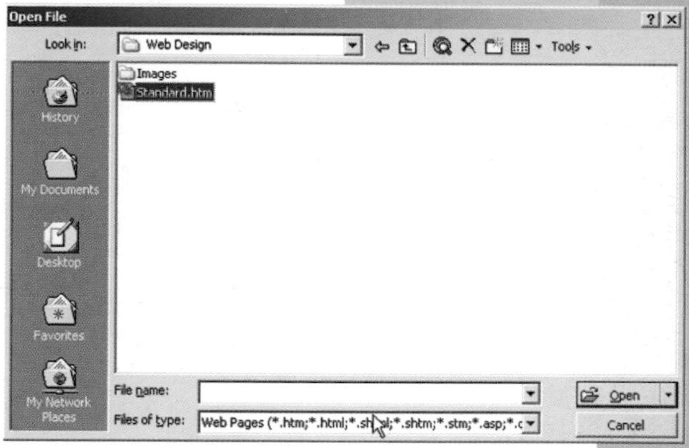

Create Web Pages

In Exercise 42 you created a standard layout page for a site. You are now going to create the remaining pages of the site. The site is being developed for a small business who provide a guinea pig hotel for families going on holiday who need their pets cared for while they are away. The pages are:

Home Page   -   Introduction to the site

Contact Page -   Form to allow users to register

Advice Page   -   Advice about keeping guinea pigs

FIGURE 309
**Page
Properties**

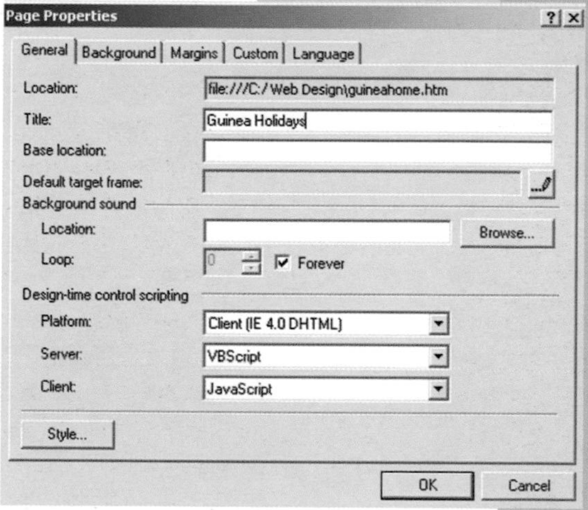

About Page   -   Description of the service offered

Guinea Holidays Site Map

Figure 306 shows the map of the Guinea Holidays site.

Design brief for Home Page

1. Design a web page in accordance with the House Style Guidelines and insert the specified content. Save your page as the html document guineahome.htm

2. Page Title: Guinea Holidays

3. Additional meta tag: Guinea Holidays provides high quality care of guinea pigs while their owners are away

4. Insert the text file Homeguinea.txt and image file guinea.gif as shown in Figure 307.

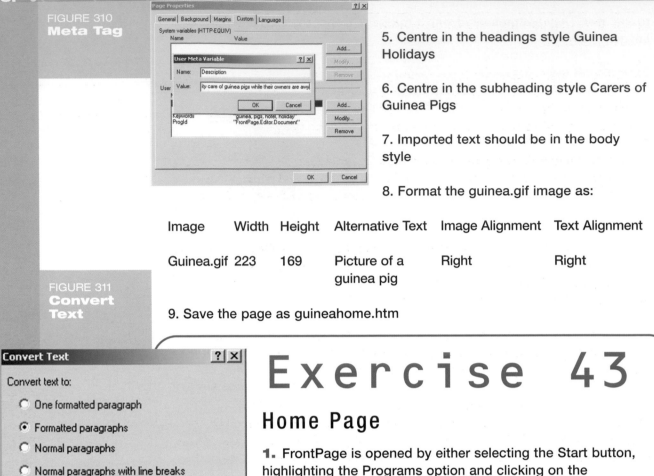

FIGURE 310
Meta Tag

5. Centre in the headings style Guinea Holidays

6. Centre in the subheading style Carers of Guinea Pigs

7. Imported text should be in the body style

8. Format the guinea.gif image as:

Image	Width	Height	Alternative Text	Image Alignment	Text Alignment
Guinea.gif	223	169	Picture of a guinea pig	Right	Right

FIGURE 311
Convert Text

9. Save the page as guineahome.htm

Exercise 43

Home Page

1. FrontPage is opened by either selecting the Start button, highlighting the Programs option and clicking on the FrontPage option or by double clicking on the FrontPage icon on the Windows desktop.

2. The application will open with a new page in the work area. If the window is not maximised then use the standard buttons in the top right hand corner of the window to display it filling the screen. Select the File menu and click on the Open option to reveal the Open File window. Change the Look in: box to read Web Design and your file standard.htm should appear. Double click on the file to load it into FrontPage (Figure 308).

3. Select the File menu and click on the Save As option to reveal the Save As window. Change the Save in: box to read Web Design and enter guineahome.htm in the File name: box then click on the Save button. It is sensible to rename your file (page) early to avoid accidentally overwriting the standard file.

4. Right click on the page to open a menu. Click on the Page Properties

FIGURE 312
Guinea Holidays Home Page

option to reveal the Page Properties window (Figure 309). Insert the new title Guinea Holidays.

5. Click on the Custom tab to allow you to add another meta tag (Figure 310). Click on the Add button to reveal the User Meta Variable window. Enter Description in the Name box and Guinea Holidays provides high quality care of guinea pigs while their owners are away in the Value box.

7. Insert the image guinea.gif into the page by selecting the Insert menu and highlighting the Picture option to reveal the submenu. Select the From File option to locate the picture file in the Images subfolder of the Web Design folder.

8. Right click on the image to open a menu and select the Picture properties option which will reveal its window. In the General Tab enter in the Alternative Representations Text box – Picture of a guinea pig. Select the Appearance tab and change the alignment to right. Click on the OK button.

9. Enter the Main Heading Guinea Holidays on the top line below the navigation table in Arial (sans serif), size 6 text, bold and centre the text. Leave a blank line and enter the subheading 'Carers of Guinea Pigs'.

10. You are now going to insert a text file into the page by selecting the Insert menu and clicking on File to reveal the window Select File. Change the Look in: box to show the Web Design Folder in which all your files are stored. Double click on homeguinea.txt. The Convert Text window will appear (Figure 311). Select Normal paragraphs and click on the OK button to insert the text.

11. Highlight the new text and change the font to Arial and the size to 3 (House Style).

12. Highlight the text again and change the line spacing to double by selecting the Format menu and the Paragraphs option.

13. Select the File menu and click on the Save option. Figure 315 shows the page.

14. Close the application by selecting the File menu and the Exit option or click on the application close button in top right hand corner.

Forms

When designing websites there are many occasions when you want to gain information from your users. You may want users to register themselves on your site. This is often required if your site is a commercial one or you want to know who your users are to help you meet their needs. If you are selling a product or service you will need information from your customers (e.g. credit cards details, delivery addresses etc.). FrontPage allows you to create interactive forms so that you can capture information from your users.

FIGURE 313
Contact Page Layout

Guinea Holidays Register
Please enter your details

1. Name:
2. Address
3. E-mail address
4. Please tell us about your pets
We will send you details of our service

Insert copyright statement here

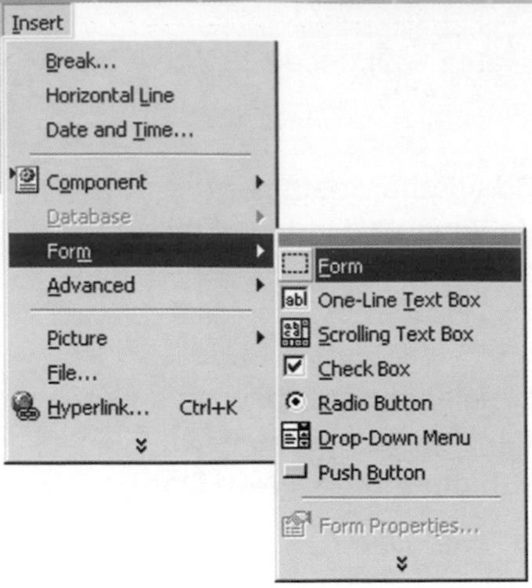

FIGURE 314
**Form
option**

Insert

Break...
Horizontal Line
Date and Time...

Component
Database
Form
Advanced

Picture
File...
Hyperlink...   Ctrl+K

Form
One-Line Text Box
Scrolling Text Box
Check Box
Radio Button
Drop-Down Menu
Push Button

Form Properties...

To create a form select the Insert menu and highlight the Form option to reveal a submenu (Figure 314). Click on the Form option. A small box will appear with two buttons Submit and Reset (Figure 315). Submit is intended to send the information supplied to a designated location while Reset allows you to clear the information inputted and to start again. To create a form you need to enter the different features that make up a form these are one line text, scrolling text and check boxes, drop down menus, push buttons as well as the Submit and Reset buttons.

FIGURE 315
Form

Submit Reset

These are placed at the cursor within the form area by using the submenu options. Text can be entered from the keyboard or pasted into the area to explain to users what the purpose of the elements are.

These elements need have their attributes set (i.e. name and value). To set the attributes you need to double click on the element (Figure 318) and a properties window will appear. This allows you to set the name of the element and its initial value.

The form's properties also need to be established so that the form knows what to do with the users input. Select the Insert menu, highlight the Form option and click on the Form Properties option. This opens the Form Properties window (Figure 319) which will allow you to enter the form details and decide where the information is to be sent.

FIGURE 316
Text Form

1. Name

2. Address

3. E-mail address

4. Please tell us about your pets

We will send you details of our service

Submit Reset

It is important to test the form to ensure that it is operating in the way you need it to. That is, the desired information is being collected and sent to the appropriate location.

Design brief for Contact Page

1. Design a web page in accordance with the House Style Guidelines and insert the specified content. Save your page as the html document guineacontact.htm

2. Page Title: Guinea Holidays Register

3. Additional meta tag: Customer register of interest

4. Insert the text file Contactguinea.txt as shown below (Figure 313):

5. Centre in the headings style Guinea Holidays Register

6. Centre in the subheading style Please enter your details

7. Imported text should be in the body style

8. Turn the imported text into an interactive form (Method = POST, Name = Register action = http://guineaholidays.co.uk/cgi-bin/script):

Name	One-line Text Box
Address	Scrolling Text Box
E-mail	One-line Text Box
Please tell us about your pets	Scrolling Text Box

9. Element Attributes

Name characters	Name, width 30
Address characters and 6 lines	Address, width 30
E-mail characters	Customer, width 60
Please tell us about your pets characters and 10 lines	Comments, width 30
Submit button Submit, value = Send your details	
Reset button Reset, value = Clear the entry	

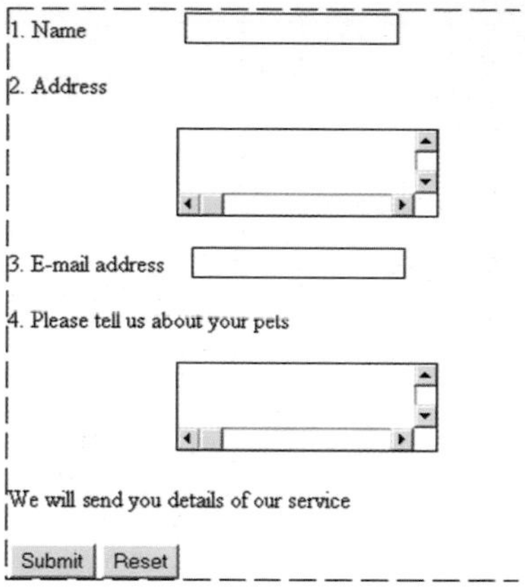

FIGURE 317
Completed Form

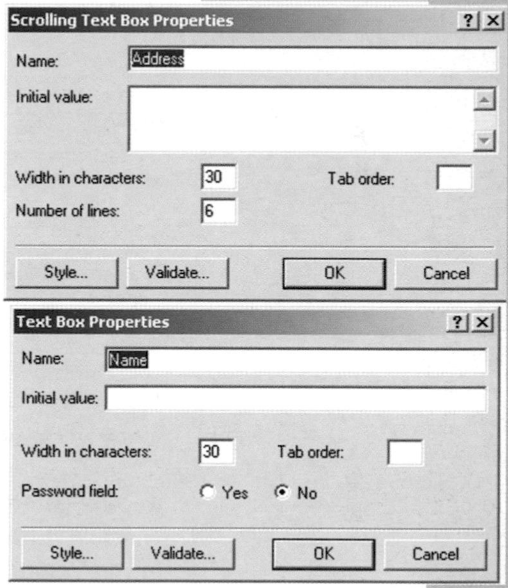

FIGURE 318
Properties Box

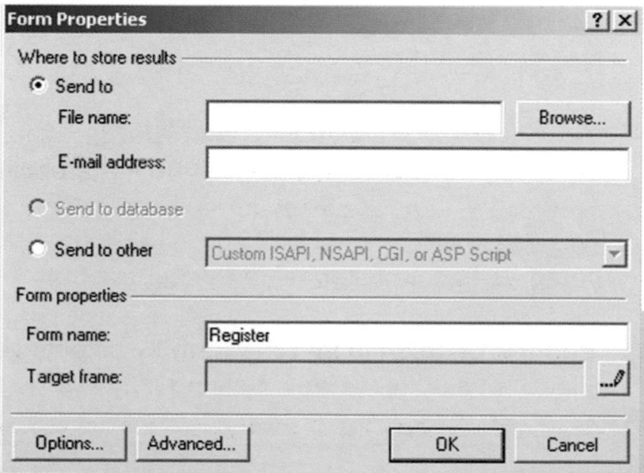

FIGURE 319
Form Properties

FIGURE 320
Contact Page

Exercise 44

Contact Page

1. FrontPage is opened by either selecting the Start button, highlighting the Programs option and clicking on the FrontPage option or by double clicking on the FrontPage icon on the Windows desktop.

2. The application will open with a new page in the work area. If the window is not maximised then use the standard buttons in the top right hand corner of the window to display it filling the screen. Select the File menu and click on the Open option to reveal the Open File window. Change the Look in: box to read Web Design and your file standard.htm should appear. Double click on the file to load it into FrontPage.

FIGURE 321
Advice Page Layout

Guinea Holidays Advice

Guinea Pig Image

Guinea Pigs are _____

Insert copyright statement here

3. Select the File menu and click on the Save As option to reveal the Save As window. Change the Save in: box to read Web Design and enter guineacontact.htm in the File name: box then click on the Save button.

4. Right click on the page to open a menu. Click on the Page Properties option to reveal the Page Properties window. Insert the new title Guinea Holidays Register.

5. Click on the Custom tab to allow you to add another meta tag. Click on the Add button to reveal the User Meta Variable window. Enter Description in the Name box and Customer register of interest in the Value box.

6. Enter the Main Heading Guinea Holidays Register on the top line below the navigation table in Arial (sans serif), size 6 text, bold and centre the text. Leave a blank line and enter the subheading Please enter your details in Arial, size 4 and centred.

7. You are now going to create a form. Select the Insert menu, highlight the Form option and click on the Form item (Figure 314).

This will insert a small box surrounded by a dotted line (Figure 315). The cursor is flashing alongside the submit button.

7. Insert a text file into the form by selecting the Insert menu and clicking on File to reveal the window Select File. Change the Look in: box to show the

Web Design Folder in which all your files are stored. Double click on contactguinea.txt. The Convert Text window will appear. Select Normal paragraphs and click on the OK button to insert the text (Figure 316).

8. To turn this layout into a form you need to add the form elements (e.g. single line boxes). Position your cursor alongside the Name label and select the Insert menu, highlight the Form option and click on the Form item (Figure 317). Click on the One-Line Text Box and it will be inserted alongside Name. Repeat this action to insert:

Address	Scrolling Text Box
E-mail	One-Line Text Box
Please tell us about your pets	Scrolling Text Box

9. Figure 317 shows you the completed form

10. You have now created a layout but you need to define what each element will accept. Click on each element and it will reveal a properties box (Figure 318). Enter the name of the element, width and number of lines.

11. Now set the attributes of the two buttons Submit and Reset by double clicking on them to reveal the Properties window. Change the Name and value to align with the Design Brief. Notice the label on the button changes.

12. The final stage of designing your form is to decide what you are going to do with the information. Select the Insert menu, highlight the Form option and click on the Form Properties item (Figure 314). This will open the Form Properties window (Figure 319) which allows you to name your form, enter the file name of the form details, an e-mail address to send details to or another action. In this case, if you enter invented information you may crash when you test the page or receive messages such as the site is unavailable, etc. You may also get error messages when entering invented information. In the assessment you will be provided with the correct details that will work with your form.

13. If you click on the HTML tab, you will see the language associated with the creation of the form.

```
<form method="POST" name="Register"
action="http://guineaholidays.co.uk/cgi-bin/script.cgi">
```

The HTML tag associated with creating an interactive form is Form. It has an attribute called method that indicates the way that the form details will be transferred from the browser to the computer server to the script processor. The script processor will handle the information. Method can have two values which determine how the information is sent. These are POST and GET.

FIGURE 322
**Advice
Page**

Action is another attribute of the form tag. It contains the name of the script that will process the form details. It will look like:
action="http://www.guineapig.co.uk/cgi-bin/script.cgi">.

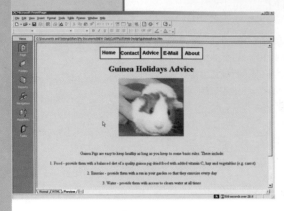

14. Your final design can be viewed using the Preview tab. Figure 320 provides our effort.

15. Select the File menu and click on the Save option.

16. It is important to test your form and in particular that the information is sent to the chosen location In this exercise we have provided you with ficticious website to send data to so testing is limited but you can enter information and try out the form. You will probably be presented with error messages when you submit your data.

17. Close the application by selecting the File menu and the Exit option or click on the application close button in top right hand corner.

Design brief for Advice Page

1. Design a web page in accordance with the House Style Guidelines and insert the specified content. Save your page as the html document guineaadvice.htm

2. Page Title: Guinea Holidays Advice

3. Additional meta tag: General advice about the care of guinea pigs

4. Insert the text file Adviceguinea.txt and image file guinea2.gif as shown in Figure 321.

5. Centre in the headings style Guinea Holidays Advice

6. Imported text should be in the body style

FIGURE 323
**About Page
Layout**

7. Format the guinea2.gif image as:

Image	Width	Height	Alternative Text	Image Alignment	Text Alignment
Guinea.gif	251	225	Picture of a	Centre	Centre

8. Save your page as guineaadvice.

FIGURE 324
About Page

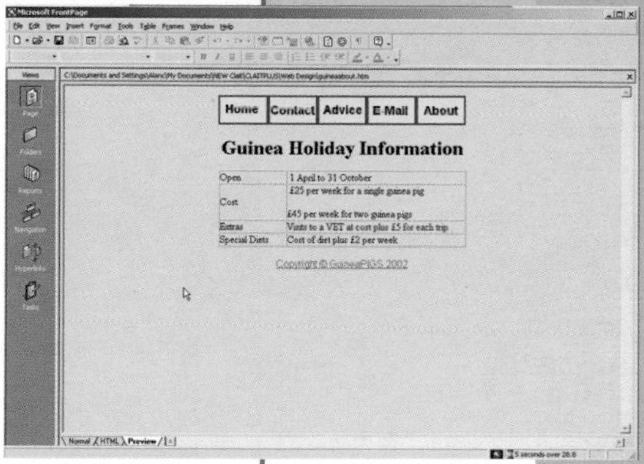

Exercise 45

Advice Page

1. FrontPage is opened by either selecting the Start button, highlighting the Programs option and clicking on the FrontPage option or by double clicking on the FrontPage icon on the Windows desktop.

2. The application will open with a new page in the work area. If the window is not maximised then use the standard buttons in the top right hand corner of the window to display it filling the screen. Select the File menu and click on the Open option to reveal the Open File window. Change the Look in: box to read Web Design and your file standard.htm should appear. Double click on the file to load it into FrontPage.

3. Select the File menu and click on the Save As option to reveal the Save As window. Change the Save in: box to read Web Design and enter guineaadvice.htm in the File name: box then click on the Save button.

4. Right click on the page to open a menu. Click on the Page Properties option to reveal the Page Properties window. Insert the new title Guinea Holidays Advice.

5. Click on the Custom tab to allow you to add another meta tag. Click on the Add button to reveal the User Meta Variable window. Enter Description in the Name box and General advice about the care of guinea pigs in the Value box.

6. Enter the Main Heading Guinea Holidays Advice on the top line below the navigation table in Arial (sans serif), size 6 text, bold and centre the text.

7. Insert the image guinea2.gif into the page by selecting the Insert menu and highlighting the Picture option to reveal the submenu. Select the From File option to locate the picture file in the Images subfolder of Web Design folder.

8. Right click on the image to open a menu and select the Picture properties option which will reveal its window. In the General Tab enter in the Alternative Representations Text box – Picture of a guinea pig. Select the Appearance tab and change the alignment to centre. Click on the OK button.

9. Insert a text file into the page by selecting the Insert menu and clicking on File to reveal the window Select File. Change the Look in: box to show the

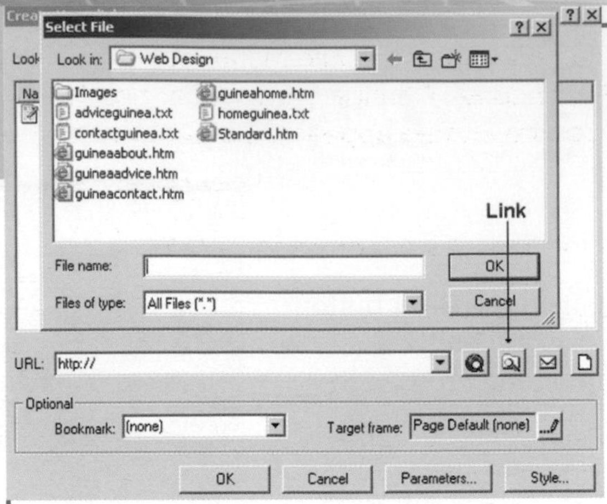

FIGURE 325
**Link to
Contact
Page**

Select File

Look in: Web Design

Images   guineahome.htm
adviceguinea.txt   homeguinea.txt
contactguinea.txt   Standard.htm
guineaabout.htm
guineaadvice.htm
guineacontact.htm

Link

File name: [   ]   OK

Files of type: All Files (*.*)   Cancel

URL: http://

Optional
Bookmark: [none]   Target frame: Page Default (none)

OK   Cancel   Parameters...   Style...

Web Design Folder in which all
your files are stored. Double click
on adviceguinea.txt. The Convert
Text window will appear. Select
Normal paragraphs and click on
the OK button to insert the text.

10. Centre the imported text.

11. Preview your page to check it
conforms to the design brief
(Figure 322).

12. Select the File menu and click on the Save option.

13. Close the application by selecting the File menu and the Exit option or
click on the application close button in top right hand corner.

Design brief for About Page

1. Design a web page in accordance with the House Style Guidelines and
   insert the specified content. Save your page as the html document
   guineaabout.htm

2. Page Title: Guinea Holidays Information

3. Additional meta tag: Background information about Guinea Pig Holidays

4. Insert the table as shown in Figure 323

5. Centre in the headings style Guinea Holidays Information

6. Table should be centred in the body style

7. Save your page as guineaabout

Exercise 46

About Page

1. FrontPage is opened by either selecting the Start button, highlighting the
Programs option and clicking on the FrontPage option or by double clicking
on the FrontPage icon on the Windows desktop.

2. The application will open with a new page in the work area. If the window
is not maximised then use the standard buttons in the top right hand corner

of the window to display it filling the screen. Select the File menu and click on the <u>O</u>pen option to reveal the Open File window. Change the Look in: box to read Web Design and your file standard.htm should appear. Double click on the file to load it into FrontPage.

FIGURE 326
**Testing
with a
Browser**

3. Select the <u>F</u>ile menu and click on the Save <u>A</u>s option to reveal the Save As window. Change the Save in: box to read Web Design and enter guineaabout.htm in the File <u>n</u>ame: box then click on the <u>S</u>ave button.

4. Right click on the page to open a menu. Click on the Page Properties option to reveal the Page Properties window. Insert the new title Guinea Holidays Information.

5. Click on the Custom tab to allow you to add another meta tag. Click on the Add button to reveal the User Meta Variable window. Enter Description in the Name box and Information about Guinea Holiday service in the Value box.

6. Enter the Main Heading Guinea Holidays Information on the top line below the navigation table in Arial (sans serif), size 6 text, bold and centre the text.

7. Insert a table into the centre of the page with 2 columns and 4 rows and a border size of 1 by selecting the <u>T</u>able menu, highlighting <u>I</u>nsert option and clicking on the <u>T</u>able item. Enter the number of columns, rows, size of border and centre alignment.

Open	1 April to 31 October
Cost	£25 per week for a single guinea pig £45 per week for two guinea pigs
Extra	Visits to a VET at cost plus £5 for each trip
Special Diets	Cost of diet plus £2 per week

8. To adjust the column widths you place your pointer over the column divide line and it will change shape to a double arrowed pointer. If you hold down the mouse button you can drag the line to the position you desire.

9. Preview your page to check it conforms to the design brief (Figure 324).

10. Select the <u>F</u>ile menu and click on the <u>S</u>ave option.

11. Close the application by selecting the <u>F</u>ile menu and the <u>E</u>xit option or click on the application close button in top right hand corner.

Hyperlinks

The World Wide Web is a nonlinear environment and you navigate around the websites and within sites using links. These connect the different pages and provide the routes between the different parts of the site. You can even link within a page. You have considerable freedom when creating links. You can create multiple links from a page to many others or a single connection. The choice is yours. Your links can be to:

• Another page of the same website
• Another page of a different website
• An e-mail system so that you can send messages
• A bookmarked/anchored section within a page

This freedom to create many and different types of links can lead to users getting confused when using the site so you need to carefully consider your reasons for the link. In the exercises you have consistently employed a navigation bar with icons to link to different parts of the site. This provides a consistency that will help users to navigate the site. Each icon serves as a link to another page or to an e-mail system.

Links can be anchored to both text and images and need to be consistently employed to assist users to understand your approach. Text links are normally underlined to indicate that they are a connection to another page. Image links are normally shown by the mouse pointer changing shape when it moves over the link. Links between pages normally take you to the top of the new page but you can also link to particular parts of a page. FrontPage calls these areas bookmarks but they are sometimes called anchors. They are often useful within a long webpage so that you can move quickly between the different sections without scrolling down. Figure 301 shows the bookmark box in the optional area at the bottom of the window. Figure 327A shows the use of anchors within a long page.

Anchors provide a useful means of helping users navigate within a page. Often they offer a link to return to the original location so that users avoid being confused about where they are. To a user it is often difficult to distinguish between a link within a page or to a new page or even to a new site.

You have now created all four pages that make up the website and it remains for you to create the hyperlinks between the pages which will produce the site. Exercise 47 concentrates on creating hyperlinks.

Exercise 47

Linking

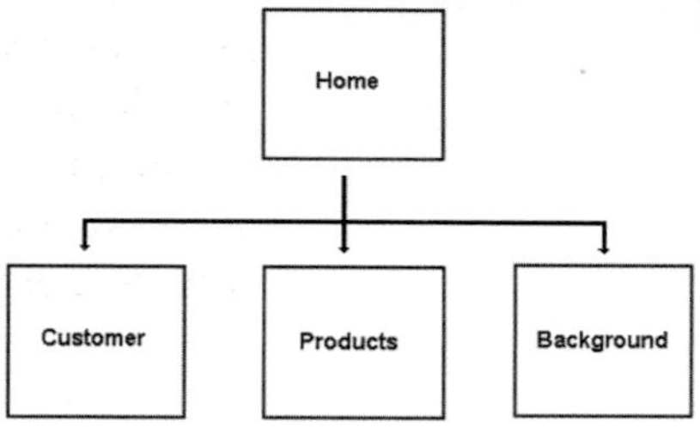

1. FrontPage is opened by either selecting the Start button, highlighting the Programs option and clicking on the FrontPage option or by double clicking on the FrontPage icon on the Windows desktop.

2. The application will open with a new page in the work area. If the window is not maximised then use the standard buttons in the top right hand corner of the window to display it filling the screen. Select the File menu and click on the Open option to reveal the Open File window. Change the Look in: box to read Web Design and your file guineahome.htm should appear. Double click on the file to load it into FrontPage.

3. You need to create links between the home page and the contact, advice and about pages. In addition you will also link the image to an external site.

4. Click on the Contact button and select the Insert menu then click on the Hyperlink option to reveal the Create Hyperlink window. Click on the make a hyperlink to a file on your computer (Figure 325). This will open the Select File window. Change the Look in: box to Web Design folder and double click on guineacontact.htm.

5. Repeat this process for the Advice and About button linking them to advice and about pages.

6. You can check that the links work by using the Preview tab.

7. To create an external link from the image, click on the guinea pig image to enclose it in a frame then select the Insert menu and click on the Hyperlink option. Enter the URL of the site you want to link to (select a site you would like to link to e.g. http://www.hodderclait.co.uk) and click on the OK button. You can also use your browser to locate the site.

8. Select the File menu and click on the Save option

9. You have now linked the home page to the other pages but you now need to link the other pages to each other. This will provide you with plenty of practice of linking.

10. Preview each page to check the links.

FIGURE 327
Site Map

FIGURE 328
Home Page Layout

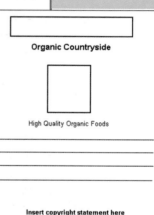

Organic Countryside

High Quality Organic Foods

Insert copyright statement here

FIGURE 329
**Customer
Page
Layout**

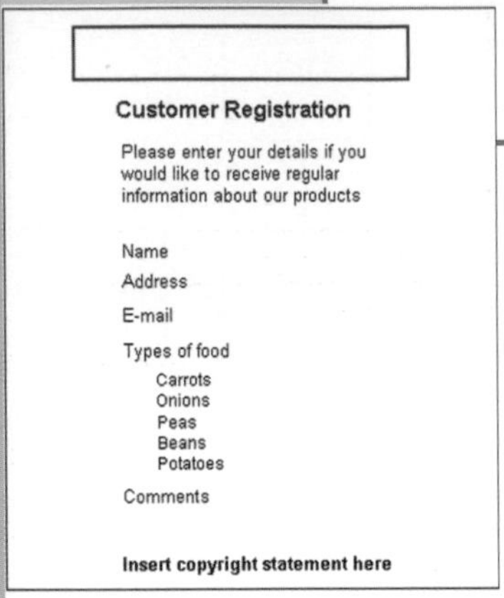

Customer Registration

Please enter your details if you
would like to receive regular
information about our products

Name
Address
E-mail
Types of food
 Carrots
 Onions
 Peas
 Beans
 Potatoes
Comments

Insert copyright statement here

11. Select the File menu and click on the Save option for each page.

12. Close the application by selecting the File menu and the Exit option or click on the application close button in top right hand corner.

Testing

You have created a small website and tested it using the Preview tab within FrontPage. However, this is not a substitute for testing your site using a browser. So open your browser by clicking on the browser (e.g. Internet Explorer) icon on your desktop or select the Start button, highlight the Programs option and click on the browser (e.g. Internet Explorer) option.

Enter the path to your file guineahome.htm (e.g. C:\web design\guineahome.htm) and press enter. Your home page should appear in the browser work area. You can now try each link. This process is essential in that you are testing the pages in the real environment.

Testing is important to ensure your users are not fustrated when using the website. However, even when the links operate perfectly it is easy for a user to become disorientated in a site.

One way of reducing disorientation and users getting lost is to provide a site map to help navigation. It is also useful during the design process in that it provides an overview of the whole site.

More Practice

Context

You are going to create a site that is intended to sell organic food. The site will have four pages – home, customer, product information and background about the location.

House Style

Site Structure

• all files must be saved to Organic folder
• all image files should be stored in a sub-folder of Organic called Images
• all links to files and images on the website should be relative, not absolute

Standard Page Properties

• Title – specified in Design Brief

• Background Colour - #008080 (Hexadecimal code of the colour Teal)

Standard Text Properties

• Text Colour - #000000 (Hexadecimal code of the colour Black)
• Link Colour – #0000FF (Hexadecimal code of the colour Blue)
• Visited Link Colour – #800080 (Hexadecimal code of the colour Purple)
• Active Link Colour - #0000FF (Hexadecimal code of the colour red)
• Typeface (font) – sans serif
• Text Size:

  - Main Heading – HTML size 7 (36 pt)
  - Subheading – HTML size 5 (18 pts)
  - Body Text – HTML size 3 (12 pts)

Image Properties

• Image height and width must be accurately specified
• Image borders set to zero
• Alt text specified by Design Brief

Design Brief - Standard

This is the design brief for the standard layout page on which all the pages will be based.

Meta Tags

Each page should have the following meta tag information:

Name	Content
Author	Your name and centre number
Keywords	rural, organic, food
Description	see individual page design brief

Navigation Table

Table of navigation icons must be placed at the top of each page

Width 400, Height 48, columns 5, Rows 1, Centred, Cellspacing 0, Cellpadding 0 and Border 0

Home	Customer	Products	E-Mail
Background			

FIGURE 330
Product Page Layout

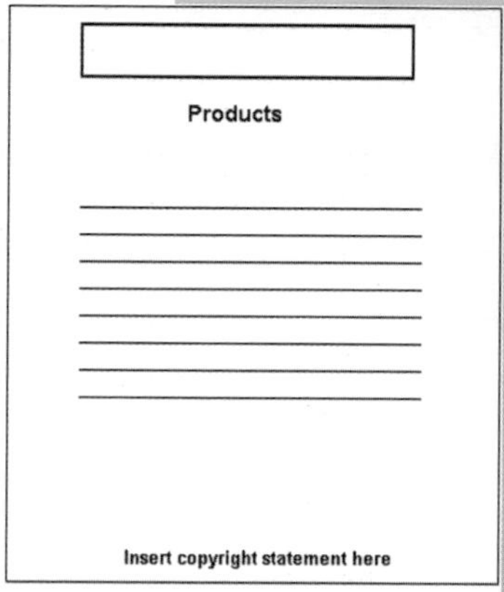

Products

Insert copyright statement here

FIGURE 331
Background Page Layout

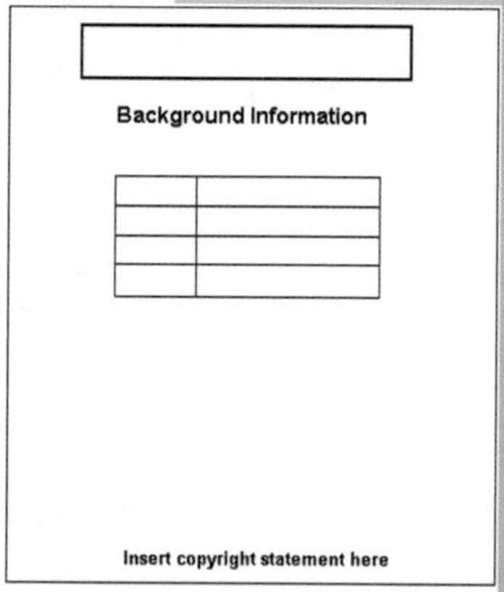

Background Information

Insert copyright statement here

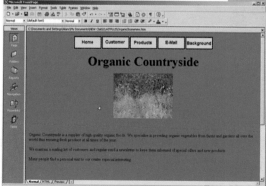

FIGURE 332
Organic Countryside HomePage

The images are all width 106 and height 48.

Image	Alt Text	Link
Home	Home Page	Homenew.htm
Customer	Book a holiday	Booking.htm
Products	Information about the organic products	Product.htm
E-Mail	Messages	E-mail link to organic@countryside.co.uk
Background	Background information about the location	Background.htm

Copyright Notice

Each Page should have this notice at the bottom:
Copyright © OrganicCountryside 2002, centred, body text size and linked to organic@countryside.co.uk

Organic Site Map

Figure 327 shows the map of the Organic site.

Design brief for home page

1. Create a web page in accordance with the House Style Guidelines and insert the specified content. Save your page as the html document homenew.htm

2. Title of the page: Organic Foods

3. Add the following meta tag: Organic Countryside are suppliers of high quality organic foods

4. Add the text file Homenew.txt and image file countryside.gif as shown in the layout below (Figure 328):

5. Centre in the headings style Organic Countryside

6. Centre in the subheading style High Quality Organic Food

7. Imported text should be in the body style with the text double spaced

8. Format the countryside.gif image as:

Image	Width	Height	Alternative Text	Image Alignment	Text Alignment
country--side.gif	230	173	Picture of a countryside	Centre	Centre

9. Save the page as homenew.htm

Design brief for Customer Page

1. Design a web page in accordance with the House Style Guidelines and insert the specified content. Save your page as the html document booking.htm

2. Page Title: Customer Registration

3. Additional meta tag: Customer can register on the mailing list
4. Insert the text file registration.txt as shown below (Figure 329):

5. Centre in the headings style Customer Registration

6. Centre in the subheading style. Please enter your details if you would like to receive regular information about our products

7. Imported text should be in the body style

8. Turn the imported text into an interactive form (Method = POST, Name = Register action = http://organiccountryside.co.uk/cgi-bin/script):

Name   -   One-line Text Box

Address   -   Scrolling Text Box

E-mail   -   One-line Text Box

Types of Food

   Carrots   -   radio button
   Onions   -   radio button
   Peas   -   radio button
   Beans   -   radio button
   Potatoes   -   radio button

   Comments   -   Scrolling Text Box

9. Element Attributes

Name   -   Name, width 20 characters

  Address   -   Address, width 30 characters and 5 lines

  E-mail   -   Customer, width 50 characters

  Radio Button   -   Food, value = Carrots,

Radio Button	-	Food, value = Onions
Radio Button	-	Food, value = Peas
Radio Button	-	Food, value = Beans
Radio Button	-	Food, value = Potatoes

Comments   - Comments, width 30 characters and 8 lines

Submit button   - Submit, value = Send your details

Reset button   - Reset, value = Clear the entry

Design brief for Products Page

1. Design a web page in accordance with the House Style Guidelines and insert the specified content. Save your page as the html document products.htm

2. Page Title: Products

3. Additional meta tag: Information about the available products

4. Insert the text file information.txt as shown in Figure 330.

5. Centre in the headings style Products

6. Imported text should be in the body style

7. Save your page as product.htm.

Design brief for Background Page

1. Design a web page in accordance with the House Style Guidelines and insert the specified content. Save your page as the html document background.htm

2. Page Title: Background

3. Additional meta tag: Background information about the location of Organic Countryside

4. Insert the table as shown in Figure 331

5. Centre in the headings style Food Information

6. Table should be centred in the body style

Directions Take the M1 to junction 24 and ....

Opening Hours 9 to 6 pm Mon to Sat

Refreshments   Green Vegetable Hotel
Car Parking   Spaces for 50 cars

7. Save your page as Background.htm

Figure 332 shows the Home page of Organic Countryside within the
FrontPage work area.

Summary

1. Load Microsoft FrontPage

Select the Start button, highlight the Programs option and click on the FrontPage option or double click on the FrontPage icon on the Windows desktop.

2. Background Colour

Select the Format menu and click on the Background option to reveal the Page Properties window. Select the Background tab. Click on the down arrow alongside the Background box and a small palette of colours will appear. Select the colour of your choice.

3. Text Colour

Select the Format menu and click on the Background option to reveal the Page Properties window. Select the Background tab. Click on the down arrow alongside the Text box and a small palette of colours will appear. Select the colour of your choice.

4. Link Colour

Select the Format menu and click on the Background option to reveal the Page Properties window. Select the Background tab. Click on the down arrow alongside the Hyperlink box and a small palette of colours will appear. Select the colour of your choice.

5. Visited Link Colour

Select the Format menu and click on the Background option to reveal the Page Properties window. Select the Background tab. Click on the down arrow alongside the Visited Hyperlink box and a small palette of colours will appear. Select the colour of your choice.

6. Active Link Colour

Select the Format menu and click on the Background option to reveal the Page Properties window. Select the Background tab. Click on the down arrow alongside the Active Hyperlink box and a small pallete of colours will appear. Select the colour of your choice.

7. Hexadecimal Colours

Colours are shown using their hexadecimal code in HTML so:

- #00FFFF - aqua
- #008080 - teal

8. Meta Tags

Additional meta information can be inserted directly into the HTML code

For example

<meta name="Author" content= "Your name and centre number">
<meta name="Keywords" content=" guinea, pigs, hotel, holiday ">

or

Right click to reveal a menu, click on the Page Properties option to reveal the Page Properties window. Select the Custom tab and in the User variables, click the Add button. Add Name and Value (i.e. content).

9. Insert Table

Select the Table menu, highlight the Insert option to reveal the Table option. Click on Table to open the Insert Table window.

10. Insert Graphic

Select the Insert menu, highlight the Picture option and click on the From File option to reveal the Select File window.

11. Hyperlinks

Select the Insert menu and click on the Hyperlink option to reveal the Create Hyperlink window. There are four small buttons alongside the URL box. These relate to different types of links.

12. Image Attributes

Right click on an image to reveal a menu. Click on the Picture Properties option to reveal the Picture Properties window. The Appearance tab opens a window which allows you to change alignment, border thickness and size. Different styles of borders are also available from the General tab display by selecting the Style button, clicking on the Format button and selecting a Border from a drop down list.

13. Page Properties – Meta tag

Right click on the page to open a menu. Click on the Page Properties option to reveal the Page Properties window. Click on the Custom tab which lets you add another meta tag. Click on the Add button to reveal the User Meta Variable window.

14. Image - Alt tag

Right click on the image to open a menu and select the Picture Properties option which will reveal its window. In the General Tab enter your text in the Alternative Representations box. Click on the OK button.

15. Forms

Select the Insert menu, highlight the Form option and click on the Form item.

16. Form Elements

Position your cursor where you want to place the element and select the Insert menu then highlight the Form option. Click on the desired element (e.g. One-Line Text Box).

17. Form Element - attributes

Click on each element to reveal a properties box. Enter the name of the element, width and number of lines etc.

18. Testing

Click on the Preview tab within FrontPage.

or

Open your browser. Enter the path to your file (e.g. C:\web design\guineahome.htm) and press enter.

Electronic Communications

This chapter will help you to:

- Use advanced e-mail features to co-ordinate information

- Set up distribution lists and use an address book

- Use PIM software to organise schedules and business data

- Manage mailbox and folders

- Publish/print calendar dates

This chapter covers Unit 8 (Electronic Communication). There are no pre-conditions for studying this unit. However, its content does assume that you have the skills and understanding that are provided by the OCR Level 1 ICT course New CLAIT (e.g. Unit 3 - Electronic Communication, Unit 11 - Becoming Webwise and Unit 1 - Using a Computer).

Assessment

After studying Unit 8 your skills and understanding are assessed during a 3 hour practical assignment. This is set by OCR and marked locally. However, the marking will be externally moderated by OCR. This ensures that the standard is being applied correctly across the many different providers of OCR CLAIT Plus. If you are unsuccessful then you can be re-assessed using a different assignment.

Microsoft Outlook

Microsoft Outlook is an application designed to help you organise your working life. It provides you with a variety of systems including:

- A comprehensive e-mail system
- A personal and group work scheduler
- A contact and address book
- A desk diary
- A project manager
- A work monitor

The application is illustrated in Figure 333. This shows the view of the Outlook e-mail inbox. The application is divided in a series of areas. These are from left to right:

- Shortcuts – there are three sets (i.e. Outlook, My Shortcuts and Other Shortcuts)

- Folder List

- List of E-mails in the inbox – top area

- Preview of the current e-mail – bottom area

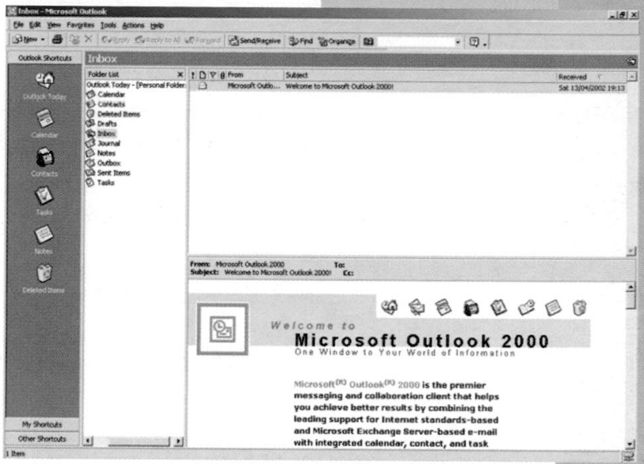

FIGURE 333
Microsoft Outlook

Across the top of the application are the normal menu and tool bars which are a part of many windows applications.

The Shortcuts area provides a list of icons that link you to the various functions of Outlook. The three sets of shortcuts are accessed by buttons at the bottom of the area. The Outlook Shortcuts are displayed by default and provide you with connections to:

- Outlook Today
- Calendar
- Contacts
- Tasks
- Notes
- Deleted items

The My Shortcuts provide links to:

- Inbox
- Drafts
- Journal
- Outlook Update

The Other Shortcuts provide links to:

- My Computer
- My Documents
- Favourites

These allow you to access to the files and folders of the other applications on the computer.

Creating an E-mail message

E-mail is an effective communication medium for business users. It combines a rapid transmission method with useful record keeping features. The e-mail system automatically records the date and time the message is sent while the sender's details are attached so that the recipient can easily identify who has

FIGURE 334
Creating an E-mail

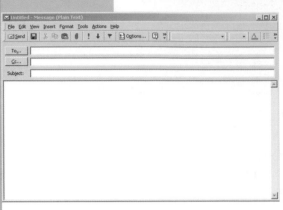

sent the communication. The initial message is retained in the reply making it is simple to understand the context of the message without having to look at files or other records. E-mail can be stored in an appropriate folder enabling complete records of business dealings to be maintained.

E-mail provides you with the means of keeping a complete record which is dated and holds the senders and recipients details. This is very useful if misunderstandings happen or people disagree about decisions that have been made. Paper communications suffer from often only providing a partial record in that dates, names and details are sometimes missing. It is often not clear what they are responding to or who has been sent copies. E-mail automatically provides this information and filing is a simple matter. Paper records are more easily lost or misfiled.

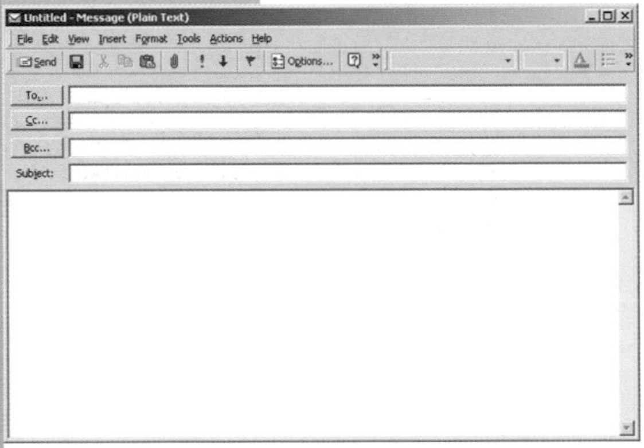

FIGURE 335
Bcc Options

E-mails are created by selecting the New button on the standard toolbar to reveal the Message window (Figure 334). This is divided into two main areas:

• The address area in which you place the e-mail address of the person(s) you are e-mailing (i.e. To... box), the address of any other people you want to copy the message to (i.e. Cc) and finally the subject of the message. When you address an E-mail it is critical to ensure that you are accurate. A single mistake (eg. reversing a letter, misspelling etc.) will ensure that the message is not received. There is also the danger that the message will be sent to the wrong person. Perfection is required with all addresses.

• The message area where you enter your communication

There is an extra box called Bcc which you can add to the message. This enables blind copying in which you copy the message to another person or persons but their names will be hidden in the recipient's copy of the message. Blind copying is used to maintain confidentiality. The option is added to the message by selecting the View menu and clicking on the Bcc option. The new message window is shown in Figure 335.

FIGURE 336
High Importance

Priorities

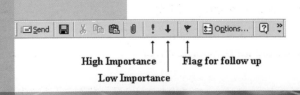

High Importance   Flag for follow up

Low Importance

When you send e-mails it is possible to indicate whether the message is important by adding a particular symbol. This is achieved by clicking on the icon indicated by an exclamation mark (Figure 336). Other related options are low importance and follow up flag.

Most e-mail users get a large number of messages so that it is useful to indicate when one is important so that recipients can identify those which need their immediate attention.

FIGURE 337
Practice Message

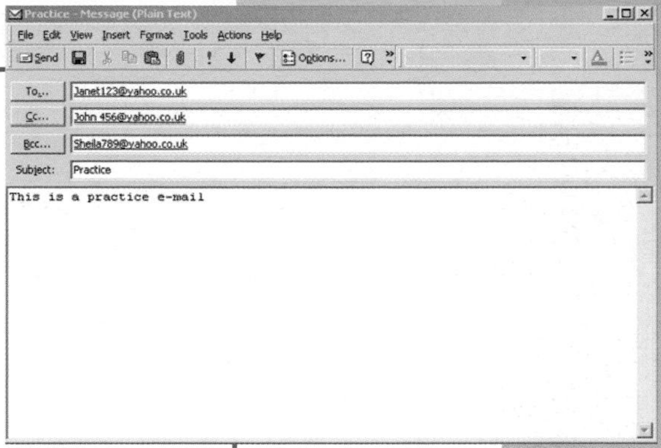

Exercise 48
Creating an E-mail

1. Outlook is opened by either selecting the Start button, highlighting the Programs option and clicking on the Outlook option or by double clicking on the Outlook icon on the Windows desktop

2. Create a new e-mail by clicking on the new icon to reveal the message window (Figure 334). Add a blind copy option to the message window by selecting the <u>V</u>iew menu and clicking on the <u>B</u>cc option. You will notice an extra line is added to the message window (Figure 335).

3. Create the message below:

FIGURE 338
Outbox

To: Janet123@yahoo.co.uk
Cc: John 456@yahoo.co.uk
Bcc: Sheila789@yahoo.co.uk

Practice

This is a practice e-mail

If you are working with a group of other learners then substitute the three e-mail addresses with those of your peers. Send the e-mail and see how it appears to the recipient (Figure 337).

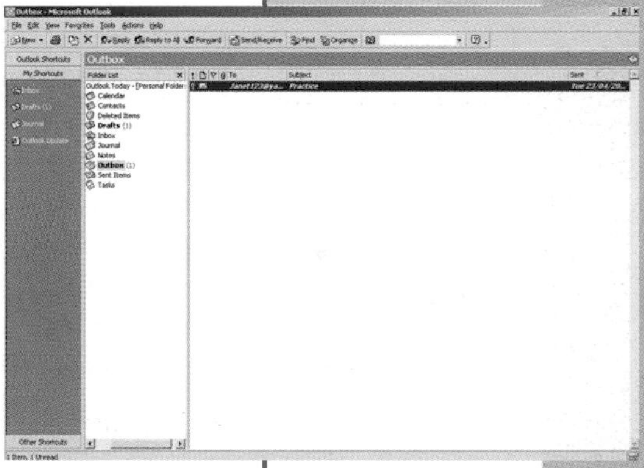

4. Give the message a high priority by selecting the High Importance icon on the toolbar.

5. If you are interrupted before you can finish your e-mail then you can save it to complete later. Select the <u>F</u>ile menu and click on the <u>C</u>lose option. A message will appear asking you if you want to save your message. Click on the Yes button. Your message will be saved as a draft in the folder list (i.e. Draft (1)) and you will see the number of drafts increased by one. To retrieve it simply click on Drafts and a list of them will appear in main work area. Click on the Practice message and send the e-mail.

FIGURE 339
Signatures

6. To send the message click on the Send button on the toolbar. If your system is connected to the Internet the message will be sent. If not, it will be stored in the Outbox until the next time you make a connection (Figure 338). Observe in the folder list that the Outbox item has a number in brackets indicating the number of messages waiting to be sent.

7. Close Outlook by selecting the File menu and clicking on the Exit option or click on the Close button in the top right hand corner of the application. You may be presented with a message informing you that there are unsent messages in your Outbox and asking if you would still like to close the application. Say yes.

Receiving E-mails

E-mails may be received every time you connect to the Internet. They will be held in your Inbox until you are ready to open them. Figure 333 shows the Inbox with a single message listed in the top box while the contents of the e-mail are shown in the preview box. If you have more than one message then the one highlighted is previewed.

Mail Folders

Most people find that the number of e-mails you receive rapidly grows when you begin to use e-mail. This indicates their value but to benefit from e-mail once their numbers start to grow you need to be organized. You will often want to refer back to messages in order to take advantage of them so that you need to store them in a way that makes retrieving them a straightforward process. The normal way of storing e-mails is to establish a series of mail folders for the main people who send you messages. By creating a series of folders in which to store mail you make it quicker to locate the ones you need. If they are all stored in a single folder you will quickly find hundreds if not thousands of messages stored in it so that finding a particular one is very difficult. A single folder is the equivalent of keeping all your papers in a pile on your desk. You will find it difficult to find the papers you need.

FIGURE 340
New Signatures

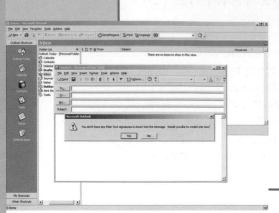

To create a new mail folder select the File menu, highlight the New option and click on the Folder option. This will open the Create New Folder window.

The folder is created by entering the folder name and then highlighting where to locate the folder in the Select where to place the folder area. In Figure 341a the folder will be placed within the inbox folder. When you are ready click on the OK button to create the mail folder.

Once you have created a series of mail folders you may want to move messages between them. This can be achieved by dragging and dropping in that you open the mail folder in which the messages are stored, click on the selected message and hold down the mouse button. The message can then be dragged over the new folder and the button released. The message will have moved to the new location (folder). Dragging and dropping needs to be practiced but is an efficient and effective way of moving messages between folders.

FIGURE 341
**Insert
Window**

Signatures

You can add a signature to your e-mail by selecting the Insert menu on the toolbar of the message window then highlighting the Signature option to reveal the More option. Click on this and you will be presented with a message asking you if you would like to create a signature. Click on the Yes button (Figure 339). This will open the Create New Signature window (Figure 340). You can now enter your name and click on Next to complete the process. When you next select, you will find available the signature you have created.

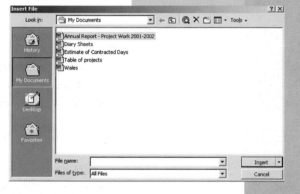

An alternative approach is to select the Tools menu on the main application and click on the Options item then on Mail Format tab. This will reveal a section called Signature.

Attachments

One of the major advantages of using e-mail is that you can attach files of information to your messages. These can be of any type but you must always remember that in order to open the attached file your recipient must have access to the application that created or a compatible one. Otherwise the file cannot be opened and this is unfortunately a regular problem with e-mail attachments. You can reduce this problem by considering what applications your recipients is likely to have or by asking them. If you do not know if a recipients has the particular application it is sometimes useful to convert files into generic formats.

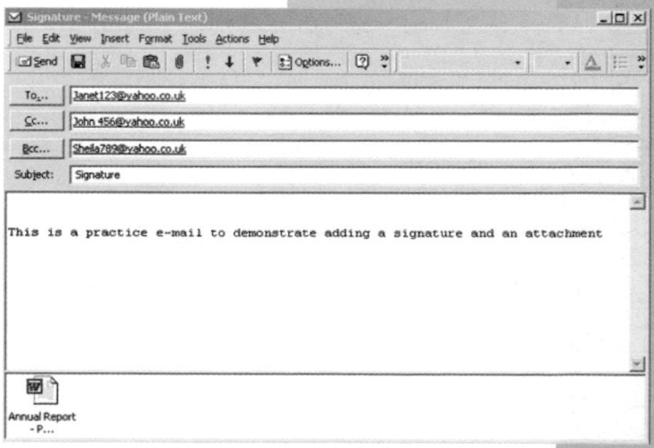

FIGURE 342
Attachment

For example

Word File – convert into a text file or a rich text file – these

FIGURE 343
Address Book

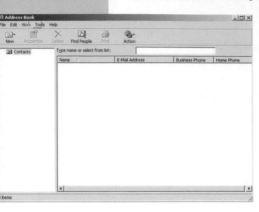

are opened by most word processors

You can attach many files to a single e-mail and they can be a mix of different formats. However, it is useful to consider the size of each file and the overall size of them all. Some e-mail systems limit the size of e-mails that they will accept so that you may have your messages refused unless you limit their size. Also if you are sending a message with attachments to a home computer they are likely to have a low speed connection to the Internet so that large attachments will mean that they are downloaded very slowly. Few home recipients will be pleased if your e-mail takes twenty, thirty or sixty minutes to download. They are paying the telephone costs.

It is good practice to consider file sizes and if they are too large to send several e-mails with a single attachment or to compress the files so that their size is reduced.

FIGURE 344
New Contact or New Group

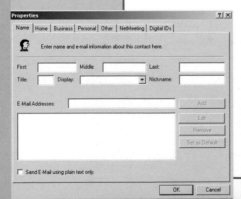

FIGURE 345

Exercise 50

Signatures and Attachments

1. Outlook is opened by either selecting the Start button, highlighting the Programs option and clicking on the Outlook option or by double clicking on the Outlook icon on the Windows desktop.

2. You are going to create a new signature so select the Tools menu and click on the Options item to open the Options window. Click on the Mail Format tab and the Signature Picker button to reveal the Signature Picker window. Click on the New button and Create New Signature will open (Figure 340). Enter your name and click on Next then Finish buttons. Close the open windows. You will now be able to select your name as a signature for your messages.

3. Click on New to create a new e-mail message. Select the Insert menu, highlight the Signatures option to reveal the signatures you can choose from. Select your own name.

4. Now enter the following message

To: Janet123@yahoo.co.uk
Cc: John 456@yahoo.co.uk
Bcc: Sheila789@yahoo.co.uk

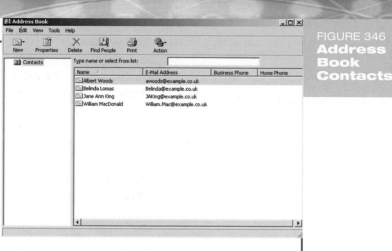

FIGURE 346
**Address
Book
Contacts**

Signature

This is a practise e-mail to demonstrate adding a signature and an attachment

If you are working in a group then address your e-mail (To: Cc: and Bcc: to other members of the group). This will allow everyone else to practise receiving e-mail and let you to see what your message looks like when it is received.

5. E-mails are not limited to the message you enter at the keyboard. You can attach files of any type. To add an attachment, select the Insert menu and the File option to reveal the Insert File window (Figure 341). Change the folder in the Look in: box to locate the file of your choice. Select it to add to your message (Figure 342). You can add many files to some E-mail by repeating the process.

6. Send the message by clicking on the Send button on the toolbar.

7. Close Outlook by selecting the File menu and clicking on the Exit option or click on the Close button in the top right hand corner of the application. You may be presented with a message informing you that there are unsent messages in your Outbox and asking if you would still like to close the application. Say yes.

FIGURE 347
**Properties
Window**

Address Book

In addition to sending and receiving messages, you can also store e-mail addresses and details of your contacts. Without these components you would need to maintain a paper address book. An electronic system not only duplicates the features of a paper address book but it is possible to establish mailing lists or groups, allowing you to send a message to a group of users as easily as sending one to an individual. This is very useful in any organisation.

Microsoft Outlook provides you with an address book (Figure 343). You can enter new contacts or create distribution lists.

FIGURE 348
**Group
Members
Window**

FIGURE 349
Select Names

FIGURE 350
Distribution List

Select contacts
from the Address
Book

Create new
contacts

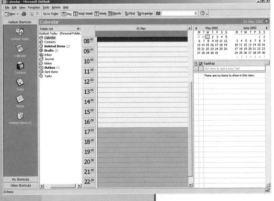

FIGURE 351
Calendar

Exercise 51

Address Book

1. Outlook is opened by either selecting the Start button, highlighting the Programs option and clicking on the Outlook option or by double clicking on the Outlook icon on the Windows desktop.

2. Select the Tools menu and click on the Address Book option. This will reveal the address book (Figure 343). To add a new contact or new group (i.e. distribution list) click on the New icon (Figure 344). Two options will be shown to you. Click on the New Contact option to reveal the Properties window (Figure 345). You will notice that a series of tabs across the top of the window that allow you to categorise your information. Explore the different tabs until you are familiar with them.

3. Return to the Name tab and enter the following contact:

Ms Jane Anne King, JAKing@example.co.uk

Accuracy is important since you will later rely on this entry for your e-mails. Check each entry carefully.

Click on the Add button and see the e-mail address appear in the work area. Click on the OK button. The properties window will disappear and you will see the new contact information appear in the address book.

4. Add the following contacts:

Dr. William MacDonald, William.Mac@example.co.uk
Miss Belinda Lomas, Belinda@example.co.uk
Mr Albert Woods, awoods@example.co.uk

FIGURE 352
**Organise
Tasks**

Figure 346 shows the address book after the contacts have been added. You will notice that you have no entries for business and home telephone numbers. Extend your entries by double clicking on the item (i.e. Albert Woods) which will open the properties and allow you to extend it by selecting other tabs and entering the new data. Obviously you could have entered all the information when you first added the new contact but there are occasions when you initially have only partial data.

This is a note

02/05/2002 03:21

5. The other option available from the New icon is to create a new group. If you click on the New Group option you will reveal the Properties window (Figure 347). Enter a group name – Example - and click on the Select members button to reveal the Select Group Members window (Figure 348).

6. You can create a group based on existing contacts, new contacts or a mix. To add existing contacts to your group, highlight the contact and click on the Select button. Add the four contacts you created earlier to your group. To add a new contact click on New Contacts button to reveal the Properties window and enter a contact in the normal way. As soon as you click on the OK button the entry appears in the list of existing contacts for you to select for your group. When you have completed your selections click on the OK button to return to the Example Properties window. Click on the OK button again and your group will be added to your list of contacts.

FIGURE 353
**Change the
Date**

◄	May 2002						June 2002					►
M	T	W	T	F	S	S	M	T	W	T	F	S	S
29	30	1	2	3	4	5						1	2
6	7	8	9	10	11	12	3	4	5	6	7	8	9
13	14	15	16	17	18	19	10	11	12	13	14	15	16
20	21	22	23	24	25	26	17	18	19	20	21	22	23
27	28	29	30	31			24	25	26	27	28	29	30
							1	2	3	4	5	6	7

7. Close the Address Book by clicking on the Close button in the top right hand corner of the window. To access the address book contacts, open a new e-mail by clicking on the New icon on the toolbar to reveal the message window. Select the To... button to show the Select Names window (Figure 349). You can place any contact or group into the To, Cc or Bcc fields by highlighting the entry and clicking on the appropriate field button.

8. Practise using the window to select different contacts until you are confident that you can use the address book.

9. Outlook also provides you with the means to print your contacts and groups. Select the Print icon on the address book toolbar to open the Print window. Choose the print ranges (i.e. all or selection) and print styles (i.e. memo, business card or phone list). Experiment with the different selections until you are confident that you understand the different choices.

View

   Current View ▸

   Go To ▸

✓ Outlook Bar

▤ Folder List

1 Day

5 Work Week

7 Week

31 Month

   TaskPad View ▸

▤ Preview Pane

   Toolbars ▸

FIGURE 354
**Different
Views**

FIGURE 355
**Actions
Menu**

10. Close all the open windows by clicking on the Close button in the top right hand corner of each window.

11. Close Outlook by selecting the File menu and clicking on the Exit option or click on the Close button in the top right hand corner of the application. You may be presented with a message informing you that there are unsent messages in your Outbox and asking if you would still like to close the application. Say yes.

FIGURE 355
**Actions
Menu**

FIGURE 356
**Appointment
Recurrence**

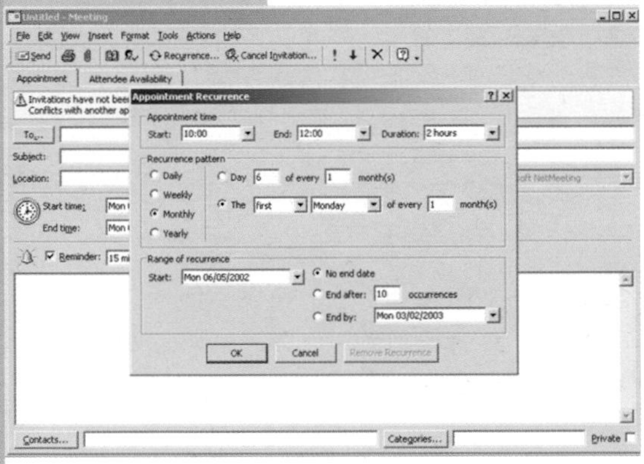

Alternative approach to creating a group/distribution list

There is an alternative method of creating a distribution list. Select the File menu, then highlight the New option to reveal a menu of choices. Click on the Distribution List option to open the Distribution List window (Figure 350). To select from the existing address book contacts you need to click on the Select Members button. New contacts are added to the list by clicking on the Add New button.

Personal Information Manager

Microsoft Outlook provides a number of functions to help you to organise your life. The three main ones are:

• A calendar (Figure 351)
• A To Do list (Figure 351)
• Notes (Figure 351)

The calendar allows you to schedule your work on a daily, weekly or monthly basis over many months while the To Do list lets you create a list of tasks you need to complete. The notes are essentially the electronic equivalent of post-it notes – brief pieces of information, reminders and useful items of data.

The To Do list of tasks can be presented in a variety of ways. Select the View menu, then highlight the Current Views item to reveal a list of options (Figure 352).

FIGURE 357
Task Window

Exercise 52

Planning your work

1. Outlook is opened by either selecting the Start button, highlighting the Programs option and clicking on the Outlook option or by double clicking on the Outlook icon on the Windows desktop.

2. You are going to create a calendar of a typical business person, complete with a To Do list of tasks and notes.

3. Click on the Calendar icon in the Outlook Shortcuts list on the left hand side of the display. It will open the calendar and To Do list (Figure 351). The calendar will show the date you are working on and offers you the choice of a complete twenty-four hour period to book appointments in. If you want to change the date you simply click on the desired one of the monthly calendar (Figure 353). Change the date to your birthday – you can change the month by clicking on the arrow buttons to move backwards and forwards through the year.

4. You can change the view of your calendar to show a single day, a working week (i.e. 5 days), a seven day week or a month by selecting the View menu and clicking on the options (Figure 354). Explore the different options and return to a single day view once you are confident.

5. In the calendar you are going to enter the appointments for the first Monday in May (i.e. in my case 6th May 2002), so change the date. The appointments for this day are influenced by the organisation always having a staff meeting on the first Monday of every month. Enter Staff Meeting at 10.00. As you enter Staff Meeting you will notice it is enclosed in a box. If you place your mouse

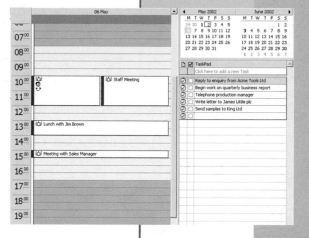

FIGURE 358
Task List and Calendar

FIGURE 359
Notes

Find out if the enquiry from Benn Ltd has been answered

Remember to ask Mary a...

This is a note

257

FIGURE 360
Print Preview

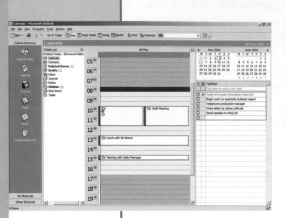

FIGURE 361
Confirm Delete Window

pointer over the box outline it will change shape and you can drag the box to cover more time. Your staff meeting will last two hours (e.g. 10 to 12).

6. The staff meeting is a recurring appointment every month and the calendar allows you to set them up without having to enter the same information 12 times. Select the Actions menu (Figure 355) and click on New Recurring Meeting to reveal the Appointment Recurrence window (Figure 356). Click on the monthly radio button in the recurrence pattern area and you will see that the first Monday of each month is offered as an option. Click on the radio button alongside the option to set the pattern. You can also set the end date for the recurrence – no end date, end after a set number of events or end by a given date. Set it to end after 10 occurances. Click the OK button to close the window and set the meeting.

7. You will notice that the window under the Appointment Recurrence window is still open. It is called Untitled-Meeting. This lets you name your meeting and also invite other people to participate in the meeting using e-mail. If you are working in an organisation with an electronic network, Outlook can be used to schedule meetings by sending e-mails to everyone who needs to attend. This adds an extra dimension to managing your individual information. Close the window.

8. If you double click on the appointment in the calendar the window will reappear. In the middle of the window is a picture of a bell and Reminder item. This enables you to ask Outlook to remind you about your appointments. The down arrow next to the reminder provides you with a range of choices of how long before the meeting or appointment do you want to be reminded. Explore the options and choose 2 hours.

9. Now enter a lunch appointment at 1.00 for one hour with Jim Brown and a meeting with the Sales Manager at 3.00 for 30 minutes.

10. It is good time management to write lists of the key tasks that need to be done. In this case we are going to create a new list:

- Reply to the enquiry from Acme Tools Ltd
- Begin work on the quarterly business report
- Telephone the production manager
- Write a letter to James Little plc
- Send samples to King Ltd

11. Click in the area "Click here to add a new task" (Task Pad) and when you have completed an entry then click elsewhere to see it added to the list. Enter all five tasks. Figure 358 shows a completed list and calendar. When you have completed a task, click in the radio button alongside it to insert a tick and see a line placed through it to show the task has been completed.

12. Explore the different ways of presenting the To Do list by selecting the View menu then highlighting the Current View to show the list of options. Consider each option in turn. If you double click on any of the To Do tasks or on the Click here to add a new task area then the Task window will open (Figure 357) letting you add more detail to your tasks.

13. Revise each of your To Do list entries to show start and finish dates:

Start Date: Monday
Finish Date: Wednesday
Reply to enquiry from Acme Tools Ltd

Start Date: Monday
Finish Date: Tuesday
Begin work on quarterly business report

Start Date: Tuesday
Finish Date: Thursday
Telephone production manager

Start Date: Wednesday
Finish Date: Thursday
Write letter to James Little plc

Start Date: Thursday
Finish Date: Friday
Send samples to King Ltd

14. Most days you will need to make a note of events, pieces of information or simply things to remind you to take action. Outlook allows you to do this by selecting the File menu, highlighting the New option and clicking on Note to reveal a blank note Enter "Remember to ask Mary about the statistic report". Close the note by clicking on the X button. Enter another note – "Find out if the enquiry form Benn Ltd has been answered". Close the note when you have finished.

15. Notes are of little use if you cannot recall them. Click on the Notes icon on the Outlook Shortcuts area to the left of the display. Figure 358 shows you your notes. If you double click on the one you want to see, it will expand. To remove the message, highlight the note with a single click and press the delete key.

16. You can copy and paste into your notes using the menu

FIGURE 362
Folder

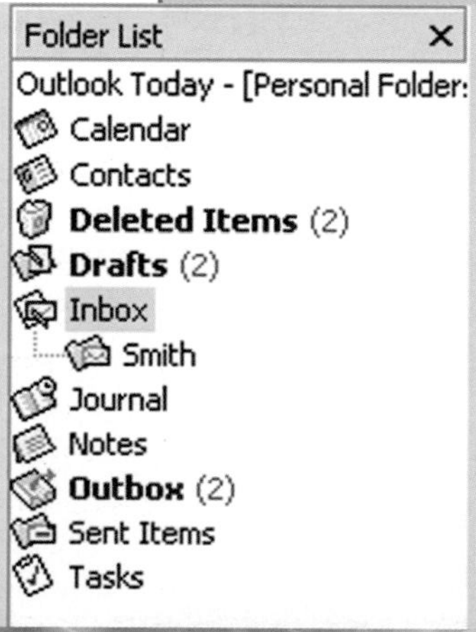

Folder List ✕
Outlook Today - [Personal Folder:
📂 Calendar
📂 Contacts
📂 **Deleted Items** (2)
📂 **Drafts** (2)
📂 Inbox
  📂 Smith
📂 Journal
📂 Notes
📂 **Outbox** (2)
📂 Sent Items
📂 Tasks

FIGURE 363
Attachment

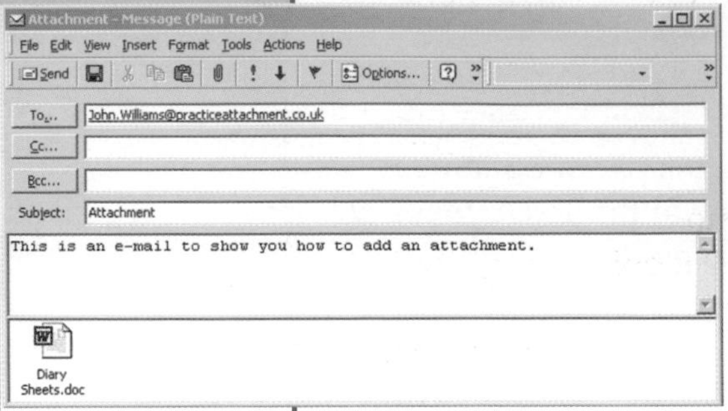

available when you right click in the note. This enables you to insert large amounts of information into a note including the contents of a file.

17. To print the calendar, select the <u>F</u>ile menu and click on Print Pre<u>v</u>iew (Figure 360). If the preview is satisfactory then click on the <u>P</u>rint button.

18. To print a note with it visible on the screen (click on the Note icon) select the <u>F</u>ile menu, click on the <u>P</u>rint option and the OK button.

19. To print a To Do list, click on the Tasks icon so the list is visible then select the <u>F</u>ile menu, click on the <u>P</u>rint option and the OK button.

20. Print your calendar, To Do list and both notes. Hardcopy is useful since there are many occasions when you need to know your schedule, To Do lists or notes while away from the computer.

21. Close Outlook by selecting the <u>F</u>ile menu and clicking on the E<u>x</u>it option or click on the Close button in the top right hand corner of the application. You may be presented with a message informing you that there are unsent messages in your Outbox and asking if you would still like to close the application. Say yes.

Updating your Calendar

Establishing a calendar is only a part of the overall task since it is just as important to be able to change entries or even delete them.

To remove an item you need to single click on the item to highlight it then select the <u>E</u>dit menu and click on the <u>D</u>elete option. This will remove the entry unless it is a recurring item when it will open the Confirm Delete window (Figure 361) where you can delete the single item or all occurring items.

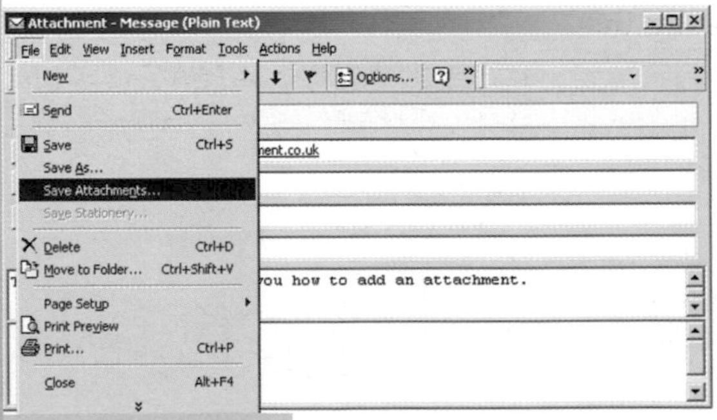

To alter a calendar item all you have to do is to highlight it. You can then change the text, add extra items or a new entry.

If you double click on the item then the appointment window will open allowing you to change start and end times, set the alarm reminder and invite attendees.

It is important to keep your calendar up to date, including removing any conflicting appointments. A calendar's effectiveness is seriously reduced by inaccurate information. If it is not maintained then it will lead to mistakes. You will not gain anyone's confidence if you miss an appointment or prepare for one which has actually been cancelled.

FIGURE 364
Save As

FIGURE 365
Page Setup

Exercise 53

Creating an E-mail with an attachment

1. Outlook is opened by either selecting the Start button, highlighting the Programs option and clicking on the Outlook option or by double clicking on the Outlook icon on the Windows desktop

2. Create a new e-mail by clicking on the new icon to reveal the message window.

3. Create the message below:

To:
Frank.Williams@practiceattachment.co.uk

Attachment

This is an e-mail to show you how to add an attachment.

If you are working with a group of other learners then substitute the e-mail address with one of your fellow learners. You can send the e-mail and see how it appears to the recipient..

FIGURE 366
Page Setup Style Window

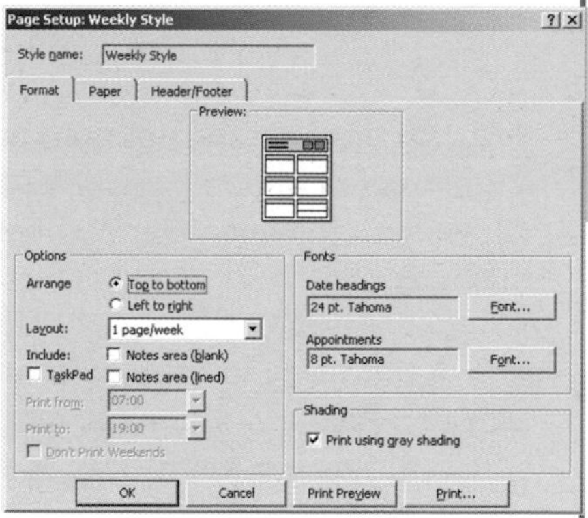

4. Add an attachment by clicking on the Insert file icon (it looks like a paperclip). This opens the Insert File window. Select the folder in which your attached file is stored in the Look in: box then highlight the file and click on the Insert button. Your attached file will appear in the message area of your e-mail (Figure 363). You can attach several files by repeating the process.

FIGURE 367
Header and Footer

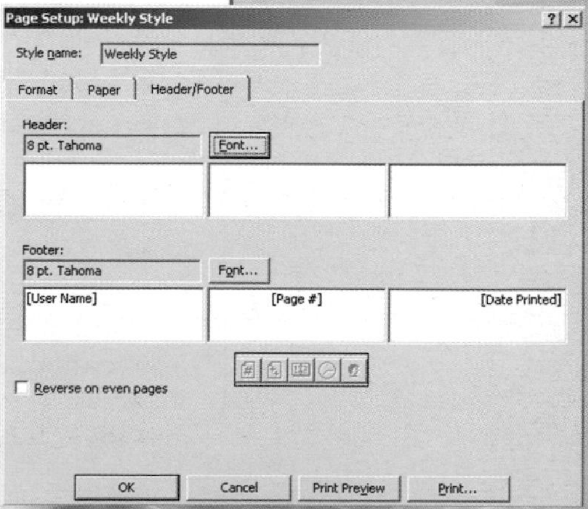

5. To send the message click on the Send button on the toolbar. If your system is connected to the Internet the message will be sent. If not, it will be stored in the Outbox until the next time you make a connection. Observe in the folder list that the Outbox item has a number in brackets indicating the number of messages waiting to be sent.

6. Practise sending messages with attachments either to imaginary addresses or preferably to other learners on your

FIGURE 368
**Page
Setups
Others**

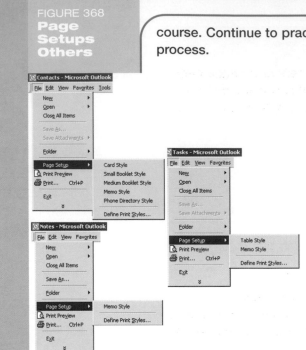

course. Continue to practise until you are confident that you understand the process.

7. Encourage your colleagues to send you e-mails with attachments but if you are on your own, you can send yourself a message.

8. When you receive an e-mail with an attachment you can read the file by double clicking on it. This will open the file providing you have the associated application software on your system (e.g. word files require Microsoft Word etc.). You can save the file using the application software in the normal way anywhere on the system and read the attachment later using the application software. Practise with the attachments.

9. If you do not have a suitable application then you will be presented with a warning message.

10. An alternative to opening a file is to select the File menu and the Save Attachments option (Figure 367) to reveal the Save Attachments window that allows you to save your file in any folder. Practise saving your attachment in this way.

11. A third way to save your attachment is to select the File menu and the Move to Folder option. You can save the e-mail and attachment to a folder within the mail system. This is useful should you want to save messages to particular folders.

12. A fourth way of saving an attachment is to simply drag it to your new folder. Highlight the attachment and hold down the mouse button then drag it to the new folder and release. It will have been copied to the new location. Copy the attachment to the notes icon and your attached file will now be available from within a note. This is useful when you are dealing with several e-mails and want to refer to the attachment as soon as you have completed dealing with the messages.

13. It is important to spend as much time as you can practising the different approaches to dealing with attachments.

14. Close Outlook by selecting the File menu and clicking on the Exit option or click on the Close button in the top right hand corner of the application. You may be presented with a message informing you that there are unsent messages in your Outbox and asking if you would still like to close the application. Say yes.

Page Setup

You may want to display or print your calendar in a variety of formats. With the Calendar selected and displayed you can change its appearance by selecting the File menu then highlighting the Page Setup option to reveal a menu of choices (Figure 365).

The choices include:

• Single page for each day
• Single page for a week (i.e. seven days shown)
• Single page for a month (i.e. whole month shown)
• Trifold style – current day, to do list and week view all on one page
• Memo style

When you click on the option the Page Setup Style window opens (Figure 366) providing additional choices. In particular you can add a header and footer to the printout to identify the calendar (Figure 367). Simply enter the text into the template provided in Figure 367.

With the calendar, the To Do list, notes or contacts displayed you can choose from a variety of Page Setups to show and print them. Figure 367 shows the different options.

Printing

E-mail, calendars, To Do lists and electronic notes are all extremely useful but they do not eliminate the need for paper. If you are away from your office then unless you have everything stored on laptop computer you will need a copy of the key documents and messages. In many locations it is difficult to use a laptop while paper can normally be studied in almost any location. When traveling a printout of your calendar is very useful. If you add copies of contact details for the people you are meeting and any relevant e-mail messages then you are well prepared.

Microsoft Outlook provides extensive facilities for printing messages, calendars and contact details. To print e-mails, calendars or contact details requires that you select the File menu and click on either the Print or Print Preview options. It is good practice to preview before you print. If you are then satisfied with the appearance of the printout you can simply click on the Print option within the preview window. If it is not correct then you close the window and select the Page Setup option to change its appearance (Figure 368).

More Practice

1. Add these new contacts to your address book:

Name:	Mrs Wendy James
Title:	Personnel Manager
Address:	Queens Ltd
	23 Long Lane
	Leicester
	LE12 9LL
Telephone:	0116 567 4599
E-mail:	wendy.james@queensleicester.co.uk

Name:	Ms Lori Davis
Title:	Personal Assistant
Address:	Square Paints Ltd
	Alliance Drive
	Manchester
	M34 9RL
Telephone:	0161 777 9999
E-mail:	ld_Square@squarepaints.co.uk

Name:	Dr Paul Brookes
Title:	Director
Address:	Unicorn Ltd
	West Way
	Nottingham
	NG38 9KK
Telephone:	0115 678 9888
E-mail:	Paul_Brookes@unicorntoday.co.uk

Name:	Ms Jane Raymonds
Title:	Human Resource Manager
Address:	Highways Ltd
	567 South County Road
	Mansfield
	NG45 7JK
Telephone:	0999 567 3400
E-mail:	Jane.Raymonds@highways.co.uk

Name:	Mr Tom Jenkins
Title:	Personnel Officer
Address:	Sunshine Ltd
	Kingsway
	Liverpool
	L89 3DD
Telephone:	0151 768 1111
E-mail:	Tomj@sunshine.co.uk

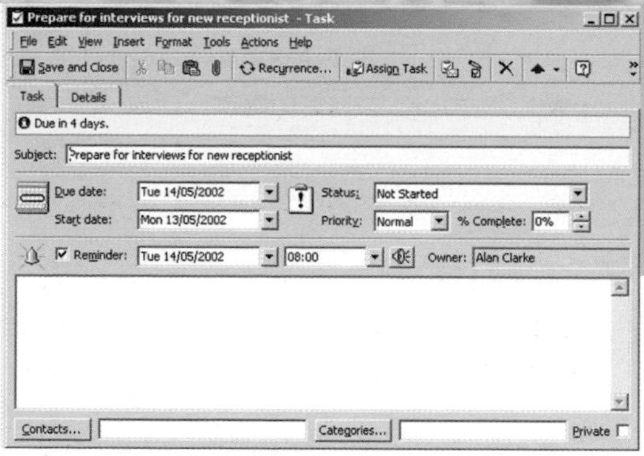

2. Establish an e-mail group based on the five contacts called Humanresources

3. Create a signature for yourself:
Your Name
Centre Number

FIGURE 369
Task Window Start and Finish Dates

4. Create a folder to store e-mails about human resource matters from the five contacts and any internal messages. Name the folder Human.

5. Create a folder to store confidential messages called Confidence.

6. Enter the following appointments and meetings into your calendar:

Day	Start Time	Finish Time	Appointment/Meeting	Notes
Monday	10.00	11.00	Staff Meeting	Recurring every week
Tuesday	9.00	9.30	Conference Update	
	11.00	15.00	Interviews for Receptionist	
	16.00	17.00	Annual Review – David Jones	
Wednesday	10.30	11.45	Telephone Conference	
	14.30	16.00	Meeting with Training Manager	
Thursday	9.00	9.45	Progress Report	
	15.00	16.30	Review of Annual Report	
Friday	10.45	11.45	Meeting with Dr Lord	
	12.30	14.00	Lunch meeting with Production Director	

7. For the same week prepare list of tasks to do. Enter the list below:

Subject	Due Date
Prepare for interviews for new Receptionist	Tuesday
Make notes for the telephone conference	Wednesday
Read Annual Report	Thursday
Confirm lunch with Production Director	Friday

8. You need to make some notes. Create the two notes below:

Note 1:

Key points for the telephone conference on Thursday

- costs must be covered by the project

- project completion date is likely to be missed
- we need an extra month to finish our tasks

Note 2:

Annual Report

Check that in the report:

- the department has been accurately described
- details of all the personnel mentioned are correct – job titles, spelling of
  names etc.
- costs and sales Figures are right

9. Print copies of your contacts, calendar/schedule, To Do list and notes:

Contacts – print as small card style

Calendar – print a single page for a week

To Do list – print in Table Style

Notes – print both notes in Memo Style

For all four printouts add a header containing your name, centre number and date

10. After you have read the Annual Report you need to contact the editor of the report to comment on the contents. If you are working within a group ask a colleague to act the part of the editor and reply to your comments.

To: Janet@madeup.co.uk (substitute the correct address)

Subject: Annual Report

Dear Janet,

I have now had an opportunity to study the Annual Report. I liked the new layout which I thought presented the information better. However, there are one or two small errors in the spelling of people's names which need to be corrected. I have attached a file of staff names.
Best Wishes

Alan

Attach a file to this e-mail to practise sending an attachment.

11. If you are working in a group, ask one of your colleagues to send you a similar e-mail with an attachment.

12. Drag and drop the attachment into the notes to copy the file.

13. Save the e-mail into the Human folder.

14. You need to amend your calendar of meetings and appointments. The new calendar is:

Day	Start Time	Finish Time	Appointment/Meeting	Notes
Monday	10.00	11.00	Staff Meeting	Recurring every week
	14.00	14.30	Meeting with Linda	
Tuesday	9.00	9.30	Conference Update	
	11.00	15.00	Interviews for Receptionist	
	15.00	16.30	Annual Review – David Jones	
Wednesday	10.30	11.45	Telephone Conference	
	14.30	16.00	Meeting with Training Manager	
Thursday	9.00	9.45	Progress Report	
	11.00	12.00	Monthly Management Statistics	
	15.00	16.30	Review of Annual Report	
Friday	10.45	11.45	Meeting with Dr Lord	
	12.30	14.00	Lunch meeting with Production Director	

15. Amend your To Do list to add the start dates (Figure 367e)

Subject	Start Date	Due Date
Prepare for interviews for new Receptionist	Monday	Tuesday
Make notes for the telephone conference	Tuesday	Wednesday
Read Annual Report	Tuesday	Thursday
Confirm lunch with Production Director	Wednesday	Friday

16. Close Outlook by selecting the File menu and clicking on the Exit option.

Summary

1. Open
Select the Start button, highlight the Programs option and click on the Outlook option or double click on the Outlook icon on the Windows desktop.

2. Create an E-mail
Select the New button on the standard toolbar to reveal the Message window.

3. Blind Copies (Bcc)
Select the View menu in the message window and click on the Bcc option.

4. Priorities – High Importance
Click on the icon indicated by an exclamation mark (i.e. High Importance) in the message window.

5. Create a Signature
Select the Insert menu on the toolbar of the message window, highlight the Signature option and click on the More option. A message asking you if you would like to create a signature will appear. Click on the Yes button to open the Create New Signature window.

or

Select the Tools menu on the main application and click the Options item then on Mail Format tab to reveal a section called Signature.

6. Address Book
Select the Tools menu and click on the Address Book option. This will reveal the address book.

7. Add New Contact
Click on the New icon. Click on the New Contact option to reveal the Properties window.

8. New Group/Distribution List
Click on the New icon. Click on the New Group option to reveal the Properties window.

or

Select the File menu, highlight the New option and click on the Distribution List option to open the Distribution List window.

9. Calendar

Click on the Calendar icon in the Outlook Shortcuts list on the left hand side of the display.

10. Change Date Click on the desired date of the monthly calendar.

11. Change Calendar View

Select the View menu and click on the option of your choice.

12. Recurring Appointments

Select the Actions menu, click on New Recurring Meeting to reveal the Appointment Recurrence window.

13. Notes

Select the File menu, highlight the New option and click on the Note option.

14. Print

Select the File menu. Click on Print Preview and then on the Print button.

15. Page Setup

Select the File menu, highlight the Page Setup option to reveal a menu of choices and select your option.

16. New Folder

Select the File menu, highlight the New item and click on the Folder option to reveal the Create New Folder window.

or

Click on the New button on the toolbar.

17. Attachment

Click on the Insert file icon (i.e. a paperclip) to open the Insert File window.

18. Save an Attachment

Double click on the attachment to open the file in the associated application software (e.g. spreadsheet files require Microsoft Excel etc.). Save the file using the application software.

or

Single click on the file to highlight it and then select the File menu and the Save As option to reveal the Save As window.

or

Drag the attachment to a folder. Highlight the attachment and hold down the mouse button to drag the attachment to the new folder then release.

19. Save Messages and Attachments to Folders

Select the File menu and the Move to Folder option to reveal Move Item to window which lists mail system folders.

20. Enter Tasks

Click in the area "Click here to add a new task" (Task Pad) and enter the item.

21. Change Task Views

Select the View menu and highlight the Current View item to reveal a list of options.

22. Task Details

Double click on the entry to reveal the Task window

Graphs and Charts

This chapter will help you to:

• Select and control data sources

• Present data using graphs and charts

• Format axes and labels

• Format the presentation of graphs and charts

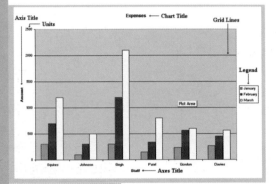

FIGURE 370

• Use graphs to extrapolate information to predict future values

This chapter covers Unit 9 (Graphs and Charts). There are no pre-conditions for studying this unit. However, its content does assume that you have the skills and understanding which are provided by the OCR Level 1 ICT course New CLAIT (e.g. Unit 7 - Graphs and Charts, Units 4 - Spreadsheets and Charts and Unit 1 - Using a Computer).

Assessment

After studying Unit 9 your skills and understanding are assessed during a 3 hour practical assignment. This is set by OCR and marked locally. However, the marking will be externally moderated by OCR. This ensures that the standard is being applied correctly across the many different providers of OCR CLAIT Plus. If you are unsuccessful then you can be re-assessed using a different assignment.

Font Families

Clait Plus uses font families rather than font names. Chapter 1 explains font families and gives examples of the fonts that they relate to them.

Examples:
Serif - Courier New and Times New Roman
Sans Serif - Tahoma and Arial

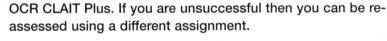

FIGURE 371

Graphs and Charts

Often numbers are more easily understood if provided in a visual form.

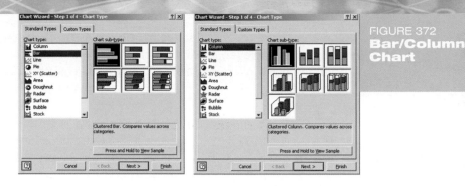

Microsoft Excel provides you with the means of converting data into a graph or chart. Figure 370 illustrates a chart and shows the different labels that can be applied to it.

The main chart or graph labels are:

- title - this is optional in an Excel chart or graph and provides a name for the chart. The title should relate to the content of the chart or graph.

- axis titles - these identify the units that measure the chart or graph.

- labels - these are used to identify the different elements in a chart or graph (eg. label the slices of a Pie chart).

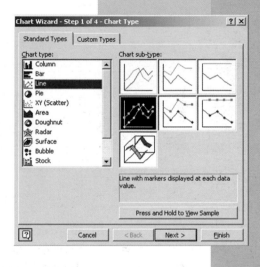

- legend - this provides the key to understanding the data series (eg colour coding in a bar chart). Without a legend to correctly identify the displayed data series the chart or graph is effectively meaningless.

You can set the chart or graph labels by using Excel's Chart Wizard. The exercises in this chapter will help you to ubderstand how to set them.

The main types of charts and graphs are:

- Pie charts (Figure 371)
- Bar/column charts (Figure 372)
- Line graph charts (Figure 373)
- XY shatter graphs (Figure 374)

You can also combine line graphs and column charts to gain another useful way of presenting information.

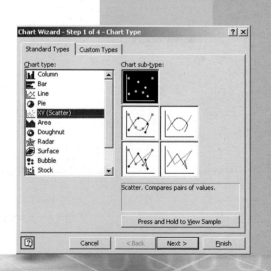

Figure 371 shows the Chart Wizard for Pie charts which is obtained by selecting the appropriate data in your spreadsheet then the Insert menu and clicking on the Chart option to reveal the Chart Wizard.

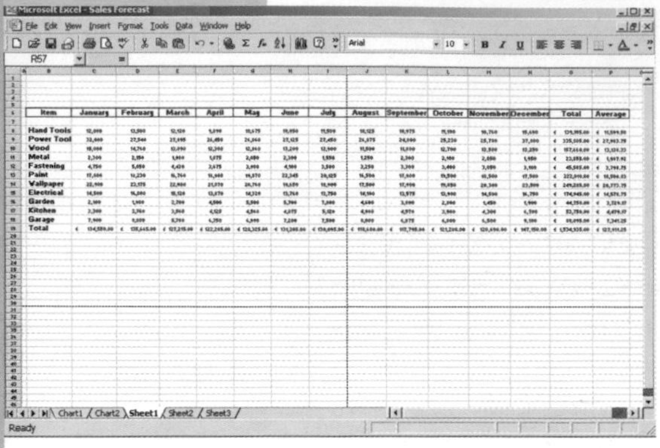

FIGURE 375
Sales Forecast

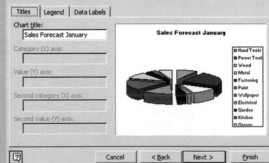

Pie charts are a very effective means of visually presenting a set of values. There are, however, more than one type. For example, the left hand and the middle charts of second row of choices are exploding and three-dimensional exploding pie charts (Figure 371).

Figure 372 shows both the Bar and Column Charts, Figure 373 illustrates a Line Graph and Figure 374 shows a Scatter Graph. A bar or column chart is useful in comparing side by side a range of results (e.g. rainfall for different months of the year) while a line graph is used to show the relationship between two variables (e.g. how income changes over a period of time).

A scatter graph presents two sets of variable data compared to each other. Often they do not show an obvious relationship in that, as the name suggests, the data points are scattered over an area. However, it is possible to draw a line through the points to illustrate the trend of the variables against each other.

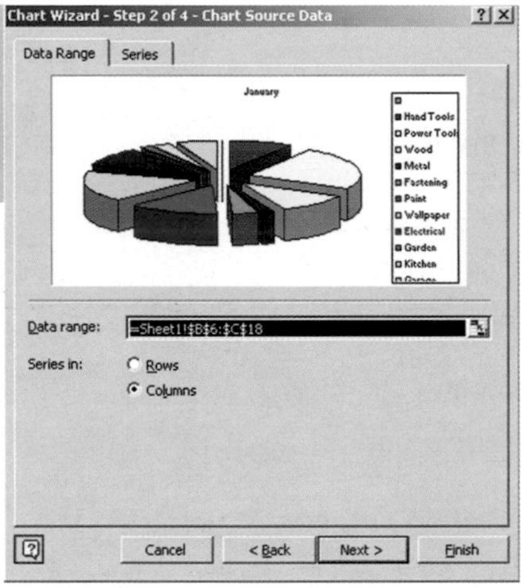

FIGURE 376
Chart Wizard Step 2

Select Data Sets

The charts and graphs that you create depend on the data that you select to base them on. You are free to select a whole spreadsheet, a subset of the data or data from non-adjacent areas. To select data you need to highlight it. If you click in the top left hand corner of the data you want to select and hold down the mouse button you can drag the mouse to the bottom right corner of the data. The subset of data is highlighted when you release the mouse button.

FIGURE 377
Chart Wizard Step 3

An alternative way of selecting data is to import the data from another application. There are several ways of importing or opening information/data from other applications within Microsoft Excel. The most straightforward is to use the Copy and Paste functions if you are importing data from another Microsoft Office application. An alternative is to use the Open option within the File menu to reveal the Open window. Excel can import files in a variety of formats. The file formats depend on the application that was used to create it. The compatible formats are shown in the Files of type box in the Open window. The file you want to import is located using the

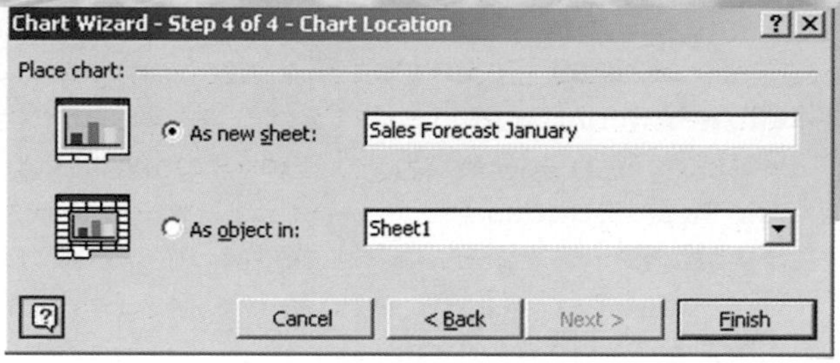

Look in box to identify the floppy disk, drive or folder. The files and folders are shown in the work area and are selected by either highlighting the file with a single click and then clicking on the Open button, or by double clicking on the file. The chosen file needs to be converted into Excel format. To undertake this task you are helped by an Excel Wizard which opens automatically when you import a file. The use of the wizard is explained in chapter 2.

FIGURE 378
Chart Wizard Step 4

In Chapter 2 you created a spreadsheet called Sales Forecast (Figure 374). You are going to use this information to practise choosing different data sets and creating charts.

FIGURE 379
Three-Dimensional Exploding Pie Chart – Sales Forecast

Set Parameters

What makes a chart or graph meaningful are the titles, data labels, legend and units that you employ. If you simply produced a chart or graph without these labels it would be very difficult to understand. The legend is particular important in that it is specifically intended to provide a key to the colours used to identify different data series. If a legend is missing or incorrect then it is almost impossible to understand. It is rather like showing the chart which uses colour coding in black and white.

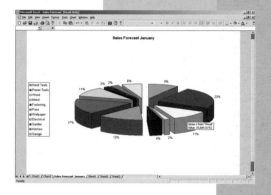

The Chart Wizard allows you to enter the title, position and show the legend and select data labels. The initial step in using the wizard is to select the data set and then to select the Insert menu and click on the Chart option. This opens the Chart Wizard. Figure 374 shows Step 1 of 4 of the Wizard in which you select the type of chart or graph you want to create. By clicking on the Next button you move to Step 2 and subsequently to steps 3 and 4. In several of the steps there are tabs which provide access to other functions. In step 2 the tab Series allows you to name, add and remove different data series. The data series can be added or removed and named in the bottom half of the window in the Series area.

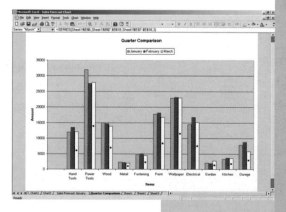

In Step 3 of the Wizard you are provided with a series of tabbed windows which provide access to different functions. The titles tab allows you to give the chart or graph a title as well as naming the axis.

FIGURE 380
Quarter Comparison

If you click on the Legend tab then you reveal a window which allows you to show or remove the legend and also to select where to position it (i.e. Bottom, Corner, Top, Right and Left) by clicking on the various check boxes and radio buttons.

If you click on the Data Labels tab then you reveal a window which allows you to choose not to apply data labels or to chose between different types of label (e.g. names or values).

Exercise 54

Create an Exploding Pie Chart

1. Insert your floppy disk which contains the Sales Forecast file into the A: drive.

FIGURE 381
Bar Chart

2. Load Microsoft Excel using either the Programs menu or the Excel icon on the desktop. Open the file Sales Forecast by selecting the File menu and clicking on the Open option to reveal the Open window. Change the Look in:box to select the floppy disk and the file name will appear in the work area. Double click Sales Forecast or single click it and then click the OK button. The spreadsheet will open in Excel (Figure 375).

3. Highlight the first two columns (i.e. Items and January) excluding the Total row. Select the Insert menu and the Chart option. Click on the Pie Chart option and either the two or three-dimensional exploding items (i.e. left hand or the middle options of the second row). Check the chart by clicking and holding down the mouse button on the Press and Hold to View Sample. This allows you to see the chart. Release and click on the next button to move to step 2 of the Chart Wizard (Figure 376).

FIGURE 382
Page Setup

4. Consider the data range =sheet1!$B$6:$C$18 translates to the area top left hand corner cell B6 to cell C18. The chart shows a blank item in the legend above Hand Tools. This corresponds to the blank and Item rows, so change the range to B8 to C18 (i.e. =sheet1!$B$8:$C$18) by clicking, deleting and entering new values.

5. Click on the Next button to reveal Step 3.

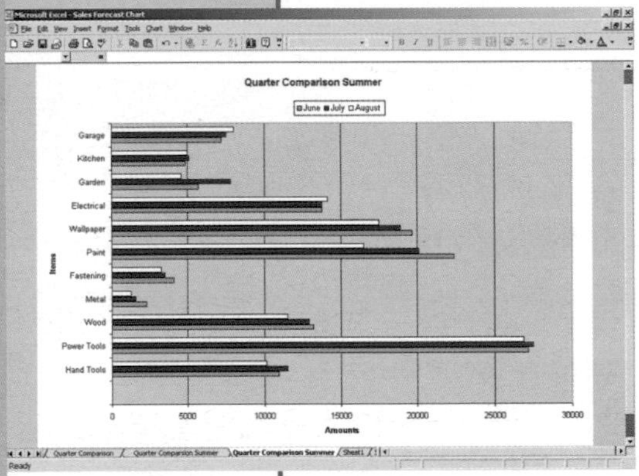

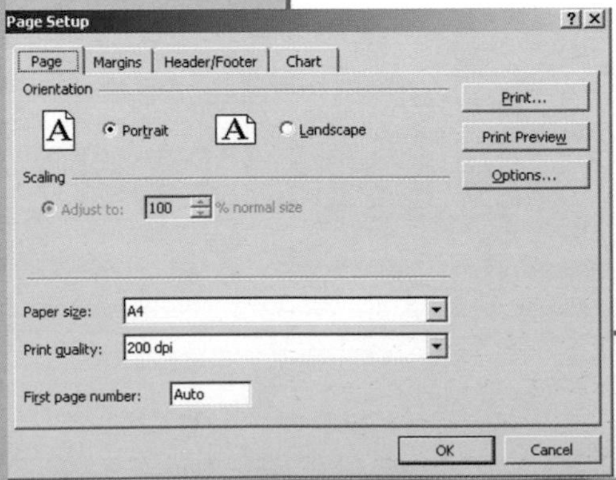

6. Click on the Title and enter Sales Forecast January (Figure 377). Click on the Legend tab and select left. Click on the Data Labels tab and select the Show percent option. Click on the Next button to reveal step 4.

7. Click on the As new sheet option and Sales Forecast January (Figure 378). Click on the Finish button. The Exploding Pie Chart will appear (Figure 379) on a new sheet linked to your Sales Forecast Data. If you place your mouse pointer on any of the segments of the Pie chart you will see an explanation of what the data represents (e.g. Wood Value 15,000 11%). Take a moment to consider the image and notice how a three-dimensional exploding pie chart is a powerful representation of the data. The size of each segment is shown in relation to the others so that it's value is emphasised.

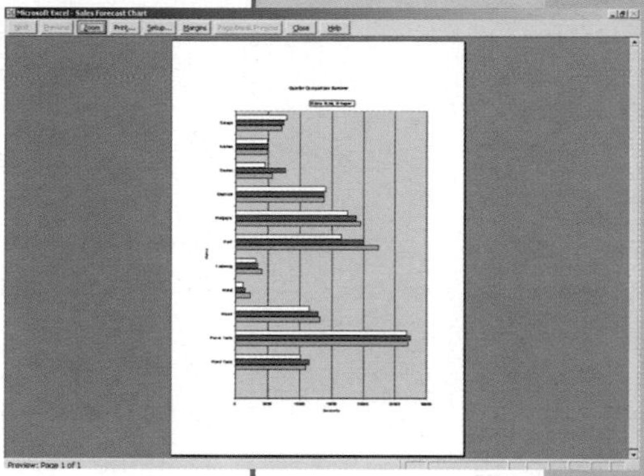

8. Save your chart by selecting the File menu and the Save As option to reveal the Save As window. Save your file as Sales Forecast Chart on your floppy disk.

9. Close Excel by selecting the File menu item and clicking on the Exit option or by clicking on the close button in the top right hand corner of the application window.

FIGURE 383
Print Preview

Rows and Columns Presentation

In step 2 of the Chart Wizard (Figure 376) are two options Rows and Columns. These options change the presentation of the chart. Figure 376a compares the same chart in row and column presentation. In column presentation the bars reflect the column values of January and February while the axis show the row items. In Rows presentation the bars reflect the row values while the axis show the column items (i.e. the bars are grouped by month).

FIGURE 384
Hand Tools Line Graph

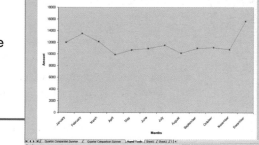

Exercise 55

Selecting Data Sets

1. Insert your floppy disk into the A: drive.

2. Load Microsoft Excel using either the Programs menu or the Excel icon on the desktop. Open the file Sales Forecast Chart by selecting the File menu and clicking on the Open option to reveal the Open window. Change the Look in:box to select the floppy disk and the file name will appear in the work area.

FIGURE 385
Line
Column
Graph

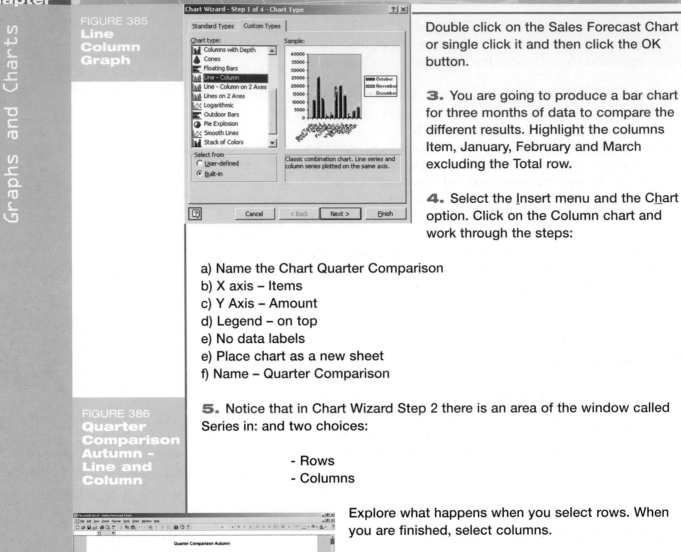

FIGURE 386
Quarter
Comparison
Autumn –
Line and
Column

Double click on the Sales Forecast Chart or single click it and then click the OK button.

3. You are going to produce a bar chart for three months of data to compare the different results. Highlight the columns Item, January, February and March excluding the Total row.

4. Select the Insert menu and the Chart option. Click on the Column chart and work through the steps:

a) Name the Chart Quarter Comparison
b) X axis – Items
c) Y Axis – Amount
d) Legend – on top
e) No data labels
e) Place chart as a new sheet
f) Name – Quarter Comparison

5. Notice that in Chart Wizard Step 2 there is an area of the window called Series in: and two choices:

- Rows
- Columns

Explore what happens when you select rows. When you are finished, select columns.

6. Save the chart by selecting the File menu and the Save option on to your floppy disk or a location of your choice.

7. Figure 380 illustrates the Quarter Comparison Chart

8. Repeat this process but select the column Item and the months June, July and August. Highlight the Item column and then holding down the CTRL key, highlight the other three columns excluding the Total row. Select the Chart option. Create a bar chart. Use the same axis, legend position and entitle the column chart Quarter Comparison Summer.

You have created a chart using data from non-adjacent columns.

9. Figure 381 shows the Bar chart.

FIGURE 387
**XY Scatter
Graph**

10. Save the chart by selecting the File menu and the Save option on to your floppy disk or a location of your choice.

11. You can present the chart in either portrait or landscape mode by selecting the File menu and clicking on the Page Setup option to reveal the Page Setup window (Figure 382). Click in the appropriate radio button. To check how the chart would appear if printed, click on the Print Preview button (Figure 383). To print the chart, click on the Print button.

12. Print your Bar chart in both portrait and landscape modes.

13. Close Excel by selecting the File menu item and clicking on the Exit option or by clicking on the close button in the top right hand corner of the application window.

Line Graphs

FIGURE 388
Chart Menu

A line graph shows the relationship between two variables. If you plotted the sales forecast for hand tools against months you would obtain a line graph showing how sales of these products fluctuated across the twelve months. It is also possible to combine a line graph with a column chart so that both appear together.

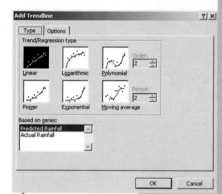

Exercise 56

Line and Column Graphs

1. Insert your floppy disk into the A: drive.

2. Load Microsoft Excel using either the Programs menu or the Excel icon on the desktop. Open the file Sales Forecast Chart by selecting the File menu and clicking on the Open option to reveal the Open window. Change the Look in:box to select the floppy disk and the file name will appear in the work area. Double click Sales Forecast Chart or single click it and then click the OK button.

FIGURE 389
Trendline

3. Highlight the top three rows of Sales Forecast excluding columns Total and Average then select the Insert menu and click on the Chart option. Select one of the line graphs (whichever appeals) and create it using the wizard. However, select:

a) Not to show the legend
b) Title – Hand Tools

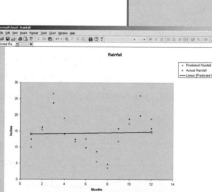

FIGURE 390
**Format
Trendline
Window**

c) X Axis – Months
d) Y Axis – Amount
e) No grid lines

f) No data labels
g) As new sheet called Hand Tools

4. Figure 384 shows the Line Graph that you have created.

5. Save the chart by selecting the File menu and the Save option on to your floppy disk or a location of your choice.

6. Print your Line Graph in either portrait or landscape.

7. You are now going to produce a graph displaying both a line and columns. Highlight columns Item and October, November and December excluding the Total row. Remember that to highlight non-adjacent columns you need to hold down the CTRL key. With the columns highlighted, select the Insert menu and click on the Chart option.

FIGURE 391
**Page Setup
Window**

8. Select the Customs Types tab and the Line Column chart (Figure 385). Follow the Chart Wizard. Choose the title to be Quarter Comparison Autumn, X Axis – Items, Y axis – Amount, Legend – Bottom and as new sheet called Quarter Comparison Autumn.

9. Figure 384 illustrates a line and column graph. October and November are shown as columns while December is displayed as a line.

FIGURE 392
**Header and
Footer**

10. Save the chart by selecting the File menu and the Save option on to your floppy disk or a location of your choice.

11. Print your Line and Column Graph in either portrait or landscape.

12. Close Excel by selecting the File menu item and clicking on the Exit option or by clicking on the close button in the top right hand corner of the application window.

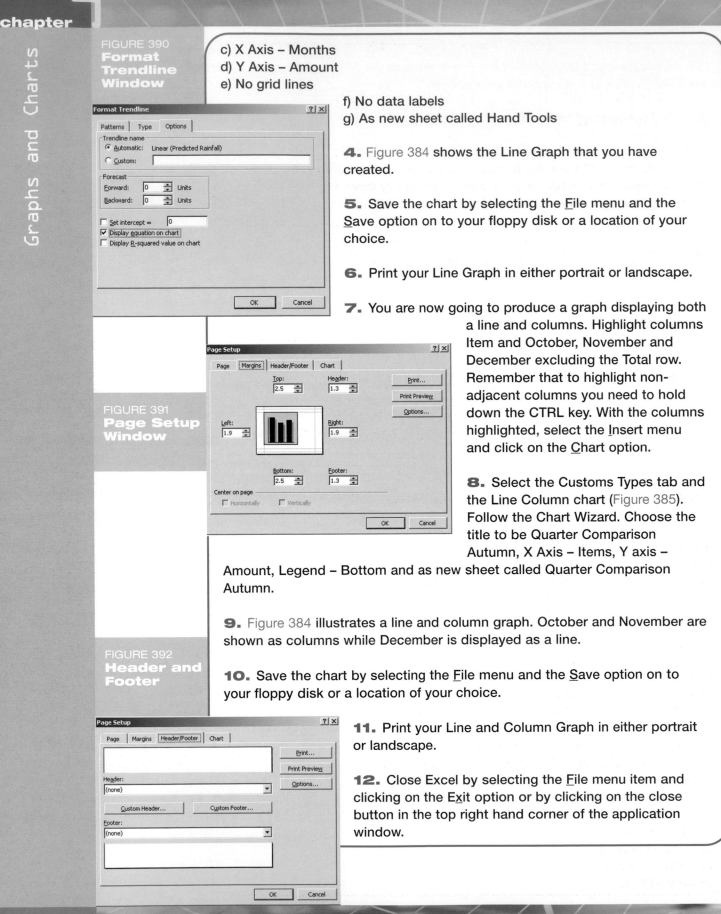

FIGURE 393
Draw Toolbar

↑
Text Box

XY Scatter Graph

XY scatter graphs are used to plot the values of two or more variables against each other in order to show the relationship between them. They are often used to present the results of engineering, laboratory or other experimental work.

Exercise 57

XY Scatter Graphs

1. Normally you will be provided with the data on which your charts and graphs will be based. In this exercise the table below shows the relationship between actual and predicted rainfall at monthly intervals.

2. Load Microsoft Excel using either the Programs menu or the Excel icon on the desktop. Enter the data below and save the spreadsheet on to a floppy disk as a file called Rainfall.

Months	Predicted Rainfall	Actual Rainfall
January	12.50	10.00
February	16.25	15.50
March	23.75	26.55
April	14.15	18.90
May	12.50	11.75
June	9.85	12.55
July	8.65	5.50
August	4.75	3.55
September	15.75	11.85
October	18.75	17.25
November	19.85	25.95
December	15.65	17.45

3. Highlight the whole of the information. Select the Insert menu and click on the Chart option. Select one of the XY Scatter graph and create it using the wizard. However, select:

a) Title – Rainfall
b) X Axis – Months
c) Y Axis – Inches
d) No grid lines

FIGURE 394
Text Box

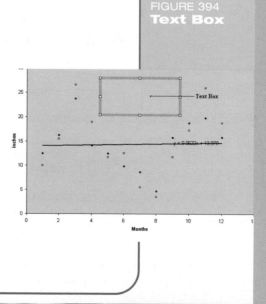

FIGURE 395
**Format
Data
Series**

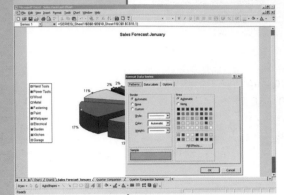

e) legend – Corner
f) no data labels
g) as new sheet called Rainfall

4. Figure 387 shows the XY Scatter Graph that we have created.

5. Save the chart by selecting the File menu and the Save option on to your floppy disk or a location of your choice.

6. Print your XY Scatter Graph in either portrait or landscape.

7. To help understand the graph, it is possible to add a trendline by selecting the Chart menu (Figure 388) to open the Add Trendline window. Select the Linear Trend/Regression type and the series the line is based on (i.e. Predicted or Actual Rainfall). Figure 391 shows the Scatter Graph with a trendline. The line helps you to predict the rainfall across the year or predict future rainfall by extending the line while the actual line allows you to consider the variation across the year.

8. It is possible to display the equation by clicking on the trendline so it is highlighted (i.e. each end of the line will have a square handle). Select the Format menu and click on the Select and Trendline option to reveal the Format Trendline window. Select the Options tab and click on the Display equation on chart radio button (Figure 390). The trendline equation is displayed near the graph.

FIGURE 396
**Editing
Data
Labels**

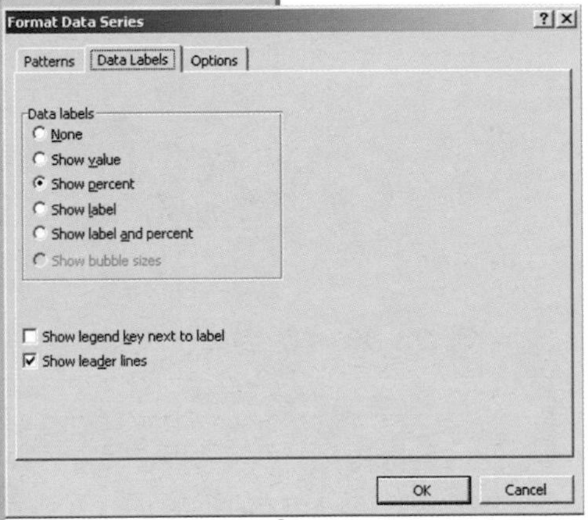

9. Save the chart by selecting the File menu and the Save option on to your floppy disk or a location of your choice.

10. Print your XY Scatter Graph with Trendline and Equation in either portrait or landscape.

11. Close Excel by selecting the File menu item and clicking on the Exit option or by clicking on the close button in the top right hand corner of the application window.

Page Setup

You can adjust the display of your charts and graphs by selecting the File menu and the Page Setup option to reveal the Page Setup window (assumes chart and graph is being displayed). Figure 391 illustrates the Page Setup window. This allows you to adjust all four margins – top, bottom, left and right. In addition, you can change the size of the header and footer.

By clicking on the Header/Footer tab you can add them to your chart or graph (Figure 392).

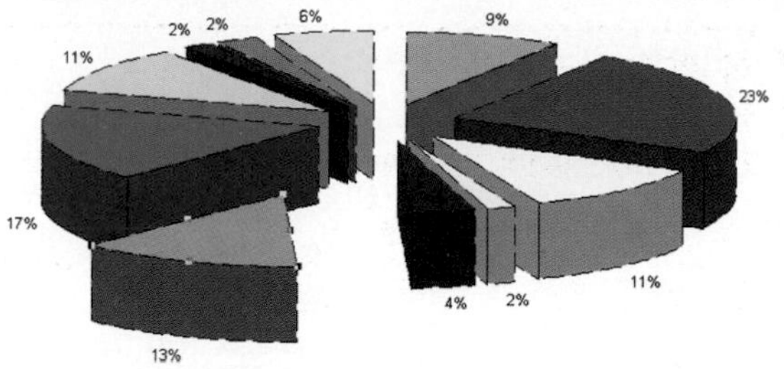

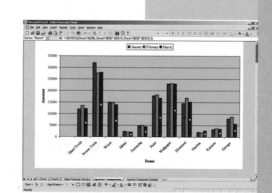

FIGURE 397
Moving a Slice

Text Box

Although an image is often said to be worth a thousand words it can be enhanced by the addition of some text. Charts and graphs are useful ways of presenting information but in many cases they need a short statement to help your audience to fully understand their content. Words can be added to charts and graphs using a text box. Click on the Text Box icon on the Draw Toolbar (Figure 393) to reveal a new mouse pointer. Draw a box by holding down the mouse button and dragging the box open (Figure 394). Text then can be added to the open box.

FIGURE 398
Format Chart Title

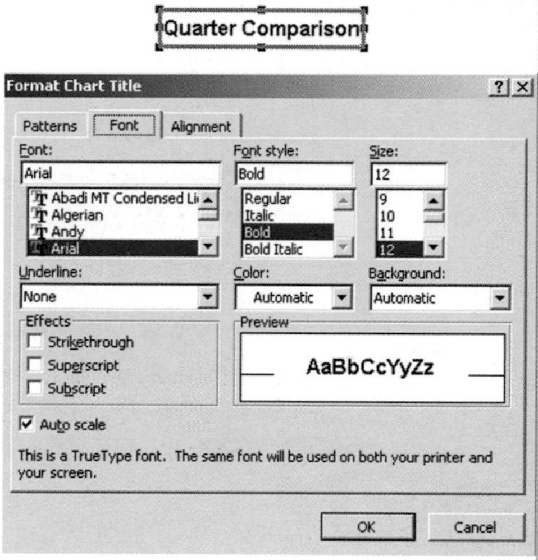

House Style

In order to ensure a consistency in organisational documents and publications house styles are often developed. These provide a series of guidelines for staff to follow and an example is given below. In the More Practice section, you will be asked to produce charts and graphs using them. House styles are often employed to ensure that a minimum standard of quality is adhered to by employees.

Example House Styles Guidelines:

FIGURE 399
Edited Chart

Pie Charts

Font (typeface)   serif (e.g. Times New Roman)

Character (Text) Size

Title   20, bold
Sub-title   20, bold
Data Labels   14
Legend   14

Bar/column, line and XY Scatter charts and graphs

Font (typeface)   serif (e.g. Times New Roman)

FIGURE 400
Format Data Series – Scatter Graph

Character (Text) Size

Title	20, bold
Sub-title	20, bold
X Axis Title	14, bold
Y Axis Title	14, bold
Other text/numbering on the x axis	12
Other text/numbering on the y axis	12
Legend	12
Text box Labels	12, border invisible
Trendline Equation	12

Headers and Footers

Your name and centre number must be inserted in either the header or footer.

Format Graphs and Charts

It is possible to edit your charts and graphs employing the techniques that you have learned from using other Microsoft Office applications. You can change the fonts, character sizes, effects (e.g. bold), apply superscript and subscript effects, change the style and thickness of lines and alter the colours of your charts and graphs.

FIGURE 401
Lines – Scatter Graph

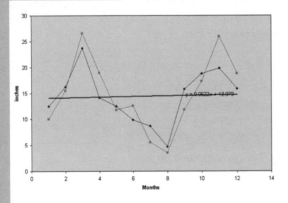

To edit a chart or graph you must double click on the element that you are seeking to change. A window will appear (e.g. Format Chart Title, Format Axis, Format Plot Area, Format Legend, Format Data Labels, Format Data Series). Figure 395 illustrates the Format Data Series for the Sales Forecast January exploding pie chart that you created earlier. The element that you have double clicked will be highlighted by being enclosed in a frame with small black squares.

The format window is divided into three tabs – Patterns, Data Labels and Options. Each of these is similarly divided but in a way appropriate to the element. In the case of Data Labels you can alter the colours, fill effects and lines. In the Data Labels tab you can adjust the labels (Figure 397) while in Options you can change the angle of the pie slices. You should notice that the options are customised to the type of chart or graph.

You can move the various slices of the pie by clicking on a segment and holding down the button to drag it. This is a useful way to emphasise that slice (see Figure 392a).

If you click on the axes then the Format Axis window will open. This allows you to change the upper and lower limits, intervals on the axes and change numeric formatting. The different functions are grouped together under the various tabs across the top of the window. Figure 397 compares three windows of Format Axis, the Scale, Number and Pattern tab. The Scale tab allows you to change the minimum and maximum values of the axis and the unit intervals while the Number tab provides you with a wide range of numeric formats for the axes (e.g. fractions, currency, decimal places, date, negative signs and minus signs). The Pattern tab provides you with the means to change the markers on the chart or graph lines using the options indicated by radio buttons on the right side of the window.

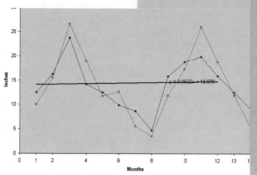

FIGURE 402
Prediction

If you select the Font tab which is available in many of the Format windows then you will reveal the options to change the fonts including type, style, size and effects. The effects include choosing Strikethrough, Superscript and Subscript by clicking on the appropriate check boxes. Figure 398 shows the Font display.

If you double click in the plot area then you will open the Format Plot Area. This allows you to change the background colour of the plot or to choose to have no background colour (i.e. none option radio button). You select the colour by clicking on the colours displayed in the palette and you are shown a sample of the colour. There is also a button Fill Effects which provides access to a variety of fills. When you wish to apply the changes to the background you click on the OK button.

In a similar way to changing the background colour of the chart or graph you can change the colour of a data series bars by doubling clicking on one of the bars. This will open the Format Data Point window. This is identical in appearance to Figure 392c except for the title. The new bar colour is chosen from the palette or from the Fill Effects options. To apply the new colour or fill you need to click on the OK button.

Exercise 58 provides you with the opportunity to explore many of these options.

Exercise 58

Editing

FIGURE 403
More Practice Pie Chart 1

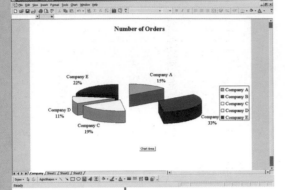

1. Insert your floppy disk into the A: drive.

2. Load Microsoft Excel using either the Programs menu or the Excel icon on the desktop. Open the file Sales Forecast Chart by selecting the File menu and clicking on the Open option to reveal the Open window. Change the Look in:box to select the floppy disk and the file name will appear in the work area. Double click Sales Forecast Chart or single click it and then click the OK button.

3. Select the Quarter Comparison by clicking on the tab. You are now going to edit this chart so that it corresponds with the House Style Guidelines. Double click on the Title to open the Format Chart Title and click on the Font tab to show the options (Figure 398). Select the Times New Roman font, character size 20 and embold the text. You should also explore the other options including the effects (e.g. Srikethrough, Superscript and Subscript). When you have completed the changes to align with the House Style, click on the OK button.

4. Double click on the legend to open the Format Legend window and select Times New Roman and size 12.

5. Double click on the X and Y axis in turn and change them to Times New Roman, emboldened and size 14.

6. Double click on the text along each axis and change it to Times New Roman and size 12.

FIGURE 404
More Practice Pie Chart 2

7. The chart should now conform to the House Style. However, you should take the opportunity to explore some other editing possibilities.

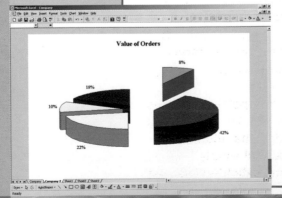

8. If you double click in the plot area you will open the Format Plot Area window which will allow you to change the background colour or remove it. In the Scale tab you can change the minimun, maximum and interval of an axsis. Experiment with different options until you find one you prefer.

9. If you double click on the Amount Axis line you will open the Format Axis window. This provides five tabs – patterns, scales, font, number and alignment. Explore the different options. You can select specific

FIGURE 405
**More
Practice
Bar Chart**

numeric formats for your axis. This can be very useful in other charts. In Patterns tab you will notice three sets of marks (e.g. Major tick mark type). Experiment with the different options.

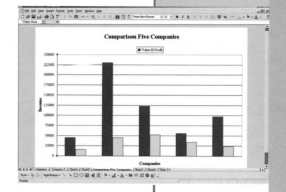

10. Double click on one of the data bars and you will open the Format Data Series window. Explore the different options but choose a new colour for this bar and the other two. Also change the line thickness using the same windows.

11. Figure 399 illustrates the changes that we have made. Compare your own efforts with it. There is no need to be identical except in respect to the House Style Guidelines.

12. Save the chart by selecting the File menu and the Save option on to your floppy disk or a location of your choice.

13. Print your edited chart in either portrait or landscape.

14. Close Excel by selecting the File menu item and clicking on the Exit option or by clicking on the close button in the top right hand corner of the application window.

XY Scatter Graph Editing

Within XY Scatter Graph editing, a key factor is that you can join up the scatter points with a line. If you double click on a point then you will open the Format Data Series window (Figure 400). For a scatter graph the radio button None is selected. If you want to join up the points, select Custom then you can choose the Style, Color and Weight (thickness) of the line.

Figure 401 shows the Rainfall Scatter Graph with the actual and predicted points joined up.

Prediction

Graphs and charts are powerful ways of presenting numerical information. They can make complex data understandable. Pie, column and bar charts allow you to compare different sets of information so that it is straightforward to understand. However, graphs can also help with predicting the future by extending or extrapolating the lines into the future. This requires a graph or chart with one axis being time (e.g. hours, days, months or years).

Figure 402 shows the actual and predicted rainfall lines extrapolated over the next two months (i.e. January and February of the next year). This allows you to estimate rainfall. However, you always need to consider what the data represents. In this case rainfall is likely to be seasonal so that simply extending the lines is likely to be inaccurate. Compare the extended lines with

FIGURE 406
More Practice XY Scatter Graph

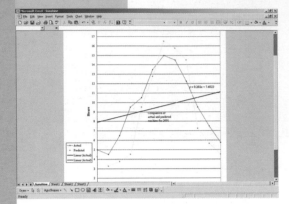

the values of months one and two (i.e. at the start of the scatter graph). They are reasonably accurate provided you do not extend the lines too far into the future. Month 1 extended is very similar to the actual first month but month 2 extended is very different from the actual.

It is often useful to extend lines into the future providing you are careful about considering the context of the information. In this case there is a distinct cycle to the rainfall throughout the year which if you consider alongside the extrapolations will provide greater accuracy in your predictions. Weather forecasts are often limited to a few days ahead.

More Practice

House Style Guidelines

Pie Charts

Font (typeface) serif (e.g. Times New Roman)

Character (Text) Size

Title	20, bold
Sub-title	20, bold
Data Labels	14
Legend	14

Bar/column, line and XY Scatter charts and graphs

Font (typeface)	serif (e.g. Times New Roman)

Character (Text) Size	
Title	20, bold
Sub-title	20, bold
X Axis Title	14, bold
Y Axis Title	14, bold
Other text/numbering on the x axis	12
Other text/numbering on the y axis	12
Legend	12
Text box Labels	12, border invisible
Trendline Equation	12

Headers and Footers

Your name and centre number must be inserted in either the header or footer.

FIGURE 407
**More
Practice
Line
Column**

Exploding Pie Chart

You will normally be provided with a set of data on which to base your charts and graphs. The table below shows the orders received from five companies in terms of their number, value and profit in 2001.

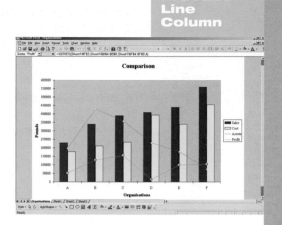

	Orders	Value	Profit
Company A	156	45000	16,000
Company B	345	230000	45,000
Company C	198	123000	52000
Company D	112	56000	34000
Company E	234	97000	24000
Total	1045	551000	171000

1. Create an exploding pie chart (either two or three-dimensional one) to show the number of orders received from the five companies following the House Style Guidelines.

2. Title – Number of Orders

3. Place your legend on the right side of the chart.

4. Data Labels should show both a percentage and a label.

5. Drag the largest slice out from the rest of the chart to emphasise it.

6. Show the chart in landscape orientation and print it in this way.

7. Save your chart. Figure 403 shows our efforts.

8. Now create a second exploding Pie Chart based on the five companies and the value of their orders.

9. Title – Value of the Orders.

10. No legend.

11. Data Labels should show only a percentage.

12. Drag the smallest slice out from the rest of the chart.

13. Show the chart in portrait format and print it in this orientation.

14. Save your chart. Figure 404 shows our efforts.

Bar/Column Chart

1. Create a horizontal bar (column) chart of the value and profit of the orders received from the five companies following the House Style Guidelines.

2. Title – Comparison Five Companies.

3. X Axis – Companies.

4. Y Axis – Income.

5. Y Axis Labels should be aligned 90 degrees.

6. X Axis format – scale minimum 0, maximum 250,000, interval 25,000.

7. Legend on the top of the chart.

8. Remove background colour from the plot area.

9. Remove markers from axes.

10. Select style and weight of lines so they are clear.

11. Select colours for the bars which highlight them.

12. Remove markers from axes.

13. Show the chart in landscape format and print it in this orientation.

14. Save your chart. Figure 405 shows our efforts.

XY Scatter Graph

You will normally be provided with a set of data on which to base your charts and graphs. The table below shows the relationship between the actual hours of sunshine in each month of 2001 compared to the predicted amount.

Months	Hours of Sunshine Actual	Hours of Sunshine Predicted
January	5.00	4.25
February	4.50	3.25
March	6.50	3.75
April	9.50	4.50
May	10.50	9.50
June	13.50	12.75
July	15.00	16.50
August	14.50	15.75
September	12.25	14.50
October	9.50	7.25
November	7.50	5.65

December	5.75	4.50

1. Create an XY Scatter Graph showing the relationship between the actual and predicted hours of sunshine following the House Style Guidelines.

2. Title - Sunshine

X Axis - Months

Y Axis - Hours

3. Format the X Axis - minimum value = 1, maximum value = 12 and interval is 1

4. Format the Y axis – minimum value 0, maximum value = 18 and interval is 1 Numbers set to 2 decimal places

5. Draw the trendline and show the lines equation.

6. Legend on the left

7. No labels

8. Remove markers from axes.

9. Remove background colour from the plot area ensuring that axes are still visible.

10. Join up the series of plots selecting suitable styles, weights and colour of lines.

11. Add a text box to read "Comparison and actual and predicted sunshine for 2001" and place the text below the trendline. Consider the overall trend of the information.

12. Show the chart in portrait format and print it in this orientation.

13. Save your chart. Figure 406 shows our efforts.

Line-Column Graph

You will normally be provided with a set of data on which to base your charts and graphs on. The table below shows the relationship between sales, costs, fixed assets and annual profit.

Organisation	Sales	Cost	Assets	Profit
A	230000	178000	198000	52000
B	340000	212000	430000	128000
C	390000	234000	357900	156000
D	410000	395000	230000	15000
E	440000	340000	178000	100000
F	560000	456000	76000	104000

1. Create a line column graph showing the sales and costs as columns and assets and profits as lines.

2. Title – Comparison

X Axis - Organisation

Y Axis – Pounds

3. Place legend on right.

4. Format the Y axis minimum = 0, maximum = 600000, interval = 50,000

5. Apply a colour fill to the plot area but ensure that the contrast with the columns and lines is suitable when chart is printed.

6. Select suitable colours for the column files and lines to maximise legibility.

7. Show the chart in landscape format and print it in this orientation.

8. Save your chart. Figure 407 shows our efforts.

Summary

1. Load
Select Start button, highlight Programs and click on the Microsoft Excel option

2. Open a File
Select the File menu, click on the Open option to reveal the Open window. Change the Look in:box to select the folder and the file name will appear in the work area.

3. Select Data
Highlight the whole area of data

4. Chart Wizard
a) Select the Insert menu and the Chart option. Click on the chart/graph option.

b) Check the chart by clicking on and holding down the mouse button on the Press and Hold to View Sample. Click on the next button to move to step 2 of the Chart Wizard.

c) Consider the data range (e.g. =sheet1!$B$6:$C$18 translates into the area top left hand corner cell B6 to cell C18). Click on the Next button to reveal Step 3.

d) Click on the tab of your choice (e.g. Legends). Click on the Next button to reveal step 4.

e) Click on the radio button of your choice. Click on the Finish button.

5. Save
Select the File menu and the Save As option to reveal the Save As window.

6. Close
Select the File menu item and click on the Exit option.

or

Click on the close button in the top right hand corner of the application window.

7. Present in Landscape or Portrait
Select the File menu and click on the Page Setup option to reveal the Page Setup window. Choose portrait or landscape by clicking in the appropriate radio button.

8. Print Preview

Select the <u>F</u>ile menu and click on the Print Pre<u>v</u>iew option.

9. Trendline

With the Chart visible, select the <u>C</u>hart menu and click on Add Trendline option to open the Add Trendline window. Select the equation type the series the line is based on.

10. Header and Footer

With the chart or graph visible, select the <u>F</u>ile menu and the Page Set<u>u</u>p option to reveal the Page Setup window. Click on the Header/Footer tab

11. Text Box

Click on the Text Box icon in the Draw Toolbar to reveal a new mouse pointer which allows you to draw a box by holding down the mouse button and dragging the box open.

12. Format Graphs and Charts

Double click on the chart or graph element then the Format window will appear (e.g. Format Chart Title, Format Legend, Format Data Labels, Format Data Series).

13. XY Scatter Graph – Joining Points

Double click on a point to open the Format Data Series window. Select Custom radio button then you can choose the <u>S</u>tyle, <u>C</u>olor and <u>W</u>eight (thickness) of the line.

14. Types of Charts and Graphs

There are several different types of charts and graphs. The main ones are:
- Pie Charts – useful way of visually presenting a range of results (e.g. sales results for four quarters of a year)
- Bar/column Charts – useful way of comparing results side by side (e.g. car sales by garage)
- Line Graphs – useful way of showing the relationship between two variables
- XY Scatter Graphs – useful way of comparing two variables which do not have an obvious relationship

Glossary

Analogue: This is continuous data as opposed to discrete information or digital data.

Application: An application is a software program designed to perform a task such as word-processing, e-mail or spreadsheets.

Baud: This is the number of changes in voltage across a communication channel and is used to measure the rate of flow of information.

Boot: The process that occurs when you switch on the computer. It involves the loading of the operating system (e.g. Windows 2000) and checking of the equipment to ensure that everything is ready for you to use.

Browser: A browser is an application which allows you to access a World Wide Web site. Each site has a unique address which is called a URL (Uniform Resource Locator) which, when entered into the browser, allows it to find the site and view its contents.

Byte: The basic measure of memory. A byte is sufficient memory to store one character (e.g. a letter or a number).

Bps (bits per second): A bit is the smallest unit of information (i.e. 1 or 0) that can be used by a computer or sent across a communication link. Bits per second are often the measure of the flow of information.

CD-ROM: Compact Disk – Read Only Memory is the computer equivalent of an audio compact disk and is used to store large amounts of information.

CD-RW: A specialist form of CD-ROM that allows information to be both read from the disk and also written to it.

Clipboard: A special area of memory in which applications in Windows can store information. It is used to copy and cut information to in order to paste from it later.

CPU see **Central Processing Unit**

Central Processing Unit: The silicon chip which controls the operation of the computer.

Desktop: The main display of the operating system and normally the first display you see after the computer has loaded the operating system (i.e. Windows).

Digital: Digital information is made up of patterns of noughts and ones.

DOS: This is an operating system called the Disk Operating System.

E-mail see **Electronic Mail**

Electronic Mail: The process of sending a message through the Internet.

Field: An individual piece of information stored on a database usually as part of a record.

File: A collection of digital (computer) information. There are many types such as word-processing, graphic and spreadsheet files.

Flame: A flame is an angry e-mail message.

Floppy: A floppy is a small magnetic disk on which you can store a small amount of information in the form of files.

Folder: This is a location on the computer in which you can store files and folders.

Footer: Essentially a standard item that is placed on the bottom of each page. It is often a graphic image such as a company logo but it can be text only or a mixture of text and graphics (see also Header).

Font: Characters can be printed and displayed in many different styles. These styles are known as fonts.

Format: A way of structuring the computer information stored in a file on a disk or drive. There are many different types of file format.

Freeware: Software that is free both in terms of price and restrictions. Freeware is sometimes called 'Open Source' software since the original source code is available for adaptation and development.

FTP: File Transfer Protocol is the means by which you can transfer a file of information from one web site to another or to your own computer.

Gb: A gigabyte is a measure of memory (i.e. approximately one billion bytes of information).

Greyed out: If an icon or menu items is faded this means that the option is not currently available.

GUI see **Graphical User Interface**

Graphical User Interface: A type of interface display which combines icons, windows and a mouse pointer to produce an easy to use environment.

Gutter: The extra space allowed in the margin for pages to be bound together or the space between columns.

Hard disk: Large magnetic disk located inside the computer on which a large amount of information can be stored.

Hardware: The physical components which make up the computer.

Header: Essentially a standard item which is placed at the top of each page (see also footer).

HTML: Hypertext Markup Language is a specialist language which is used to design documents and World Wide Web sites so that they can be read using a browser.

Hypertext: Pages of a web site are linked together through a number of hypertext connections. These are shown by underlined words, coloured words, icons and graphic pictures. The links allow the user to jump between different parts of the site or even between sites.

Icon: A small image that is used to represent a computer function or application.

Information Society: The name given to the society which is evolving from the change brought about by the impact of information and communication technology.

ISDN see **Integrated Service Digital Network**

ISP: Internet Service Providers are commercial companies who provide connections to the Internet for individuals and companies.

Integrated Service Digital Network: A high speed, broadband link which is specially designed for digital data transmission.

Internet: The word wide network of individual computers and computer networks which links millions of users.

Justification: A way of laying out text e.g. left justification means that text is aligned so that its left edge is parallel with the paper's edge when it is printed.

Kb: A Kilobyte is a measure of memory (i.e. 1024 bytes).

LAN: see also Local Area Network

Laptop: A portable computer with a screen built into its cover.

LCD: Liquid Crystal Display is a type of screen used in some portable computers.

Local Area A group of computers linked by cables so that they
Network: can communicate with each other in order to share resources. See also LAN, WAN and ISDN.

MB: A Megabyte is a measure of computer memory (approximately a million bytes).

Memory: A measure of the computer's capacity to perform tasks and to store information.

Menu: A method of displaying options.

Mhz (mega hertz): This is a measure of the speed of the computer.

Modem: A device for linking computers together via a telephone line. The modem converts digital (computer) output into an analogue signal so that it can be sent down a telephone line. The signal is then converted back by a second modem so that the information can be understood by the second computer.

Motherboard: The main circuit board within the computer.

Multitasking: The carrying-out of several tasks in parallel. Windows operating system allows you to undertake multitasking.

Network computer: A computer connected to many other computers.

Open Source software: see Freeware

Operating System: The operating system is the software system (e.g. Microsoft Windows 2000) that links the hardware and software together and provides many of the standard features of the computer. These include saving information on to the hard and floppy disks, printing documents, linking the keyboard and mouse to the application and presenting the information on the monitor.

Palmtop: A palmtop is a small battery-powered computer (pocket sized) which usually does not have all the functions of either a laptop or a desktop computer.

PC: Personal Computer

Pixel: Graphic image are made up of many small rectangular areas which are called pixels.

Personal Computer: A personal computer is essentially a machine designed for individual use. It consists of a monitor, system box, keyboard, mouse, various drives, CPU, motherboard and a variety of electronic cards.

PoP: ISPs provide you with a telephone number which is called a Point of Presence (PoP). Your communication software dials this number when you try to access the Internet and links you through your modem to the ISP's computer. The ISP is linked to the Internet. Many ISPs have several PoPs throughout the country.

Primary Key: A unique identifier of a database record (e.g. staff number and national insurance number)

PSDN see **Public Switched Data Network**

Public domain software: Software that is entirely free of conditions and users can use the software in any way they choose.

Public Switched Data Network: The world telephone network is called the Public Switched Telephone Network.

QWERTY: The order of the top line of alphabetical keys on the keyboard.

RAM see **Random Access Memory**

Random Access Memory (RAM): The working memory in which the computer carries out its functions once it is switched on. It only exists while the machine is on. If the power is switched off, so is the memory.

Record: A group of related fields of information that you normally find in a database.

ROM see **Read Only Memory**

Read Only Memory: This is the permanent memory built into the computer through the silicon chips which make up the system.

RSI see **Repetitive Strain Injury**

Repetitive Strain Injury: RSI is an injury brought about by carrying out an action in such a way that it places a strain on a person's body (e.g. arms, wrists and fingers). It can cause serious harm to you.

Search Engine: A search engine is an application that allows you to search for a web page containing information on a specific topic.

Shareware: Software which is provided on a try before you buy it system.

Software: Computer programs written to allow you or the computer to carry out certain tasks such as constructing databases.

Spam: Unsolicited e-mails which are often advertisements.

Surfing: The process of wandering around the World Wide Web in search of interesting information.

Table: A table is part of a database on which information is stored as a series of records and fields.

URL: URL (Uniform Resource Locator) is the unique address of a World Wide Web site that allows a browser to find a site.

VDU: Visual display unit is another term for monitor.

Virus: Viruses are pieces of software which are designed to replicate themselves and to damage your computer system. They can delete your files, change your computer settings and fill up your storage with rubbish.

WAN see **Wide Area Network**

Wide Area Network: This is a network of computers over large geographical areas. A WAN can cover an individual town, county or even continent.

World Wide Web: A large network of millions of websites spread across the world as part of the Internet.

Web site: A web site is a collection of pages on the Internet.

Window: A window is a rectangular area of the screen in which computer applications and information is displayed.

Wizard: Many Windows applications include a Wizard. These are used to perform complex tasks more easily by allowing the user to choose between options.

WWW see **World Wide Web**

Index

Page numbers in italics refer to illustrations.
The following abbreviations are used: Acc –Access; CD – CorelDraw;
CPP – CorelPHOTOPOINT; Exc –Excel; FP – FrontPage; PP – PowerPoint; Wd - Word